The Deoband Madrassah Movement

DIVERSITY AND PLURALITY IN SOUTH ASIA

The **Diversity and Plurality in South Asia** series, wide in scope, will bring together publications in anthropology and sociology, alongside politics and international relations, exploring themes of both contemporary and historical relevance. This diverse line in the social sciences and humanities will investigate the plurality of social groups, identities and ideologies, including within its remit not only interrogations of issues surrounding gender, caste, religion and region, but also political variations, and a variety of cultural ideas and expressions within South Asia.

The Deoband Madrassah Movement

Countercultural Trends and Tendencies

Muhammad Moj

ANTHEM PRESS

Anthem Press India
An imprint of Wimbledon Publishing Company India Private Limited (WPCIPL)
WPCIPL is a subsidiary of Wimbledon Publishing Company Limited (UK)

This edition first published in India 2015
by ANTHEM PRESS INDIA
www.anthempress.co.in

First published in UK and USA 2015
by ANTHEM PRESS
www.anthempress.com

ISBN-13: 978 93 80601 71 7 (Hbk)
ISBN-10: 93 80601 71 9 (Hbk)

FOR SALE IN SOUTH ASIA ONLY

Digitally Printed at Replika Press Pvt. Ltd

In memory of my loving parents
Alive, they were close to me
Departed, they are closer

CONTENTS

PREFACE

This book explores the history and evolution of Deobandi Islam, a South Asian Sunni sect whose origin dates back to 1866 when a *madrassah* movement was launched in the small North Indian town of Deoband. Since its inception, Deobandi Islam has survived and spread mainly through its *madrassah* network, which has produced Deobandi prayer leaders, preachers and politicians on the one hand and has paved the way for the creation of extremist Deobandi organizations like the Taliban and Lashkar-e-Jhangwi on the other. The latter role of the Deobandi movement makes it all the more relevant in the present scenario, whereby a global wave of extremism and terrorism has seriously threatened world peace.

Unlike the existing literature that has studied the Deobandi movement in the context of political Islam and religious reform, this book endeavours to interpret this *madrassah*-based movement from a countercultural perspective. By employing an offbeat approach, this book tries to explain the background of the perennial conflict between the Deobandi sect and mainstream Muslim society in the subcontinent. An attempt has also been made to identify the countercultural currents in the 150-year-long history of the Deobandi movement. In addition to that, a comparative analysis of the values and attitudes of the students of a Deobandi *madrassah* and a mainstream educational institution has been included to underline the countercultural mindset of Deobandi Islam. In its concluding section, the book looks at some probable scenarios with respect to the future of Deobandi Islam as a counterculture.

The main objective of this work is to understand Deobandi Islam from a different perspective. This work is expected to be of ample interest and importance to the intelligentsia and academia on the one hand and politicians and policymakers on the other. By giving an insight into the making of the mindset of the Deobandi Taliban, this work also hopes to add considerable value to the ongoing policymaking process vis-à-vis the future of the Pak-Afghan region, especially after the withdrawal of NATO forces from Afghanistan.

While working on this book, I immensely benefitted from the efficient editorial oversight and valuable secretarial support offered by Anthem Press. In thanking the publishing staff for their efforts on my behalf, I do not, of course, absolve myself of responsibility for the shortcomings of this work.

PROLOGUE

This book identifies countercultural trends and tendencies in the Deoband Madrassah Movement (DMM) during its 150-year-long history, with a particular focus on Pakistan. Religious schools or *madaris* (plural of Arabic *madrassah*: 'place of learning') of Pakistan have acquired greater significance since the terrorist attacks of 11 September 2001. Since then, there has been a substantial increase in the literature concerning madaris in Pakistan. However, most of that literature has focused on madaris from the perspective of securitization. According to Malik, 'Few of those studies are well grounded in empirical research – in fact most of them lack research altogether.' The majority of recent studies on madaris suffer from 'sensationalized overgeneralization' and do not take into account the history of the religious education and the factors influencing the demand and supply of madaris (Malik 2008, 1). Recent research on madaris has also been 'predicated on observational accounts and anecdotes' (Ali 2009, 85), while ignoring the social context and historical background (Riaz 2008, 36).

The major focus of post-9/11 madrassah literature has been the rise in the number of madaris and their possible links to extremism. Just before 9/11, the Western media had already begun to highlight the madrassah–terrorism nexus during the rise of the Taliban in Afghanistan. In the year 2000, Jessica Stern, Jeffery Goldberg and Stephen Cohen each published articles that specifically focused on Pakistani madaris and their links with jihadism and terrorism. Immediately after 9/11, as the intensity of this discourse increased, Peter Singer (2001) pointed out that madaris were displacing the public education system and some of these had 'extremely close ties with radical militant groups and played a critical role in sustaining the international terrorist network'. Andrew Coulson (2004) called madaris 'weapons of mass instruction'. Even the *9/11 Commission Report* referred to madaris as 'incubators of violent extremism' (2004, 385). Ali Riaz (2008, 39–40) studied the coverage of nine Western media outlets between 12 September 2001 and 31 March 2005 and identified two thematic similarities with regard to their portrayal of Pakistani madaris: the depiction of madrassah children as enemies-in-the-making and the framing of the madrassah environment as repressive.

At the same time, some revisionist literature on madaris appearing after 9/11 has questioned the sensationalism of certain media reports as well as academic essays. Peter Bergen and Swati Pandey (2005) studied the backgrounds of 75 terrorists behind major attacks on Western targets and concluded that only 9 of them were linked to madaris. Earlier, Mark Sageman (2004) had reached a similar conclusion in a study of 137 terrorists, out of which only 23 (17 per cent) had attended Islamic religious schools.

William Dalrymple (2005) also provided a somewhat positive account of madaris in South Asia by highlighting the contribution of these institutions with respect to education and shelter for poor children. Akbar S. Ahmed (2002) also regarded madaris to be a 'cheaper, more accessible and more Islamic alternative to education', while Mumtaz Ahmad (2003) stressed the apolitical tone of the traditional curriculum of madaris. A World Bank–funded study tried to downplay the sensationalism against Pakistani madaris by stating that madrassah enrolment may account for less than 1 per cent of total students in Pakistan (Andrabi et al. 2005). These findings actually refuted the much-discussed 2002 report of the International Crisis Group, which had claimed that about one-third of all students in Pakistan were enrolled in madaris. Recent academic works by Hefner and Zaman (2007), Jamal Malik (2008), Ali Riaz (2008) and Saleem Ali (2009) have tried to interpret madaris in the overall historical context, with particular focus on the growth, evolution, syllabus and sectarian outlook of South Asian madaris.

Before 9/11, madaris in the subcontinent were studied mostly in the context of a religious reform movement. After 9/11, almost all the literature on madaris has tried to explain these institutions from the political perspective while focusing on issues like extremism and terrorism. Although both these approaches are vital, there is still some need to study these madaris at a deeper level in order to understand the whole madrassah phenomenon in the Indian subcontinent generally and in Pakistan particularly. So far, no such research has been conducted to explain this phenomenon in the sociocultural context. This book has tried to bridge that research gap by studying the madrassah phenomenon from a countercultural perspective.

This book studies the growth and evolution of the Deobandi denomination of madaris, which form bulk of the total madaris in Pakistan. The percentage of Deobandi madaris is placed between 60 per cent (Akbar 2010) and 70 per cent (Rehman 2008) of total madaris in the country. According to Rehman (2008, 64), other madrassah denominations in Pakistan include Barelwi (16 per cent), Ahle Hadith (4 per cent), Shia (4 per cent) and Jamaat-e-Islami (5 per cent).

However, it is interesting to note that the above percentage of madaris is not compatible with the overall sectarian composition of Pakistani society. According to cursory estimates about the sectarian divide in Pakistan, around 60 per cent of Pakistani Muslims represent the Barelwi sect. About 20–25 per cent belongs to the Deobandis and less than 5 per cent to Ahle Hadith. Shia Islam is represented by 10–15 per cent of Pakistani Muslims (Akbar 2010). However, said sects find these statistics unacceptable, each claiming for itself a far greater share among Pakistani Muslims.

Furthermore, the aforementioned sectarian composition is not watertight in the sense that a huge majority of Sunni Muslims in Pakistan do not claim strict adherence to any particular sectarian denomination. Rather, they follow a very tolerant and broad-minded version of Islam, which is strongly linked to the spiritual and *Sufi* religious traditions of the region. This charitable version of Islam can broadly be called folk Islam, whose norms, values and practices are largely represented by the Barelwi school of thought. It is predominant in villages and small towns, where more than 75 per cent of Pakistanis live, but it also enjoys a significant following in urban areas (Jafferlot 2002, 232–4). Therefore, one may argue that it represents mainstream Muslim society in Pakistan. According to

Ahmad (1991, 158), folk Islam has 'an emphasis on *sufism*, veneration of saints, idolization of the Prophet and one's spiritual preceptors, and popular and festive display of syncretic religious rituals'.

It is quite remarkable that the Deobandis have not only maintained far more madaris than their share in the population but have also managed to influence both the state and the society in Pakistan despite being a minority sect. Similarly, all the madaris that have been linked to jihadism or terrorism also belong to the Deobandi sect. This dubious distinction qualifies the Deobandi madaris as the focus of this book, which studies Deobandi Islam in a countercultural context.

The Deoband Madrassah Movement (DMM) was launched in 1866 to protect the religious capital of Indian Muslims (Arshad 2005, 29) against the backdrop of the fall of Muslim rule and the introduction of a secular education system by the British in India. After their defeat in the war of 1857, Muslims had lost hope of gaining any political power in India and there was a general feeling of social isolation, a condition which Westhues (1972, 19) considers to be a source of counterculture. A counterculture is a set of norms and values of a group that contradict the prevalent norms and values of the society of which that group is a part (Yinger 1982, 3). Unable to attack the power structure, the DMM founders decided to convert their social isolation into physical isolation by setting up an independent chain of madaris. Through the establishment of these madaris, the DMM were actually setting up isolated communities where they could preach and practice their own value system, which they perceived to be threatened by the British and Hindu cultures on the one hand and the sociocultural practices of folk Islam on the other. Taking inspiration from Shah Waliullah's eighteenth-century movement, the DMM aimed to reform the social customs and cultural practices of Indian Muslims.

Existing literature on the DMM has explained this movement mainly from two perspectives (Pemberton 2009). First is the political interpretation, which focuses on the efforts of the DMM to establish an Islamic state governed by *Shariah*. The second perspective is based on 'interiorization', which sees the DMM as a religious reform movement more concerned with the perfection of faith and the moral development of ordinary Muslims and less with the assertion of a political agenda. A possible third perspective focuses on the intellectual contributions of the DMM (Pemberton 2009). Taking its lead from the 'interiorization' perspective, this research introduces a fourth perspective by interpreting the DMM from a sociocultural standpoint. It focuses on the conflict of the Deobandi movement with the social customs and cultural practices of folk Islam in the subcontinent. This conflict is the outcome of the DMM's aim 'to resuscitate classical Islam to rid the Muslims of theological corruptions, the ritual degradations and the material exploitation to which they have fallen prey' (Smith 1943, 320).

Without discounting the interpretations offered by the existing three perspectives on the DMM, this book identifies the countercultural inclinations of the movement by studying it in the context of Milton Yinger's theory of counterculture. Yinger (1960, 629) defined the concept of counterculture as a 'normative system of a group which contains, as a primary element, a theme of conflict with the values of the total society'.

This book addresses the following major research question:

How can the Deoband Madrassah Movement be understood from a countercultural perspective?

Based on the hypothesis that the seeds of counterculture were sown in the origins of the Deoband Madrassah Movement, this major question has been answered through the following two secondary questions:

i. *Which countercultural tendencies has the Deoband Madrassah Movement (DMM) shown from its origin to the partition of India (1866–1947) on the one hand and in Pakistan since 1947 on the other?*
ii. *How do the values and attitudes of the Deobandis differ from those of mainstream Muslim society in Pakistan?*

These secondary questions have been researched in two stages. At the first stage, the research questions were addressed through a detailed survey and analysis of the available literature on the DMM. The second stage of research involved fieldwork, which included a) a review of three Deobandi journals to identify countercultural recent trends in the DMM; and b) semi-structured qualitative interviews of students of a Deobandi madrassah and a mainstream postgraduate college in order to compare their values and attitudes. Details of the theoretical framework and methodology for this exploratory research are given in Chapter 1.

Organization of the Book

Apart from this prologue, this book has been organized into the following chapters.

Chapter 1: The Deoband Madrassah Movement: Research Context

This chapter is broadly divided into three sections. The first section focuses on the origin of madaris in Islam as well as the background and emergence of the DMM in the subcontinent, with a particular focus on Pakistan. Apart from briefly touching upon the curriculum and courses of Pakistani madaris, this section also looks into the various viewpoints on the objectives and goals of the DMM as elucidated in the published research. The second section discusses social and religious movement theories before explaining the theoretical context, based on Milton Yinger's counterculture theory. This section also elaborates the concept of counterculture along with its boundaries and three types: ascetic, activist and mystic. The last section provides the details of the research methodology, which includes a literature survey, a review of Deobandi journals and field interviews.

Chapter 2: Origin of the DMM: Seeds of a Counterculture

This chapter has been divided into two parts. The first part traces the links of the DMM to Shah Waliullah's eighteenth-century movement and the countercultural trends it passed on to the DMM. This section not only discusses Waliullah's ideology and legacy but also spotlights the DMM founders' direct affiliation with his movement. It also illustrates how the DMM merely became a narrower version of that earlier movement, which was itself influenced by the Salafi movement of Muhammad bin Abdul Wahhab of Arabia. The second part of the chapter defines the factors that caused DMM leaders to withdraw from mainstream society in the wake of the fall of the Mughal Empire in 1857 and the rise of the British Raj. While discussing this 'inward turn' of the DMM, which focused on perfecting Islamic life and practice instead of being involved in the external exigencies of British rule and impending modernity, this section proposes that the DMM during its early years behaved, in Milton Yinger's terminology, as an 'ascetic' counterculture.

Chapter 3: The DMM in United India: Activist Countercultural Trends

This chapter argues that the DMM gradually adopted an activist approach by preaching its values on the one hand and opposing the customs and traditions of folk Islam in India on the other. This chapter also highlights the countercultural activism of the DMM in the political arena, where it placed itself in opposition to the political groups who represented mainstream Muslim society in India. Most importantly, this chapter also examines Deobandi resistance to the popular movement for Pakistan from a countercultural perspective. Further, this chapter touches upon the initiative of some Deobandi leaders to form the Tablighi Jamaat (literally, 'proselytizing group'), which behaved somewhat like a 'mystic' counterculture.

Chapter 4: The DMM in Pakistan: Countercultural Politics and Extremism

This chapter discusses in detail the role of the DMM in Pakistan from 1947 to the present, and spotlights the factors leading to different phases and trends in the DMM. The chapter also focuses on the shifting stances of the Jamiat-ul-Ulama-e-Islam (JUI), a major Deobandi political party in Pakistan. A significant shift in the DMM's approach towards extremism after its involvement in the Afghan 'jihad' (1979–89) provides the pivot for this chapter. The chapter also identifies terrorist trends in the DMM, suggesting a fourth variety of counterculture (i.e. 'extremist') in addition to the three types proposed by Milton Yinger. Further, it elaborates the countercultural character of the DMM through a case study of the Deobandi Taliban government in Afghanistan.

Chapter 5: Deobandi Islam: Countering Folk Islam and Popular Custom

While highlighting the differences between the Deobandi movement and popular folk Islam, this chapter details the beliefs and practices of the DMM that contradict the values and norms of the majority of Muslims in Pakistan. The chapter explores how the DMM employed Islamic theology to castigate the established religious and sociocultural values and practices of folk Islam, followed by the majority of Pakistani Muslims. Deobandi arguments against prevalent religious practices, popular customs and even sports and entertainment activities are juxtaposed with the counterarguments of non-Deobandi scholars in order to highlight the countercultural disposition of the DMM.

Chapter 6: The DMM versus Mainstream Society: Viewpoints of Deobandi Journals and Students

This chapter has been divided into two sections. The first section reviews three prominent Deobandi journals published by large madaris in three of the four provinces of Pakistan. The review focuses on four major themes: popular values and practices, politics, the educational system and the role of women in society. This review clearly exhibits the countercultural character of the Deobandi movement by spotlighting a sharp contrast between the values and beliefs of the DMM and mainstream Muslim society in Pakistan. The second section compares the values and attitudes of the students of a Deobandi madrassah and a mainstream postgraduate college in the light of the qualitative interviews conducted during the fieldwork for this research. The findings of this fieldwork further substantiate the countercultural constitution of the DMM specifically with reference to the four themes covered in the first section.

Epilogue

This concluding chapter not only recaps the major findings of the research but also touches upon the impact of the DMM on Pakistani society. It also discusses possible scenarios with regard to the future of the DMM in Pakistan. Further, it indicates possible avenues for future research on the Deobandi movement.

Chapter 1

THE DEOBAND MADRASSAH MOVEMENT: RESEARCH CONTEXT

They see their values and conceptions of the good life disappearing, and they can find no way within the system to restore them.

Milton Yinger, *Countercultures: The Promise and Peril of a World Turned Upside Down* (1982, 210)

This chapter spells out the research areas and schema of this book. The chapter unfolds at three levels. At the first level, it presents a brief history of madaris on the one hand and the DMM on the other. Secondly, it narrates the different interpretations of the DMM in the existing literature. At the third level, it explains the theoretical context as well as the research methodology.

1.1 Madaris in Islam

The Arabic word *madrassah* (plural: *madaris*) literally means 'school' (Riaz 2008, 2) or 'place of learning' (Malik 2008, 1). It originates from the word *dars*, which means 'lesson' or 'instruction'. In the Arabic-speaking societies, the word madrassah can be applied to a wide variety of institutions (Berkey 2007, 40). However, in non-Arabic-speaking regions, this word is generally used to refer to a special kind of institution devoted to the training of *ulama* (religious scholars, plural of *alim*) through instruction about the Quran, the Hadith (traditions of the Prophet), *fiqh* (jurisprudence) and Islamic law (Riaz 2008, 2).

The tradition of madrassah is as old as the history of Islam itself. Although the word madrassah was not used as such, a study circle or *halaqah* was established for learning in the mosque of the Prophet Muhammad (peace be upon him, PBUH) in the city of Madinah. The ones who participated in that *halaqah* used to sit on an elevated platform called a *suffah* and were called *Ashab al-Suffah* (Arshad 2005, 21). Even during the life time of Prophet Muhammad (PBUH), nine such *halaqahs* had been established inside Madinah (Khalid 2002, 89). These non-formal educational arrangements, based in the mosques or in the homes of the Prophet's companions, were the precursors of madaris and continued during the era of the first four caliphs and even later (Riaz 2008, 53–4). Imdad Sabri has pointed out the existence of systematic education at primary level during Caliph Umar's reign (632–44 CE) whereby the educational requirements of Muslims were fulfilled through a *maktab* or *kuttab*, an institution attached to a local mosque (Arshad 2005, 23).

A. L. Tibawi has added that 'the *maktab* could be held in a private house, shop or any other place and was presided over by a *mu'allim* (teacher)' and that it was aimed at the 'removal of illiteracy and the teaching of reckoning, grammar, poetry, history (*akhbar*) and above all, the Quran' (quoted in Riaz 2008, 55). During the first four centuries of Islamic education (seventh through tenth century CE), the majority of Muslims who sought instruction stopped at the *maktab* level, and so seekers of higher knowledge had to join the circles of well-known scholars and mystics because madaris did not exist as independent institutions.

It is hard to trace the exact period when madaris began to appear as independent and exclusive educational institutions. It is generally agreed that the Madrassah al-Nizamiya of Baghdad, established in 1067, is the first institutionalized madrassah (Khalid 2002, 91; Malik 2008, 4; Rizwi 2005, 68). This madrassah was established by Nizam ul-Mulk Tusi (1017–92), who was the *vizir* (prime minister) of the Seljuk Turk Sultan Alp Arsalan under the Abbasid Caliphate. However, Arshad (2005, 22) and Riaz (2008, 54) mention several madaris established well before Madrassah al-Nizamiya. Riaz (2008, 54) has even traced the history of institutionalized madaris to the reign of al-Mamun (786–833 CE) of the Abbasid Caliphate.

Although Madrassah al-Nizamiya is not the first institutionalized madrassah in the history of Islamic education, its founder Nizam ul-Mulk Tusi holds the distinction of providing a model for other madaris. He established a chain of madaris in several cities in the Seljuk sultanate, which stretched from the Hindu Kush to Eastern Anatolia and from Central Asia to the Persian Gulf (Arjomand 1999). He also set up *auqaf* (plural of Arabic *waqf*: trust) for these madaris in order to ensure income generation, which in turn provided independence and autonomy to these institutions (Arshad 2005, 22–3). This tradition later became the standard practice and helped in spreading the network of madaris throughout the regions under Muslim rule. These madaris were typically patronized by the ruling elite. Apart from the pursuit of knowledge, the rapid rise in the number of madaris after the tenth century was also associated with at least three other factors: rivalry between Shias and Sunnis, contention between various Sunni schools of thought (*madhabs*), and philosophical debates between the rationalist Mutazilites and orthodox Asharites (Riaz 2008, 56).

As far as the Indian subcontinent is concerned, it is hard to find a discernible pattern among the Islamic educational institutions before the rise of Mughal Empire in the sixteenth century. After Muslims began to arrive in the region during the early eighth century, mosques and *khanqahs* (*sufi* hospices or monasteries) were initially used as the centres of informal religious education. The first formal madrassah was set up in 1191 in Ajmer by Muizzuddin Muhammad Ghauri (d. 1206), founder of Turkish rule in India (Khalid 2002, 93; Riaz 2008, 58). Saleem Ali (2009, 18) has pointed out that the first recorded madrassah in the subcontinent was the Madrassah Firozi in Multan established by Nasiruddin Qabacha. The earliest madaris in the subcontinent were reportedly established in the regions of Sindh and Multan (Arshad 2005, 24), when Arab scholars migrated there following Muhammad Bin Qasim's invasion of Sindh leading to the establishment of new cities like Mansura during the early eighth century.

In Delhi, Shams-ud-din Iltutmish (d. 1236) established the first madrassah, named Madrassah Muizziah in the memory of Sultan Ghauri (Arshad 2005, 24). Qutbuddin Aibak (d. 1210) of the Slave Dynasty and Muhammad bin Tughluq (d. 1351) and Feroze Shah (d. 1388) of the Tughluq Dynasty were the most enthusiastic founders of madaris in the subcontinent (Arshad 2005, 24; Khalid 2002, 93; Riaz 2008, 58). According to Miqrizi, during the reign of Muhammad bin Tughluq (1324–51) there were about one thousand madaris present in Delhi alone (Rizwi 2005, vol. 1, 72). However, that figure seems to be unrealistic given that even today, while the Muslim population of Delhi has increased enormously since the fourteenth century, there are still less than twelve hundred madaris there. Apparently, Miqrizi included in his calculation of madaris the *maktabs* attached to mosques, which provided basic Islamic education with a special focus on recitation of the Quran.

Most of the early madaris in the Indian subcontinent were established by the rulers of different dynasties and regional kingdoms that emerged in the wake of the Delhi Sultanate's weakening in the fifteenth century. Thus the curricula of these madaris varied to reflect the background of the scholars and saints who influenced a particular ruler. Despite having no single educational model, these early madaris had some common features: operational autonomy, freedom to choose syllabus, instruction of both revealed (*manqulat*) and rational (*ma'qulat*) sciences, and producing graduates who were to serve in the royal courts and state administration (Riaz 2008, 60–61).

After the establishment of the Mughal Empire, there was a marked increase in the number of madaris owing to the political stability and the royal policy to support education and learning. Muslim education during the Mughal period (1556–1858) can be divided into three categories; elementary, secondary and higher education. Elementary or primary education was provided at the *maktab*, which was almost invariably attached to a mosque. Occasionally, *maktabs* were based in private houses. Secondary education was imparted at *khanqahs*, *dargahs* (shrines) or sometimes at mosques. These institutions, which focused on mystical and theological ideas, acted as supplements and feeders to the madaris, which in turn imparted higher education. These madaris were present in important towns and cities and provided advanced studies in three types of sciences: *illahi* or divine sciences, consisting of theology and the means of acquiring the knowledge of God; *riazi* or mathematical sciences, which also included astronomy, music and mechanics; and *tabi'i* or physical sciences (Ojha 1975, 76–80).

The curriculum of madaris (i.e. higher education) during the first half of the Mughal era put great emphasis on the study of rational sciences (*ma'qulat*), which took on 'new importance' and made 'great strides towards popularity' during Emperor Akbar's reign (Ikram and Bilgrami quoted in Riaz 2008, 64). This emphasis on rationalist content continued under Emperor Jahangir despite efforts by some *ulama* like Shaikh Abdul Haqq Muhaddis Dehlwi, who tried to revive the *manqulat* (revealed) tradition. Later, Aurangzeb, who is considered the most orthodox Mughal ruler, patronized the Farangi Mahall madrassah in Lucknow as a major institution of learning.

The Farangi Mahall tradition also stressed *ma'qulat* more than *manqulat*. In fact, Mulla Nizamuddin Sihalvi (d. 1748) of this tradition expanded and compiled the curriculum of madaris by including a number of books on *ma'qulat*, while the Quran (two commentaries) and the Hadith (one abridgement) were given marginal focus (Metcalf 1982, 31). The Farangi Mahall syllabus, known as *Dars-e-Nizami*, has since dominated religious education in the subcontinent – of course, with some modifications. Nadwi (1970, 300) considered the modern *Dars-e-Nizami* to be an inferior form of the original syllabus, which focused more on the subjects than on books. However, Robinson (2001) has pointed out that *Dars-e-Nizami* was not a strict syllabus; rather it was more like a method of teaching whereby the teachers introduced books according to the ability of students rather than teaching them all the suggested books for a particular subject (Sanyal 2008, 25).

In a period marked by political instability, Farangi Mahall became one of the largest centres of learning by the early eighteenth century. While preparing *qadhis* (judges) and *muftis* (jurists) for the Muslim courts, this school also revived the tradition of combining scholarly and mystic learning (Metcalf 1982, 31–2), a tradition which had been eclipsed during the early period of Mughal rule that was marked by growing influence of the *ulama* vis-à-vis the *sufis* (Riaz 2008, 61). Another revival which occurred during the same period was related to the *manqulat* tradition, which was given more weightage in the curriculum of madaris. This revival was made possible by Shah Waliullah (1703–62), who not only emphasized the teaching of *tafsir* (exegesis) of the Quran but also included *Sihah-e-Sittah* (six authentic collections of Hadith) in the syllabus for his Madrassah Rahimia in Delhi. While urging the need and value of study of *manqulat* in bringing people closer to the teachings of Islam, Shah Waliullah, a contemporary of Muhammad bin Abdul Wahhab of Nejd, explicitly dismissed *ma'qulat* as mere intellectual exercises and a source of confusion (Metcalf 1982, 38).

Unlike Farangi Mahall, Waliullah's madrassah advocated a more independent and political role for *ulama* vis-à-vis the rulers. At a time marked by the decline of the Mughal Empire and the rise to power of the Marathas, Waliullah launched a movement from his madrassah to restore Muslim rule under a central authority. To achieve this, he developed a two-pronged strategy. First, he influenced the ruling elite through his teachings and wrote to Nizam ul-Mulk of Hyderabad, Najib ud-Daulah of Rohilkhand and even to Ahmad Shah Abdali of Afghanistan to take the initiative to revive stable Muslim rule (Metcalf 1982, 35). Second, Waliullah influenced the general Muslim population through a class of *ulama* which was prepared through the madaris set up in different parts of India (Sindhi 2008, 45–6). The first initiative of Waliullah proved to be short-lived and in vain. However, his intellectual work on religious thought succeeded in creating a class of *ulama* which was to play an important role in the future of Islamic education as well as Muslim politics in the subcontinent.

After Waliullah's death in 1762, the focus of his movement narrowed as his original ideas of *tatbiq* (intellectual synthesis), *ijtihad* (independent reasoning in matters relating to Islamic law) and religious harmony were ignored by his descendants. The movement gradually adopted *taqlid* (strict following) of the Hanafi *madhab* and contributed to disharmony among the Muslims through its criticism of Shias on the one hand and Sunni folk Islam on the other. For example, Waliullah in his book *Izaltul Khifa* had tried to address some misunderstandings between Shias and Sunnis, but his son Abdul Aziz in his book *Tohfa-e-Athna Ashari* aggressively dismissed Shia Islam. Similarly, in his will Waliullah had called on his heirs to forsake 'the customs of Arabs (pre-Islamic Arabia) and *hunud* (the Hindus)' (Ikram 2011, 572), but Abdul Aziz resolved to issue *fatawa* (plural of *fatwa*, a religious edict) concerning proper conduct on the tombs of saints.

Later on, condemnation of the popular customs of Indian Muslims became the major thrust of this movement, especially after Waliullah's grandson Muhammad Ismail wrote *Taqwiatul Iman*, a book inspired by Muhammad bin Abdul Wahhab's *Al-Tawhid*, which advocated a very strict and puritan concept of monotheism (Sindhi 2008, 70). This book by Ismail created a storm of protest by mainstream *ulama* and is still considered a controversial book (Faruqi 1963, 18). While stating that God alone was entitled to worship and homage, Ismail denounced all practices and beliefs that seemed to compromise faith in *tawhid* (the transcendent unity of God). Three sources were identified as threats to *tawhid*: false *sufism*, Shia Islam and popular customs (Metcalf 1982, 56–7). By aggressively attacking these sources, the movement adopted a 'practical approach' that eclipsed the original intellectual approach of Shah Waliullah.

As shall be discussed in the next chapter, Waliullah's intellectual tradition finally came to an end when his great grandson Muhammad Ishaq left the family madrassah in Delhi and migrated to Makkah in 1842 (Sindhi 2008, 98), leaving behind a group of dedicated students who were supposed to keep the movement alive. This group included Abdul Ghani Dehlwi, Mamluk Ali and Syed Nazir Ahmed (Metcalf 1982, 71; Sindhi 2008, 98). The first two persons were to play a vital role in the genesis of the DMM, while the third was to establish a distinctive sect called Ahle Hadith – a group which is *ghair muqallid* (who do not observe *taqlid* or following of any of the four *madhabs*, i.e. Hanafi, Shafi'i, Maliki and Hanbli). Compared to the DMM, the Ahle Hadith school of thought is considered closer to the teachings of Muhammad bin Abdul Wahhab of Nejd.

1.2 A Brief History of the DMM

As the East India Company took control of the subcontinent after assuming power in Bengal in 1765, they initially kept the old education system intact. Madaris and *maktabs* continued to operate with state support. Persian remained the official language and for 'the first fifty years of the Company's rule, the Musalmans [*sic*] had the lion's share of state patronage' (Hunter 1871, 141). Even when the company established an educational institution for Muslims in Bengal in 1780, it was called Calcutta Aliya Madrassah and adopted the *Dars-e-Nizami* curriculum until changes were eventually introduced in 1791 (Riaz 2008, 68). The 1831 charter of the East India Company indicated for the first time that English was to be introduced to the Indian educational system alongside vernacular languages.

In 1835, Parliament approved Thomas Macaulay's 'Minute on Education', introducing English as well as the Western education system to India, which resulted in the discontinuation of government support for madaris and other traditional educational institutions (Riaz 2008, 69). Before that, the East India Company, in an effort to increase its revenues, had acquired the *auqaf* (trusts) of madaris (Arshad 2005, 26), a step which made it virtually impossible to run these institutions. After English replaced Persian as the official language and medium of the higher courts in 1835, and once Governor-General Henry Hardinge decided in 1844 that only people with Western-style education and knowledge of English were eligible for state-sector jobs, the employability of madrassah graduates reduced remarkably (Riaz 2008, 70). On the other hand, the rapid growth in attendance at Western-style government schools was equally remarkable (Robinson 1974, 35).

The steps taken by the East India Company in the decade after 1835 reflected a shift in its earlier policies, which since 1765 were marked by moderation as well as determination to let Muslim power expire by slow natural decay (Hunter 1871, 117). As the previous policy helped to avert Muslim rebellion, the deviation from that policy after 1835 was likely to stir the sentiments of local populations, especially those linked to traditional institutions, both social and political. The result of this new policy was the War of Independence or the 'Mutiny' in 1857, represented by both Muslim and Hindu populations. That rebellion failed and consequently British rule was established all over India. British response to the rebellion was ruthless, especially against Muslims, who as the last rulers of India were disproportionately blamed for their part in the Mutiny. The whole population of Delhi was expelled for some time, thousands of Muslims were shot, several mosques were desecrated and many madaris were razed (Metcalf 1982, 84–5).

An important casualty of the Mutiny of 1857 was Delhi College, which had been established by the British in 1825. The college had been set up on the recommendations of the General Committee on Public Instruction, which lamented the state of private madaris. The goal of the college was the education of respectable people in order to enable them to find suitable jobs (Metcalf 1982, 72). There were two branches of the college, English and Oriental. The head of the Arabian department of the Oriental branch, Mamluk Ali, was closely associated with the Waliullah family and had been taught by a student of Abdul Aziz (Rizwi 2005, vol. 1, 97). Among the students of Mamluk Ali were Muhammad Qasim and Rasheed Ahmed, who were to launch a madrassah movement from Deoband in 1866.

After the failure of the 1857 war and the removal of even the symbolic presence of the Mughal Empire in India, the original dream of the Waliullah *ulama* to form an Islamic state was completely shattered and they were somehow persuaded that the British were invincible. Further, they realized that the introduction of the Western education system and the marginalization of madaris had endangered the intellectual tradition of Waliullah. Similarly, the British decision in 1864 to do away with Muhammadan law officers (Hunter 1871, 118) was considered a direct blow to the Islamic way of life. In addition, the activities of Christian missionaries were seen as a threat to Muslim culture in India.

The above-mentioned factors put those *ulama* in a completely defensive mode. Their proactive role for the expansion of Islam was replaced by the reactionary activity of 'protecting and preserving the Muslim cultural and religious life – an activity which manifested itself in a new form, inward-looking and primarily concerned with the Islamic quality of individual lives' (Metcalf 1982, 85–6). The madrassah at Deoband established in 1866 (some books say 1867) was the outcome of this reactionary approach and is considered a continuation of Shah Waliullah's movement under a different strategy (Sindhi 2008, 98; Shahjahanpuri 2004, 120).

Deoband is a small town in the district of Saharanpur in North India. It is located at 144 kilometres to the north-west of Delhi. The origin of the madrassah at Deoband was quite modest. It was started with just one teacher and one student, both named Mahmood, who started their first lesson under the pomegranate tree in the courtyard of a small mosque called Chhatta Masjid. Muhammad Qasim of Nanautah and Rasheed Ahmed of Gangoh, supported by several of their companions from Delhi College, were the founding fathers of this madrassah, which was to become the precursor of a huge movement in the coming years.

The major aim of the founders of this madrassah was to save the religion as well as the religious capital of Muslims in India (Arshad 2005, 29), while taking extra care to avoid any conflict with the British rulers (Metcalf 1982, 85). The madrassah would run on small public donations from Muslims and would accept no government funding (Khalid 2002, 100; Durrani 2001, 34).

Although the modest beginnings of the madrassah at Deoband pointed towards an informal system of education, the founders planned to establish it in the British bureaucratic style for educational institutions (Metcalf 1982, 93). According to Sindhi (2008, 98), it was founded on the model of Delhi College. Therefore, it was to have a fixed institutional character with permanent salaried staff, distinct classrooms and library, a fixed course of study, and regular examinations and convocations (Berkey 2007, 49). The administration worked at three levels: the *sarprast* or rector, who acted as patron and guide; the *mohtamim* or chancellor, who was chief administrative officer; and the *sadr mudarris* or principal, who was to look after instruction (Metcalf 1982, 95). So, long before this madrassah became a *darul ulum* (a term used for a higher level of religious education) in 1879, it was already structured as a university.

Since the founders' vision was to protect and preserve Muslim culture in India, one madrassah would not be enough to achieve their goal. Therefore, several new madaris were set up initially in the Upper Doab region of North India. By the end of 1880, at least fifteen madaris were operating on the pattern of the mother school at Deoband. By the end of the nineteenth century, more than fifty madaris had been established under the DMM.

Following the practice of Farangi Mahall and the Shah Waliullah schools, the DMM upheld the traditional role of their religious leaders as saints and scholars. However, the religious leaders belonging to the DMM stressed a responsible, reformist interpretation of the faith for their followers, while dismissing any intercession or miraculous intervention (Metcalf 1982, 140). In terms of Arthur Buehler's distinction, the DMM's spiritual leaders were 'teaching' *shaikhs* as opposed to the traditional 'mediating' *shaikhs* (Naeem 2009). Owing to this distinction, the DMM was able to detach itself from the traditional folk Islam that centred on *sufi* saints and their *khanqahs* and shrines. The Deobandis thus abandoned the popular *sufi* traditions and institutions of the subcontinent in favour of their own madaris, through which their particular version of Islam was to be preserved and preached.

While isolating itself from the institutional set-up of folk Islam, the DMM simultaneously opposed the popular beliefs and practices of Indian Muslims. These included celebrating the birthday of the Prophet (*Eid Milad-un-Nabi*), annual festivals of the saints (*urs*), distributing sweets upon completion of the Quran, and the belief that the Prophet shared God's knowledge of the unknown (*ilm-ul-ghaib*). The *ulama* belonging to the DMM also opposed elaborate marriage, birth and funeral ceremonies on the pretext that these were un-Islamic. This Deobandi opposition was in line with the 'practical' tradition of Waliullah's movement, as shall be explained in the next chapter.

For their opposition of the practices of the folk Islam, the DMM *ulama* faced severe criticism from their opponents. The fiercest opposition to Deobandi Islam came from the Ahle Sunnat wal Jamaat or Barelwi movement, which was launched in the 1880s under the leadership of Ahmad Raza Khan of Bareilly (Rohilkhand), whose father had earlier refuted the ideas of Syed Ahmed and Muhammad Ismail. Ahmad Raza (1856–1921) continued that tradition and issued a *fatwa* that Qasim and Rasheed of the DMM were no longer Muslims as they had shown disrespect to the Prophet (Metcalf 1982, 309).

The Barelwi school of thought later established its own madaris to counter the DMM. Although the Barelwis shared the Hanafi *madhab* with the Deobandis, they accepted the prevailing customs among Indian Muslims and championed the cause of saint worship (Faruqi 1963, 127) as well as veneration of the Prophet. As opposed to the DMM, the Barelwis 'wanted to preserve Islam unchanged: not Islam as was idealized in texts or the historical past, but Islam as it had evolved to the present' (Metcalf 1982, 296). As such, the Barelwis upheld the folk Islam followed by the majority of Muslims in the subcontinent.

Despite opposition from the *ulama* of other schools of thought, the DMM managed to establish itself in India. The growth of the DMM was mainly caused by two factors: a core of *ashraaf* (social elite) donors, and the effective use of modern communication methods such as the printing press and mail and money order services. Since the initial students and staff were mostly *ashraaf*, they were able to attract donors from their own class, including government servants, religious leaders, traders and land holders. This urban class was most adversely affected by the fall of Muslim rule on the one hand and the subsequent policies of the colonial rulers on the other (Metcalf 1982, 252–3). The DMM was now supposed to provide them with a sense of cultural pride and self-esteem. However, this pattern changed by the end of the nineteenth century when the student body of the DMM was dominated by children from the lower classes (*ajlaaf*) of rural areas, whose objective was to find better employment and enhance their social status. Its effective use of modern communication allowed the DMM to consolidate the core of donors by sending letters of invitation and publishing the list of sponsors along with their individual contributions. Posters and pamphlets distributed by the DMM also helped to attract more students.

Another factor which contributed to the growth of the DMM was the deliberate decision of its founders to stay away from political issues in an effort to avoid conflict with the British government. In fact, the DMM occasionally showed signs of loyalty to the British by celebrating coronation events and offering prayers for the Queen's health (Metcalf 1982, 154–5). However, this loyalty appears to have been a calculated move by the founders to avoid offending its colonial rulers. As shall be discussed in Chapter 3, the DMM largely stayed away from political activity from its inception in 1866 until the 1920s; it was only through joining the religious party Jamiat-ul-Ulama-e-Hind

(JUH; Association of Indian theologians) that the DMM finally decided to take part in political activities in the early 1920s. Later, the Deobandis opposed the Pakistan movement, which was launched in 1940 by the All-India Muslim League (AIML), a party representing the majority of Indian Muslims.

It is quite enigmatic that the DMM, which earlier appeared to follow Shah Waliullah's ideal of forming an Islamic state, suddenly performed a *volte-face* when the possibility was about to be realized in the shape of Pakistan. Instead of owning the idea and going all out for it, the DMM did the opposite and joined the Hindu-dominated Congress Party to work against the creation of Pakistan.

During the Pakistan movement, the AIML claimed to be the sole representative of the entire Muslim community of the subcontinent. By 1945, the popularity of the league and the idea of Pakistan had greatly increased. Spiritual leaders of different *sufi* orders had already shown support for Pakistan. Most of the Barelwi *ulama* were also in favour of Pakistan, and even a section of the Farangi Mahall *ulama* declared their support for the idea. However, an important group of Indian *ulama* represented by the DMM and JUH was still campaigning, in alliance with Indian National Congress, against the creation of Pakistan. The Jamaat-e-Islami of Maulana Maududi opposed Pakistan as well as the views of the JUH. In this scenario, the AIML contacted different *ulama* of the JUH to garner their support and finally succeeded in winning over Shabbir Ahmed Usmani, who in 1946 was elected president of a new Deobandi party called the Jamiat-ul-Ulama-e-Islam (JUI). This party later gained official support from the government of Pakistan (Binder 1961, 31) and would provide guidance and support to Deobandi madaris in the newly established state.

Until the creation of Pakistan in 1947, most Deobandi madaris were established in those areas which were to become part of India after independence. During the first 35 years of the DMM, almost fifty madaris were established, out of which only four were set up in areas which are now part of Pakistan (Metcalf 1982, 134). There is no exact figure available for the number of Deobandi madaris in those areas at the time of partition; however, Hafiz Nazar Ahmed (1960) has stated that there were 134 madaris of all denominations just before partition. At that time, several small Deobandi madaris were operating in big cities like Karachi, Lahore and Peshawar (Metcalf 1982, 134). In the year 1947, several important Deobandi madaris were established, including Jamia Ashrafia of Lahore, Khairul Madaris of Multan, Jamia Rasheedia of Sahiwal, Darul Ulum Al-Islamia of Hyderabad and Darul Ulum Haqqania of Akora Khatak (Shahjahanpuri 2004, 129) as shown in Figure 1.1 below. This trend continued under the leadership of JUI. By 1960, a total of 464 madaris had been established in Pakistan, out of which at least 50 per cent can be estimated to be Deobandi in the light of the later trend of denominations.

Since Pakistan is a predominantly Sunni country, most of the madaris belong to that sect. Less than 2 per cent of madaris represent the Shia sect. Within the Sunnis, there are three subsects (Deobandi, Barelwi and Ahle Hadith), which have their own brands of madaris. Apart from that, Jamaat-e-Islami also has its own madaris, which promote a non-sectarian approach. Each of these denominations has its own umbrella organization or central board, as shown in Figure 1.2.

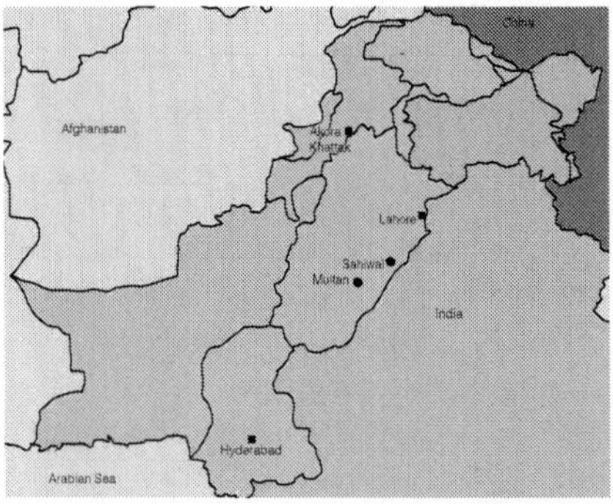

Figure 1.1. Cities of (West) Pakistan where Deobandi madaris were established in the year 1947.

Name of the sect/subsect	Name of umbrella organization	Date established
Deobandi	Wifaqul Madaris Al-Arabiyya	1959
Barelwi	Tanzeemul Madaris	1959
Ahle Hadith	Wifaqul Madaris Al-Salfia	1955
Jamaat-e-Islami	Rabtat ul Madaris Al-Islamia	1983
Shia	Wifaqul Madaris Shia	1959

Source: Khalid (2002, 143)

Figure 1.2. Umbrella organizations of madaris in Pakistan.

Although the number of madaris in Pakistan has always been on the rise, there was a remarkable increase in that number during the 1980s in the wake of Afghan resistance against Soviet occupation. Mostly Deobandi madaris benefitted from this increase and since then their share has always been more than 60 per cent of total madaris. The remarkable rise of madaris in Pakistan continued even after the Soviet withdrawal from Afghanistan. During the period 1988–2002, more than five thousand new Deobandi madaris were established, reflecting an increase of almost 300 per cent. Figure 1.3 shows the denominational increases in the number of madaris in Pakistan.

According to latest available figures, there were about thirty to thirty-five thousand madaris in Pakistan in 2009 (Akbar 2010, 147). Out of these, 60–70 per cent belonged to

Denomination/sect	Number of madaris		Increase 1988–2000 (%)
	1988	2002	
Deobandi	1,779	7,000	294
Barelwi	717	1,585	121
Ahle Hadith	161	376	134
Jamaat-e-Islami/others	97	500	415
Shia	47	419	792

Source: Rehman (2008, 64–5)

Figure 1.3. Increase in number of madaris in Pakistan.

the obandi sect, 20–25 per cent to Barelwi and 2–3 per cent to Ahle Hadith. About 3 per cent of madaris belonged to Jamaat-e-Islami and the share of Shia madaris was less than 2 per cent. In 2014, the website of the umbrella organization of the DMM, Wifaqul Madaris Al-Arabiyya (WMA), claimed to have an affiliation of 17,687 madaris with an enrolment of about 2.2 million. More than one-third of these madaris only provides initial or primary level education, which focuses mostly on reading and memorizing the Quran. WMA declares itself an educational and non-political organization whose aims and objectives include developing and updating curricula for affiliated madaris, holding examinations and issuing certificates and degrees, training teachers, and taking effective measures to protect Deobandi madaris.

As regards the madaris' curricula, Darul Ulum Deoband originally scheduled a course of ten years, later reduced to six (Metcalf 1982, 100). The school basically taught the *Dars-e-Nizami* – the curriculum devised by the Farangi Mahall school of thought. However, the Deobandis reduced Farangi Mahall's emphasis on rational studies (*ma'qulat*) and offered six Hadith books in line with Shah Waliullah's tradition.

Although all denominations of madaris in Pakistan call their bachelor-level course *Dars-e-Nizami*, there is some difference in terms of recommended books as well as interpretations of the texts. Even within the same denomination, madaris do not strictly follow a standardized curriculum. Notwithstanding such variations, the typical curricula of Pakistani madaris span eight years and hold some common elements, as shown in Figure 1.4.

Year 1	Biography of the Prophet (*Seerat*), conjugation/grammar (*sarf*), syntax (*nahw*), Arabic literature, chirography (*khush-navisi*), chant illation (*tajvid*)
Year 2	Conjugation/grammar, syntax, Arabic literature, jurisprudence (*fiqh*), logic, chirography, chant illation
Year 3	Quranic exegesis, jurisprudence, syntax, Arabic literature, Hadith, logic, Islamic brotherhood, chant illation, external study (Tareekh-e-Millat and Khilafat-e-Rashida Indian and Islamic movements)
Year 4	Quranic exegesis, jurisprudence, principles of jurisprudence, rhetoric, Hadith, logic, history, chant illation, modern sciences (sciences of cities of Arabia, geography of the Arab Peninsula and other Islamic countries)
Year 5	Quranic exegesis, jurisprudence, principles of jurisprudence, rhetoric, beliefs (*aqa'id*), logic, Arabic literature, chant illation, external study (history of Indian kings)
Year 6	Interpretation of the Quran, jurisprudence, principles of interpretation and jurisprudence, Arabic literature, philosophy, chant illation, study of the Prophet's traditions
Year 7	Sayings of the Prophet, jurisprudence, beliefs, responsibility (*fara'iz*), chant illation, external study (Urdu texts)
Year 8	Ten books by various authors focusing on the sayings of the Prophet

Source: Anzar (2003, 15)

Figure 1.4. Overview of curricula of madaris in Pakistan.

The courses covered in the *Dars-e-Nizami* syllabus are taught after the enrolled student has completed primary-level education from a *maktab* or a mainstream school. Several madrassah boards include in their curricula some 'secular' subjects in addition to *Dars-e-Nizami*, as shall be discussed in Chapter 4.

The eight-year course of *Dars-e-Nizami* is equivalent to a bachelor's degree called *Shahadatul Aliya*. After this, a two-year postgraduate degree of *Shahadatul Alamiya* is offered in bigger madaris. A few madaris even offer studies beyond this level, called *Takhassus* or specialization. A comparison of the levels of madrassah education with those of the mainstream education system is given in Figure 1.5.

Level in madaris	Duration	Madrassah *sanad* (diploma)	Equivalence to mainstream certificate
Ibtadaiya (naazra/tajvid)	4–5 yrs	*Shahadatul Tahfizul Quran*	Primary/5th grade
Mutawassata	2–3 yrs	*Shahadatul Mutwassat*	Middle/8th grade
Sanviya Aama	2 yrs	*Shahadatul Sanviya Aama*	Matric/10th grade
Sanviya Khasa	2 yrs	*Shahadatul Sanviya Khasa*	Intermediate/FA
Aliya	2 yrs	*Shahadatul Aliya*	Bachelor's
Alamiya	2 yrs	*Shahadatul Alamiya*	Master's

Source: Fair (2009, 52)

Figure 1.5. Comparisons of degrees of madaris and mainstream education.

Coming back to the sectarian divide, there is at least one political group or party in Pakistan to represent and propagate each of the above-mentioned denominations in the political arena. The Shia sect is represented by groups like Majlis-e-Wahdat-e-Muslimeen (MWM), Islami Tehreek Pakistan and the Hazara Democratic Party. Barelwi political groups include Sunni Tehreek, Jamiat-ul-Ulama-e-Pakistan (JUP) Noorani, JUP Sawad-e-Azam and the Sunni Ittehad Council. Jamaat-e-Islami is more of a political party than a sect. Deobandis are active in politics through Jamiat-ul-Ulama-e-Islam (JUI) and Ahle Sunnat wal Jamaat (ASWJ). Ahle Hadith is represented by Jamiat Ahle Hadith, which is further divided into two subgroups. JUI and Jamaat-e-Islami are the most active religio-political parties among these groups. JUI is further divided into three factions: the main faction is called JUI (F), headed by Maulana Fazal-ur-Rehman, while the minor factions are JUI (Nazariyati) under Maulana Asmatullah and JUI (S) under Maulana Samiul Haq, who also runs Darul Ulum Haqqania, the alma mater of several Afghan Taliban leaders. The politics of Deobandi groups is the subject of Chapter 4.

It is pertinent to add here that the DMM in Pakistan kept alive the original spirit of Darul Ulum Deoband by focusing on the 'practical tradition' of Shah Waliullah's movement regarding the need for an Islamic state as well reforming the customs and practices of Muslims. Further, the links of the DMM with Afghanistan since 1979 are reminiscent of the approach of Waliullah and his followers. However, the DMM in Pakistan seems to have ignored the intellectual tradition of Waliullah.

Even on the 'practical tradition', the DMM has shown signs of a marked decline in the sense that opposition to the prevailing practices of Muslim society has gradually intensified to the extent of intolerance and violent reaction against the followers of such practices. In that sense, the DMM has pitched itself against mainstream Muslim society, which mostly follows the traditional folk Islam long preached by *sufi* saints of the subcontinent.

Apart from condemning several customs and practices of folk Islam in Pakistan, the DMM's approach towards Shia Islam has moved from radical to fanatic. This extremist approach has led to the rise of several sectarian organizations that have been supported directly or indirectly by the DMM. This extremist trend in the DMM is the direct outcome of its involvement in the Afghan *jihad* against the Soviets as well as its subsequent links with the Taliban, who also follow Deobandi Islam. In fact, many Taliban leaders studied in the Deobandi madaris established by the DMM in the Pak-Afghan border areas to cater to the children of millions of Afghan refugees. Besides that, many Deobandi madaris sent their Pakistani students to Afghanistan to fight for the Taliban (Rashid 2008, 91–2) with the connivance of Pakistan's military intelligence agencies, who helped set up military training camps on the Pak-Afghan border to train madrassah students and other volunteers who were to take part in *jihad*.

The Afghanistan connection gave the DMM access to money, weapons and military training. Owing to this newly acquired strength, some sections of the DMM decided to put their radical ideas into practice through the use of force, leading to the formation of many extremist sectarian Deobandi parties such as Sipah-e-Sahaba Pakistan (SSP) and Lashkar-e-Jhangwi (LeJ). At first, these subgroups of the DMM asked that Shias be declared non-Muslims and later physically attacked them, as shall be explained in Chapter 4.

During the last decade, Deobandi extremist organizations have been alleged to be involved in attacks on major *sufi* shrines in Pakistan. These shrines are visited daily by thousands of devotees, who pay homage to the saints through various rituals which are considered *shirk* (polytheism) by DMM *ulama*. Some Deobandi sectarian organizations have also joined hands with Tehreek-e-Taliban Pakistan (TTP), an extremist organization and largely a Deobandi outfit. TTP was established in 2007 by two-dozen tribal militias and other groups from Punjab and Kashmir with the aim to take over Pakistan and turn it into a *Shariah* state under their rule (Rashid 2010, 239). Details are given in Chapter 4.

1.3 The DMM and Social Movements

In modern times, there have been many Islamic movements that resulted from the decline of Muslim states. The earliest among these movements was that of Muhammad bin Abdul Wahhab (1703–92), and the best known of recent times is that which culminated in the Iranian revolution of 1979 (Metcalf 1982, 3). There is no single convenient rubric under which these movements can be placed. Depending on their central ideologies, these have been called movements of primary resistance, social reform, religious syncretism, nationalism, modernization and even reaction and rebellion (Metcalf 1982, 3). Several Islamic movements have also been explained through the theories of social movement.

The study of religious movements from the perspective of 'social movement theory' is a recent phenomenon. Specialists in the fields of religious and social movements have, more often than not, failed to recognize the common grounds in which the two types of movements are rooted, opting instead to address different problems and formulate separate paradigms (Hannigan 1991). Despite the fact that the two commanding figures in modern sociology, Durkheim and Weber, situated religion within the wider study of social change, there has long been ideological opposition to the inclusion of religious movements as a legitimate topic for study within the field of social movements. According to this view, religion is the pillar of the status quo, and religious movements are treated as withdrawals from, rather than encounters with, social change. Taking the lead from Karl Marx's well-known maxim that religion is the 'opiate of the masses', Adorno (1974) supported the view that religion is a 'false' alternative to collective political action. More contemporary attempts by Turner and Killian (1972), Smelser (1962) and Rose (1982, 17) to classify social movements have also treated religious movements separately, relegating them to a marginal form (Hannigan 1991).

In recent decades, a theoretical renaissance has occurred in which scholars have identified much in common between social and religious movements both structurally and ideologically. According to Hannigan (1991), social movement theorists have been exploring a variety of new approaches that seek to reconcile traditional resource mobilization and action-oriented paradigms so as to explain more fully how and why social movements arise (Cohen 1985). At the same time, religious movements have also opened up to several promising reconceptualizations, notably those that view religious movements primarily as sources of personal empowerment (Beckford 1983) and those that treat contemporary religious movements as part of a more extensive world order (Wuthnow 1982) or 'globalization' process (Robertson 1989). However, this new synthesis between religious and social movements is mostly rooted in and orientated towards the highly differentiated, technologically advanced and politically open societies of the West, a fact that undermines its ability to account adequately for the dynamics of social activisms in the societies of the global South, especially in Muslim countries. Bayat (2005) has questioned the applicability of prevailing social movement theories to the complexities of socio-religious movements in contemporary Muslim societies.

As mentioned above, Islamic movements had been excluded, until recently, from the mode of inquiry developed by social movement theorists in the West. Scholars who have lately attempted to bring Islamic activism into the realm of 'social movement theory' often present contemporary Islamic movements as highly homogenous and coherent social units which are to be identified by the discourse of their ideologues. Besides that, Bayat (2005) has identified two types of interpretations regarding the spread of Islamic activism in modern times. The first type presents Islamism as a reactive movement, which is both anti-West and antidemocratic. The second type interprets Islamic movements as the manifestation of, and a reaction to, postmodernity. In this framework, these movements represent a quest for cultural autonomy and alternative polity vis-à-vis the universalizing secular modernity.

There seems to be a good deal of plausibility in such representations, and they offer important vantage points from which to view and interpret the movements of Maulana

Maududi in Pakistan, Syed Qutb in Egypt, Ayatollah Khomeini and Ali Shariati in Iran, and Abdul Salaam Yassin in Morocco. However, much of the research on social movement dynamics has been presented almost entirely in terms of the effect of external factors on a social movement (notably the structure of political opportunity), whereas the relevant civil societies, behaviours, attitudes, cultural symbols and value systems have mostly been ignored (Bayat 2005). Similarly, there is a strong tendency in the dominant interpretations to deduce the character of Islamist movements from 'Islam', which they often regard as a fixed and unique doctrine linked to the idea of a unitary *ummah* (Muslim community). This view, in a sense, ignores the influence of national cultures on the perception and practice of Islam across different national boundaries despite the fact that by now it has been established that there is not one but many Islams (Bayat 2005).

Metcalf (1982, 5) has also highlighted the above-mentioned limitations by stating that Islamic movements in modern times have differed in their approach and outlook, depending on the cultural and political constraints within which the Muslims of a particular region have found themselves. However, the traditional trend in studying the Islamic movements has taken a position whereby the vitality and creativity in Islam is a high cultural phenomenon limited to the classical age and the Middle East. In this regard, the DMM has not been an exception, as discussed below.

As far as the Indian subcontinent is concerned, it has had more than its share of Islamic movements, hence Albert Hourani's declaration that the eighteenth century was the 'Indian century' of Islam. One reason behind the spread of Islamic movements in South Asia may be the extreme form of political loss after the Mughal Empire disappeared. A second reason surely is the particular form of colonial control established by the British, whose interests sustained the old elites and simultaneously strengthened communal cleavages, as well as disseminating high forms of Hindu and Muslim culture. In dramatic contrast to this, the French in colonial North Africa co-opted the old religious elites while undermining the autonomy and vitality of traditional religious institutions (Metcalf 1982, 7–8).

Islamic movements in South Asia were mainly the result of three responses to the weakening of Muslim rule and the ensuing political instability during the eighteenth century (Metcalf 1982, 8–9). One response came from the *ulama* of the imperial capital of Delhi under the leadership of Shah Waliullah and his family. This movement later gave birth to the Deobandi and Ahle Hadith movements in the nineteenth century. Another response came from the *ulama* of the Farangi Mahall tradition in Lucknow, who, not unlike the Delhi *ulama*, aimed to preserve religious learning and maintain the old relationship between the ruler and the scholar. The third response was from the shrine-based *sufis* and *pirs* (saints) of the Punjab and Sindh. Originally led by the politically motivated landlord *pirs*, this response became the Barelwi movement of the nineteenth century, which was mainly concerned with preserving the popular values and practices of folk Islam by opposing the ideas of the Deobandi and Ahle Hadith movements.

As regards the DMM, it has been interpreted differently by different scholars. This diversity of opinion can be identified even within the writings of Deobandi scholars. The original constitution of the madrassah at Deoband included in its objectives the teaching of Islamic education as well as the propagation and protection of Islam, while simultaneously avoiding the influence of the colonial government (Rizwi 2005, vol. 1, 142). The official history of the Darul Ulum Deoband describes how the movement was launched for the survival and protection of the religious and collective lives of Muslims in the subcontinent (156). According to Muhammad Yaqub, the first principal of the Darul Ulum Deoband, 'This madrassah was set up for the revival of Islamic knowledge [at a time] when it appeared as if Islamic studies would vanish' (143). Deobandi scholars have not only given their movement the credit for the renaissance of Islam in India but also for the freedom of India from British rule (506–15).

Non-Deobandi scholars have mostly interpreted the DMM from 'modernist' perspectives. Metcalf (1982) has termed the DMM an Islamic reform and revival movement that was launched in the wake of British rule and Christian missionaries on the one hand and Hindu fundamentalist movements on the other. Murphy (2013, 25) regards the DMM as a revivalist and reformist movement that espoused 'a more literal and markedly austere interpretation of Islam'. Arshad (2005, 29) thinks that the DMM, like the Aligarh educational movement, was the product of a defeatist mindset in the post-Mutiny period and that its founders stressed only saving the religion and religious capital of Indian Muslims. Ahmed Rashid (2008, 88) is of the view that the Deobandis aimed to train a new generation of learned Muslims who would revive Islamic values based on intellectual learning, spiritual experience, *Shariah* law and *Tariqah* (spiritual path).

Saleem Ali (2009, 22) has stated two goals of the DMM: '(i) providing a more puritanical interpretation of Islam that would eschew the accretion of other diluting influences such as ritual visits to shrine; (ii) to organize a religious educational movement against British occupation'. However, Ali (2009, 84) has simultaneously added that the current madrassah establishment in Pakistan is quite conscious of being an inertial institution and acting as a 'cultural conservatory'. Riaz (2008, 73) has observed that the objective of the DMM was to correct the defective state of Islam and Muslim life in India. This correction was to begin with the revival of faith and piety. According to Riaz, the Deobandis were 'scripturalists' in their orientation and felt that Indian Muslims were facing threats not only from colonial rulers but also from within the community. The latter threat included the modernist efforts of Sir Syed Ahmad Khan of Aligarh, the practices of folk Islam including the *sufi* tradition, and Shias. Jonathan Berkey (2007, 49) has also termed the Deoband model 'scripturalist' as it focuses on the Quran and the Hadith and promotes 'the idea that through them [the Quran and the Hadith] rather than through the extensive medieval apparatus of commentary, one could discern the precise parameters' of the Muslim community and Islam. Berkey has also pointed out that by jettisoning much of the informal pattern of traditional Muslim education, the DMM model (inspired by the fixed British education model) undermined the highly personalized and polyvocal tradition of transmitting religious knowledge, which had encouraged flexibility and creativity in medieval Islamic educational and intellectual life.

Faruqi (1963, 24–5) has linked the DMM to the safeguarding of Indian Muslims' religion and culture, which were threatened by the official British educational system. Khalid (2002) has also described the DMM as a religious educational movement that was launched in reaction to the British education system, and as a result of that it is still averse to modern education. On the other hand, Rahman and Bukhari (2006) are of the view that madaris in Pakistan have never been considered part of the educational system and the state has always treated them as religious or social institutions.

Zaman (2007, 61–82) has explained the DMM phenomenon against the backdrop of madrassah learning as a tradition as well as an instrument for expanding the sphere of influence of the *ulama*. Alam (2003) has pointed out how the DMM model served the *ulama* as 'a tool for hegemony and control over the masses' through which they could transform ordinary Muslims into pious 'personally responsible Muslims'. According to Robinson (1971, 273–4), the DMM was launched to revive and strengthen the Islamic sciences with an emphasis on strict adherence to *Shariah.* Smith (1943, 320) has stated that the DMM's aim was 'to resuscitate classical Islam to rid the Muslims of theological corruptions, the ritual degradations and the material exploitation to which they have fallen prey since the British occupation'.

Hussain (2007, 78) has termed the Deobandis 'akin to Saudi Wahhabis'. According to him, the founders of the DMM drew their spiritual guidance from Waliullah; the movement, which originally sought to revive puritan Islam, later became radicalized after the call for *jihad* against the Soviet occupation of Afghanistan (Hussain 2007, 64). The Barelwi movement, which came into being as a reaction to the Deobandis, has also termed them Wahhabis for their attack on the Barelwi-supported 'meditational, custom-laden Islam, closely tied to the intercession of the *pirs* of the shrines, that was characteristic of the area [i.e. the subcontinent]' (Metcalf 1982, 296).

Rashid (2002, 121–2), while defining Deobandism and Wahhabism separately, has found some commonality between the two in terms of their 'tradition, which sees the seizure of power only as a way to impose *Shariah* and transform social behaviour'. This Deobandi–Wahhabi tradition is different from the 'Ikhwan-based movements, which seek to [first] seize state power and then transform each country into an Islamic political state'. According to Rashid (2002, 44), Deobandism, which helped radicalize Islamic thought in Pakistan, Afghanistan and Central Asia, is characterized by three features: abhorring Shia Islam, restricting the role of women in society, and reintroducing *jihad* in the latter half of the twentieth century.

To sum it up, the DMM has been explained mainly from two perspectives. First is the political interpretation, which focuses on the efforts of the DMM to establish an Islamic state and implement *Shariah.* The second perspective is based on the 'interiorization' thesis, which sees the DMM as a religious reform movement more concerned with the perfection of faith and moral development of ordinary Muslims, and less with asserting a political agenda (Pemberton 2009). Most of the literature on the DMM has focused on the first interpretation. Barbara Metcalf's 1982 work seems to have addressed the second perspective by stating that the 'interiorization' process after the disastrous 1857 uprising made the *ulama* undertake 'an inward turn focusing on cultivating a perfect Islamic life and practice instead of involving themselves with the external exigencies of British Rule and impending modernity' (Naeem 2009). Zaman (2003) has critiqued Metcalf's views, stressing the continuing participation of *ulama* in the public sphere as well as their engagement with the modern world. However, Naeem (2009) has found a middle ground by pointing out that Metcalf's work focuses on the early period of the DMM (1866–1900), while Zaman's major focus is the period after 1900. Naeem (2009) has also hinted that Metcalf's thesis does not exclude the political and public activities of the DMM and as such it is not a pure 'interiorization' thesis. In that sense, there appears to be a research gap with respect to interpretation of the DMM from a purely sociological rather than a political perspective. This book aims to fill that gap by focusing on the sociocultural milieu of the DMM.

Keeping in view the above discussion about the DMM as well as the limitations regarding the study of Islamic movements in the context of 'social movement theory', one may argue that the DMM is not an archetypal social movement. According to Gecas (2008, 349), a social movement is 'typically identified as representing and advocating one or a few specific values, such as equal rights, pro-choice, pro-environment'. The DMM, on the other hand, was apparently launched to protect the whole Islamic value system. As a matter of fact, the goals of the DMM, unlike a social movement, were never defined clearly. It is also interesting to note that the phenomena involved in social movements generally do not reflect an alternative culture in their purview (Westhues 1972, 22). On the other hand, one of the major objectives of the DMM was to preserve and purify the culture of Indian Muslims.

Furthermore, the history of the DMM does not fit in with the well-recognized four stages of a typical social movement lifecycle: emergence, coalescence, bureaucratization, and decline or institutionalization. Unbefitting the emergence stage, the origin of the DMM did not owe to 'widespread discontent' (Hopper 1950) against certain policies or social values. Rather, the DMM was a continuation of an earlier movement of Shah Waliullah, as reported by both Deobandi (Sindhi 2008, 108; Rizwi 2005, vol. 1, 27; Shahjahanpuri 2004, 120; Gilani n.d., vol. 1, 254) and non-Deobandi writers (Hussain 2007, 78; Metcalf 1982, 71–2; Faruqi 1963, 24–5; Smith 1943, 320). Similarly, the DMM did not pass through the coalescence stage, which is characterized by mass demonstrations to express public discontent (Christiansen 2009). On the contrary, the DMM took an inward-looking approach and initially preferred to isolate itself from mainstream society by restricting itself behind the walls of its madaris (Metcalf 1982, 85–6). As regards bureaucratization, the DMM did introduce this concept at the level of individual madaris (Metcalf 1978) but as a movement its madaris continued to enjoy a lot of independence and autonomy from the Darul Ulum Deoband due to a lack of any centralized bureaucratic system. This situation still continues in Pakistan, where Deobandi madaris are only loosely affiliated with their umbrella board, mostly for conducting examinations. Similarly, various Deobandi political and sectarian groups operate independently. The fourth stage of the social movement lifecycle is marked by repression, co-optation, success and failure (Miller 1999). Likewise, these features cannot be consistently applied to the DMM in terms of its decline or institutionalization.

As regards the four major theories of social movement (i.e. collective behaviour, resource mobilization, new social movement and action-identity approaches), neither of these concepts can be employed to understand and explain the DMM. Each of these theories was developed for the analysis of a distinct kind of social movement in a particular social and political context. For example, the 'collective behaviour' approach has been used to interpret social movements of a totalitarian type, such as fascist or communist movements. The 'resource mobilization' approach is mainly employed for the analysis of movements for citizens' rights of the 1960s and 1970s and special interest groups such as the feminist, anti-nuclear and other movements of semi-integrated minorities. The 'action-identity' approach is generally associated with analysis of the social and political movements of the late 1960s and 1970s, such as anti-nuclear mobilizations and urban protests. The 'new social movements' approach analyses movements of the 1970s and 1980s such as ecological, anti-nuclear and feminist movements (Mamay 1991). The genesis and evolution of the DMM as described is not in keeping with these theories.

1.4 The DMM in a Countercultural Context

Despite the above-mentioned incongruence between the DMM and a typical social movement, the former still shares a few features with the latter. Taking the lead from the definition by De la Porta and Diani (2006, 20), the DMM is 'involved in conflictual relations with clearly identified opponents' (i.e. followers of folk Islam); is linked by an informal network (i.e. madaris); and holds a collective identity. However, it is interesting to note that the DMM does not openly declare its conflict with folk Islam and prefers to indirectly criticize the beliefs and practices of mainstream Muslim society in Pakistan. Further, the madaris under this movement are practically independent and autonomous in their operations. As such, the DMM can be considered at most a loose form of social movement. According to Scott (1990; cited in Haenfler 2004), social movements exist on a continuum of structure, with fully bureaucratized, formal organizations on the one extreme and very diffuse movements on the other. Therefore, the DMM can be termed at best a diffuse social movement, if at all.

However, it is quite difficult to develop a conceptual framework to study the DMM as a diffuse movement because 'theoretical development of examples at the diffuse extreme is less common [and the] precise role of collective identity in diffuse, culture-based movements has yet to be fully explained' (Haenfler 2004, 786). In this regard, one may refer to the literature that explains social movements from a countercultural perspective. The leading contributors to such literature are Milton Yinger and Kenneth Westhues. Yinger (1960) defined the concept of counterculture as a 'normative system of a group which contains, as a primary element, a theme of conflict with the values of the total society'. Later on, Yinger further refined the concept and defined counterculture 'as a set of norms and values of a group that sharply contradict the dominant norms and values of the society of which that group is a part' (1982, 3). It is pertinent to add here that the DMM has also been involved in condemning the social and cultural norms of Muslims of the subcontinent. Further, the Deobandi madaris in Pakistan fit more closely with Westhues's depiction of counterculture, which he described as 'a social island existing in society's sea' (1972, 20).

In view of the above considerations, this book aims to study the DMM in a countercultural context in order to understand it at a deeper level. Without discounting the political role as well as impact of the DMM, this book shall explore whether or not the DMM has manifested countercultural tendencies, and if so, then the extent to which this is the case. As such, this research aims to add a new perspective to the study of Islamic movement in general and the DMM in particular.

1.4.1 What is a counterculture?

The term counterculture is generally considered to have been coined by Theodore Roszak, who used it to illuminate the 1960s phenomenon of 'youthful dissent', which included 'the mind-blown bohemianism of the beats and hippies [and] the hard-headed political activism of the student New Left' (1968, 56). Sweeping through Continental Europe and the United States, this youth movement was marked by rejection of both the socialist and capitalist models of society and the search for new forms of social organization (Klineberg et al. 1979). Roszak found the rising culture of the youth 'so radically disaffiliated from the mainstream assumptions of our society' that he referred to the phenomenon as a 'counterculture' (1968, 42). According to Roszak, the revolt of the youth was there to counter the technocracy, which he defined as 'the society in which those who govern, justify themselves by appeal to technical experts who, in turn, justify themselves by appeal to scientific forms of knowledge' (1968, 8). Against the backdrop of the youth movement, Musgrove has further suggested that countercultures are linked to 'steep population growth and intensive migration associated with great economic transformations' (1974, 196).

Despite the fact that Roszak (1968) is generally given credit for coining the term counterculture, the concept was actually introduced quite earlier by Milton Yinger (1960), at a time prior to the youth movement. The origin of the word 'counterculture' can be traced back to Parsons (1951, 522), who mentioned it as a flippant substitute for subculture. But the term later became so closely associated with the phenomenon of youth dissent in 1960s that it almost became a synonym for the movement. The emergence of the youth revolt was so forceful, and received so much attention from the Western media and academia, that the concept of counterculture, which was intently attached to this revolt, lost its independent interpretation. Therefore, as the youth movement gradually declined in 1970s, the term counterculture lost its significance.

This marginalization of the concept of counterculture was so remarkable that it has even been suggested to be nothing more than an early explanation of a disorganized phenomenon (Jonsson 1981, 178). For instance, Bash (1972) was so critical that he declared that counterculture was 'neither a theoretical nor an empirical term but rather an interpretation of an observable' (Jonsson 1981, 179). Similarly, Buchdahl (1977, 467) suggested that the term counterculture was 'merely a sign that was applied over-hastily to a complex and continuing process of cultural change'.

Since the term 'counterculture' became associated primarily with the youth movement of the 1960s, scholars endeavoured to interpret the concept in that narrow context as the movement progressed, evolved and declined. Later on, the concept became even more marginalized when other terms were introduced in the 1970s to explicate the changes in the phenomenon of the youth movement especially with respect to its relationship with the mainstream society. Those terms included: utopian community, deviant adaptation, subculture, Aquarian Frontier, New Age, soft revolution and the Human Potential Movement (Jonsson 1981, 179–80). Charles Reich (1970, 217) called it 'Consciousness III', which led to the 'Greening of America' (1970, 349). He suggested that Consciousness I was marked by individualism and capitalism, while Consciousness II was represented by the rise of the corporate state after World War II. With the introduction of so many terms in the literature on youth movement, the independent concept of counterculture gradually became more indistinct.

Although there is a lot of literature available on counterculture, almost all of it can be termed a 'period piece' in the sense that it was written against the backdrop of youth culture in the 1960s. Westhues (1972, 8) noted that most of the literature on counterculture 'is a straightforward description of the contemporary youth scene, and the reader is left by default with the impression that this is the only counterculture that the world has ever known'. However, Milton Yinger, who introduced the concept in 1960 as 'contra-culture', has conducted a detailed study of different countercultures in the Western world, to show that 'countercultures are not simply bizarre and marginal sets of standards and activities, but important elements in the process of social change' (1982, ix).

By employing an historical approach, Yinger has been able to identify and explain the presence of countercultures in the fields of politics, religion and economics. In politics, Yinger (1982, 200–205) has discussed in terms of counterculture the 'new left' movement on the one hand and the 'far right' groups like the Ku Klux Klan on the other. Similarly, he has also identified in this regard several anarchist groups like the 'Situationists' in France, 'Kommune I' in Germany and the 'Provos' in the Netherlands. Among the disadvantaged, Yinger (1982, 179–84) has described several African American movements like the Black Muslims, the Nation of Islam and the Black Panthers as countercultural.

As regards the counterculture in economics, Yinger (1982, 212) has built his argument around four themes that seemed to dominate attacks on economic institutions: concentration of economic power through control of the major means of production; great inequality in income distribution; materialism (i.e. overemphasis on the human value of possessions); and technocracy. For Yinger, Marxism in its fullest sense contained all these four themes to qualify as an economic counterculture. Among other economic countercultures, Yinger has included 'anti-technology', 'no work' or 'anti-work' groups as well as protest movements against state capitalism of the 1960s and 1970s. Demodernizing movements of 1930s in Japan and Germany have also been linked to economic countercultures. While referring to numerous movements in Germany during the Hitlerian period that equated 'modern' with alien, Jewish and Western as opposed to traditional German folk, Yinger (1982, 218) has pointed out that such countercultural movements occurred because Germany, like Japan, had implemented industrialization into a society that still contained many feudal qualities. It is interesting to note that Yinger has termed the emerging breed of 1970s businessmen in the United States 'countercultural capitalists' who attended schools for 'entrepreneurs' (222). During the last four decades, such capitalists have become part of the dominant culture and can no more be called counterculturalists. This development is in line with Yinger's assertion that 'what is countercultural today may also be tomorrow, or it may disappear, or it may flow into the dominant cultural stream' (46).

As for the countercultural religions, Yinger (1982, 227) has stated that 'Christianity was, at first, countercultural mainly to Judaism, from which most of its early converts as well as many of its beliefs – and much of its opposition – came. In a few generations, however, it was more drastically at odds with the Roman Empire.' Within Christianity, Yinger (1982, 229–33) has examined Gnosticism, the Church of Satan and the Unification Church from the countercultural perspective. Further, some quasi-religious groups like the Church of Scientology and *est* (Erhard Seminars Training) as well as cults like Hare Krishna as well as the Meher Baba and Rastafari movements have also been depicted as countercultural (Yinger 1982, 239–47).

Apart from Yinger, Westhues (1972) has also investigated the sociology of countercultures from a broader perspective. He has described a counterculture as 'a set of beliefs and values which radically reject the dominant culture of a society' (1972, 9–10). According to Westhues (1982, 437), counterculture is represented by a 'group which breaks with the mainstream order more sharply, detaches itself more completely and establishes its own relatively self-contained way of life'.

This research will employ Yinger's counterculture theory. Yinger has stated that the central questions regarding social order and change should be approached in a paradoxical manner, by looking for explanations of disorder, rather than order (1982, 3–4). He has formulated his theory by focusing on the disorderly side of three theories of social order. The first theory, in this regard, defines social order as the product of *reciprocity* whereby behaviour occurs in anticipation of rewards from others. The second theory posits social order as a consequence of the *power* of some to command compliance from others and the behaviour in this sense is caused by coercion. The third theory states that social order is a product of a mutually shared *normative system* (culture) and behaviour here occurs in harmony with values and norms to which one has been socialized (1982, 4). The three components of the 'reciprocity–power–normative system' social order provide the fundamentals for Yinger's theory.

According to Yinger (1982, 6), individuals and groups attack a frustrating social order by protesting against the above-mentioned three components: reform movements primarily strike at the reciprocity component and attempt to change social bargains; rebellions mainly attack the power component and strive to change the rulers; countercultural movements predominantly strike at the normative component and focus on the reorganization of culture; revolutions attack all three components to change the whole social order. Westhues (1972, 18), who otherwise included the power component as a target of counterculture movements, has simultaneously stated that 'discontent with existing power structure [...] does not lead to attempts at political change [because] in most cases, counterculture lacks the power to destroy its parent society'. Further, Westhues (1972, 11) has also highlighted the difference between reform and counterculture movements by stating that 'a counterculture that would be satisfied with some modification of the wider culture is no counterculture at all'.

Although a counterculture is primarily a protest against the normative values of a society, there is also an opposition at secondary level. This secondary protest hits at both the power structure and reciprocity patterns only where they are linked to normative values (Yinger 1982, 6). As a result of this protest by a counterculture movement, new normative systems emerge in opposition to the prevailing culture, along with the groups and individuals who are proponents and carriers of the oppositional culture. Apart from proposing this cultural–countercultural dialectic as a tool for resolving problems of analysis and interpretation, Yinger has also described the study of countercultures as a way of explaining normative aspects of social change (4–8). He also emphasized that if one sought to select one theme for the study of the cultural–countercultural dialect, religion would be the wisest choice (226). As such, this research shall also be significant with respect to the potential impact of the DMM on Pakistani society.

1.4.2 Boundaries of counterculture

A countercultural movement is a combination of behavioural and symbolic streams, which respectively represent non-conformity and criticism of society's values. These streams are never entirely separate. Some individuals in a countercultural movement might be both the exemplars and theoreticians of the cultural inversions while others could be identified primarily with either the symbolic or the behavioural stream (Yinger 1982, 23–4).

According to Yinger,

> The term counterculture is appropriately used whenever the normative system of a group contains as a primary element, a theme of conflict with the dominant values of society, where the tendencies, needs, and perceptions of the members of that group are directly involved in the development and maintenance of its values and whenever its norms can be understood only by reference to the relationship of the group to the surrounding dominant society and its culture. (1982, 22–3)

The term 'values' in this definition refers to 'the states and objects towards which behaviour is preferentially directed', while norms are 'the culturally approved procedures and objects believed necessary to optimize the realization of values in particular sets of condition' (Yinger 1982, 23). As regards the conflicts, Yinger (1982, 38) has used the term counterculture to refer to normative and value conflicts *within* a society (intra-societal), not to those *among* societies (inter-societal).

While stating that it is unlikely to 'draw the boundaries around the territory of countercultures with sufficient clarity or completeness', Yinger has attempted to define some broad parameters of counterculture (1982, 24–39). According to him, countercultural behaviour is a form of group-supported deviation, which is nonconformist but not aberrant as such. This distinction can be understood by the fact that the nonconformist takes pride in his deviant acts and believes they are moral, but the aberrant feels guilty and believes his acts are immoral or wrong. For example, illegal behaviour is not countercultural by definition when the violation is aberrant or when the violated law does not represent the prevailing norms. However, illegal behaviour becomes countercultural 'if it is nonconformist, if it is accepted by a group as an expression of its normative system, and if it does not have substantial support, overt and covert, from the larger society' (35). For instance, terrorism as a way of life is countercultural. Similarly, the legend of Robin Hood would be countercultural and so would be the participants in the civil rights movement who sought to get a cup of coffee in a 'legally' segregated restaurant in the United States. These examples also underscore an important point: 'To call something countercultural is not to applaud it or lament it' (35). As far as religious movements are concerned, Yinger has emphasized that 'the presence of countercultural religions is not intrinsically good or bad' (27).

Yinger has also pointed out that 'the values of a group can be moderately or extensively countercultural: a few, several, or a large number of the institutional patterns can be opposed' (1982, 26). As such, it is not the quantity of dominant norms and values challenged by a particular group that qualify it as a counterculture. Mostly it is the mixture of countercultural elements and sometimes it is just the intensity of a few such elements that make a group countercultural. Similarly, the flow of a counterculture varies at different points of time; it is 'now a torrent, now a trickle, at one time underground, at another fully visible' (11). Yinger has also suggested that some countercultures may have reactionary qualities referring to a retreat to earlier values (36). These are blended, however, with new elements and utopian elements to produce standards sharply at odds with the dominant contemporary system of values.

1.4.3 Types of counterculture

Milton Yinger (1982, 91) has identified the following three types of countercultural groups. These are analytic distinctions, of course, not empirical descriptions.

i. Radical prophetic *activist* counterculture 'preaches, creates or demands *new* obligations'. It attacks the dominant culture and its institutional expressions.
ii. Communitarian *ascetic* counterculture 'withdraws into a separated community where the new values can be lived out with minimum hindrance from an evil society'. It works for the purification of values.
iii. Bohemian *mystic* counterculture is represented by 'those who are searching for the truth and for themselves'. It does not so much attack society as disregard it.

According to Yinger (1982, 91), 'Every countercultural group tends to be a mixture; the strains and the splits they experience often result from the sharply contrasting views of the best way to realize their oppositional values'. In this regard, he gives the example of the 'new left' movement of 1970s that combined revolutionary (activist) and hippie (mystic) ideas. The 'activist' counterculturalists of the movement later concluded that the tendency of 'mystic' participants to 'define political problems in terms of personal issues, often in the language of alienation, seems a terrible deflection from the basic goal of achieving a society based on new values' (Clecak 1973; quoted in Yinger 1982, 91).

Referring to different amalgams of the above-mentioned types in single countercultural movements, Yinger (1982, 94) has observed that such 'mixtures are common but unstable because of the mutually contradictory qualities of both the means seen as effective in attaining the various goals and of the goals themselves'. As shall be discussed later, the DMM has also shown the rise of these three types of countercultural trends at various points of the movement's history. This work goes one step further by proposing a fourth type (i.e. *extremist* counterculture, which is marked by terrorist attacks on the followers of folk Islam who visit *sufi* shrines) that has emerged in the DMM during the last decade.

1.5 Research Methodology and Approach

A counterculture is not an independent culture. It develops out of conflict with the dominant tradition or culture (Yinger 1982, 187). So what, then, is cultural about counterculture? In line with Yinger's approach, this research has focused on culture as a blueprint of a society, a system of normative guidelines. Here, the most relevant definition of culture would be that of Kluckhohn and Kelly (1962, 54). According to their definition, culture is 'all those historically created designs for living, explicit and implicit, rational, irrational, and non-rational, that exist at any given time as potential guides for the behaviour of men [*sic*]'.

For this research, the culture in question is that of the Muslim society in colonial India (1866–1947) as well as that in Pakistan (1947 to date). The counterculture for this research comprises the norms and beliefs of the DMM which came into sharp conflict with those of mainstream Muslim society in the above-mentioned periods. Instead of examining the overall Muslim culture in the Indian subcontinent, this research has simply examined, through a historical approach, the DMM's countercultural reversals of the prevailing beliefs and practices of Muslim society at different periods of time.

According to Yinger (1982, 41), a counterculture is defined primarily by its reversal of the dominant norms and beliefs. He further states that 'every counterculture has unique elements that for some purposes are appropriately the focus of attention'; hence countercultures have been studied from many different perspectives (11). This book has adopted a research approach whereby countercultural reversals in the case of the DMM have been identified in the first instance and then the dominant behaviour has been explained afterwards. This inverted approach to the study of such reversals as well as the 'disorderly' aspects of the normative system is quite in keeping with the concept of the counterculture itself (4). This selective approach of looking only for the countercultural hues in the DMM while ignoring other aspects is in line with American literary theorist Kenneth Burke's (1897–1993) notion that 'a way of seeing is also a way of not seeing'. In other words, this work mostly looks at the DMM through a countercultural lens. However, since the cultural blueprint of a society can be ambiguous and difficult to decipher (31), in this book the countercultural deviations of the DMM have in part been defined situationally and politically.

This work basically addresses the following major research question:

How can the Deoband Madrassah Movement be understood from a countercultural perspective?

Based on the hypothesis that the seeds of counterculture were sown in the origins of the Deoband Madrassah Movement, this major question has been answered through following secondary questions.

i. Which countercultural tendencies has the Deoband Madrassah Movement (DMM) shown from its origin to the partition of India (1866–1947) on the one hand and in Pakistan since 1947 on the other?
ii. How do the values and attitudes of the Deobandis differ from those of mainstream Muslim society in Pakistan?

Taking the lead from Yinger's methodology to identify and measure countercultures (1982, 44), the above-mentioned sub-questions have been researched in two stages.

The first stage addressed the first sub-question through a detailed survey of the literature on the DMM from its inception in 1866 to the present day. This work has reviewed the relevant literature in both English and Urdu, the latter including material written by Deobandi scholars mostly during the twentieth century. This inclusion of Deobandi literature is important in the sense that it is equally valid and reliable in terms of identifying countercultural tendencies and values, because 'countercultures tend to be defined, both by themselves and by others, as much by what they are set against as by their own normative system' (Yinger 1982, 41). This first stage of the literature review has relied on measured observations to record the oppositional values and behaviour of the DMM vis-à-vis the prevailing practices of Muslim society. Accordingly, countercultural tendencies in the DMM have been identified at different stages in its 150-year-long history with a particular emphasis on the post-independence period in Pakistan. The DMM in postcolonial India and Bangladesh has not been included in the scope of this research.

Countercultural ideas are promoted both in social settings as well as through printed material and in today's world through electronic media including the Internet. Accordingly, the second stage of research in this work aimed to look into these instruments of dissemination through fieldwork in Pakistan, which operated at two levels: a review of Deobandi journals and interviews with students from madaris and mainstream educational institutions. The Deobandi print media was selected for review due to the fact that DMM has little presence in the electronic media, which is itself a target of the DMM's countercultural opposition. This review focused on three Deobandi journals to identify countercultural trends in the DMM during the last two decades. The second level of fieldwork comprised 40 semi-structured qualitative interviews with students of a Deobandi madrassah and a mainstream postgraduate college with the objective of comparing their values and attitudes.

With respect to fieldwork research, it would be relevant to add here that values are generally conflated with attitudes. But values are different in the sense that these are more abstract than attitudes (Rokeach 1973; Hitlin and Piliavin 2008). Values are 'conceptions of the desirable' (Kluckhohn 1951; cited in Wuthnow 2008) whereas an attitude is 'an organization of several beliefs around a specific object or situation' (Rokeach 1973; cited in Spates 1983, 30). Further, values are beliefs, which transcend specific actions and situations and serve as standards and criteria to guide attitude and behaviour (Schwartz 2006).

There is a lack of standardized methods for measuring values and attitudes. As regards the measurement of values, the most systematic and influential approaches have been the Rokeach Value Survey (RVS) and Schwartz Value Survey (SVS), which respectively employ ranking and rating techniques. Rokeach (1973) developed a list of 18 instrumental (means) values and 18 terminal (ends) values, while Schwartz (1994) identified 10 values, each defined in terms of its motivational goal (Hitlin and Piliavin 2008). The instrumental values of RVS mainly focus on self-directed competence, restrictive conformity and pro-social personal concerns, while terminal values are concerned with individual self-definition, positive affiliation, mature accomplishment, universal pro-social values and a life without inner and outer conflicts (Debats and Bartelds 1996). The values included in SVS are achievement, benevolence, conformity, hedonism, power, security, self-direction, stimulation, tradition and universalism (Spini 2003). Later on, Schwartz (2006) put forward a theory of seven cultural value orientations that form three cultural value dimensions: embeddedness versus autonomy (intellectual and affective), egalitarianism versus hierarchy, and harmony versus mastery. Despite a great deal of empirical cross-cultural support for these surveys, their value items may not be valid for a study in Pakistan, because these instruments have primarily focused on the developed countries (Hitlin and Piliavin 2008) and hence are biased towards Western values (Spini 2003). Most of the values defined in these surveys are either not relevant for this research or they might carry a different connotation in Pakistani society. Schwartz (2006, 144) has stated that 'values whose meanings differ across cultures should not be used in cross-cultural comparison'.

Therefore, this work has not, as such, included the values described in the above-mentioned surveys. Instead, the values of madaris have primarily been identified through a review and analysis of the literature on the DMM. As regards attitudes, the fieldwork for this research mainly focused on four themes: popular customs and practices, politics, education and the role of women in Pakistani society.

It may not be out of place to reiterate here that this book aims to point out countercultural trends in the DMM without disregarding the existing interpretations of this movement. In other words, this book intends to explain the history, evolution and behaviour of the DMM specifically from a countercultural standpoint. Therefore, it is not unlikely that anyone employing a different context would be tempted to disagree with the observations and findings of this research. However, such disagreement shall not be in conflict with this research's overall objective to add a new perspective to the study of Islamic movements like the DMM.

Chapter 2

ORIGIN OF THE DMM: SEEDS OF A COUNTERCULTURE

A new cultural pattern does not emerge out of nothing – the seed must already be there.

Philip Slater, *The Pursuit of Loneliness* (1971, 111)

This chapter establishes the case that the DMM continued what Shah Waliullah began. It also explains that some countercultural currents were present in his movement, but these were overshadowed by its larger intellectual canvas. Those countercultural trends gradually became more prominent after Waliullah's death, when a 'practical' rather than intellectual tradition became dominant. This chapter argues that the DMM was the continuation of the 'practical' version of Waliullah's movement. Finally, the chapter suggests that the DMM's intellectual decline brought forward the countercultural countenance of the movement, which came into conflict with several social and cultural norms and values of mainstream Muslim society in India.

2.1 Shah Waliullah's Movement

Shah Waliullah (1703–63) was born in Delhi four years before the death of the Mughal emperor Aurangzeb, whose death is considered to mark the beginning of the end of Muslim rule in India. In the fifty years following Aurangzeb's death, the Delhi court saw ten emperors, only four of whom died a natural death (Mian 1988, 76). As the palace intrigues weakened the central authority of the Mughal Empire, many regional power centres sprang up in India. Marathas took control of South India and later also gained influence in the Delhi court after their victory against the Mughals in 1736 (Mian 1988, 86). Rohailas set up their government north-east of Delhi, while Sikhs became strong in North West India (Abbott 1962). In 1737, Afghan ruler Nadir Shah attacked and looted Delhi, killing thousands of people. After that attack, North West India and Punjab were completely cut off from the Delhi sultanate. On the eastern front, Bengal, Bihar and Orissa also severed ties with the central government of Delhi. These regions were later occupied by the British East India Company after the Plassi war in 1757 (Mian 1957, vol. 2, 36–7).

The period after Aurangzeb's death was also marked by the rise of Shia Islam in India. The last Mughal emperor, Bahadar Shah Zafar, in fact introduced Shia practices at the imperial court during his rule from 1837 to 1857. Zafar, a poet and a devout follower of *sufi* Islam, presided over an empire that barely extended beyond Delhi's Red Fort in the wake of the rise of the British East India Company. Later on, the Lucknow court of

Oudh became the centre of Shia culture. The rulers and nobles of Hyderabad, Amroha and Rampur also patronized Shia Islam (Metcalf 1982, 41). This official patronage led to notable conversions to Shiaism throughout India. Under the rising influence of Shia Islam, even ordinary Sunni Muslims began to observe Shia practices, such as taking part in mourning assemblies and processions in the Islamic month of Muharram to mark the martyrdom of Imam Hussain, son of Caliph Ali and grandson of the Prophet Muhammad (PBUH). The orthodox Sunni *ulama* opposed such Shia practices, marking the beginning of sectarian differences among Indian Muslims during the eighteenth century.

Under these circumstances, Waliullah decided to launch a movement for the revival of Islam as well as Muslim rule in India. The centre for his movement was the Madrassah Rahimia in Delhi. That madrassah was founded by his father, Shah Abdur Rahim, who was himself a renowned religious scholar. Unlike the *ulama* of his time, Shah Abdur Rahim was averse to work in royal courts and actually declined an invitation to join the Delhi court during Emperor Aurangzeb's reign (Mian 1957, vol. 2, 25). Waliullah received religious education from his father at Madrassah Rahimia and in 1821 took over as head after his father's death. Later, he went to the Hijaz for about two years to study the Hadith (Mian 1957, vol. 2, 4–5).

In fact, it was during his stay in the Hijaz that Waliullah developed his vision for a revivalist Islamic movement. Waliullah was a contemporary of Muhammad bin Abdul Wahhab of Nejd (1703–87). Both studied in Madinah in almost the same period, had at least one teacher in common and were deeply influenced by the revivalist teachings of Ibne Taiymiyah (1263–1328), a fourteenth-century jurist of Damascus (Alan 2005). However, the major influence on Waliullah during his stay in the Hijaz was his teacher Shaikh Abu Tahir, who was a follower of Ibne Taiymiyah. Shaikh Abu Tahir's father Shaikh Ibrahim Kurdi was also a great scholar, who not only respected the teachings of Taiymiyah but was also convinced of the greatness of Spanish *sufi* mystic Ibne Arabi (1165–1240), whose ideas were emphatically refuted by Taiymiyah. Waliullah himself later followed Kurdi's approach in accepting the teachings of both Taiymiyah and Arabi (Sindhi 2008, 67) with more of a focus on conformity than conflict.

After returning to India, Waliullah began his movement by influencing the Muslim political elite of Delhi on the one hand and creating a class of *ulama* on the other (Sindhi 2008, 45–6). Waliullah's movement operated at three levels: intellectual, social and political. At the intellectual level, the movement focused on the renaissance of Islam in India through the study and teaching of the Quran and the Hadith. Troubled by the social, political and religious disorder among Muslims, Waliullah 'sought to stem the tide of decline by consolidating and classifying the entire body of Islamic tradition' (Metcalf 1982, 36) through *tatbiq* – a term used to define the process of finding a common ground between apparently contradicting statements or ideas. The principle of *tatbiq* is the hallmark of Waliullah's work. For example, he favoured *ijtihad* (effort) over strict *taqlid* (following) of a particular school of *fiqh* (Islamic jurisprudence). *Ijtihad* is the making of a decision in *Shariah* by individual effort independent of Islamic jurisprudence, whereas *taqlid* is unquestioned adherence to one of the four schools of jurisprudence or *madhabs* (i.e. Hanafi, Shafi'i, Maliki or Hanbli). Forensically speaking, *ijtihad* is 'a process of legal reasoning and hermeneutics through which the jurist-*mujtahid* derives or rationalizes law on the basis of the Quran and the Sunnah' (Hallaq 2005, 208). Waliullah suggested that the writings of the Imams of the four *madhabs* should be interpreted by the *ulama* in the light of the Hadith. He believed that *manqulat* or revealed sciences were more likely to bring people to the central teachings of Islam as opposed to *ma'qulat* or rational sciences, which he considered a source of confusion (Metcalf 1982, 38).

Through his *tatbiq* approach, Waliullah aimed to end divisions and deviations among Indian Muslims with respect to their beliefs and practices, hoping to bring some unity and reconciliation between Shia and Sunni Islam. Shias venerate Ali bin Abu Talib, the fourth caliph. They believe that Ali was the best among the companions of the Prophet Muhammad (PBUH) and was his natural successor. Sunnis generally believe that the first three caliphs were superior (or equal) to Ali in the order of their succession. Waliullah unsuccessfully tried to find some *tatbiq* between the two sects by stating that not all three but the first two caliphs were superior to the fourth (Metcalf 1982, 42).

Waliullah also claimed to have created a synthesis beyond even that of Al Ghazali, uniting not only reason (*aql*) and tradition (*naql*) but the gnosis (*ma'rifat*) of the *sufi* as well (Metcalf 1982, 43). He wanted his followers to take guidance not only from *fiqh* and the Hadith but also from *tasawwuf* or spiritual Islam. In fact, he wanted these three streams to combine in a true Islamic scholar. In one of his writings, he declared that those who do not adhere to such multifaceted scholars are not among his followers (Sindhi 2002, 200). Waliullah not only preached but exemplified the ideal of a religious leader being both a saint and an *alim*. He was even able to find *tatbiq* between the two opposing views in Indian *sufism*: *wahdatul wajud* (unity of being) and *wahdatush shahud* (unity of witness). *Wahdatul wajud*, formulated by Ibne Arabi, is defined as ontological or existential monism. This *wajudi* school of thought emphasizes the singleness of God and suggests that the human spirit is a direct emanation from the divine. This view was opposed by the *shahudi* school on the ground that it denies *tawhid* (Islamic monotheism) and encourages the believer to be lax in matters of *Shariah* (Metcalf 1982, 39).

On the other hand, *wahdatush shahud*, propagated by Shaikh Ahmed Sarhandi (1564–1624), is defined as phenomenological monism. This view asserts that *wahdatul wajud* does not represent the ultimate nature of reality, but is rather a mere perception of unity superseded by perceptions associated with yet higher stages of spiritual advancement. Waliullah found a common ground between these two views by arguing that the *wajudi* position was not only legitimate but it also confirmed the *shahudi* position if properly understood. Although Waliullah, like his father, followed *wahdatul wajud*, he was not in favour of discussing such matters in public because of the risk that ordinary Muslims might be misled through such debates (Metcalf 1982, 39). This was part of Waliullah's strategy to make a deliberate distinction between the *khas* (special) and the *aam* (ordinary) among Indian Muslims. The *khas* was to include a particular class of *ulama* who followed Waliullah's movement, whereas the *aam* were the rest of the *ulama* and ordinary Muslims.

Although the strategy of differentiating between the *khas* and the *aam* apparently contrasted with the concept of *tatbiq*, Waliullah through this delicate distinction aimed at avoiding any confusion and disunity among the overall Muslim community. Most Sunni *ulama* considered this division of society into *khas* and *aam* wise and prudent on the grounds that a man of understanding would speak to others in accordance with their capacity for understanding (Metcalf 1982, 42). However, by encouraging the *khas ulama* to do *ijtihad*, Waliullah's intellectual tradition at the same time came into conflict with the prevalent practice of *taqlid* (Metcalf 1982, 38–9). Waliullah controlled this conflict by prescribing *taqlid* for the *aam*. Through these strategies, Waliullah managed to maintain the existing harmony and unity among Indian Muslims despite facing some criticism for his unconventional intellectual approach (Butt 2002, 19).

As regards the social and political aspects of Waliullah's movement, these are together considered the 'practical' tradition, which was less prominent than the intellectual tradition of the movement. This practical tradition was mainly concerned with the revival of Muslim rule in India through political and sociocultural reforms. As regards political reforms, Waliullah wanted to form a strong central Muslim state in India in which the *ulama* would collaborate with political leaders as their teachers and advisors (Metcalf 1982, 43). As for sociocultural reforms, Waliullah sought to reinvigorate faith among Muslims through the true following of the practices of the Prophet and his companions. In this regard, he criticized many local customs as *bidah* (wrongful innovation) and *shirk* (polytheism). However, he did not preach intolerance in this regard and placed less emphasis on this sociocultural aspect than on the intellectual and political aspects.

On the political front, Waliullah also introduced a combination of *zahiri khilafat* (outer caliphate) and *batini khilafat* (inner caliphate). This was derived from the 'pious sultan' theory, which in turn had been extracted from a pre-Islamic Iranian tradition and proposed that the king or caliph must acknowledge *Shariah* as interpreted by the *ulama* (Hardy 1971, 16–17). More recently, this theory has been linked to the articulation of classic Sunni political theory by Ibne Taiymiyah on the Islamic model of legitimate power. This articulation, which recognized the legitimacy of the first four caliphs, rejected the necessity of having a single caliphate and allowed for the existence of many emirates and sultanates provided that the ruler strictly applied religious law, while his subjects were obliged to obey the established authority except where it required disobedience to God. Despite the legitimacy of 'pious sultans', the ruler could not become absolute because a basic restraint was placed upon him by *Shariah*, which provided him the divine sanction for his authority (Olesen 1995, 9). In practice, this legitimacy model did not in principle allow for any popular representation. Rather, it depended upon a 'concordance' between the ruler and the *ulama*, who were the chief intermediaries of the 'divine sanction' of the former (Olesen 1995, 63). In line with this articulation, Waliullah thought that the outer caliphate or the ruler was to be responsible for securing order and stability while the inner caliphate of the *ulama* was supposed to guide the ruler and instruct the Muslim community.

In the troubled period of the mid-eighteenth century, which he perhaps considered the end of an age, Waliullah propagated a far more activist role for the *ulama*. This was in sharp contrast to his contemporaries like the Farangi Mahall *ulama*, who preferred the traditional role of institutional and curricular development and the compilation of mere commentaries (Metcalf 1982, 36). Waliullah on the other hand was very concerned with the political developments of the time and therefore tried to influence the political elite through his movement. However, he was not particularly in favour of reviving the declining Mughal Empire (Mian 1957, vol. 1, 26).

Waliullah was actually looking to form a strong central Muslim state where his ideas could be put into practice to uplift the Muslims of India in an era of disorder and decline. He not only patronized Najib ud-Daulah of Rohilkhand to play a role in this regard but later also invited Ahmed Shah Abdali of Afghanistan to invade India and help strengthen Islam in the subcontinent (Mian 1957, vol. 2, 26–7). Simultaneously, Waliullah was gradually convinced that the Muslim revival in India would be brought about by Afghan rather than Indian Muslims (Sindhi 2008, 53).

2.1.1 Shah Waliullah's legacy

Waliullah's work was mainly addressed to the religious and political elite. His ideas could be implemented by this elite only in a situation where Muslim political leadership could be restored in line with the pious sultan theory. He expected his work to be continued and implemented by his four sons, Abdul Aziz, Rafiuddin, Abdul Qadir and Abdul Ghani. For his successors, their father's manifold legacy was based on four pillars: a sense of their importance as leaders; commitment to the study of the Hadith and Islamic law; acting as role models for Muslims; and a desire for Muslim unity (Metcalf 1982, 43).

However, after Waliullah's death in 1762, his successors found themselves in a situation where the decline of Muslim rule was being hastened by the rise of British power in India. Thus, the possibility of finding a 'pious sultan' was becoming even more remote. Therefore, in order to deal with this less-than-ideal situation, Waliullah's successors, under the leadership of his eldest son, Abdul Aziz (1746–1822), had to alter their strategy for upholding their mentor's legacy. This improvisation gradually changed the character of Waliullah's movement.

In the absence of a central Muslim state, Waliullah's successors were unable to find an outer caliph or ruler whom they could guide as inner caliphs. Similarly, there was limited scope for their second responsibility, to instruct the Muslim community. The decline of Muslim rule led to a marked decrease in the direct influence of *ulama* on the community through their role in the royal courts. Their indirect influence through state-sponsored madaris also declined as the Mughal Empire became too preoccupied with its own survival to support such madaris in a hitherto generous manner.

In response, Waliullah's successors adopted a peculiar approach that allowed them to act as inner caliphs without having an outer caliph. Unlike most other *ulama* of the late eighteenth century, including those belonging to the famous Farangi Mahall tradition, the *ulama* of Waliullah's movement were not ready to join the weak regional states or small kingdoms of Muslim rulers in India. In the absence of their ideal outer caliph (i.e. a powerful sultan of a central Islamic state) the inner caliphs utilized the institution of public *fatawa* to fill that legal void. Traditionally, such *fatawa* were issued by the courts of Muslim rulers through officially appointed jurists to administer Islamic law. Without any power to ensure compliance to Islamic law, although they continued to look for an outer caliphate, these self-proclaimed inner caliphs decided, perhaps temporarily, to take up for themselves the role of the outer caliph by directly advising the Muslim community on social, political, economic and religious issues in addition to their traditional role of guiding people on personal matters (Metcalf 1982, 51–2).

The mass publication of such edicts through the newly available printing presses also strengthened the institution of public *fatawa*. These edicts exemplified the kind of guidance Abdul Aziz 'saw as ever more important, guidance that could create a community substantially self-contained not only on matters of faith but in everyday behaviour' (Metcalf 1982, 52). Issuing public edicts became a major activity of Waliullah's sons and other *ulama* of the post-Mughal period. Although Abdu Aziz was trying to realize his father's dream, his approach and level of focus was different. He was in fact trying to do through the larger Muslim community what his father had tried through the Muslim political elite (Sindhi 2008, 12).

For the next sixty years, his eldest son Abdul Aziz was to play the role of top inner caliph with the added burden of outer caliph with respect to directly approaching the Muslim community through thousands of his edicts. Other members of the Waliullah family supported him as junior inner caliphs. This additional responsibility of the outer caliph actually transformed the original character of Waliullah's movement. The purely intellectual role of the *ulama* or inner caliphs was gradually expanded to allow for an activist approach. This combination of the intellectual and practical tradition was the most vital factor in defining the future direction of the movement.

At the same time, Waliullah's sons tried their best to uphold the four pillars of their father's legacy, taking it upon themselves to carry the movement forward. They committed themselves to the study and teaching of the Hadith and Islamic law through their father's madrassah in Delhi. In fact, their contribution to reviving the study of the Hadith in India is unprecedented. One non-Indian scholar touring different cities of the subcontinent wrote that he did not find a single Hadith scholar who was not a student of the Waliullah family, directly or indirectly (Rizwi 2005, vol. 1, 94). In fact, Abdul Aziz was considered the top authority on the Hadith in India, and apart from issuing religious edicts he also wrote commentary on the Quran. His most famous *fatwa* declared India *darul harb* (the territory of war) in 1803 in the wake of the decline of Mughal Empire, which by that time had been mostly restricted to the Red Fort of Delhi after the rise of British power. This *fatwa* declared that India was no longer under Muslim rule. Later on, it was to be employed by Syed Ahmed and Muhammad Ismail to justify *jihad* against the British in India (Metcalf 1982, 50–52), as discussed later in this section.

As Waliullah's movement broadened its scope by including middle-class Muslims in its ambit (Sindhi 2008, 57), his sons adopted a simple and plain language to convey their father's ideas to ordinary scholars, for whom it was not easy to understand Waliullah's intellectual message. For example, Abdul Aziz wrote an exegesis of the Quran entitled *Fathul Aziz*, which was actually a means of explaining his father's Quranic commentary *Fathur Rehman* (Sindhi 2008, 59). Similarly, his brothers Abdul Qadir and Rafiuddin translated the Quran into the Urdu language for less-educated Muslims. This was in fact an effort to widen their audience – much like Waliullah, who had earlier translated the Quran into Persian for the highly educated Muslim elite.

As regards the third element of Waliullah's legacy, his sons also successfully presented themselves as role models in their personalities and achievements. They faithfully followed the spiritual rituals practiced by their father. Similarly, they acted upon his advice to take pride in the Arabic language and civilization while trying to avoid the practices of Hindu culture (Sindhi 2008, 62). They also wrote many books for Indian Muslims so that they might reform their lives in the light of Waliullah's teachings.

On the fourth front of Waliullah's legacy, his sons undoubtedly still felt a desire for unity among Muslims. However, some disunity was to be expected as the scope of the movement expanded. Differences did appear over the *fatwa* declaring India *darul harb.* Many *ulama* did not agree with Abdul Aziz's verdict on the grounds that Indian Muslims were free to practice Islam and there was still a nominal Muslim ruler in Delhi. Then there were disagreements on the interpretation of that *fatwa.* Although Abdul Aziz did not call for war, many of his followers later used that *fatwa* to wage *jihad* against the British. Similarly, Shia–Sunni differences (which never died down even in Waliullah's time) re-emerged after Abdul Aziz wrote a book on Shia Islam entitled *Tohfa-e-Athna Ashari.* Abdul Aziz declared Shias to be apostates or *murtadeen* – those who have renounced their religion (Meeruthi 1908, vol. 1, 166).

As regards Sunni Islam in India, unity among Muslims was by and large not threatened by the teachings of Waliullah's sons, who were quite sensitive to their father's instruction, especially with respect to maintaining a delicate balance between the *khas* and the *aam.* That was in itself a great achievement by Waliullah's sons, who had to play the role of inner caliphs without the support of an outer caliph. However, these early successors, being the religious *khas*, compromised on Waliullah's idea of *ijtihad* by inclining towards a general *taqlid* of Hanafi *madhab*, which was originally suggested for the *aam.* Perhaps this compromise was deliberate, with the intention to promote unity among Muslims through adherence to one school of thought. Another reason for this compromise could be the political uncertainty in the absence of an outer caliph – a situation which called for preservation of the existing *Shariah* law rather than its reinterpretation through *ijtihad.*

While Waliullah's sons managed to carry forward his vision, the next generation reinterpreted the movement in a manner that clearly showed a drift in his legacy. This new generation was led by Muhammad Ismail (1776–1831) and Abdul Hayee (d. 1828). The former was Waliullah's grandson and the latter was son-in-law of Abdul Aziz. While the earlier generation under Abdul Aziz had interpreted the revival of Islam mostly at an intellectual level, this new generation emphasized the revitalization of Islam in practical form.

This radical shift actually occurred once Syed Ahmed of Rai Bareli joined Waliullah's movement and influenced the younger generation of the family. Both Muhammad Ismail and Abdul Hayee took *bay'ah* (the oath of allegiance) to Syed Ahmed as their *shaikh.* This was a deviation from family tradition, in which the younger generation had to take *bay'ah* to the elders of the family. Under the charismatic influence of Syed Ahmed, the younger generation rejected the gradualist and pragmatic approach of their elder Abdul Aziz, who had hoped that scholarly guidance could transform the life of Indian Muslims (Metcalf 1982, 52). The new generation, on the other hand, was more focused on reforms through practical rather than intellectual endeavours. As Gilani (n.d., vol. 1, 74) observes, Syed Ahmed was focused on practical tradition because he believed that the intellectual work had already been accomplished by Waliullah and his sons.

Syed Ahmed (1786–1831) belonged to a family of Syeds (descendants of the Prophet) in Rai Bareli, Oudh. His family was well respected throughout Oudh for piety and spiritual influence (Mian 1957, vol. 2, 86). He first arrived in Delhi at the age of 18 and became a student of Abdul Qadir, Waliullah's son. Being more inclined towards spiritual than scholarly activities, he could not complete his religious education and left for Central India. There, he joined the forces of Amir Khan (1768–1836), who, alongside Maratha leader Jaswant Rao Holkar, was resisting the advance of British power in India (Metcalf 1982, 53). However, in 1816 when Amir Khan surrendered and was made Nawab of Tonk, Syed Ahmed, who was not in favour of surrender, decided to return to Delhi (Mian 1957, vol. 2, 88).

Upon his return to Delhi, Syed Ahmed quickly assumed leadership among some of the most respected *ulama*, including those belonging to the Waliullah family (Metcalf 1982, 54). When the members of the younger generation of that family took *bay'ah* to Syed Ahmed, they not only accepted his leadership but also expected him to later take the role of an outer caliph in the making. Under the influence and leadership of Syed Ahmed, both Ismail and Hayee introduced major shifts in Waliullah's movement. Abdul Aziz, an old man approaching his death, was not expected to actively resist this marked shift. However, Aziz bypassed both Ismail and Hayee and appointed his grandson Muhammad Ishaq as his successor. Ishaq was supposed to carry forward the intellectual tradition of the movement as head of the family madrassah at Delhi. Although Ishaq was made the official leader of the movement, the practical tradition of Syed Ahmed, Ismail and Hayee dominated after Aziz's death.

It may be noted that while Abdul Aziz introduced his father's movement to the Muslim middle class, Ismail and Hayee took a step further under Syed Ahmed's guidance to take the movement to ordinary Muslims belonging to the lower socio-economic strata. Their practical tradition was mainly focused on popular reform of customs and practices on the one hand and preaching *jihad* against the British and the Sikhs on the other. The decision of *jihad* was apparently inferred from Abdul Aziz's 1803 *fatwa* declaring India *darul harb*. However, Abdul Aziz himself had never called for *jihad* in his *fatwa* or anywhere else. In fact, some writers have hinted that Aziz might have even opposed *jihad* (Metcalf 1982, 55). But most Deobandi writers believe that Abdul Aziz approved the *jihad* that was launched, after his death, under Syed Ahmed. Sindhi (2008, 75) thinks that although Aziz had agreed to *jihad*, the *jihadis* failed because they diverted from his exact advice to run the Islamic government through an advisory board rather than choosing an *ameerul momineen* (leader of the faithful), who was none other than Syed Ahmed.

Coming to the practical tradition, the concept of reforming popular customs was not in any way derived from the teachings of Waliullah, who had written in *wasaya* (plural of *wassiya*: will or bequest) about the superiority of Arabic language and customs over local practices derived from Hindu traditions. Although Abdul Aziz had issued edicts on many practices like proper conduct on the tombs of saints, he refrained from exactly defining the customs which were to be followed or eradicated. Actually, one major reason why he did not preach for reform was the fact that any such initiative could easily jeopardize Muslim unity – one of the major pillars of his father's legacy. Secondly, Waliullah's advice regarding Arab and local customs was specific to his successors, the *khas*. But the younger generation of his family decided to go ahead with such reforms among all the Muslims of India, without support from within the family.

In fact, the elders of the family in some cases refused to abandon what came to be seen as suspect practices by the next generation. For example, Abdul Aziz continued to follow certain practices such as determining an auspicious time for work, using particular healthcare rituals, and distributing food after offering prayer (*fatihah*) at his father's grave (Mujeeb 1967, 508–11). Similarly, Abdul Qadir, younger son of Waliullah, allowed women in his family to follow the custom of *bibi ki sahnak*, whereby they would offer food in the name of Fatimah, daughter of the Prophet. Young reformers like Ismail and Ishaq used to show their disapproval by quietly moving away whenever the family held such events (Metcalf 1982, 55).

Despite their differences on some customs and practices, relations between the two generations of Waliullah family remained mutually respectful. In fact, the older generation was generous enough to concede to a few ideas of the young reformers. For example, at the insistence of Ismail, Abdul Qadir stopped the women of his family practising *bibi ki sahnak*. Similarly, Abdul Aziz did not criticize Ismail's *shaikh* Syed Ahmed, who had opposed the established spiritual practice of *tasawwar-e-shaikh* – meditation on the image of one's spiritual leader (Metcalf 1982, 55).

Such leeway might have been given by the older generation not only to maintain unity in the family but also on the pretext that the ideas of the new generation could be tolerated as long as they were being preached among the *khas*. Outside the family, neither Abdul Aziz nor Abdul Qadir ever openly preached or even appreciated the new ideas of the younger generation, though they were accepted or respected inside their homes. So it appears that for the older generation, the reforms of customs and practices which Waliullah had mentioned in his *wasaya* were fundamentally addressed to his successors and the *khas*. The elders must have known that preaching such reforms among ordinary Muslims or the *aam* could destroy their father's fundamental philosophy of *tatbiq* and create differences and disunity among Indian Muslims.

However, the younger generation under Syed Ahmed's guidance was ready to compromise on the vital issue of maintaining a distinction between the *khas* and the *aam*. Their priorities were different from those of their elders in the sense that they hoped to unite Muslims through the revival of Muslim rule or at least creating a Muslim state where the ideas of Waliullah could be implemented. They had even found an outer caliph in the shape of Syed Ahmed, who now needed a Muslim state to rule. In order to achieve this, Syed Ahmed along with Ismail and Hayee campaigned for Indian Muslims to participate in *jihad* against the alien British rule. In line with the classical notion of *jihad*, they decided to launch warfare from an independent and free Muslim area – the tribal region of the north-west frontier. Since the *fatwa* declaring the whole of India *darul harb* had been disputed by several *ulama*, Syed Ahmed decided to initiate *jihad* against the Punjab, which could be more easily declared *darul harb* because its Sikh rulers did not owe any allegiance to the weak Muslim emperor in Delhi (Metcalf 1982, 61–2).

As Syed Ahmed and the younger generation of Waliullah apparently tried to unite Indian Muslims in the name of political revival through *jihad*, their practical tradition created fissures in Muslim society through their ideas about religious and sociocultural reform, as discussed below.

2.1.2 The rise of practical tradition in Waliullah's movement

Under the energetic influence of Syed Ahmed, the new leadership of the Waliullah movement concluded that the major reason for the decline of the Islamic rule in India was the lack of religious commitment among Muslims. Their solution to slowing this descent was to purify and revitalize Islam through popular reform of customs and practices. In a striking parallel to other nineteenth-century movements, 'they rejected their local "classical style" of Islam in favour of a scripturalist emphasis on the original practice of the faith' (Metcalf 1982, 56). Like the contemporary Wahhabis in Arabia, the foremost focus of Syed Ahmed's teachings was the centrality of *tawhid*. Muhammad Ismail stressed the paramount importance of *tawhid* in his two widely published books, *Siratul Mustaqeem* (straight path) and *Taqwiatul Iman* (Strengthening of the Faith). The two works stressed above all the centrality of *tawhid* and denounced all those practices and beliefs that were held in any way to compromise that fundamental tenet of Islam (Metcalf 1982, 56).

The followers of Syed Ahmed argued that God alone was entitled to worship and homage. The old tradition of showing excessive veneration and reverence to the prophets and saints was execrated. In fact, they denounced all those customs, practices and beliefs that were held in any way to compromise *tawhid*. Such practices were declared *shirk* – an unpardonable sin in Islam.

This strict and uncompromising emphasis on *tawhid* was not very dissimilar to what Muhammad bin Abdul Wahhab had preached in Arabia. In 1822, Muhammad Ismail along with Syed Ahmed had visited Arabia to perform *hajj*; there they had the opportunity to learn more about the teachings and strategy of Muhammad bin Abdul Wahhab. It was actually on his return from Arabia that Muhammad Ismail wrote *Taqwiatul Iman*, which was inspired by Muhammad bin Abdul Wahhab's *Al-Tawhid* (Sindhi 2008, 70). According to Hunter (1871, 47), Syed Ahmed became a fanatical disciple of Muhammad bin Abdul Wahhab after returning from Arabia.

Despite accepting some influence from Muhammad bin Abdul Wahhab, Waliullah's movement was otherwise quite different from the Wahhabis of Arabia. The followers of Muhammad bin Abdul Wahhab were far more extremist and aggressive in their approach than Waliullah's acolytes. Even on the fundamental issues of *tawhid* and *shirk*, Muhammad Ismail to some extent allowed *tawassul fid-dua* – praying to God to ask for something indirectly through the mediation of a pious person such as a prophet or a saint. Wahhabis on the other hand did not allow such practice at all.

Similarly, Ismail divided *shirk* into two categories, major and minor. He proclaimed, unlike Wahhabis, that committing a minor *shirk* did not place a Muslim outside the pale of Islam (Sindhi 2008, 176–7). For example, if a person calls upon a saint from far away by requesting that he pray to God for that person, it would be *shirk* because the saint had been called upon with the belief that he is capable of hearing from afar – a quality that is attributed to God alone. However, it would be minor *shirk* because prayer is ultimately directed to God (Ismail n.d., 74). Further, Waliullah's movement under Syed Ahmed did not denounce *sufism*, as did the Wahhabis. However, Syed Ahmed tried to reform *sufism* by introducing his own spiritual order called Tariqat-e-Muhammadia (The way of the Prophet Muhammad, PBUH), which was characterized not by internal devotions but by external obedience to *Shariah* (Metcalf 1982, 57).

In short, Syed Ahmed's rise was marked by a clear division of Waliullah's movement into two traditions: intellectual and practical. The intellectual tradition carried by the sons of Waliullah was passed on to Muhammad Ishaq, who was to head the Madrassah Rahimia after the death of his maternal grandfather Abdul Aziz in 1824. This tradition was to focus mainly on the study of the Hadith and Islamic law. The practical tradition, on the other hand, was to be carried forward by Muhammad Ismail and Abdul Hayee under the leadership of Syed Ahmed. This tradition was further divided into political and sociocultural categories; the former focused on *jihad* and the establishment of an Islamic state, while the latter centred on the reform of the prevalent beliefs and practices of Indian Muslims. The wellspring of the practical tradition was the basic Islamic tenet of *tawhid* that was to be revived in a purified form among Indian Muslims. Any threat to the purity of *tawhid* was to be opposed. The followers of Syed Ahmed identified three sources of threat to their strict version of *tawhid*: prevalent *sufism*, popular custom, and Shia doctrine and practice (Metcalf 1982, 57).

As mentioned earlier, Syed Ahmed, unlike the Wahhabis, did not denounce *sufism* as such. Rather he was himself perceived as a *sufi shaikh* among his followers. He tried to reform some of the established practices that he considered to be deviations from true *sufism*. For example, he believed that a *shaikh* cannot play the role of an intermediary between his disciples and God. He opposed the traditional discipline of repeating the name of a saint or meditating on his image (*tasawwar-e-shaikh*). He also condemned the prevalent practice of calling upon saints, imams and angels for help or even naming children after them. He also criticized prostration at shrines and pilgrimages that entailed special dress, animal sacrifice and the burning of lights for saints. Although he allowed a simple *fatihah* ceremony at shrines or graves, fixing a particular date for such ceremonies (e.g. birth or death anniversaries) was condemned (Metcalf 1982, 57–8).

The primary idea behind this execration of ceremonies connected to the dead was that one should not propitiate saints or expect any favour in return – this was declared *shirk*. Muhammad Ismail wrote in *Taqwiatul Iman* that the only purpose of performing a good deed for the deceased is *isal-e-sawab* (transfer of merit). He stated that attributing any favour to the dead was akin to putting the crown of a king on the head of a *chimar* or shoemaker (Ismail n.d., 58).

While condemning popular *sufi* practices, Muhammad Ismail described four categories of *shirk* with God: *shirk* in knowledge, *shirk* in disposing, *shirk* in worship and *shirk* in daily chores. According to him, *shirk* in knowledge involved calling or invoking the name of a saint or prophet for help and meditating on the image or grave of a saint with the belief that they are cognizant of one's affairs. *Shirk* in disposing meant a belief that human beings or angels have the authority to award health and sickness, poverty and abundance, victory and defeat or prosperity and distress. *Shirk* in worship included travelling long distances to visit the graves of saints or prophets, offering cloth sheets as a covering for the graves, bowing or prostrating before the graves, standing there with folded hands, lighting lamps on shrines, offering supplications and making wishes, and distributing specific sweet dishes in the name of particular saint (e.g. *halwa* for Sheikh Abdul Haq, *maleeda* for Shah Madar and *siwayyan* for Bu Ali Qalandar). As regards *shirk* in daily chores, it involved, among other things, invoking a vow (*mannat* or *nadhr*) to a saint or prophet with the intention of facilitating a difficult assignment, dedicating animals or farm produce in the name of anyone other than God, and giving one's children such names as Abdul Nabi (slave of the Prophet), Peer Bakhsh (granted by the saint), etc. He even considered standing up for other people in respect an act of *shirk* (Ismail n.d., 50–54).

Muhammad Ismail proclaimed that all prophets and saints were averse to intercession and never interceded on behalf of anyone who adhered to un-Islamic social customs and defied the injunctions of *Shariah*. He explained that intercession was only possible when God directs a prophet or saint to do so on behalf of those who seek God's support exclusively (Ismail n.d., 87–8). He also forbade Muslims from showing excessive praise or veneration for Prophet Muhammad (PBUH) in case it led to polytheistic expressions (Ismail n.d., 143). He declared, 'He whose name is Muhammad or Ali, has no authority over anything' (Ismail n.d., 47).

Apart from prevailing *sufi* practices, Syed Ahmed and his followers also reprehended many other popular customs. For example, they condemned traditional ceremonies associated with weddings, circumcisions and burials. Syed Ahmed considered these customs to be harmful to one's spiritual as well as worldly well-being (Metcalf 1982, 59). He also attacked the prohibition of remarriage for widows – a practice that was followed by many Muslim families in imitation of Hindu traditions. Muhammad Ismail was the first to follow Syed Ahmed in this regard when he convinced his elder sister (an ageing widow suffering from ill health) to marry Abdul Hayee (Gilani n.d., vol. 2, 9).

Apart from this, Syed Ahmed's party rarely attributed the deviations in Muslim practices to Hindu influence, but rather blamed Muslims themselves (Metcalf 1982, 59). This is in contrast to the narrative constructed by most Deobandi writers with regard to the sociocultural practices opposed by the movement. Although Ismail did mention in *Taqwiatul Iman* (n.d., 110) some Hindu customs followed by Muslims (e.g. believing in bad omens, propitious times of day, the influence of the moon and planets, etc.), the movement actually never sought explicit distinction between Muslims and Hindus. On the contrary, the movement adopted a conscious approach to avoid conflict with Hindus. In fact, Syed Ahmed stopped Ismail from preaching at Hindu fairs so as not to antagonize them.

One may argue here that it was perhaps the huge majority (about 80 per cent) of Hindus in India that deterred Syed Ahmed from opposing their idolatrous and pantheistic practices, which could be blamed for adulterating the Islamic way of life. However, it does not apply in this case because in the urban areas of North India (the main target of Syed Ahmed's movement) the demography was not so unfavourable. Muslims not only made up about 40 per cent of the population in North India but also had a sizeable share among influential groups like government servants, small traders and landlords (Robinson 1974, 13–23). As such, Syed Ahmed could have built a strong support base. Conversely, his movement chose to avoid linking Hinduism with acts of *shirk*, while criticizing those socio-religious and spiritual practices of Indian Muslims that had long been established even among Muslims in other parts of the world.

It may be argued that through this approach, Syed Ahmed might have wanted to avoid communal disharmony in India. However, the fact of the matter is that his movement was primarily focused on the 'intra-societal' conflict that challenged the prevalent sociocultural and religious practices of the majority of Indian Muslims rather than the 'inter-societal' differences between Hindus and Muslims. Looking from this perspective, the movement was behaving in a countercultural manner.

Apart from popular custom and *sufism*, the third source of threat to Syed Ahmed's purist version of *tawhid* was the influence of Shia doctrine and practices. Shia influence had been increasing in India since the death of Aurangzeb, who had restricted Shia practices through the propagation of a puritanical version of Islam. Later on, the decline of the Mughal Empire was accompanied by a simultaneous rise of Shia influence in India. Interestingly, Deobandi writer Gilani (n.d., vol. 2, 60) has observed that whenever the belief in *tawhid* among Muslims is weakened or whenever there is a decline in Islamic rule, it is the Shia version of Islam that becomes popular among the Muslim community. Syed Ahmed particularly opposed the Shia practice of keeping *taziyahs* – replica tombs of the martyrs of Karbala carried in procession in the first Islamic month of Muharram to observe the death anniversary of Hussain, grandson of Prophet Muhammad (PBUH). At that time, the practice was also followed by many Sunni Muslims. Ismail declared *taziyahs* to be *shirk*, preaching in *Taqwiatul Iman* that they should be broken down and such an act should be considered as virtuous as the destruction of idols. Syed Ahmed reportedly smashed thousands of *imam bargahs* – Shia-owned buildings where *taziyahs* are kept and mourning meetings are held (Hassan 1950, 124).

This aggressive approach towards Shias was quite different from that which Waliullah and his sons had adopted earlier. Although Waliullah had himself criticized Shia Islam, he was very conscious not to create fissures within the overall Muslim community. Similarly, Abdul Aziz also opposed Shia Islam in his writings, but his approach was gentle persuasion compared to what Muhammad Ismail preached and Syed Ahmed practiced against Shias. Their practical approach was a marked shift from the original intellectualism of Waliullah and the first generation of his successors (Gilani n.d., vol. 1, 74).

Although Abdul Aziz had nominated Muhammad Ishaq to carry on the intellectual tradition of the movement, the aggressive activism of Syed Ahmed and Ismail pushed the old tradition into the background. Muhammad Ishaq, unlike his grandfather, failed to openly disapprove of the practical tradition. Rather, he tacitly approved it: it has been reported that he provided financial support to Syed Ahmed's party when they launched *jihad* against the Sikhs (Sindhi 2008, 94).

On their return from Arabia in 1824, Syed Ahmed and his two lieutenants, Ismail and Hayee, planned for *jihad* to set up an independent Muslim state. This strategy was not all that different from that of Muhammad bin Abdul Wahhab's followers in Arabia, who had earlier set up a state in Nejd with the support of the Derai'yeh tribe. Syed Ahmed and his party selected the north-west frontier to set up the new state. Their *jihad* was to be initiated against the Sikh government of the Punjab with the support of the tribal Afghan leaders.

Syed Ahmed launched a public campaign for men and money, travelling more than three thousand miles across India and preparing an army of more than two thousand *mujahideen* (plural of *mujahid*: holy warrior). These *mujahideen* then migrated in 1826 to the north-west frontier (Sindhi 2008, 78), where they soon won the allegiance of the local tribes to defeat the Sikhs at Akora Khattak. In January 1827, a provisional Islamic government was established and Syed Ahmed was declared *ameerul momineen* – a title traditionally assumed by the Muslim caliphs. Abdul Hayee was initially the top advisor of Syed Ahmed and acted as the 'inner caliph' to his 'outer caliph'. Despite his respect for Syed Ahmed, Abdul Hayee showed enough courage as inner caliph to guide and direct his outer caliph, even openly reprimanding him for coming late to the morning prayers (Sindhi 2008, 79; Meeruthi 1908, vol. 2, 272).

When Abdul Hayee died in 1828, Muhammad Ismail was to play the role of inner caliph and guide to Syed Ahmed. However, his influence was not as strong as that of Abdul Hayee, under whom the provisional government remained symbolically attached to the weak Mughal Empire in Delhi and was thus more acceptable to Indian Muslims. After Hayee, the provisional Islamic government became completely independent and even opposed the emperor (Sindhi 2008, 80).

As the provisional government began to behave as a permanent central Islamic government under the dictatorship of Syed Ahmed, the already weak Mughal Empire in Delhi became even weaker, allowing British East India Company to further strengthen its control in the subcontinent (Sindhi 2008, 80). At the same time, Syed Ahmed and his *mujahideen* developed differences with some Afghan leaders who opposed his decision to reform local customs that he considered un-Islamic, including the ban on widows remarrying as well as other strict tribal traditions like dowry, which delayed the marriage of Afghan girls. Syed Ahmed criticized such practices and even encouraged Afghans to marry their daughters to Indian *mujahideen.* It was acceptable in Afghan society to intermarry with Muslims of other nationalities, and Syed Ahmed himself married an Afghan woman. However, things became controversial when some of his followers forced Afghans to marry their daughters to the *mujahideen* (Sindhi 2008, 85), creating serious acrimony among some tribal leaders.

Apart from that, some tribal leaders also resented having a non-Afghan as their leader, which was considered against their traditions. Therefore, the *mujahideen* had to fight against both the Sikhs and some Afghan groups who opposed the reforms and leadership of Syed Ahmed. In this regard, the tribes of Peshawar and Mardan offered the most resistance. In 1830, Syed Ahmed defeated them and established his rule in Peshawar. However, he allowed the tribal heads to act as local leaders as long as they were willing to pay taxes to his government. These local tribal leaders later conspired against the *mujahideen* over the forced marriage of an Afghan girl to an Indian *mujahid.* In order to take revenge, the Afghans killed hundreds of Syed Ahmed's tax collectors and other office bearers in one night, marking the end of the provisional government in Peshawar. Later, Syed Ahmed decided to shift his movement's headquarters to Kashmir (Sindhi 2008, 91).

On their way to Kashmir in 1831, Syed Ahmed and about one thousand *mujahideen* were trapped at Balakot at the opening of the narrow Kaghan Valley (Metcalf 1982, 62) by around twenty thousand Sikh troops under the crown prince of Punjab, Sher Singh. Syed Ahmed, Muhammad Ismail and the *mujahideen* were all killed (Sindhi 2008, 92). After that, the followers of Syed Ahmed regrouped in the Sittana area of the north-west frontier and kept the embers of *jihad* alive for many decades under the leadership of Wilayat Ali and Inayat Ali of Patna. However, this later resistance was gradually delinked from Waliullah's movement, which was to be led by Muhammad Ishaq, head of the Madrassah Rahimia at Delhi.

After Balakot, Muhammad Ishaq tried to revive Waliullah's movement in Delhi. However, his major contribution was the introduction of strict *taqlid* of Hanafi *madhab* among his followers (Sindhi 2008, 97). That decision actually proved to be a death blow to the intellectual tradition of Waliullah. The door of *ijtihad* was henceforth closed and there was no room left for the application of intellectual synthesis or *tatbiq* to bring about unity among Indian Muslims.

2.2 The Link between Waliullah's Movement and the DMM

In 1842, just a decade after Balakot, Muhammad Ishaq along with his brother Muhammad Yaqub migrated to the Hijaz. Before leaving India, Ishaq set up a board of scholars under Mamluk Ali to continue Waliullah's movement in India. Other members of the board included Abdul Ghani, Muzaffar Hussain, Qutbuddin, Fazlur Rehman, Nazir Hussain and later Imdadullah (Sindhi 2008, 98; Metcalf 1982, 71–2). Abdul Ghani (1819–78), a disciple of Abdul Aziz, became head of the Madrassah Rahimia, which was now to be run for the first time by a person not belonging to the Waliullah family.

As regards the members of the board, they had supported the Mughal rulers of Delhi during the Mutiny against the British, with the exception of Nazir Hussain, who stayed neutral. After the fall of the Mughal Empire in 1857, the members of the board dispersed as Madrassah Rahimia had also been demolished by the British. Nazir Hussain founded a movement of *ghair muqallideen* (those who do not follow a particular *madhab*). During the early twentieth century, this movement developed into a new sect called Ahle Hadith, which was heavily influenced by the teachings of Muhammad bin Abdul Wahhab and Ibne Taiymiyah. Abdul Ghani and Imdadullah migrated to the Hijaz in 1857. Mamluk Ali had already died before the Mutiny. The following discussion highlights the connection between Waliullah's movement and the founding fathers of the DMM.

Mamluk Ali, leader of the board of scholars appointed by Muhammad Ishaq, originally belonged to Nanautah, a small town in North India. He completed his education in Delhi and later joined Delhi College as head Arabic teacher. He was closely associated with Waliullah's family and came to Delhi explicitly to study under them. His teacher Rashid-ud-Din Khan was a student of Abdul Aziz (Metcalf 1982, 76). In Delhi, Mamluk Ali kept a close connection with the family of Waliullah and even accompanied Muhammad Ishaq in 1842 when he decided to migrate to the Hijaz. However, after performing *hajj*, Mamluk returned next year to fulfil his duties at Delhi College, and his commitment to the Waliullah movement remained strong (Metcalf 1982, 75).

Mamluk Ali was a skilled teacher; he knew Persian, Urdu and Arabic and translated several classical Arabic works on the Hadith, history and mathematics into Urdu. Along with his companions Abdul Ghani and Imdadullah, he kept the spirit of Waliullah's movement alive until his death in 1851. He brought many of his relatives from Nanautah to join him and study at Delhi College. These included his son Muhammad Yaqub and his nephews Ahsan, Mazhar and Qasim as well as two distant relatives, Zulfiqar Ali and Fazlur Rehman. This group of people later played a major role in setting up a madrassah in the town of Deoband near Nanautah in 1866. However, the most conspicuous among them was Muhammad Qasim (1833–80), who along with Rasheed Ahmed (1829–1905), another student of Mamluk Ali, was to become the spirit behind the DMM.

During their stay at Delhi, the two future founders of the DMM, Muhammad Qasim and Rasheed Ahmed, were thoroughly influenced by the followers and leaders of Waliullah's movement. Both of them received their formal religious education as private students of Mamluk Ali (Gilani n.d., vol. 1, 222–7); they were not regular students of Delhi College. They studied the Hadith from Abdul Ghani, the successor of Muhammad Ishaq at Madrassah Rahimia (Gilani n.d., vol. 1, 254), and their spiritual leader was Imdadullah, another prominent leader of Waliullah's movement (Metcalf 1982, 79). Imdadullah (1815–99) was a spiritual disciple of Syed Ahmed (Rehman 1997, 7; Sherkoti 1965, 175). Like Syed Ahmed, he was not trained as an *alim*. However, he held the unique position of being a spiritual guide or *shaikh* to some seven or eight hundred *ulama* of North India (Meeruthi 1908, vol. 1, 47).

It is worth noting that the leadership that was to launch the DMM was influenced by Waliullah's movement as it stood in the early nineteenth century. In fact, the movement by that time had come a long way from its origins about a century beforehand. The four pillars of Waliullah's legacy (i.e. taking leadership of Indian Muslims, studying the Hadith and Islamic law, acting as role models and promoting Muslim unity) had already been shattered by the middle of the nineteenth century. His family had already abdicated leadership after Ishaq and his brother Yaqub migrated to the Hijaz. Their Madrassah Rahimia, even before the Mutiny, was neither very active nor very popular among Indian Muslims, especially after the British introduced the modern education system to India. After the Mutiny, the madrassah was razed by British forces. The desire for its religious leaders to become role models had already been destroyed after Syed Ahmed and Ismail deviated from Waliullah's principle of maintaining the delicate distinction between the *khas* and the *aam*. By fiercely preaching the model of the religious elite to ordinary Indian Muslims, Syed Ahmed and Ismail had hurt Muslim unity by challenging people's established beliefs and practices. Even Syed Ahmed's *jihad* on the frontier divided more than it united the Indian Muslims, the majority of whom were ambivalent about the legality and religious sanction of the war.

In short, the DMM's founding fathers aimed to follow Waliullah's ideas, but these ideas had metamorphosed in the intervening generations. The shifts had occurred on a number of levels, which included debates on the intellectual versus practical relevance of religious knowledge, the question of *khas* and *aam*, inner and outer caliphs and the place of *jihad* in Islam as well as the purpose of Islamic revivalism. In other words, the founders of the DMM were more influenced by the metamorphosed version of Waliullah's movement than his original ideas. As such, the DMM was to mainly inherit the practical tradition of Waliullah's movement as elaborated by Syed Ahmed and Ismail. It may be added here that the founders were clearly drawing inspiration from Syed Ahmed and Ismail. Their limited armed resistance against the British during the Mutiny (discussed in the next chapter) was part of their desire to revive Syed Ahmed's *jihad*. Further, Muhammad Qasim was deeply influenced by the teachings and preaching style of Ismail. His teacher Mamluk Ali once likened the two by stating that 'people recall Muhammad Ismail but they would also see my Ismail [i.e. Qasim] in future' (Gilani n.d., vol. 1, 267).

To sum it up, this chapter not only establishes links between Waliullah's movement and the founders of the DMM but also suggests that the latter mostly inherited the practical rather than the intellectual tradition of the former. That practical tradition, which carried the seeds of a counterculture, mainly focused on two fronts: internal and external. On the internal front, it had to purify Muslim society by fighting against prevailing *sufism*, popular customs and Shia doctrine. On the external front, it was concerned with *jihad* against non-Muslims to establish an Islamic state. As shall be discussed in the next chapter, there was to be little room for activity on the external front after an Indian rebellion was completely crushed by the British in 1857. Therefore, the DMM was to be left with just the internal front at its inception in 1866. At that time, the topmost concern of the founders was the survival and preservation of their version of Islam in the wake of British rule in India. The following sections discuss the countercultural characteristics of the DMM during its initial years.

2.3 The DMM's Initial Ascetic Approach

This section explains the origin of the DMM against the backdrop of the War of Independence or Mutiny of 1857. Apart from discussing the status of Indian Muslims in the post-Mutiny period, this section also provides details of the DMM's inward-looking approach during its early years, when it behaved as an ascetic counterculture.

The origin of the Mutiny of 1857 can be traced to the political and economic grievances of Indian people against the rule of the British East India Company. However, according to Sir Syed Ahmad Khan of Aligarh, the biggest causes of the Mutiny were the social and religious concerns of Indians. He wrote in his 1859 pamphlet titled *Asbab-e-Baghawat-e-Hind* (The causes of the Indian revolt) that Indians believed that the company's government was interfering in the social customs and religious practices of both Hindus and Muslims. The activities of British clergymen and their missionary schools in India were considered a threat to the social and religious practices of Indians, who regarded these activities as part of a government policy to convert them to Christianity (Khan 1903, 7–23).

Maulana Fazle Haqq Khairabadi, who was sentenced to exile in the Andaman Islands for supporting the Mutiny, wrote in his memoirs that the English were planning to destroy the culture and civilization of India (Metcalf 1982, 84). The introduction of Western education also hurt the traditional educational institutions like Muslim madaris and Hindu *pathshalas*, both of which were religion oriented. Thomas Metcalf (1964) has also identified the British proselytization of Christianity and attempts to reform indigenous customs as two of the major grievances behind the Mutiny (quoted in Metcalf 1982, 80–81).

The immediate events that triggered the Mutiny were also related to religious issues. In January 1857, news spread among the local Indian soldiers that the cartridges provided for their rifles carried fat contents derived from swine and cow, animals whose meat are prohibited in Muslim and Hindu religions respectively. On this pretext, the local soldiers, both Hindu and Muslim, refused to use those cartridges despite assurances by the British officers that no such fat contents were used in the ammunition. For such disobedience, Mangal Panday, a Hindu soldier, was hanged by the British military authorities on 6 April 1857 in Barakpur near Calcutta. As the news of Panday's death reached North India, local soldiers in Meerut revolted and after killing their British officers on 10 May they marched towards Delhi, where they were welcomed by both Muslims and Hindus (Mian 1957, vol. 4, 84–104). In Delhi, these rebels not only killed British soldiers but also murdered civilians of British origin despite the appeals and edicts of religious leaders against such brutalities.

Later on, more local soldiers from other parts of India also reached Delhi and independence from the government of the East India Company was announced. The Mughal king, Bahadar Shah Zafar, who was only a titular head under the company's rule, was declared the emperor of India (Mian 1957, vol. 4, 102–3). Afterwards, this mutiny of sepoys, combined with civil rebellion, spread across North India to challenge the hold of the British on the subcontinent. However, the British forces ruthlessly crushed the revolt within a few months.

The cataclysm of the Mutiny was followed by general political quietude among Indian Muslims, who seemed to be finished as a political force in the subcontinent. British rule in India had been passed from the East India Company to the Queen's government in England. The rebellion had been brutally and completely crushed by the colonial government, and prominent political and religious Muslim leaders who had participated in the Mutiny were either sentenced to death or exiled. According to Ikram and Spear (1955, 185), Muslims were now being 'looked upon as traitors by the British and an easy target by their erstwhile Hindu subjects to pay off old scores. Sandwiched between the two, Muslim frustration deepened, and Muslims began to sink lower and lower in the economic, political, and educational spheres.'

The post-Mutiny events had 'sobered' the Indian Muslims and their *ulama*, who were gradually convinced that the British were invincible (Metcalf 1982, 87). Apart from political and economic losses, the Muslim community was also suffering from deep psychological scars at that time. That 'defeatist mindset' gave rise to two movements among Indian Muslims (Arshad 2005, 29) who felt marginalized after the fall of the Mughal Empire in 1857. These two movements were named after the towns in which they were founded: Aligarh and Deoband. Although these two movements appeared to be educational in form, they were sociocultural in spirit. Later on, they would play vital roles in Indian politics.

The Aligarh Movement was led by Sir Syed Ahmad Khan (1817–98), who was of the opinion that Muslims, like Hindus, should compromise with the British rulers and try to work for their economic, political and social uplift with the help of modern education. Sir Syed had initiated his reform efforts immediately after the fall of Delhi. In 1859, he established a Persian school at Moradabad during his posting there as a court officer.

The school was established in the modern tradition of the British educational system, but it was independent from the government and was founded with the aid of a committee of local notables, both Hindus and Muslims (Robinson 1974, 91–2).

Later, Sir Syed set up the Muhammadan Literary and Scientific Society of Calcutta in 1863 and the Scientific Society of Ghazipur in 1864. The latter was shifted to Aligarh upon Sir Syed's transfer there. Before that, he had also established an independent school in Ghazipur where the English language was introduced. In 1866, a building named the Aligarh Institute was erected for the Scientific Society, which launched its journal *Aligarh Institute Gazette* in the same year. In 1870, Sir Syed founded a monthly magazine, *Tahzib-ul-Akhlaq* (Muslim social reformer), with a goal 'to reconcile Indian Islam to rationalism, and to induce Muslims to acquire education on modern lines' (Faizi 1970, 152–3).

In 1875, the Muhammadan Anglo-Oriental (MAO) College was founded in Aligarh by Sir Syed with an emphasis on modern Western learning. Later on, the college was upgraded as Aligarh University. Initially, Sir Syed faced strong opposition from the *ulama* and the orthodoxy of North India, who were not ready to accept his new approach to Islam, which focused on reason and modernity (Robinson 1974, 109). However, he persisted with his approach and gradually influenced 'the way of thinking of Muslim intelligentsia and the attitude of the Muslims in general towards the new order of things' (Faizi 1970, 153).

As the Aligarh Movement gathered momentum, it succeeded in attracting to its fold a number of eminent scholars (Ikram and Spear 1955, 186). Sir Syed's influential team included statesmen like Nawab Mohsin-ul-Mulk (1837–1907) and Nawab Viqra-ul-Mulk (1841–1917), poet Maulana Altaf Hussain Hali (1837–1914), novelist Deputy Nazir Ahmed (1836–1912), historian Maulvi Zakaullah (1832–1910), religious scholar Maulvi Chiragh Ali (1844–95) and academic Maulana Shibli Naumani (1857–1914). Through his movement, Sir Syed not only filled 'the big void created in the life of the Muslim community by the disappearance of Muslim rule', but also 'bridged the gulf between the Medieval and Modern Islam in India' (Ikram and Spear 1955, 188). In other words, the Aligarh Movement's chief contribution was to mainstream the Muslim community, which had been marginalized after the War of Independence.

The second movement of Indian Muslims in the post-Mutiny period was launched in a small town of North India called Deoband, where a madrassah was established in the old tradition of Muslim religious schools, with a particular inclination towards Waliullah's movement. The Deoband Madrassah Movement was led by Muhammad Qasim and Rasheed Ahmed, whose primary objective was to protect the religious capital of Indian Muslims (Arshad 2005, 31). 'While Sir Syed Ahmad Khan was seeking to extricate his co-religionists from the slough of despondency through Western education and cooperation with the British' (Ikram and Spear 1955, 190), the founders of the DMM 'considered that the Muslim community was facing threats from the colonial power as much as from within the community' (i.e. from the Aligarh Movement; Riaz 2008, 73).

The DMM from the very beginning opposed the modernist approach of Sir Syed. Unlike the Aligarh Movement, which aimed to mainstream marginalized Islam, the DMM's major objective was to protect and preserve 'true' Islam. DMM leaders generally identified 'true' Islam with that propagated by Waliullah's movement under

Syed Ahmed and Muhammad Ismail during the early nineteenth century. The major concern of the DMM was to preserve and revive the values of that movement. In line with Waliullah's philosophy, the DMM considered the practices of folk Islam to be a bigger threat to 'true' Islam than British or Hindu culture. The real threats were those identified by Muhammad Ismail, including popular custom, traditional *sufi* doctrine and Shia practices (Metcalf 1982, 57). These threats were considered even more menacing in the wake of the 'growing influence of liberal Muslim leaders under Sir Syed who favoured English education and closer cooperation with the British colonial administration' (Riaz 2008, 73).

Interestingly, the DMM's opposition to the rise of modernists like Sir Syed in the post-Mutiny scenario correlates with the attitude of the DMM's founders and other *ulama* of the Waliullah tradition during the Mutiny, when they chose not to support the mainstream religious forces who had issued a *fatwa* to declare the revolt as *jihad*. One may argue that this attitude during and after the Mutiny reflected the Deobandis' approach to eschewing the majority and the mainstream – an approach not unlike a counterculture. The following discussion highlights the peculiar positions taken by the DMM during and after the Mutiny.

The *ulama* of the Shah Waliullah tradition were divided on joining the Mutiny (Mian 1957, vol. 4, 133). The apparent reason for this difference of opinion was the lack of unanimity in interpreting the revolt as *jihad*. Another important reason behind the reticence of these *ulama* was their disinclination to bear allegiance to the Mughal emperor under whose leadership the Muslims were fighting against the British. The emperor was inclined towards Shia Islam as well as the practices of folk Sunni Islam (e.g. visiting shrines), which these *ulama* considered un-Islamic (Khan 1859, 9). Therefore, the majority of the *ulama* belonging to the Waliullah tradition stayed neutral during the Mutiny (Sindhi 2008, 106), while others, like Nazir Hussain, Sheikh Muhammad Thanawi, Khawaja Ziauddin and Mahboob Ali, openly opposed it (Khan 1880, 675).

When an official *fatwa* was issued in Delhi to declare the Mutiny as *jihad*, very few *ulama* of the Waliullah tradition supported it. The *fatwa* was issued under the influence of the rebel commander Bakht Khan, who was a follower of Sarfraz Ali, a disciple of Syed Ahmed (Mian 1957, vol. 4, 177). The Delhi *fatwa* helped increase the participation of Muslims in the Mutiny. At that time, the future founders of the DMM, Muhammad Qasim and Rasheed Ahmed, were staying with their spiritual leader Haji Imdadullah in Thana Bhawan, Muzaffar Nagar district. Initially, they were reluctant, like many other followers of the Waliullah tradition, to join the rebellion. There is some ambiguity about the exact reasons for their much-delayed decision to join the Mutiny just a couple of weeks before the fall of Delhi on 19 September 1857. It may be noted that the active rebellion had been going on since early May 1857.

Most Deobandi writers believe that the decision to join the rebellion was delayed because there were differing views on declaring the Mutiny as *jihad* (Madni 1931, 274). It has also been reported that the future founders of the DMM also sent one of their associates, Rehmatullah, to Delhi to gather the views of other *ulama* on this issue. Rehmatullah was subsequently convinced, and signed the Delhi *fatwa* for *jihad* at the end of July 1857

(Mian 1957, vol. 4, 73). However, it is still not clear why the future DMM leaders took about two months to join the rebellion after the Delhi *fatwa*.

One may argue that this group of *ulama* in Thana Bhawan was apparently reluctant to launch *jihad* under the Mughal emperor as they felt his observance of the practices of folk Islam made him ineligible to become their leader in *jihad*. They may also have had in their minds the interpretation according to which *jihad* becomes obligatory when declared by the *ameer* (leader) of an Islamic state (Okon 2013). Perhaps that is why they first set up an Islamic government in Thana Bhawan under the leadership of Imdadullah to declare *jihad* (Gilani n.d., vol. 2, 125–6). Muhammad Qasim was designated as the military chief, while Rasheed Ahmed was appointed as the *qadhi* or chief justice of that small Islamic state (Mian 1957, vol. 4, 276). Thousands of *mujahideen* later joined them to attack and conquer the neighbouring town of Shaamli (Madni 1931, 452), an event referred to by Deobandi writers as the 'Jihad of Shaamli'.

It may be noted that the small Islamic state set up by the future founders of the DMM somewhat resembled the rebel government established by Syed Ahmed in North West India about three decades beforehand. Imdadullah, like Syed Ahmed, was not trained as a traditional scholar and was more inclined towards spiritual learning. Similarly, he was supported by Qasim and Rasheed, just like Syed Ahmed was assisted by Muhammad Ismail and Abdul Hayee. In fact, Muhammad Qasim tended to idealize Ismail and revered his teachings and traditions (Gilani n.d., vol. 1, 400; vol. 2, 18–19). However, the little Islamic state in Thana Bhawan was too superfluous to have any impact on the Indian polity. Immediately after the fall of Delhi, the British forces recaptured Shaamli as well as Thana Bhawan and the leaders of this small pocket of resistance went underground.

Despite the fact that most Deobandi writers have glorified the events in Shaamli as *jihad* against the British, the biographers of both Muhammad Qasim (Gilani n.d.) and Rasheed Ahmed (Meeruthi 1908) have described the events as a local dispute. Both biographers have explained the events in a manner that shows loyalty of the two leaders to the British (Gilani n.d., vol. 2, 89–141; Meeruthi 1908, vol. 1, 73–80). In fact, Meeruthi (1908, vol. 1, 76) has presented the events as if the *ulama* were fighting against Indians who had rebelled against the 'kind government' of the British.

This stance is in sharp contrast to the nationalist approach of the DMM propagated by the majority of later Deobandi writers. Interestingly, such nationalist accounts of the events of Shaamli and Thana Bhawan appeared only in secondary sources written after 1920 (Metcalf 1982, 82), when Deobandis finally joined hands with the Indian National Congress to become part of the anti-British nationalist movement in India. These later writings have tried to interpret this stance in terms of the DMM's efforts to avoid conflict with the British authorities as well as to evade the government ban on these publications. The official historian of the DMM, Muhammad Mian, who has been given the title *Muarrakh-e-Millat* (historian of the nation), has tried to explain away this discrepancy by stating that Rasheed Ahmed's biographer (i.e. Meeruthi) was a pro-British writer, while that of Muhammad Qasim (i.e. Gilani) did not focus much on political events (Mian 1957, 270–73).

Irrespective of the reasons behind the revolt in Muzaffar Nagar, the attack on Shaamli was noted in a British account as Islamic in motivation (Metcalf 1982, 83).

After the Mutiny, the British authorities issued arrest warrants for Muhammad Qasim and Rasheed Ahmed along with their spiritual leader Imdadullah, and the three of them went into hiding (Meeruthi 1908, vol. 1, 77). Later, Imdadullah migrated to Makkah, while Rasheed Ahmed was arrested but finally released after six months due to lack of evidence of his involvement (Meeruthi 1908, vol. 1, 84–5). Muhammad Qasim remained in hiding until 1861, even after a general amnesty had been announced by the Queen in 1858 (Gilani n.d., vol. 2, 192–3)

The events of Shaamli highlight how far the views on *jihad* had evolved in this movement within five decades. In 1803, Abdul Aziz issued a *fatwa* to declare India *darul harb* and the British *kuffar* (infidels), yet he gave no call to military action and apparently wanted Muslims to behave politically as if India were *darul Islam* as Mughal rule was still in place. In the 1820s, Syed Ahmed and Muhammad Ismail used that *fatwa* to launch *jihad* in India, though not against the British. Rather, they targeted Sikh rule in the Punjab and North West India, which could clearly be interpreted as *darul harb* in the absence of any Muslim ruler there. In 1857, the future founders of the DMM declared *jihad* against the British even though a Muslim emperor was still present in Delhi. Further, their *jihad* was independent of the main *jihad* declared by the *ulama* of Delhi, who recognized the weak Mughal emperor as a legitimate Muslim ruler.

The 'Jihad of Shaamli' was a marked deviation from the classical legal view, which saw *jihad* in the context of conflict in a world divided between *darul Islam* (territory under Islamic control) and *darul harb* (territory of war, comprising all lands not under Muslim rule), with the objectives to defend and expand *darul Islam* (Knapp 2003). In the case of Shaamli, the boundaries of *darul harb* and *darul Islam* were ill-defined on the one hand, and on the other, setting up an Islamic state in Thana Bhawan was itself a rebellion against the Muslim ruler in Delhi. It can be argued that by establishing their own state in Thana Bhawan, the founders of the DMM were taking the lead from Ibne Taiymiyah, who had declared that a ruler would forfeit his right to rule if he failed to enforce the *Shariah* rigorously in all aspects (Knapp 2003). It appears that for the *jihadis* of Shaamli, Thana Bhawan was *darul Islam* and the rest of India was *darul harb*. It may not be out of place to add here that the concept of *jihad* was to further evolve under the DMM during the twentieth century, when the Deobandis would launch a militant campaign against Shia Muslims in Pakistan. There is a consensus on the view that Islamic law condemns all warfare that does not qualify as *jihad*, specifically any warfare among Muslims themselves. Thus, the use of force against Muslims is justified only by denying them the status of Muslims (Knapp 2003). Accordingly, the Deobandi *ulama* were to issue a *fatwa* in 1987 to declare Shias non-Muslims (Hassan 1988) in order to justify an anti-Shia *jihad*.

As regards the DMM's approach in post-Mutiny India, the ruthless and vengeful ways of the colonial government after 1857 deterred the DMM leaders from a public campaign to revive their version of 'true' Islam. They knew that it was not possible to openly preach or propagate the teachings of Syed Ahmed and Muhammad Ismail, whose followers were considered rebels and 'Wahhabis' by the British government. At the same time, Muslim society itself was resisting criticism from Ahmed and Ismail regarding the popular customs and practices of folk Islam. Maulana Naqi Ali Khan (d. 1880), father of Ahmad Raza Khan Barelwi (1856–1921), aggressively refuted through his writings the ideas of Ismail and Syed Ahmed, whom he considered 'Wahhabis' (Sanyal 2008, 23). Later, Ahmad Raza carried forward his father's mission by launching the Barelwi movement, which had sizeable support in small towns and rural areas of the United Provinces and the Punjab (Metcalf 1982, 297).

In this scenario, the founders of the movement opted for an isolationist approach vis-à-vis the government as well as the mainstream Muslim community, which they considered a threat to their purified version of Islam. Their primary goal after the events of 1857 was to protect and preserve the Islamic value system they had inherited from Syed Ahmed's movement. Faced with the question of survival, the founders of the DMM set up madaris as separate communities where they could practice and preach their values and norms. In line with Westhues's definition of counterculture (1972, 20), they added physical isolation to their already existing political and social isolation by establishing closed communities in the form of madaris. According to Westhues (1972, 11), 'Countercultural beliefs lead to their adherents cutting themselves off from mainstream society and severing the ties that bind them to the dominant order.'

One may also argue that the early madaris set up under the DMM were to represent an ascetic counterculture, which 'withdraws into a separated community where the new values can be lived out with minimum hindrance from an evil society' (Yinger 1982, 91). The first madrassah under the DMM was established at Deoband in May 1866. Within the next six months, another madrassah was set up at Saharanpur (Rizwi 2005, vol. 1, 164). By the end of 1880, at least fifteen madaris were operating from the template of the mother school at Deoband. In terms of the location of these madaris, the DMM also followed the pattern of some earlier countercultures such as monasteries, early Mormon or Amish settlements and 'hippie' communes, who all preferred to locate themselves far from cities (Westhues 1972, 20). Just like those countercultures, the DMM decided to move away from big cities like Delhi, Calcutta and Bombay to establish their early madaris in small towns of North India like Roorki, Ambahta, Kairanah, Thana Bhawan, Amroha and Naginah.

According to Westhues (1972, 20), the strategy of isolation among countercultures serves three purposes: maintaining solidarity among members, avoiding interaction with the dominant 'evil' society, and ensuring the survival and longevity of the counterculture. Yinger (1982, 93) has also observed that an ascetic approach is vital for the survival and continuity of a counterculture – compared to an activist approach, which is highly unstable. He gives the example of the Ranters, who shifted to a more ascetic movement like the Quakers in the seventeenth century. Similarly, the hippies of 1960s later 'turned to ascetic and highly restrained religious groups – the Divine Light Mission, Hare Krishna, or Meher Baba' (Yinger 1982, 93).

During that ascetic phase, the DMM focused on two activities. The more visible of these was to set up madaris for teaching and preaching the Deobandi version of Islam inside a closed community. The less visible activity mainly focused on individual *fatawa* to differentiate Deobandi Islam from popular folk Islam. These *fatawa* are discussed in the next section. During that early period, the Deobandis were not able to make a big impression on mainstream Muslim society even in those areas where they had established madaris. Owing to its closed-door approach, the DMM was neither able to attract many local students nor to change the practices of folk Islam in India. Students of the madrassah at Deoband were mostly coming from out of town. Muhammad Qasim once complained about the indifference of the local people. He said in his address to the 1874 convocation of the *darul ulum* that outsiders had benefitted from the madrassah but the residents of Deoband had ignored it (Shahjahanpuri 2004, 133). Similarly, in his home town of Gangoh, Rasheed Ahmed was unable to prevent pilgrimages to the shrine of his ancestor Shaikh Abdul Quddus and used to leave the place during the annual celebration of *urs* (Meeruthi 1908, vol. 2, 9).

Although the DMM did not openly attack the sociocultural practices of Indian Muslims during that ascetic phase, its religious edicts in this regard were closely monitored by the *ulama* of other schools of thought. As mentioned earlier, the Barelwi movement of Ahmad Raza Barelwi was the most active defender of traditional folk Islam against the Deobandi sect. He issued a *fatwa* declaring that Muhammad Qasim and Rasheed Ahmed were no longer Muslims due to showing disrespect to the Prophet. He was even successful in finding the support of *ulama* in the Hijaz in favour of his *fatwa* (Metcalf 1982, 309). However, the DMM's approach was ascetic to such an extent that it did not even react to that *fatwa* and Rasheed Ahmed advised his followers to ignore the issue. The DMM publicly refuted the *fatwa* only when it moved from an ascetic to an activist approach, as shall be discussed in the next chapter.

As the major visible activity of the DMM was to establish madaris, it was labelled as an educational movement that was launched in response to the secular education system introduced by the British in India. In fact, the first principal of the madrassah at Deoband, Muhammad Yaqub, while addressing the convocation meeting in 1883, also said that 'this madrassah was set up for the revival of Islamic knowledge in the aftermath of the Mutiny, when it appeared as if Islamic studies would vanish and there would be no one to learn or teach Islam in the next two or three decades' (Rizwi 2005, vol. 1, 143). However, the DMM appears to have overplayed such fears because thousands of madaris continued to operate even after the introduction of secular education and in the post-Mutiny period.

At the time of the DMM's inception, many leading madaris at Farangi Mahall (Lucknow), Khairabad (Rampur), Badaun, Delhi and Punjab were still very active in imparting religious education to Indian Muslims (Arshad 2005, 26). After 1857, the graduates of these mainstream madaris 'indeed took service under the British, filling posts for which they were ideally suited by their literacy and their respectable status. Some kept up a semblance of earlier times by taking employment in the protected Muslim states of Hyderabad and Bhopal' (Metcalf 1982, 87). So it was hardly likely that the madaris (or Islamic education in the Indian subcontinent at large) would become extinct, even after the fall of Muslim rule. In fact, many Muslim states were independent even under the British colonial system and implemented the Islamic education system without any hindrance or threat.

Further, the DMM adopted the same syllabus (*Dars-e-Nizami*) that was already being taught at other madaris in India. Metcalf (1982, 102) has suggested that the curriculum at Deoband 'was not dramatically innovative' in comparison to those of other madaris operating in India. However, they followed Waliullah's tradition of preferring revealed sciences (*manqulat*) over rational sciences (*ma'qulat*). In fact, Rasheed Ahmed, who had been teaching the Hadith at his home town of Gangoh before joining Darul Ulum Deoband, initially forbade (though he later allowed) the teaching of philosophy (Meeruthi 1908, vol. 1, 87–94). Therefore, the argument that the DMM was founded to meet the challenge and threat posed by secular education does not hold much ground. The new education system was not of much concern to the DMM's founding fathers, who actually never opposed modern education as such. In fact, Muhammad Qasim was in favour of learning modern sciences (Faruqi 1963, 33) and at one time considered introducing English to the madrassah at Deoband. He even intended to learn English himself (Gilani n.d., vol. 2, 300). Earlier, Waliullah's son Abdul Aziz had also given guarded approval of learning and teaching English (Metcalf 1982, 154). Qasim also hinted at the possibility of madrassah students going into modern education after completing their religious studies (Gilani n.d., vol. 2, 281). Gilani has interpreted the 1868 decision of the DMM to reduce the duration of the madrassah syllabus from ten to six years as an attempt to link DMM graduates with the modern education system (286–7).

So, in terms of an educational movement, the DMM was offering something neither new nor unique in its syllabus, nor was it presenting itself as an alternative education system. In fact, Mahmood Hassan, the first student and later a principal of the Deoband madrassah from 1890 to 1915, himself negated the general belief that the DMM was an educational movement. He stated of the Deoband madrassah (designated *darul ulum* or university in 1879) that 'it was founded in my presence and as far as I know its objective was to compensate for the losses in 1857' (Gilani n.d., vol. 2, 226). According to Qasim's biographer, Manazar Gilani (n.d., vol. 2, 212), the DMM was not just an educational movement but a social and political one. In short, from the DMM's perspective, it was neither religious education nor Islam in general that the British system threatened. For the leaders of the DMM, it was actually a particular version of Islam and the value system they inherited from Syed Ahmed and Ismail that was at risk of becoming extinct in the face of opposition from mainstream Muslim society as well as British aggression against 'Indian Wahhabis' (followers of Syed Ahmed). So, one may argue that the madaris of the DMM were to function basically as sanctuaries where that particular version of Islam could be practiced and preserved without any hindrance from outside society.

2.4 The Countercultural Character of the DMM

The founders of the DMM apparently followed the Waliullah tradition by offering a style of composite leadership which united *Shariah* (Islamic law) and *Tariqah* (spiritual path) in the personality of a religious leader. Other schools of thought like the Farangi Mahall or the Barelwis also made similar claims to espousing a 'middle way' (Metcalf 1982, 140) by combining elements of the *alim* (scholar) and the *sufi* (saint) in their leaders. However, there was something unique about the DMM, which remained in conflict with mainstream *ulama* and *sufis*. In fact, Muhammad Qasim used to lament that 'among the *ulama* I have a bad name and *sufis* think I am stained with *maulwiyyat* [derogatory term for *ulama*]' (Gilani n.d., vol. 1, 340).

The source of that uniqueness was not Waliullah's original movement, which actually worked for *tatbiq* or synthesis of the whole range of Islamic knowledge in order to end divisions and deviations among Indian Muslims with respect to their beliefs and practices. As mentioned earlier, the DMM had dropped the idea of *tatbiq* as well as *ijtihad* in favour of strict *taqlid* of Hanafi *madhab* after Muhammad Ishaq took control of Madrassah Rahimia in 1824 (Meeruthi 1908, vol. 1, 91; Sindhi 2008, 97). Rasheed Ahmed, while declaring *taqlid* binding and compulsory for Muslims (Meeruthi 1908, vol. 1, 132–3), stated that Muslims should neither pray behind a *ghair muqallid* (who does not observe *taqlid*) nor should they listen to his *wa'az* (religious speech; Meeruthi 1908, vol. 1, 179).

It is to be reiterated here that instead of the original movement of Waliullah, the DMM owed this uniqueness to a narrow version of the former movement that emerged under the leadership of Syed Ahmed and Muhammad Ismail. From the Ahmed–Ismail movement, the DMM inherited an idiomatic approach marked by an excessive focus on the purification of *tawhid* and an aggressive attitude towards the potential sources of threat to *tawhid* (i.e. the popular customs and practices of Indian Muslims, traditional *sufism* and Shia Islam). Like the Ahmed–Ismail movement, the DMM's major focus was also to revive 'true' Islam by protecting *tawhid* from those particular threats.

In line with the strict interpretation of *tawhid* inherited from Ahmed and Ismail, Deobandi *ulama* issued several controversial *fatawa*, which Muslim society considered disrespectful to the Prophet Muhammad (PBUH) and even to God. For example, the Deobandis insisted, contrary to common Muslim belief, that the Prophet did not share God's knowledge of the unknown (*ilm-ul-ghaib*). Rasheed Ahmed deemed this so important that he forbade his followers to accept as *imam* (prayer leader) anyone who denied it (Metcalf 1982, 150).

The Deobandis believed that they had a special understanding of the nature of God and *tawhid*. This belief gave them a certain *élan* – a sense of uniqueness and pride (Metcalf 1982, 150) not unlike that found in a counterculture. According to Yinger (1982, 30), countercultural nonconformists take pride in their acts, which they believe to be moral. Rasheed Ahmed once showed this pride by stating that 'truth is what comes out of Rasheed Ahmed's tongue and [I swear] by God that guidance and deliverance in this era is achieved by following me' (Meeruthi 1908, vol. 2, 17). This 'sense of pride in their cultural tradition' (Metcalf 1982, 197) was enhanced by the fact that their position on the sociocultural and spiritual values of Indian Muslims drew attacks from mainstream *ulama* and ordinary Muslims, including the above-mentioned *fatwa* by Ahmad Raza Barelwi against Muhammad Qasim and Rasheed Ahmed.

Such attacks against the Deobandi version of Islam on the one hand and close monitoring of the DMM by the British government on the other, convinced the DMM leaders to pursue an ascetic approach during the early years. At that time, DMM leaders mostly restricted themselves to their madaris and the small communities surrounding those institutions. At that time, they preferred to live in society 'with detachment and dignity' (Metcalf 1982, 197), presenting themselves as a model of religious leadership, combining the qualities of both *ulama* and *sufis*.

Despite the DMM's claim to follow Waliullah in consolidating Islamic sciences and *sufi* orders, the main emphasis of the movement was on 'popular reform of custom, not intellectual synthesis' (Metcalf 1982, 140). The major intellectual activity of Deobandi *ulama* was restricted to the writing of *fatawa*, which were mainly derived from the teachings of Waliullah's son Abdul Aziz and grandson Muhammad Ismail. Apart from those *fatawa*, publications of Deobandi *ulama* during the early years included 'letters written to disciples and followers, biographies and biographical dictionaries, and collections of exemplary anecdotes or *hikayat*. [...] All these works reflected to varying degrees the atmosphere of controversy among the schools of thought of the *ulama*. [...] No writing served what one might call an objective or intellectual concern' (Metcalf 1982, 210).

Although the DMM leaders were against the religions of Hindus and the colonial rulers, they felt that the biggest threat to 'true' Islam did not come from non-Muslims but from the sociocultural and spiritual practices of the folk Islam followed by mainstream Muslim society in India. In fact, the DMM showed far less opposition towards Hindus and the British compared to the religious or political groups of Muslims in India. As for the colonial rulers, '[The DMM's] concern was not with the British culture in general but with British law as it affected them and British decorum as they observed it' (Metcalf 1982, 153). As regards Hindus, Rasheed Ahmed issued a *fatwa* in favour of the Hindu-dominated Indian National Congress while opposing the Indian Patriotic Association – a political organization founded by Sir Syed (Madni 1930, 481–2).

The DMM coupled its 'moral disapproval of the British with realism in their relations with them and their culture' (Metcalf 1982, 154). Rasheed Ahmed once declined a large donation of 5,000 rupees from Afghanistan's ruler Habibullah Khan so as not to offend the British (Meeruthi 1908, vol. 2, 172). In fact, the DMM initially showed symbolic loyalty to the British, and even when it later decided to oppose the colonial government, it was accomplished with the support of the Hindu-dominated Congress.

As mentioned above, the DMM was unique in its condemnation of the sociocultural and religious practices of Muslims, popular *sufism* and Shia Islam. Following the Ahmed–Ismail tradition, the DMM declared many popular customs of Indian Muslims to be *shirk* (polytheism) or *bidah* (wrongful innovation). Rasheed Ahmed was so concerned and obsessed with eliminating popular custom that he made it part of his will (Meeruthi 1908, vol. 2, 342). Muhammad Qasim declared that *shirk* is committed 'by following false custom' (Metcalf 1982, 145). Similarly, Rasheed Ahmed lamented that the harm the *sufis* had caused to Islam was greater than that of any other sect (Hasan 1950, 279).

Owing to its ascetic approach during the early years, the DMM did not aggressively attack mainstream folk Islam. However, they continued to issue *fatawa* from time to time against many prevalent customs and practices of Indian Muslims. Those *fatawa* clearly linked the DMM with the tradition of the Ahmed–Ismail movement (Metcalf 1982, 149), as shown in the following discussion. It may be added here that the only difference between the ideas of these two movements is that of scale. The concepts and boundaries of *tawhid* and *shirk* had already been defined by the Ahmed–Ismail movement with respect to certain popular beliefs and customs among Indian Muslims. The DMM simply took it further by identifying and criticizing more customs and practices which they considered to violate *tawhid*. What its predecessors could not elaborate, perhaps due to their priority for and engagement in *jihad*, was thus accomplished by the DMM, which had ample time to ponder and produce relevant *fatawa* in post-Mutiny India when it was mostly confined to its madaris. It is the detail and extent of Deobandi ideas in this regard that sometimes make the DMM look more inflexible than its predecessor.

The sociocultural practices opposed by the DMM included ceremonies associated with elaborate marriages, funerals and even Eid (a biannual Muslim religious festival). Deobandi *ulama* also 'forbade funeral prayers to be read in either mosque or graveyard, and prohibited ceremonies on fixed days after death' such as *teejah*, *daswan* and *chaleeswan* – events on the third, tenth and fortieth day after death respectively, where supplications are offered and food is distributed for the soul of the deceased (Metcalf 1982, 149). Rasheed Ahmed issued a *fatwa* forbidding participation in such events (Meeruthi 1908, vol. 1, 141), which were part and parcel of life in mainstream Muslim society. Similarly, he also declared as *bidah* the common practice of embracing and handshaking among Muslim men after the Eid prayers (Meeruthi 1908, vol. 1, 181).

The Deobandis even denounced the widely popular practice of Eid Milad-un-Nabi 'on the grounds that it encouraged the belief that a dead person was actually present [and] that it elevated the importance of a fixed day. [...] Under Rasheed Ahmad's aegis, a group jointly signed a *fatwa* opposing [its] observance' (Metcalf 1982, 150). Rasheed Ahmed wrote that not a single participant of Milad ever followed the path of the Prophet (Meeruthi 1908, vol. 1, 128–9). The Deobandis also anathematized as *bidah* several other popular customs and practices such as fasting on the 24th day of the Islamic month of Rajab, reciting certain verses in supererogatory prayers and distributing sweets after reading the Quran (Metcalf 1982, 151).

Following in the footsteps of Ahmed and Ismail, Deobandis also declared it *haram* (forbidden) to show excessive respect to parents and elders through the use of words such as *qibla* and *ka'bah* (names used for Holy *Ka'bah* in Makkah), a cultural practice that was common among the Muslims of North India (Meeruthi 1908, vol. 1, 137). Similarly, they also asked Muslims to avoid excessive veneration of the saints and prophets (Meeruthi 1908, vol. 1, 146). Further, the DMM condemned the prohibition of remarriage for widows, a practice prevalent among many Muslim families in India. Muhammad Qasim set an example, like Muhammad Ismail had a few decades beforehand, by arranging the marriage of his widowed elder sister (Gilani n.d., vol. 2, 9).

Popular *sufi* practices were a special target of the DMM's criticism. About one-third of Rasheed Ahmed's *fatawa* dealt with issues related to *sufism*. Here again, their stance was similar to that of the Ahmed–Ismail movement. For example, the DMM leaders 'consistently sought to strip away local customs that unduly elevated the status of saints and prophets [...]. Theoretical justification for this orientation was again an emphasis on *tawhid*, the singularity of God' (Metcalf 1982, 149). However, the Deobandis, unlike Arabian Wahhabis, never sought to eliminate *sufism* altogether. Rather, they hoped, like Ahmed and Ismail, to integrate *sufism* into an obedient and responsible religious life whereby a *sufi shaikh* had to offer no intercession or miraculous intervention on behalf of his followers (Metcalf 182, 140). This was a marked deviation from the established practices of traditional *sufism*.

The DMM leaders 'offered an alternate spiritual leadership, geared to individual instruction rather than to mediation, stripped of what they deemed to be a deviant custom' (Metcalf 1982, 157). They also strictly objected to customs such as *sama* or *qawwali* (mystic musical sessions to induce ecstasy), distributing food after offering prayer (*fatihah*) for the dead and pilgrimage to the tombs of saints. They also prohibited eating any food on which *fatihah* had been recited for the dead. Their approach here looks even more strict than that of Abdul Aziz and Syed Ahmed, who did not object to eating such food (Gilani n.d., vol. 2, 43–4). The Deobandis also declared as *bidah* the practice of offering utensils and clay pots at the shrines of *pirs*. Rasheed Ahmed used to break all the clay pots offered to his uncle, who was associated with the shrine of his ancestor Abdul Quddus Gangohi (Meeruthi 1908, vol. 1, 58). Later on, he stopped going to that shrine altogether because of such activities (Meeruthi 1908, vol. 2, 16).

The Deobandis also opposed many customary observances at the famous tombs of Khawaja Moin-ud-din Chishti and Nizam-ud-din Auliya, which were visited by large numbers of Muslims. One of those observances was *urs*, an annual event held at the shrines of saints, during which pilgrims recited the Quran, listened to *qawwali* or *sama*, offered money and distributed food. The Deobandis also condemned observances held by many Indian Muslims on behalf of the greatest Muslim saint, Abdul Qadir Jilani, 'whose followers observed not only the yearly anniversary of his death but a monthly one (the *giyarhwin*) as well' on the eleventh day of each Islamic month (Metcalf 1982, 181). They also declared as *haram* the meat of an animal that was slaughtered after being declared *nadhr* (gift) to a saint – another common practice among Indian Muslims (Meeruthi 1908, vol. 1, 157).

As regards intercession by *sufi* saints, the Deobandis tried to minimize the role of not only the living *shaikh* but also that of the dead saints. Rasheed Ahmad explained in one of his *fatawa* that praying to a saint to grant one's wish was wholly illegitimate, nothing less than *shirk*. Following the tradition of Syed Ahmed, he decried the idea of *tasawwar-e-shaikh* because of the possibility of *shirk* (Meeruthi 1908, vol. 2, 233, 312). Similarly, he doubted that the dead saints could even hear one's prayers (Metcalf 1982, 181–2). Muhammad Qasim, despite believing that the dead could hear, forbade his followers to call on the dead. He only allowed his followers to read a section of the Quran and offer it as *isal-e-sawab* (transfer of merit) for the dead (Gilani n.d., vol. 2, 32–3).

Apart from popular custom and traditional *sufism*, the DMM also refuted the practices of Shia Islam. Not unlike Ahmed and Ismail, the Deobandis believed that Shias 'deny the singularity of God, the humanity of the Prophet, and the finality of revelation' (Metcalf 1982, 152). Rasheed Ahmed issued a *fatwa* asking Sunni Muslims to stay away from the religious activities of Shias and to avoid offering congregation prayers with them. He was of the view that Shia *ulama* were *kafir*, whereas ordinary Shias were *fasiqeen* – sinners who openly disobey God (Meeruthi 1908, vol. 2, 286).

On the question of marriage between Shia and Sunni Muslims, Rasheed Ahmed issued a *fatwa* declaring Shias to be on a par with *ahl-e-kitab* (people of the book – a term used for Christians and Jews) and accordingly allowed marriage between a Sunni man and Shia woman but not between a Shia man and Sunni woman (Meeruthi 1908, vol. 1, 166). Following the tradition of the Waliullah family, Rasheed also wrote *Hidaya-tush-Shia* (Guidance of the Shia) to denounce Shia Islam (Meeruthi 1908, vol. 1, 200). Rasheed forbade his followers to read or listen to true events of the martyrdom of Imam Hussain in the month of Muharram on the grounds that it resembled a Shia act (Meeruthi 1908, vol. 2, 78).

Muhammad Qasim also condemned Shia Islam in his book *Hadya-tush-Shia* (Gift of the Shia; Husaini 2003, 51), believing it to be the source of many wrongful customs and practices among Sunni Muslims (Gilani n.d., vol. 2, 70). Following the tradition of Syed Ahmed, he successfully managed to stop the practice of *taziyah* among the Sunnis of Deoband (Gilani n.d., vol. 2, 77). He also tried to reinforce the common misconception among Sunni Muslims about the general inability of Shias to learn the Quran by heart. He wrote that the reason for this inability was their opposition to the third caliph, Usman, who played an extraordinary role in compiling and publishing the Quran (Gilani n.d., vol. 2, 67). He also declared that Shias were practising a *barzaghi* religion that was to be placed in between *kufr* (non-belief) and Islam (Gilani n.d., vol. 2, 63–4). *Barzakh* is a term used in Islamic eschatology to define the barrier between the physical and spiritual worlds at which the soul awaits after death until Judgement Day (*Qiyamah*).

As regards the role of the DMM in politics, the two founding fathers, Qasim and Rasheed, kept the movement completely detached from political issues for almost four decades after its inception. During that early period, the movement was never involved in any criticism or opposition of the colonial government. On the other hand, the DMM seemed to be showing loyalty and support to the British rulers until the second decade of the twentieth century. For example, Darul Ulum Deoband 'celebrated ceremonial occasions with appropriate pomp, and observed times of crises, like Queen Victoria's last illness, with fitting prayers and messages' (Metcalf 1982, 182). The DMM remained totally nonchalant to the founding of the Indian National Congress in 1885 and the All-India Muslim League (AIML) in 1906. It remained completely unconcerned with the major issues of Indian Muslims like the Urdu–Hindi dispute over separate electorates. During that period, the political concerns of Indian Muslims were mainly raised by the Aligarh Movement and later by the AIML.

The isolation of the DMM from the mainstream social and political issues was so thorough that it even refused to support many religious causes on which there was otherwise a consensus among Indian Muslims. As shall be discussed in the next chapter, the DMM refused to join Anjuman-e-Khuddam-e-Ka'bah, an organization set up to protect Muslim holy places in the wake of the decline of the Ottoman Empire after the Balkan War. Similarly, the Deobandis refused to support the pan-Islamic movement in India that was launched to bolster the weakened Ottoman Empire. The DMM was also initially reluctant to join the Khilafat Movement, launched to protect the Muslim caliphate in the wake of the Young Turk Revolution (1908) as well as World War I (1914). The details are given in the next chapter.

Keeping in view the DMM's isolation from the political arena, it can hardly be considered a political movement for that initial period. During that phase, the DMM tried to present itself as a movement that was primarily working for the protection and preservation of the religious capital of Islam. The period can be explained in the context of the 'interiorization' thesis, which sees the DMM as a religious reform movement more concerned with perfection of faith and moral development in ordinary Muslims, and less with the assertion of a political agenda (Pemberton 2009). However, as mentioned in Chapter 1, the DMM did not behave like a typical social reform movement and concerned itself with the protection of its own version of 'true' Islam and Muslim culture. Therefore, one may argue that the DMM, for the first four decades after its inception, can neither be called a prototypal social reform movement nor a political movement. For that initial period, the DMM's behaviour can at best be likened to an ascetic counterculture that decided to withdraw into a separated community where their values could be 'lived out with minimum hindrance from an evil society' (Yinger 1982, 91). That 'evil society' included mainstream Muslim society as well as the colonial government in India, which apparently threatened the Deobandi version of Islam and its values inherited from the Ahmed–Ismail movement.

The DMM continued in its ascetic mode until the death of the second founding father, Rasheed Ahmed, in 1905. The other founding father, Muhammad Qasim, had already died in 1886. This ascetic approach focused on remaining aloof, mainly from mainstream Muslim society, in order to avoid outside influence on the DMM's value system. The movement deliberately kept its distance from other Muslim movements operating at that time. In 1874, when Sir Syed of the Aligarh Movement invited the DMM's Muhammad Qasim and Muhammad Yaqub to be part of a committee to design the religious curriculum for Aligarh College, the latter two declined participation on the grounds that Shia Muslims would be among the other members (Metcalf 1982, 328–9). Similarly, Rasheed Ahmed prevented Deobandis from joining Nadwat-ul-Ulama, an association of *ulama* founded in 1891 to consolidate a single leadership for all Indian Muslims (Meeruthi 1908, vol. 1, 205). Nadwat-ul-Ulama offered a new model of education that combined modern and religious education and was overwhelmingly welcomed by all sections of Muslim society in India (Nadwi 1970, 149).

After the death of the two founding fathers, the next generation of the DMM felt less insecure about their value system. They decided to gradually open the movement to the outside world in terms of condemning the sociocultural practices of Indian Muslims as well as participating in the mainstream political activism to oppose the colonial rulers. This all began under Mahmood Hassan (1851–1920), who took up the leadership of the movement after the death of Rasheed Ahmed in 1905 and decided to introduce a somewhat activist approach to the DMM. Even before that, Mahmood Hassan, after becoming the *sadr mudarris* or principal of Darul Ulum Deoband in 1890, had started working to expand the network of Deobandi madaris. Hence, about sixty madaris with links with the parent school at Deoband had been established at the dawn of the twentieth century (Metcalf 1982, 134). Unlike the DMM's earlier preference for small towns, some of the new madaris were established in big cities like Delhi, Lucknow, Calcutta, Lahore, Peshawar and Karachi. The next chapter will discuss how the DMM moved from an ascetic to an activist mode through its involvement in politics.

Chapter 3

THE DMM IN UNITED INDIA: ACTIVIST COUNTERCULTURAL TRENDS

Countercultural deviation [...] is partly defined situationally and politically. The cultural blueprint of a society – smudged by much handling – is sometimes ambiguous and difficult to decipher.

Milton Yinger, *Countercultures: The Promise and Peril of a World Turned Upside Down* (1982, 31)

This chapter discusses the circumstances under which the DMM dropped its ascetic approach in favour of activism. Under this new approach, the Deobandis established networks of *darul ulum* alumni in India as well as the North West Frontier Province (NWFP) and Afghanistan to revive the old dream of its predecessors to set up an Islamic state. This change of approach occurred during the first decade of the twentieth century, when the second generation of leadership took control of the movement. This chapter points out that the DMM's activism was largely displayed in politics, where it adopted a nationalist approach and hence countered the Pakistan movement, which demanded a separate state for Indian Muslims. In line with the view that a counterculture is partly defined situationally and politically (Yinger 1982, 31), this chapter focuses on the countercultural behaviour of the Deobandi movement in the political arena. The chapter also suggests that in its opposition to the idea and creation of Pakistan, the DMM was motivated inter alia by its countercultural mindset.

The DMM's transition from an ascetic to an activist mode occurred during a period marked by remarkable regional and global developments. At the time the British were reviving their 'forward policy' to strengthen their grip on the Indian subcontinent. At the international level, Great Britain had allied with France and Russia at the start of the twentieth century to form the Triple Entente; the Ottoman Empire was falling apart; and Egypt was under British influence, while the French had taken control of Algeria, Tunisia and Morocco. In 1910, Italy attacked Tripoli and in 1912 the Balkan states of Serbia, Bulgaria, Montenegro and Greece launched a military offensive against the Ottoman Empire, where the rebellion of the 'Young Turks' in 1908 had led to constitutional reforms. At around the same time, Albania announced independence from Turkey. After the Balkan Wars, all areas of European Turkey went to the Balkan states in 1913 (Madni 1954, 519–41). These political upheavals were followed by World War I, in which Turkey allied with Germany and Austria-Hungary to face the Triple Entente. As a reaction to these developments, several anti-colonial and pan-Islamic movements were formed in the Muslim world.

Still going through its ascetic phase, the DMM's attitude towards the above-mentioned developments was mostly nonchalant, as shall be discussed later in this chapter. However, the movement could not for long remain unconcerned with the situation in the NWFP and Afghanistan, where many graduates of Darul Ulum Deoband had established themselves as religious leaders. In this region, both anti-colonial and pan-Islamic sentiments were flourishing under Amir Habibullah's reign (1901–19). Anti-colonialism in this region was originally a reaction to the aggressive British 'forward policy' of pushing outposts into tribal areas, recruiting local levies, paying high subsidies to some tribes while fighting others, and building railway lines to Dargai, Thal and Jamrud at the Khyber. The local response was equally aggressive, resulting in tribal raids on these outward symbols of the empire. In 1897, a frontier uprising took no less than thirty-five thousand troops to put down. As a result, the NWFP was established with a chief commissioner directly under the viceroy. However, tribal raids continued in the coming years (Olesen 1995, 102–3).

The warring tribes in the NWFP were supported on the one hand by the 'traditionalist' religious and tribal leaders of Afghanistan, represented by Sardar Nasrullah, younger brother of Amir Habibullah, and *qadhi-ul-qudhat* (chief Shariah judge) Haji Abdur Razzaq, a graduate of Darul Ulum Deoband, and on the other hand by the 'modernists', led by Mahmud Tarzi and Sardar Amnullah, who later became king of Afghanistan in 1919. Pan-Islamism in Afghanistan was mainly spread by Mahmud Tarzi through his Persian-language biweekly *Sirajul Akhbar*. Tarzi had become familiar with pan-Islamic ideas and the Ottoman nationalist movement during his forced exile to Damascus during Amir Abdur Rehman's reign (1880–1901). After returning to Afghanistan in 1904, Tarzi not only influenced the Afghan court and people but also the Muslim intellectuals of India who were already watching with concern the political developments in the Ottoman Empire (Olesen 1995, 99–102).

Apart from focusing on the NWFP, this chapter shall also highlight how the DMM responded to the political changes inside Mainland India, where a nationalist movement under the banner of the Indian National Congress was launched in 1885 to campaign for more Indian participation in the legislative process. It may be added here that the Congress largely remained a Hindu-dominated party despite explicit efforts to draw Indian Muslims into its fold. Prominent Muslim leaders like Sir Syed Ahmad Khan and Syed Amir Ali (1849–1928), the eminent lawyer and religious thinker of Calcutta, argued that the Congress could not speak for the interests of the two distinct 'communities' that comprised India. The pervasive opinion among Muslims was that identity rested in one's religious community. The Congress vision, by contrast, insisted that the interests of self, caste and community be subordinated to the 'public good' and the Indian nation (Metcalf 2002, 136–7). Against this backdrop, and in close association with the Aligarh movement of the modernist Sir Syed Ahmad (Taylor 1983, 185), the All-India Muslim League (AIML) was formed in 1906 with the objective of advancing the interests of Muslims (Metcalf 2002, 159). These changes gradually drew the Deobandis into active politics under the banner of Jamiat-ul-Ulama-e-Hind (JUH), a platform of Indian *ulama* established in 1919.

3.1 The End of the DMM's Ascetic Approach

As discussed in the last chapter, Mahmood Hassan, the first student of Deoband madrassah, was a favourite of the DMM founders. Being a close associate and confidant of Muhammad Qasim, founder and ideologue of the DMM, Hassan was well aware of the objectives of the movement (Mian 1957, vol. 5, 171–3). He joined Darul Ulum Deoband as a teacher in 1874 after his graduation (Rizwi 2005, vol. 1, 174). In 1880, he set up an alumni association named Samrat-ul-Tarbiyyat (fruit of the training), the main objective of which was to convince graduates to support their alma mater by making an annual financial contribution equalling 25 per cent of their monthly income (Rizwi 2005, vol. 1, 187).

In 1890, Mahmood Hassan was selected as the principal in a unanimous decision by the members of the *darul ulum* (Madni 1954, 547–8) who considered him to be the true successor to the DMM founders. Deobandi historian Muhammad Mian (1957, vol. 5, 171–3) declared Hassan to be the *roohani farzand* (spiritual son), *talmiz-e-khas* (special student) and *hamraaz* (sharer of secrets) of Muhammad Qasim. Another Deobandi writer, Manazar Ahsan Gilani, a contemporary of Hassan at the *darul ulum*, declared him to be Muhammad Qasim's bona fide successor and heir (Gilani n.d., vol. 2, 226). Owing to this exceptional association with the founders of the DMM as well as his constant links with its alumni, Hassan had extraordinary influence and clout in the movement. The authority and respect he inspired added unprecedented leverage to the academic post of principal alongside the powerful management posts of *mohtamim* (chancellor) and *sarprast* (patron or rector).

After 1895, when Muhammad Qasim's son Muhammad Ahmad was appointed *mohtamim* of Darul Ulum Deoband, the management focused on institutional strengthening. Muhammad Ahmad gave particular attention to raising more funds and donations, expanding the physical infrastructure, establishing new departments and building a large library (Rizwi 1974, vol. 2, 228). His primary focus seemed to be the development of the madrassah at Deoband and not the Deobandi movement as a whole. His target was to make the *darul ulum* a centre of excellence for religious education, with a peculiar emphasis on Deobandi Islam and its values. He was also very careful, like the DMM founders, not to offend the colonial government with respect to the madrassah's activities.

On the other hand, Principal Mahmood Hassan's vision for the DMM was far broader than that of the *mohtamim*. He wanted to follow the practical tradition of Syed Ahmed and Muhammad Ismail in letter and spirit. As a true successor of Muhammad Qasim, he believed that the primary purpose of the DMM was not to impart religious education. According to Hassan, the DMM was launched against the backdrop of the fall of Muslim rule in India in 1857 and that Muhammad Qasim's vision was not just to set up madaris for educational purposes. He told Manazar Ahsan Gilani that Darul Ulum Deoband had been set up as a centre to prepare people to avenge the defeat of 1857 (Gilani n.d., vol. 2, 226). Hassan wanted to pursue that vision through an activist approach.

It is interesting that both the biological and spiritual successors of Muhammad Qasim (Muhammad Ahmad and Mahmood Hassan respectively) belonged to the same

Deobandi tradition. However, their approaches were quite different with regard to the spread of their movement. Muhammad Ahmad preferred to continue with the ascetic approach adopted by the movement in the wake of the post-Mutiny situation. He wanted to preserve and propagate Deobandi Islam through madaris and religious education. On the other hand, Mahmood Hassan felt confident enough to come out of the ascetic phase. By the end of the nineteenth century, he was ready to adopt an activist approach and explore the possibilities of an Islamic state where Deobandi Islam would prevail. It can be argued that the ascetic approach of the DMM continued until Rasheed Ahmed became *sarprast* of Darul Ulum Deoband. After his death in 1905, Hassan became more influential in the affairs of the Deobandi movement as a whole, whereas Muhammad Ahmad's role was mostly restricted to managing the *darul ulum*.

In 1908, Principal Hassan and Mohtamim Ahmad decided, in view of the expansion of academic disciplines and the rise in the number of students, to strengthen the faculty by recalling some of the old graduates to teach at their alma mater. Consequently, many well-known *ulama* who were running Deobandi madaris in different parts of India joined the *darul ulum*. These included Anwar Shah from Kashmir, Ubaidullah from Sindh, Murtaza Hassan from Darbhanga, Abdus Samad from Rehrrki and Sahool Bhagalpuri from Calcutta. In addition, Hussain Ahmed Madni, former student of Mahmood Hassan, was also called back from Madinah to join the faculty (Madni 1954, 142). Madni later became the principal from 1927 until his death in 1957. During the last nine years of his life, he was also president of the Deobandi political party, Jamiat-ul-Ulama-e-Hind.

The expansion of faculty at the *darul ulum* marked the rise of an activist approach in the DMM. Most of the new teachers came under the influence of Mahmood Hassan, owing to his image as the harbinger of Muhammad Qasim's ideology (Gilani n.d., vol. 2, 226). In 1909, Hassan set up Jamiat-ul-Ansar, an alumni association of Darul Ulum Deoband, under the leadership of one of his most trusted lieutenants, Ubaidullah Sindhi (1872–1944). Through Jamiat-ul-Ansar, Hassan was able to organize Deobandi *ulama* in India as well as in Afghanistan (Sindhi 2008, 111). Housed in Darul Ulum Deoband, its apparent role was to propagate the teachings of the *darul ulum* and expand the network of Deobandi madaris (Mian 1957, vol. 5, 215–16). However, the exact aims and objectives of this organization were never defined, hence its role has been interpreted differently by different writers. According to Faruqi (1963, 57), the idea behind Jamiat-ul-Ansar was to lay the foundations of an organization of Deobandi *ulama* who could be mobilized in times of need. Deobandi historian Muhammad Mian (1957, vol. 5, 196–7) has referred to Jamiat-ul-Ansar as an 'outline' of a broader 'system', which was to be presented before the ordinary Muslims through Deobandi madaris and its *ulama*. Without giving any concrete ideas about what this 'system' involved, Mian (1957, vol. 4, 195) has hinted that Hassan's major objective was to revive the movement of Syed Ahmed and Muhammad Ismail by bringing together the NWFP of India and Afghanistan.

In order to popularize Jamiat-ul-Ansar, Hassan first used the platform of the *darul ulum*, where a large *jalsa-e-dastarbandi* (convocation) was held in 1910, attended by more than thirty thousand Muslims from all over India (Faruqi 1963, 58). Next year, a large public gathering was held under the banner of Jamiat-ul-Ansar in Moradabad, where more than ten thousand people came to participate. Maulana Ahmad Hassan

Amrohawi, who presided over the meeting, said in his speech that Jamiat-ul-Ansar was neither an old boys' association nor an embodiment of anyone's personal or worldly ambitions; rather its purpose was to urgently fulfil a series of 'necessary objectives' (Mian 1957, vol. 5, 198–9).

Although they never explicitly stated what these 'necessary objectives' were (perhaps to avoid any reaction from the colonial government), the later activities of Hassan and his followers would indicate that they were perhaps trying to achieve their predecessors' old dream of finding an 'outer caliph' and establishing an Islamic state where they could freely propagate and implement Deobandi Islam and their *ulama* could play the role of 'inner caliphs'.

During the Italo-Turkish War (1911–12) and the Balkan Wars (1912–13), Jamiat-ul-Ansar became active in collecting funds for the war victims of Turkey. Hassan used his influence on the management of Darul Ulum Deoband to temporarily close the madrassah and engage the students in fundraising for Turkey (Madni 1921, 31). According to a British report, Hassan at that time believed that the *darul ulum* should focus more on *jihad* than religious education. He had, in fact, also started mobilizing his followers and taking *bay'ah* (the oath of allegiance) from them for participation in *jihad* (Madni 1954, vol. 2, 632).

The differences between Principal Hassan and the management became apparent in 1912 when they invited the British governor of the United Provinces to visit the madrassah, where he bestowed the title *shamsul ulama* upon Muhammad Ahmad, the *mohtamim*. Hassan boycotted the whole event and preferred to stay in his office (Mian n.d., 265). In 1913, the management reacted by expelling many of his followers without consulting him. First, Ubaidullah Sindhi, head of Jamiat-ul-Ansar, was reprimanded by the management for taking part in political activities. Later on, Sindhi along with some of his companions was thrown out of the *darul ulum* in 1913 (Mian n.d., 262–5). The management also issued a *fatwa* declaring Sindhi a *kafir* (non-believer) with respect to some of his religious ideas, which were considered to be in conflict with Deobandi Islam (Robinson 1974, 270). Further, Hassan was asked to keep away from politics, though he ignored these suggestions (Faruqi 1963, 59). This rift between the management and Hassan marked the split of the DMM into two parallel streams: one preserving and practising Deobandi Islam through madaris and the other politically pursuing the goal of an Islamic state for the implementation of Deobandi Islam. This implicit division of labour in the DMM has continued since then in one form or another, whereby madaris have tried to separate themselves from the manifestations of Deobandi politics in the public space. Despite having different approaches, these two streams have managed to avoid direct conflict with each other to prevent any damage to the movement. Conversely, these parallel streams have helped sustain and strengthen the movement through their mutual links between the Deobandi madaris and Deobandi politicians, who in turn are mostly graduates of the same madaris. This is explained further in the next chapter.

This sharp division in the Deobandi movement in 1913 was clearly identified by the British government's Rowlett Committee, which investigated the activities of Hassan and his followers. The report declared the *mohtamim*, Muhammad Ahmad, and his management team loyal to the British government, as opposed to the camp represented by Hassan and Sindhi (Mian n.d., 425, 439–40, 449). While acknowledging this division in the movement, most Deobandi writers have tried to downplay and rationalize it. However, Deobandi historian Muhammad Mian has tried to give the impression that there were no actual differences between the principal and the management at all. As for their decisions to welcome the British governor and to expel Hassan's supporters, Mian has defended the management in terms of their policy of *maslehat* (short-term compromise or expediency) to avoid British intervention in the *darul ulum* (Mian n.d., 160–63, 261–5).

However, Madni (1954, 561, 661), while understating such divisions, has acknowledged that these differences owed to the management's soft approach towards the British government. The management's real fear was that the activist approach of Hassan and Jamiat-ul-Ansar would offend the British to such an extent that the government would decide to permanently close the madrassah. When Madni shared these concerns, Hassan replied, 'The founder of the Darul Ulum, Muhammad Qasim had prayed to God that the madrassah may survive for fifty years; so that period of fifty years has passed by the grace of God and the madrassah has served the purpose for which it was established' (Madni 1954, vol. 2, 623). These words (as well as his statement refuting the educational objectives of the madrassah at Deoband, linking it to revenge for the 1857 defeat; Gilani n.d., vol. 2, 226), highlight a conflict between the demeanour and intent of the DMM with respect to its goals. Deobandi writers have further mystified things by holding on to both the demeanour and intent, perhaps in order to shield their leadership from criticism. It may be argued here that if Hassan – a close confidant of the DMM founders and highly esteemed among all Deobandis – was right then it is hard to argue that the DMM was an educational movement. In that case, one can argue that the Deobandi madaris were to mainly serve as sanctuaries where the value system of a particular version of Islam was to be preserved in the face of British oppression against the followers of Syed Ahmed and Muhammad Ismail, especially in the post-Mutiny environment.

For Hassan, the time had already come to mobilize the followers of Ahmed and Ismail and revive the movement, as did the founders of the DMM when they tried to set up an Islamic state in Muzaffar Nagar during the Mutiny. Hassan, like Ahmed and Ismail, selected the region of Yaghistan to launch his movement – not only for the historical connection to the Ahmed–Ismail movement but also because many graduates of Darul Ulum Deoband lived in that particular region. The term Yaghistan (literally 'land of freedom and unrestraint') referred to those tribal areas of the NWFP that were independent from both the British and Afghanistan governments (Madni 1954, 558). Today, this region mostly forms what is called the Federally Administered Tribal Areas (FATA) of Pakistan.

After the events of 1913 at Darul Ulum Deoband, Hassan asked Sindhi to temporarily move to Delhi to work for the Nizarat-ul-Ma'rif-ul-Quran (Academy of Quranic learning). The academy had been established by Hassan in association with Hakim Ajmal Khan and Wiqar-ul-Mulk, two graduates of Aligarh University. The major objective of the academy was to instruct Western-educated Muslim youths in the Quranic teachings in a way that would enable them to shake off their ill-founded scepticism about Islamic belief (Madni 1954, vol. 2, 554–5). The objectives and activities of the academy hint at the new approach of the DMM, which tried to influence mainstream Muslim society through their own interpretation of Islam. Despite the management's insistence on continuing with the ascetic approach, the influence of Hassan had convinced many Deobandis to be more self-assured and open about their version of Islam. In fact, it was at the start of this activist phase that the DMM aggressively worked to refute the *fatawa* of Ahmad Raza Barelwi, who had declared the DMM founders and many other Deobandi *ulama* to be *kafir*. During that period, followers of the DMM collected hundreds of signatures from the Indian *ulama* and testified that the Deobandis were Sunni Hanafi Muslims (Metcalf 1982, 310).

In 1915, Hassan commanded Sindhi to proceed to Afghanistan. Within a few months of Sindhi's departure, Hassan himself left for the Hijaz in 1915 to avoid arrest, as the British government had become alert to his activities. Many Indian Muslims considered the departure of Hassan *hijrat* (migration) in line with Abdul Aziz's nineteenth-century *fatwa* declaring India *darul harb* (Mian n.d., 276). Therefore, thousands of Muslims came to see him off at different railway stations during his journey from Deoband to Bombay, where he boarded a ship for the Hijaz (Madni 1921, 38–9). There are two different opinions among Deobandi writers about the departure of Hassan. Some have interpreted it as part of his plan to garner support from the Ottoman Empire against the British. Others on the other hand think that the immediate reason for his departure was to avoid arrest (Madni 1921, 37).

In another part of the world, when Sindhi arrived in Kabul he found a number of people who enthusiastically welcomed him as a representative of Hassan. According to Sindhi (2008, 112), Hassan's influence in Afghanistan 'was the outcome of fifty years of efforts by DMM's graduates' in the tribal areas bordering Afghanistan. Interestingly, Hassan mentioned the same number of years for which the madrassah at Deoband was supposed to play its role as per the vision of Muhammad Qasim. It may be argued that the timing of Hassan's activism suggests that he was perhaps more inspired by Muhammad Qasim's vision than by some specific political plan or strategy.

The true and exact objectives of Hassan's movement are as obscure as those of Jamiat-ul-Ansar or even the DMM itself. Sindhi has stated that when Hassan directed him to go to Afghanistan, he was not given any kind of programme or plan (Faruqi 1963, 59). Deobandi writers have tried to portray Hassan's movement as a nationalist campaign for the freedom of India. However, there is hardly any evidence to prove that the goal of Hassan or Sindhi was to win independence for India from the British. Although it is true that this movement did oppose the British in the early twentieth century, there is no convincing proof to show that it was a typical freedom movement in the true sense. On the other hand, circumstantial evidence suggests that it was merely an attempt by the Deobandis to somehow replicate the earlier movement of Ahmed and Ismail, who had temporarily set up an Islamic state in the NWFP. In that sense, the ultimate goal of the DMM could perhaps be the revival of Muslim rule in India at some distant point in the future. In such a scenario, postcolonial India was to be different from the actual partition of 1947, for which the Deobandis have already tried to take credit by linking it with Hassan's movement.

The objective of Hassan's movement was not much different from that of Ahmed and Ismail. Hassan even adopted a similar approach by propagating and taking *bay'ah* for *jihad*, which was to be launched in the same region as was selected by the earlier movement. Like Ahmed and Ismail, he also planned to use the famous *fatwa* of Abdul Aziz declaring India *darul harb* (Mian n.d., 301). However, Hassan's strategy was slightly different in the sense that he tried to involve the Afghanistan government on the one hand and the Ottoman Empire on the other, as shown in the following discussion.

When Sindhi began organizing people in Kabul for *jihad*, Hassan advised many Deobandi *ulama* from North West India to move to tribal areas and motivate the people (Mian n.d., 373). As a result of that a group named Junoodullah (Armies of God) was established in tribal areas under the leadership of Haji Tarangzai of Charsadda, a close friend of Hassan (Madni 1954, vol. 2, 578–9). Junoodullah began fighting in the frontier region against the British forces, the majority of which were engaged on various fronts during World War I.

While Sindhi coordinated with Afghan government to support Junoodullah, Hassan met the Turkish governor of the Hijaz, Ghalib Pasha, in Makkah to appeal for the support of the Ottoman Empire for his movement in India. Pasha's response was positive, and was actually in line with the Ottoman Empire's tactical approach of reviving pan-Islamic ideas to strengthen its position in the war. Otherwise, pan-Islamism was on the decline in Turkey itself since the Young Turks had seized power in 1908 (Eickelman and Piscatori 1996, 139). Ghalib Pasha gave three letters to Hassan. The first was addressed to Indian Muslims and declared support for their struggle against the colonial government. The second was for Basri Pasha, governor of Madinah, asking him to help Hassan in meeting Anwar Pasha, Turkish minister for war. The third was for Anwar Pasha, stating that Hassan was a reliable person who should be provided help in the form of men and money (Madni 1954, vol. 2, 634). Later, Hassan met Anwar Pasha in Madinah to receive another letter of support (Madni 1954, vol. 2, 642).

After receiving these letters, Hassan's plan was to go to the tribal areas of Yaghistan and actively launch a *jihadi* movement with the aim of setting up an Islamic state. He requested Anwar Pasha and Turkish commander Jamal Pasha to send him to Yaghistan via Kabul using the Iranian route, but was told that the Russians had blocked the Iranian route, while the British had cut the Iraqi route to Kabul, making communication impossible between the Ottoman Empire and Afghanistan (Madni 1954, vol. 2, 607). Accordingly, Anwar Pasha advised him to go to Yaghistan through India. However, Hassan avoided that due to fear of arrest and decided to wait in the Hijaz for the time being.

Meanwhile, the letters provided by the Turkish authorities were secretly despatched to India and then onward to Yaghistan for distribution among the followers of the movement. These letters proved to be helpful in lifting the morale of Hassan's followers in both India and Yaghistan (Mian n.d., 359). Sindhi was also trying hard to lure Afghanistan into a war against the British to revive Muslim rule in India. In the tradition of Shah Waliullah, who in the eighteenth century had invited Afghan ruler Ahmad Shah Abdali to invade and rule India, Sindhi promised Habibullah that if Kabul attacked India and defeated the British, the crown prince of Afghanistan would be declared the permanent emperor of India (Mian 1957, vol. 5, 276). Sindhi also suggested appointment of a prince from the Afghan royal family as head of the rebel provisional government of India in Kabul (Mian n.d., 329). However, his efforts failed to convince the Afghan ruler.

Realizing the impending failure of the movement, Sindhi wrote a secret letter to Hassan in 1916 warning him not to come to Kabul (Mian n.d., 185). The letter was written on yellow silk cloth and was to be delivered to Hassan in the Hijaz through a reliable member of the movement (Mian n.d., 185). However, the British government in India intercepted the letter along with another addressed to Abdur Rahim Sindhi, who was to ensure safe delivery of the first letter to Hassan. In August 1916, the government launched a series of investigations to probe and expose Hassan's movement; it became known as the 'Silken Letters Conspiracy'. In the meantime, the Sharif of Makkah had rebelled against the Turks with the help of the British. Soon after that, Hassan and his companions in the Hijaz were arrested by the authorities and handed over to the British forces, who exiled him to Malta for the next three years.

During all those years of activism, Darul Ulum Deoband distanced itself completely from the followers of Hassan despite the fact that the movement was operating underground until the Silken Letters were discovered in 1916. Although Deobandi writers have tried to downplay the differences between Darul Ulum Deoband and Hassan's followers, the division was so clear and sharp that the latter strongly criticized the former for serving the interests of the British and even ignoring Hassan's family members left behind in India (Mian n.d., 358).

The management of Darul Ulum Deoband was afraid that if the colonial government found it had any links with Hassan, they might close the Deobandi madaris. Therefore, they preferred to stick to the old ascetic approach of preserving Deobandi Islam by using the madaris as sanctuaries. It was in line with this approach that the *darul ulum* passed a resolution of loyalty to the British at the outbreak of war in 1914 (Robinson 1974, 282). Similarly, the management showed no reaction to the arrest and exile of Hassan despite his rising popularity and support among the Muslim and non-Muslim nationalists of India.

Apart from the fear of reprisal from the British government, another reason for the DMM's ascetic approach under the *darul ulum*'s management was its countercultural mindset vis-à-vis mainstream Muslim society in India. Hence, the DMM had not only kept itself away from the political issues of Indian Muslims but had declined to join the Muslim community even on many purely religious matters. For example, they distanced themselves from Anjuman-e-Khuddam-e-Ka'bah, an organization that was launched to protect Muslim holy places in the Hijaz and represented all shades of Muslim society in India (Robinson 1974, 208). Clearly the DMM did not take issue with the objectives of the *anjuman*, with which no Muslim could disagree. Neither was there any risk of British reprisal as such if the DMM had joined the *anjuman*. As a matter of fact, the DMM had 'no intention of having much to do with a society in which the Firangi Mahalis [*sic*] were in command' (Robinson 1974, 209). The Farangi Mahall school of thought followed a version of Islam which the Deobandis found unacceptable. Similarly, the DMM was perhaps not comfortable with other Muslim groups in the *anjuman* who represented the folk Islam generally practiced by mainstream Muslim society.

The DMM also opposed the Lucknow Pact of 1916 between the two biggest political parties of India, whereby the AIML, the main political party of Indian Muslims, succeeded in gaining the support of the Hindu-dominated Indian National Congress to give representation to Muslims in central and provincial legislative councils according to their population. The pact also provided guarantees to the Muslim population with regard to legislation affecting their religious codes and practices – a remarkable achievement in the wake of the 'home rule' and self-government schemes announced by the colonial government.

While the AIML tried to interpret the Lucknow Pact in terms of protecting and preserving the Islamic way of life in India, the DMM chose to oppose the agreement despite itself making similar claims about Islam in India. The DMM not only objected to the authority of the AIML and its president Muhammad Ali Jinnah but also raised doubts about the likely gains of Indian Muslims through the pact. Instead, the Deobandi leader, Mufti Kifayatullah, proposed that the British government should set up Muslim *Shariah* courts to be headed by the *ulama* (Mian 1957, vol. 5, 309–20). Here again, the opposition of the DMM appears to have been inspired by its tendency to dissociate from the popular folk Islam of ordinary Muslims, which the AIML claimed to uphold.

It is interesting to note that in 1916 the DMM, which later endorsed Hassan's movement for the freedom of India, took a contradictory stance by disapproving of the Lucknow Pact, an important milestone on the road to Independence of India. The chief target of the DMM's criticism of the Lucknow Pact was the AIML, the main party claiming to represent the Muslims of India. Although Deobandi historians like Hussain Madni and Muhammad Mian have tried to portray the DMM as a pioneer of the freedom struggle in India, it actually proved otherwise by passing resolutions of loyalty to the colonial government during World War I, disowning Hassan and his followers and opposing the truly nationalist Lucknow Pact.

3.2 The DMM's Entry into Active Politics

It is interesting to note that the DMM's reaction to the nationalistic spirit of the Lucknow Pact was quite opposite to what the movement was to preach in the next few years. Commenting on the pact in 1917, the DMM's Mufti Kifayatullah stated that 'it is the duty of the Muslim public to give top priority to protecting religious independence. [...] We are first Muslims and then Hindi, Arabic, Iranian or Chinese' (Mian 1957, vol. 5, 315). In other words, the DMM, which was to later present itself as the champion of nationalism, was putting this concept on the back burner until the second decade of the twentieth century. As for their concerns about the protection of religious independence, the Lucknow Pact in no way endangered that independence for Muslims; rather it provided enough space and guarantees to block any laws which they found to be against their religious values. If one tries to understand the DMM's criticism from a countercultural perspective, the Deobandis were mainly concerned about protecting the values of their own version of Islam. This was not likely to find any representation in the proposed legislative councils, owing to the fact that the DMM at that time had no political platform of its own and neither was it willing to join other groups or parties that represented Indian Muslims.

Remarkably, in 1916, when the DMM was censuring the AIML after the Lucknow Pact, Sindhi wrote in a letter to Hassan that Darul Ulum Deoband was not only busy serving the colonial government but also feeling proud to be loyal to the royal court (Mian n.d., 358). Even if one believes the viewpoint of Deobandi writers that the DMM was actually nationalist at its core, and only showing loyalty to the British as a policy of *maslehat*, the question still arises as to why it chose at the same time to condemn the AIML by declaring it loyal to the colonial government. In fact, the Deobandis, without giving the AIML any benefit of the doubt, did not hesitate to call Mr Jinnah an agent of the British (Mian 1957, vol. 6, 169, 173).

Despite issuing occasional statements on political issues, the DMM, in line with their previous ascetic approach, kept its distance from Indian politics until 1920. The Deobandis showed no interest in joining the pan-Islamic Khilafat (Caliphate) Movement, a campaign launched after the end of World War I by Indian Muslims who felt that the British had reneged on their assurances about Turkey and the Ottoman Caliphate. They were also concerned about the Muslim holy places in the Hijaz, which, it seemed to them, would come under the control of non-Muslims (Faruqi 1963, 63). The spirit of the Khilafat Movement, like Anjuman-e-Khuddam-e-Ka'bah, was Maulana Abdul Bari of Farangi Mahall, which upheld the values of folk Islam. The DMM had earlier shown its contempt for the Farangi Mahall school by snubbing Abdul Bari as 'a busy body who could not read his Koran rightly' (Robinson 1974, 282). This time, when Abdul Bari tried to bring the *ulama* together to resist British policy on the caliphate issue, the Deobandis opposed it. In fact, the *mohtamim* of Darul Ulum Deoband, Muhammad Ahmad, took a pro-British position by declaring that 'Indian Muslims were not obliged to help their co-religionists against the British government with which they entered into a contract' (Robinson 1974, 293). Interestingly, this position was soon to be reversed, as shall be discussed in the following paragraphs. Here one may argue that, not unlike the case of Anjuman-e-Khuddam-e-Ka'bah, the DMM's refusal to join the Khilafat Movement was perhaps inspired by its unwillingness to work under the leadership of Abdul Bari (Robinson 1974, 209). Otherwise, the Khilafat Movement was launched to protect the Ottoman Caliphate and as such there was no reason for the DMM to refuse participation in it.

In this way, the DMM continued its policy of *maslehat* as well as its countercultural approach of avoiding any close association with *ulama* and Muslim political leaders not belonging to their own school of thought. This same approach allowed them to reverse their stance during World War II when the Deobandis not only urged the Muslims to oppose the British government but also commended the Hindus for their resistance against the British. On 28 September 1939, the pro-Deobandi Urdu daily *Madinah* wrote a satirical editorial in which it stated,

> It is ironical that a nation [Muslims] that had always felt pride in its martial nature and had opposed the non-violence of Hindus was standing at the door of the British in a posture of slavish respect with folded hands and stooped neck while the other nation [Hindus], which believed in avoiding war and fighting, was standing in front of the British in a bold manner with its head held high and chest straight. (Mian 1957, vol. 6, 62).

In the summer of 1920, estranged Deobandi Mahmood Hassan returned to Bombay once the British had finally ended his exile. The colonial government advised him not to take part in politics, hoping he would avoid contact with khilafatists, as had the DMM. But he ignored their advice and decided to attend the reception arranged in his honour by the Khilafat Committee of Bombay, where he was bestowed with the title *shaikh-ul-Hind* (elder of India). Abdul Bari specially travelled from his home town of Lucknow to welcome Hassan and brief him about the objectives of the Khilafat Movement and its alliance with the Congress. Gandhi also travelled from Allahabad to Bombay to meet Hassan and update him on the political situation of the country.

Contrary to the DMM's policy, Hassan not only announced his support for the Khilafat Movement but also issued a *fatwa* giving religious sanction to the non-violent, non-cooperation movement being launched jointly by the khilafatists and the Congress to resist British policies vis-à-vis India and the Ottoman Caliphate. The stature and popularity of Hassan among Indians soon convinced his Deobandi supporters to gather behind him. This situation left the DMM with little choice but to accept Hassan as well as the Khilafat Movement, which they had earlier opposed. Hassan's return marked the beginning of the Deobandis' active participation in Indian politics.

The return of Hassan to India brought together the followers of the ascetic and activist approaches in the Deobandi movement, which finally seemed to be settling under the undisputed leadership of Hassan, who, owing to his alliance with the khilafatists and the Congress, was now considered more of a nationalist than a Deobandi religious leader. When Hassan later visited Deoband, he asked *mohtamim* Muhammad Ahmad to return the title of *shamsul ulama* granted to the latter by the British government. Muhammad Ahmad found it impossible to resist Hassan and made the announcement. However, he continued to receive the periodic financial support given to such title holders (Mian 1957, vol. 5, 388).

Hassan soon adjusted to his new role as a Muslim nationalist leader by moving beyond his identity as a Deobandi activist. Therefore, he did not hesitate to join the students of Aligarh University, the old nemesis of Darul Ulum Deoband, who decided to boycott classes as part of the non-cooperation movement, which required people to sever ties with every institution that received funds from the colonial government. Despite his illness, in October 1920 Hassan presided over a ceremony in Aligarh to lay the foundations for Muslim University (which was later shifted to Delhi in 1925 and named Jamia Millia). In his speech, he seemed to have made up his mind to take the Deobandi movement into mainstream Muslim society instead of restricting it to madaris. While criticizing the government's influence on the original Aligarh University, he suggested a model for mainstream education based on the DMM, whereby educational institutions should be independent from the funds and influence of the government (Mian 1957, vol. 5, 377).

In November 1920, Hassan agreed to preside over the second annual conference of Jamiat-ul-Ulama-e-Hind (JUH), a platform of Indian *ulama* established a year beforehand through the efforts of Abdul Bari Farangi Mahall, president of the first JUH Conference in 1919. Hassan, in his presidential address, reminded the Indian *ulama* that 'God has somehow made the biggest nation of India [Hindus] your ally in achieving your noble objective [*pak maqsad*]'. He emphasized that both the Hindu and Muslim nations should work together for the independence of India; otherwise, he thought, the grip of the British government would grow even stronger and 'the already-dim imprint of Islamic rule [in India] would be erased forever' (Mian 1957, vol. 5, 363–4). Although Hassan did not explain the said 'noble objective', it can be inferred from his speech that what he visualized was perhaps more than just the independence of India. It may be added that he had already nodded towards the idea of appointing an *ameer-e-Hind* (religious leader of whole India) to implement the mandates of *Shariah* (Gilmartin 1988, 63). Another important point to be noted in what turned out to be his last speech was that he referred to Hindus and Muslims (at least five times in his short address) as two different nations, a fact that was to be completely ignored by his Deobandi successors in the coming years. Hassan died just one week later on 30 November 1920.

A closer look at Hassan's last two speeches suggests that after the failure of his movement to revive Muslim rule in India or to set up an Islamic state in the NWFP, he seemed to be convinced that the DMM alone could not succeed in establishing an Islamic state in which its *ulama* would serve as 'inner caliphs' to implement their version of Islam. As mentioned earlier, this idea of finding an 'outer caliph' or 'pious sultan' of an Islamic state had not worked during Waliullah's time, when he invited Ahmad Shah Abdali of Afghanistan to invade India. Later, Syed Ahmed and Ismail temporarily established an Islamic state in the Pashtun tribal areas, but their government soon fell owing to resistance from the Sikh forces as well as from tribal leaders who found the new state to be in conflict with their sociocultural practices. Hassan's movement was the third such failed attempt to set up an Islamic state involving Afghanistan and the NWFP tribal areas.

After his return from exile, Hassan appeared to have changed his strategy, as is evident from his last two speeches. His new strategy required the DMM and mainstream Muslim society to be able to cooperate and ignore their countercultural conflicts. On the other hand, he preferred an alliance with nationalist Hindus to fight for the freedom of India from colonial rule. For example, he said at Aligarh:

> O youth of my country, when I realized that sympathizers to my distress [at the British supremacy] are less in madaris and *khanqahs* and more in schools and colleges, I along with some sincere friends took a step towards Aligarh. [...] It is not unlikely that many well-intentioned elders would criticize my trip [to Aligarh] and declare that I deviated from the path of my predecessors. (Mian 1957, vol. 5, 375)

Further, he adopted a softer approach towards mainstream education while defending the DMM founders' opposition to Western education. He stated:

> My great predecessors never issued a *fatwa* of *kufr* against learning foreign languages or sciences and skills belonging to other nations. But yes, it was certainly said that if the final impact of Western education is that people become immersed in Christianity or they ridicule their religion and co-religionists through atheistic contempt or they begin to worship the government of the day, then it is better for a Muslim to stay illiterate than receiving such an education. (Mian 1957, vol. 5, 376)

Referring to Gandhi's statement declaring modern education as a pure and clean milk with a pinch of poison in it, Hassan said, 'Thanks to God who enabled the youth of my nation to differentiate between what is beneficial and what is harmful for them and then separate that poison from the milk through a chelating agent. [...] Muslim University is that chelating agent' (Mian 1957, vol. 5, 376).

During his other speech at the JUH meeting, Hassan stressed the need for an alliance between Hindus and Muslims. He said, 'I consider the unity and agreement between the two to be very useful and decisive.' He also preached for broadening the scope of the JUH by asking of the *ulama*, 'Through wisdom and good advice, absorb in your party those people who are presently separate from you' (Mian 1957, vol. 5, 380).

One may argue here that Hassan's post-exile strategy was based on cooperation with mainstream Muslim society on the one hand and with the Hindu-dominated Congress on the other. However, there is no evidence to suggest that Hassan's new strategy was in any way meant to drop the goal of an Islamic state. In fact, that goal seemed to be delayed until after the independence of India, which actually meant the simultaneous liberation of a vast Muslim area (Faruqi 1963, 71), thus increasing the possibility of creating a state where Deobandi Islam could be implemented. Such a strategy would have required the DMM to temporarily ignore its countercultural approach towards the sociocultural practices of ordinary Muslims. Hassan, through his visit to dissident Aligarh students, showed that he was willing to hold back that approach at least for the time being. But after his death, the Deobandi leadership both at Darul Ulum Deoband and JUH was not able to take that strategy forward, either due to their lack in understanding of Hassan's initiative or their inability to follow it as circumstances changed. However, as far as cooperation with Hindus was concerned, the Deobandis completely followed Hassan's advice, as shall be explained in the next chapter.

Hassan had already found an appropriate forum for his new strategy in the form of JUH, which he was to head. However, his death immediately after he was appointed president of JUH and the later developments in Turkey leading to the end of the caliphate changed the political horizon of India, leading to a sudden decline in the role of *ulama* in politics (Robinson 1974, 338).

To recap the preceding discussion, there were two factors that inspired the DMM to come out of its ascetic phase and adopt an activist stance: the rise in influence of religion and the *ulama* in the political field, and Hassan's new strategy to join the nationalist freedom struggle after the failure of the decade-long secret movement. Hassan's movement had created serious differences between his followers and Darul Ulum Deoband, which preferred to continue with the old ascetic approach. However, once Hassan returned to India after three years of exile, the DMM finally adopted his activist approach by developing close links between the madaris and politics.

Once the DMM had joined JUH and officially recognized its activist approach, it was not surprising that some Deobandis resisted this change after having followed an ascetic approach for more than half a century. As a result of this resistance, a group of Deobandi *ulama* decided to set up Tablighi Jamaat (Proselytizing group) under the leadership of a prominent Deobandi scholar, Maulana Muhammad Ilyas

(1885–1944). The main objective of this offshoot of the DMM was to inform ordinary Muslims in distant regions of the subcontinent about the basic tenets of Islam while strictly keeping away from the public arena of elections and parties. According to Metcalf (1993), the focus of Tablighi Jamaat (TJ) was the spiritual development of individuals.

Although TJ apparently opposed the activist approach of Mahmood Hassan in politics, Maulana Ilyas at least seemed to share Hassan's ambition to influence mainstream Muslim society while de-emphasizing the role of madaris, in line with what he considered to be the vision of the DMM's founder (Madni 1954, vol. 2, 623). Therefore, Hassan decided to adopt an activist approach by trying unsuccessfully to revive Muslim rule in India or to at least set up an Islamic state in the tribal areas of the NWFP. However, TJ adopted a different approach to both the asceticism and activism of the DMM. Instead of establishing new madaris to continue with the previous ascetic approach or aggressively opposing mainstream Muslim society, TJ seemingly adopted a 'mystic' countercultural approach. According to Yinger (1982, 91–5) a mystic counterculture is represented by 'those who are searching for the truth and for themselves'. This type of counterculture prefers to disregard mainstream society rather than attacking it.

Behaving like a mystic counterculture, TJ preferred to focus on the spiritual formation of individuals (Metcalf 1993). It stayed away from politics on the one hand and avoided criticism of the practices of folk Islam on the other. The favourite refrain of TJ missions visiting ordinary Muslims was 'We concern ourselves only with what is in the heavens above and the grave below' (Sikand 2006). Calling his movement a '*khanqah* on the move' (Troll 1994), Maulana Ilyas stated that 'the aims of modern political authority and Islam do not coincide and [...] if Islam were to make any progress, it must be divorced from politics' (Haq 1972, 170 quoted in Sikand 2006). At the same time, the Tablighi texts avoided criticism of the customary practices of Indian Muslims, which the DMM considered wrong (Metcalf 1993). TJ actually believed that 'by doing away with the material pursuit of happiness and worldliness, the Tablighi Jamaat principles help members make in-roads to a new unity between Muslims and Allah' (Ali 2003).

As the popularity and following of TJ increased outside the Indian subcontinent, it gradually acquired a separate identity to the DMM. Owing to its policy of avoiding any links with other groups, TJ attracted members and followers from different sects and *madhabs*. This diversification coupled with a soft approach towards folk Islam further separated TJ from the DMM. However, TJ continued to receive support from Deobandi mosques in the subcontinent where Tablighi missions stayed during their proselytizing tours. In this regard, TJ could be considered a pro-Deobandi organization. Otherwise, it gradually developed as a movement independent from the DMM. As such, a detailed study of TJ is beyond the scope of this book.

3.3 The Countercultural Politics of Deobandi Leadership

Jamiat-ul-Ulama-e-Hind (JUH) represented an era marked by the rise and hegemony of *ulama* in Indian politics. It was a unique platform in the sense that it brought together *ulama* of all shades of opinion. Abdul Bari had finally succeeded in bringing Deobandi *ulama* on board by offering a leading role to Mufti Kifayatullah, a graduate of Darul Ulum Deoband. Kifayatullah became president of JUH after Mahmood Hassan's death in December 1920 and continued in that position until 1938, when he was replaced by then principal of the *darul ulum* Hussain Ahmad Madni, who led JUH until his death in 1957. Although JUH initially included *ulama* of different schools of thought, it was soon dominated by the Deobandis as *ulama* belonging to other religious groups left after the decline of the non-cooperation movement and Khilafat agitation in the early 1920s.

JUH had an ambitious programme which included: providing guidance to Indian Muslims according to *Shariah*; defending Islam, the caliphate and other centres of Islam; protecting Islamic rituals and customs; organizing *ulama* on a common platform; fighting for the freedom of the country and religion according to *Shariah*; and propagating Islam in India and in foreign lands (Faruqi 1963, 68). The ultimate goal of JUH, it seemed, revolved around a single pivot (i.e. *Shariah*), which could be correctly understood and interpreted only by the *ulama*, who considered themselves its custodian; therefore the correct guidance for Muslims could come only from them (Faruqi 1963, 69–70).

The DMM saw an opportunity in JUH to make a grab for the leadership of Indian Muslims and to find some space to impose the Deobandi version of Islam upon them. It is worth noting that during the inception meeting of JUH, Syed Jalib, editor of newspaper *Humdam*, suggested that instead of setting up a separate political party, the *ulama* would better work alongside the AIML, which was already representing the Muslims of India. Deobandi leader Kifayatullah opposed this proposal, stating that the political field could not be left at the mercy of those who had no knowledge of Islam (Mian 1957, vol. 5, 237–8). The Deobandis thought that the Western-educated Muslim intelligentsia of the AIML (mostly drawn from Aligarh University) were representatives of a different culture. The cultural concerns of the Deobandis about the AIML can be illustrated by the following excerpt quoted by Faruqi (1963, 76) from an official publication of JUH written by Muhammad Mian under the title *Jamiat-ul-Ulama Kia Hai?* (What is Jamiat-ul-Ulama?):

> The situation is this, that in matters of daily behaviour and culture the western-educated class, both Hindu and Muslim, has accepted a new culture and discarded their old cultural norms. This new culture is so uniform that hardly any distinction can be made between the Hindus and the Muslims. As for the masses, their culture varies from place to place in accordance with the general culture of the majority of the area. In the Punjab and other Muslim provinces a Hindu looks like a Musalman [*sic*] while in provinces of Hindu majority the situation is the reverse.

The above-mentioned excerpt shows that the Deobandis were not ready to accept any culture except that of their own. Hence, Habib-ur-Rehman of Deoband declared JUH superior to all other Muslim organizations and conferences in India (Robinson 1974, 337). Not unlike countercultural movements, the DMM's pride in its own values and derision of others' kept the Deobandis in conflict, on the one hand, with urban middle-class Muslims (represented by the AIML) and, on the other, with the lower socio-economic class living in small towns and rural areas, where folk Islam was popular owing to the influence of the Barelwis (Metcalf 1982, 297).

The DMM's cooperation with the Muslim leadership was restricted to its short-lived association with *ulama* of different schools of thought on the JUH platform during the period 1920–24. However, it is interesting to note that even during that period the DMM was able to avoid the Barelwi *ulama*, who not only stayed away from JUH but also showed little enthusiasm for the Khilafat Movement. In the mid-1920s, after the failure of the non-cooperation and Khilafat movements, when *ulama* of different shades lost prominence on the political scene, the DMM became the sole spokesman of JUH. In line with Hassan's advice, JUH extended full cooperation to Hindus and the Congress party. However, at the same time Deobandi *ulama*, owing to their countercultural inclinations, found it hard to go along smoothly with parties and leaders representing mainstream Muslim society. Apart from expressing their original aversion to *pirs* and folk Islam, Deobandis also showed a 'deep-rooted distrust' towards political leaders in the Indian legislative councils, which were composed of members of various communities under British control (Faruqi 1963, 77).

During the mid-1920s, when several bills regarding changes to the existing laws on civil marriage, child marriage and *hajj* (pilgrimage to Makkah) were introduced in the legislature, JUH protested by organizing campaigns not only against the government but also against the Muslim legislators, whose requests for guidance were ignored by the Deobandi *ulama* (Faruqi 1963, 77). In fact, in 1924, when the Central Hajj Committee recommended that pilgrims purchase a return ticket to avoid being stranded in the Hijaz for want of money, the government drafted a bill making it mandatory to do so (prior to that many pilgrims would travel to Hijaz on a one-way ticket and be stranded for months or even years). Muslim member Muhammad Yaqub translated the draft and sent it to Darul Ulum Deoband and JUH for comments. Neither of these organizations offered any comment for a year, and when Central Legislative Assembly gave leave to introduce the bill in February 1925, the Deobandi *ulama* suddenly sprang into action by blaming the Muslim legislators and declaring their leader Jinnah the arch-conspirator (Nagarkar 1975, 157).

The Deobandi *ulama* were equally aggressive towards the introduction in September 1927 of the Child Marriage Bill, which JUH termed 'interference' in Muslim personal law. Many Muslim legislators were ready to support the bill when it was disclosed in the Indian Central Legislative Assembly that according to the 1921 census there were 1,575 married Muslim children aged below one year, 2,000 aged one to two years, 6,000 aged two to three years, and so on. This disclosure was followed by a scholarly debate between Muslim legislators, whose majority was in the favour of prohibiting child marriages. T. A. K. Sherwani of the AIML stated that 'Islam never contemplated child marriages, […] the scriptures left the question entirely to the person who wanted to marry. […] The only verse in the Koran pertaining to marriages of women contained the Arabic word *nissa*, which meant a grown-up woman and not a child. […] The early Muslim jurists had only allowed the pre-Islamic custom of child marriages to continue but the laws could be changed and were not immutable' (Nagarkar 1975, 168). He also quoted an extract from the Hadith, which says, 'Do not marry a virgin unless she gives her consent by inclination.' Sherwani added, 'In the face of this *hadis* I ask my Mussalman friends whether they can oppose this bill. On receipt of a telegram by Jamiat-ul-Ulema, I sent a long reply followed by reminders. I also quoted my authorities but I have yet to receive a reply. There is not a single verse in the Koran, there is not a single *hadis* which recommends pre-puberty marriage' (Nagarkar 1975, 168). The bill was eventually passed, supported by 13 and opposed by 6 Muslim members of the assembly.

The above discussion shows that the DMM was not a reform movement as has generally been assumed in the literature produced by writers like Smith (1943), Metcalf (1982), Berkey (2007) and Riaz (2008). In fact, the DMM was not even purely a revitalization movement in the sense that it was more concerned with opposing the prevalent customs and values than reviving those prevalent during the early period of Islam. Deobandis have used the revivalist argument mostly to condemn the customs and practices of mainstream Muslim society. Otherwise, they were ready to improvise and rationalize when it applied to their own group. For example, JUH supported and justified the Gandhian ideas of non-violent non-cooperation for the resistance movement against the British when those ideas were challenged as being alien to Islam. Mahmood Hassan gave religious sanction to the idea of non-cooperation by issuing a *fatwa* that was later ratified by around five hundred *ulama* of JUH. He declared that the 'religious standing of this issue [non-cooperation] is undeniable. In these circumstances, it is obligatory upon the honour of a true Muslim that he should: i) return official titles and honours; ii) refuse participation in modern councils of the country; iii) use only local things and products; iv) not send his children to government schools and colleges' (Madni 1954, 675). Hassan justified his position by stating that if modern weapons could be allowed for violent resistance against the enemy, then the same line of argument could be extended to resist an infidel British government through non-violent non-cooperation (Madni 1954, 679–80). However, the argument was self-contradictory vis-à-vis the DMM's earlier policy of cooperation with the British for more than half a century.

In order to justify resistance to the British in his *fatwa*, Hassan employed Quranic verses which forbade for Muslims any cooperation or friendship with *kuffar* (infidels). However, he simultaneously chose to ignore the fact that while declining cooperation and friendship with British infidels, he was allowing Muslims to join hands with Hindus, who were also *kuffar*. From a Deobandi perspective, the aforementioned *fatwa* was perhaps part of their *maslehat* policy. However, if their support to the idea of non-cooperation is viewed from a countercultural perspective, it can be assumed that the DMM accepted this idea because it was presented by Hindus who were placed outside the scope of Deobandi counterculture, which was by definition restricted to Muslim society. If the above line of argument is further extended, the Deobandis might have opposed or condemned the very same idea of non-cooperation if it had been presented or practised by mainstream Muslim society, as a counterculture is fundamentally concerned with intra-societal (Muslim, in the case of the DMM) rather than inter-societal (Hindu versus Muslim) conflict. Another example of the DMM's flexibility and improvisation to justify its own stance is JUH's decision in 1931 to support, at the Congress's insistence, the ideas of adult franchise and elections, which the Deobandis had declared un-Islamic in 1923 (Nagarkar 1975, 131, 227).

There are several examples where the DMM appeared (unlike a revitalization movement) to support or follow customs and practices which never existed during the early period of Islam. For instance, from dress to dining and from travelling to technology, the Deobandis adopted new trends and innovations while simultaneously condemning the customs and practices of other Muslims on the grounds that those were *bidah*, and did not exist during the time of the Prophet and his companions. A detailed discussion on these customs and practices is given in Chapter 5.

3.4 Deobandi Opposition to the Pakistan Movement

This section shall discuss how the countercultural disposition of the DMM influenced its political behaviour, which was more concerned with 'intra-societal' conflict within the Muslim community than the 'inter-societal' disagreements between Muslims and other religions. The following discussion on the DMM's opposition to the Pakistan movement shall also try to analyse the political position of the Deobandis whereby they extended unconditional cooperation to the Hindu-dominated Congress while never missing an opportunity to criticize the AIML, which claimed to champion the rights of Indian Muslims (Faruqi 1963, 79).

Deobandi historian Syed Muhammad Mian has repeatedly termed the AIML and its leader Jinnah agents of the British government (Mian 1957, vol. 6, 76, 85, 87, 107, 115, 165, 173–5, 257). He declares that 'the Muslim League and its Quaid-e-Azam, by dancing to the tune of British imperialism, have left no stone unturned to abase Indian Muslims in the history of independence' (Mian 1957, vol. 6, 68). Similarly, Hussain Madni, principal of Darul Ulum Deoband, wrote a pamphlet titled 'Muslim League ki aath Muslim-kush ghalatian' (Eight Muslim-cidal mistakes of the Muslim League) whereby he stated that Muslim League leaders had 'conceived a conspiracy in alliance with the Tory leadership, which included Lord Lloyd, Lord Hertford, Lord Sydenham and others. Whenever signs of weakness or defeat [of the British in India] appeared, the Tory lords whole-heartedly backed the communal leaders [of the AIML to gain their support for the British]' (Mian 1957, vol. 6, 257). In 1939, when the AIML disagreed with the Congress on the issue of war and India's future, and asked the British government not to make any future plans without the approval of the AIML, chief organizer of the Deobandi JUH Maulana Ahmed Saeed issued a statement to condemn Jinnah and his party: 'It is a well-known reality that the viceroy needed at this critical juncture a party of Muslims that he could use to beat the Congress. [...] [The British] government faced no difficulty in this as Mr Jinnah took the *bay'ah* [of the British]' (Mian 1957, vol. 6, 82–3).

These allegations of the DMM against the AIML lead to an interesting debate. If the AIML was pro-British, the Deobandis would have perhaps fared better by initially supporting the AIML on the Lucknow Pact of 1916 as well as Jinnah's policy of 'loyal' nationalism. This would have been perfectly in line with the DMM's policy of *maslehat*, whereby it maintained a pro-British stance until 1920. In that case, the colonial rulers would have shown appreciation towards the DMM for supporting their 'British agents'. However, the DMM, on the contrary, set aside its policy of *maslehat* in this case by aggressively criticizing the 'loyal' AIML while simultaneously keeping itself loyal to the

British. Here, one can only assume that either the DMM's own argument for adopting *maslehat* vis-à-vis the British government was not valid or their allegations against the AIML and Jinnah were untrue.

However, if one takes both these viewpoints to be true, then one can infer that the DMM's opposition to the AIML was so intense that they would even take the risk of offending the colonial rulers. It is quite remarkable that it took the Deobandis more than fifty years to take that risk. It was the same inability to undertake that venture that had compelled the DMM to disown the principal of their *darul ulum* for so many years. In this scenario, the DMM's opposition to the AIML (which claimed to represent the majority of Indian Muslims) can perhaps be better understood in terms of its countercultural leanings, as discussed below. The following discussion about the politics of JUH also suggests that Deobandi opposition to the idea of Pakistan was not only about politics but also counterculture.

Without discounting JUH's political stance of blaming the AIML as an agent of the British, one may argue that the hostile attitude of the Deobandi *ulama* towards the AIML reflected their condemnation of mainstream Muslim society and folk Islam, which came in direct conflict with the Deobandi sect. Faruqi (1963, 80) has highlighted the different perspectives of the AIML and the Deobandi *ulama* of JUH regarding Islam. He has stated that Deobandi *ulama* were neither intellectually well-equipped to give new interpretations to Islam nor were they committed to Shah Waliullah's tradition of *tatbiq*. Therefore, they were not likely to win the support of the Western-educated urban Muslims, who were trained in an entirely new set of traditions. Similarly, rural Muslims who followed folk Islam were also opposed to the Deobandi sect owing to its countercultural stance on popular customs and traditional *sufism*.

JUH's opposition to the AIML was also linked to earlier Deobandi criticism of Islamic modernist Sir Syed Ahmad Khan, whose Aligarh University was the alma mater of many leaders of the AIML. In 1891, the founder of the DMM, Rasheed Ahmed, had issued a *fatwa* declaring:

> [Muslims] should not keep any connection with Syed Ahmad Sahib irrespective of whether he talks about national welfare in name only or if he is a well-wisher in actuality. His involvement in the affairs of Muslims is a killer poison for both Islam and Muslims. The drink that he makes is a sweet poison that ultimately kills. Therefore, avoid joining him. [However], you may work together with Hindus. (Mian 1957, vol. 5, 163)

Taking the lead from that *fatwa*, the DMM also opposed the AIML. According to Mian:

> The Muslim League and its leaders are far ahead of Sir Syed and his associates with respect to such dangers [modernism]. Not to mention the practices of praying and fasting; they are not even properly aware of these acts of worship. For them, the commandments of the Quran are, God forbid, backward and cumbersome in terms of modern developments. [...] [They] are typically European in demeanour, have a resolute intent to end the power of the *ulama*, and are an amalgamation of the Muslims, Shias and Qadiyanis. (Mian 1957, vol. 5, 166–7)

During the early years of the AIML, the Deobandis believed that:

> [The AIML's] politics is only about gaining for Muslims a share in those rights and positions [already] claimed by Hindus. This is not true politics. Asking the government to meet people's demands is true politics and this passion derives an equal force from the religion. Owing to the absence of this [religious] force, a member of the Muslim League is unable to bear any loss and hence lacks the will power and courage. (Mian 1957, vol. 5, 291)

After 1930, when the AIML motivated Muslims for a separate Muslim state, Deobandi criticism was to take a different turn whereby they questioned the intentions of the AIML. Mian (1957, vol. 5, 166) justified that criticism in the light of the above-mentioned *fatwa* by stating that 'it is extremely dangerous to join and relate with such Muslims who achieve their personal objectives and ideas in the name of Islam'. This opposition mostly kept JUH in the opposite camp to the AIML.

The countercultural character of the Deobandis was more explicitly reflected in their politics in the 1920s, when philosopher-poet and leader of the AIML Dr Muhammad Iqbal provided the intellectual content as well as emotional vigour to the general separatist feeling among the Muslim community vis-à-vis the Hindus. Although Iqbal had been referring to the 'unconscious trends of the two communities' (i.e. their identities as separate nations) since his return from Europe in 1908, his belief in the two-nation theory was actually strengthened after the rise of Hindu revivalist movements like Shuddhi (Proselytization) and Sanghatan (Organization) in reaction to Muslim religious parties like JUH. In fact, Iqbal interpreted the Indian nationalism of the Congress as part of neo-Hinduism (Faruqi 1963, 85).

During his landmark presidential address to the annual session of the AIML at Allahabad in 1930, Iqbal declared Hindus and Muslims to be two separate nations in the light of the religious, social, cultural and historical contexts. While recognizing the right of each community to free development according to its own cultural traditions, Iqbal put forward a proposal which contained the seeds of the demand for a separate homeland for Indian Muslims: 'I would like to see the Punjab, North-West Frontier Province, Sindh and Balochistan, amalgamated into a single state. Self-government within the British Empire or without the British Empire, the formation of a consolidated North-West Indian Muslim State appears to be the final destiny of the Muslims, at least of North-West India' (Ikram 1970, 169).

The strongly negative reaction of the Deobandi leaders of JUH to Iqbal's official declaration of the two-nation theory exposed the DMM's approach towards the AIML. If principles and history were to be any guide, the Deobandis should not have opposed the two-nation theory because their leader Mahmood Hassan had himself repeatedly described Muslims and Hindus as two separate nations in his last address (Mian 1957, vol. 5, 380–81). Similarly, Hassan's predecessors, like Shah Waliullah, Syed Ahmed and Muhammad Ismail, had also pursued the idea of a Muslim state. However, the Deobandi leaders of JUH chose to ignore their history and principles. Instead, they allowed their countercultural biases to dominate their policy, which required them to oppose mainstream Muslim society, which was to be looked down upon by Deobandi Islam.

For a counterculture, the rest of the society to which it belongs is to be considered wrong and evil (Yinger 1982, 91). Therefore, any ideas from that society also need to be condemned as wrong and evil. Accordingly, JUH not only opposed the two-nation theory put forward by Iqbal of the AIML but also decided to redefine the concept of nation for Indian Muslims. Hussain Madni, principal of Darul Ulum Deoband and a top leader of JUH, stated that in modern times nations were formed by lands and that Indian Muslims should accept this view (Faruqi 1963, 88). In support of his definition of nationalism for Indian Muslims, Madni argued that if the British, in order to promote Arab independence, could declare the Turks and Arabs different nations, then all Indians (both Muslims and Hindus) should also be considered a separate nation from the British and thus deserved independence (Mian 1957, vol. 5, 574).

Madni's argument in favour of a united Indian nationalism did not appear to be convincing vis-à-vis the two-nation theory adopted by the AIML, as he was apparently trying to explain his idea of united nationalism in the context of the freedom movement while ignoring the sharp communal divisions between the Hindus and Muslims of India. Therefore, Madni's idea of composite Indian nationalism cut no ice with Muslim intellectuals and the masses, who considered it to be somewhat unusual in terms of Islamic ideology (Nagarkar 1975, 304).

By taking a modern and innovative stance, Madni chose to ignore the history of Islam as well as his own Deobandi movement, which had always looked for a peculiar and purified identity for Muslims. If one looks at this 'reinterpretation' of the Muslim nation through the countercultural lens of the DMM, one might find it akin to *bidah*. Madni was perhaps himself aware of the novelty of his interpretation of Indian Muslims' status in the context of modern nation-states. Hence, he tried to liken his united Indian nationalism with the Prophet's alliance with the Jews of Madinah (Mian 1957, vol. 5, 582). However, it was not a strong argument in the sense that the Prophet's agreement with the Jews, called the Misaq-e-Madinah (Charter of Madinah), was more like a defence treaty against outside aggression. On the other hand, JUH and the Congress never hinted at making such a formal agreement between the two communities of India. Further, there was nothing in the charter that established the Muslims and Jews of Madinah as one nation. The example was also not very appropriate in the sense that it had fallen apart within four years, when the Muslims of Madinah forced the Jewish tribe of Banu Nadheer to go into exile for violating the agreement.

The Deobandis also tried to defend their idea of united Indian nationalism by appealing to the Prophet's love for his homeland Makkah, which, much like India, was dominated by non-Muslims. This was again not a very relevant argument because the Prophet's love for Makkah was not only due to his being born there but because of the city's sacred and holy status for Muslims as a whole. India did not carry any such sacredness for Muslims. Further, the Prophet had to migrate from Makkah and he chose not to settle there even after it was conquered by the Muslims.

Madni, while asserting that united Indian nationalism was not contrary to the spirit of Islam, stated that this type of nationalism was necessary in India because people of different religions shared the same problems, the same happiness and the same miseries, despite their religious differences (Nagarkar 1975, 305). It is quite perplexing that the

Deobandis, who had always highlighted their differences with overall Muslim society, were now ready to find similarities with people of other religions, reflecting their peculiar mindset, which was more concerned about counterculture within Islam than cultures in other religions.

Dr Muhammad Iqbal was quite surprised by the unique approach that Hussain Madni and other Deobandis took to define and defend united Indian nationalism. In his presidential address delivered at the annual session of All-India Muslim Conference at Lahore on 21 March 1932, Iqbal said:

> I am opposed to nationalism as it is understood in Europe, not because, if it is allowed to develop in India, it is likely to bring less material gain to Muslims. I am opposed to it because I see in it the germs of atheistic materialism which I look upon as the greatest danger to modern humanity. Patriotism is a perfectly natural virtue and has a place in the moral life of man. Yet that which really matters is a man's faith, his culture, his historical tradition. These are the things, which in my eyes, are worth living for and dying for, and not the piece of earth with which the spirit of man happens to be temporarily associated. (Faruqi 1963, 88–9)

Later, Iqbal voiced his strong reaction to Madni's views in a poem titled 'Hussain Ahmad'. A translation of the poem is given below.

> The Ajamites do not yet know
> The fine points of our faith;
> Otherwise, Husain Ahmad of Deoband!
> What is this foolhardiness?
> A sermon-song from the pulpit that
> A nation by a homeland be!
> From the real position
> Of the Arabian Prophet
> How sadly unaware is he!
> Your self merges with Mustafa
> For all faith embodies in him!
> If you do not reach up to him
> It is all Bu Lahab's[1] idolatry! (Iqbal n.d., 67)

As Iqbal's ideas about two-nation theory caught the imagination of Muslims of India, Jinnah decided to reorganize the AIML by weaning away the Muslim masses from the Congress and Muslim nationalist organizations like JUH. By the end of the 1930s, Hindu–Muslim division had reached the point where no compromise on a united Indian nationalism was possible. The mass campaign of the Congress and JUH in favour of united nationalism had already failed (Faruqi 1963, 89–90). Jinnah had also made up his mind by then about the future strategy for a final fight with the Congress. That strategy

1 Abu Lahab was one of the worst enemies of Prophet Muhammad (PBUH).

was announced in the landmark Lahore session of the AIML in March 1940, whereby a resolution was passed demanding separate homelands for the Muslims of India comprising the Muslim majority areas. The nationalist media termed the resolution a demand for an independent Pakistan.

When the historic Lahore Resolution was passed on 23 March 1940, the Deobandis were give another opportunity to display their countercultural approach by attacking the AIML and its idea of a separate Muslim country, Pakistan. Within one month of the resolution, the Deobandis organized an Azad Muslim Conference under JUH to denounce it. On the other hand, the resolution immediately increased the popularity of the AIML in mainstream Muslim society, which chose to call Jinnah *Quaid-e-Azam* (The greatest leader). The demand for a separate homeland had remarkably broadened the appeal of the AIML, which had earlier been labelled as an organization representing the interests of the Muslim bourgeoisie. Later, when the AIML tactfully presented the demand for Pakistan in terms of religious and cultural freedom along with the cry of 'Islam in danger', the Muslim masses gathered behind the AIML and Pakistan became a common goal of the majority of Indian Muslims. As the Pakistan movement gathered momentum, the old rivalry between the DMM and Aligarh was revived as Deoband became the citadel of opposition to Pakistan, while Aligarh turned out to be the training centre of the *mujahideen-i-Pakistan* (holy warriors of Pakistan; Faruqi 1963, 104).

In view of the earlier efforts of Shah Waliullah, Syed Ahmed and Muhammad Ismail, as well as Mahmood Hassan and Ubaidullah Sindhi, the demand for an independent Muslim state should not have been an alien idea for the Deobandis. History should have ideally convinced them to at least not oppose the idea of a Muslim state even if they were not yet ready to support it. However, the immediate response of the Deobandis was that of shock and comprehensive opposition of the demand for a separate state for Indian Muslims. The potential source of their condemnation of a not-so-unfamiliar idea was the reality that it was being presented by those Muslims whose customs and values came into conflict with Deobandi Islam.

The Deobandis, *prima facie*, criticized the idea of Pakistan as being the conspiracy of the colonial government to prevent the emergence of a strong united India. They blamed, without any evidence, the AIML and Jinnah as the supposed agents of the British. They were not ready to give the AIML the benefit of the doubt despite the fact that they themselves had shown open loyalty to the British. JUH leaders also tried to oppose the creation of Pakistan in the context of the economic development of Muslims, which would be hurt in case of India's partition. They labelled it as a design to keep Muslims backward, a design the British had pursued for more than a century after ending Muslim rule in India (Faruqi 1963, 106–8). This line of argument was again based more on conspiracy theory than evidence.

Another Deobandi argument against partition was presented by Hussain Madni, who believed that the Pakistan movement would prove to be 'the death-knell for Muslims of the areas where they were in a minority' and which were to be part of Hindu-dominated India (Mian 1957, vol. 6, 136). This argument in fact implicitly supported the two-nation theory by anticipating some retaliation from Hindus, the partners of JUH in united Indian nationalism. In reply to such apprehensions, Jinnah argued that the presence of a Hindu minority in Muslim-dominated Pakistan would prove to be the surest guarantee for fair treatment of the minorities on both sides; if there were 25 million Muslims in India after partition then exactly same number of Hindus would be there in Pakistan (Mian 1957, vol. 6, 314). Jinnah's reference to this 'balance theory' was condemned as 'dubious, foolish and mad' by the Deobandis, who did not believe it would provide sufficient safeguards (Faruqi 1963, 113).

The Deobandis further criticized the 'balance theory' by stating that according to *Shariah*, future Muslim governments of Pakistan could not treat its Hindu minority unfairly in retaliation for something wrong done to Muslims in India by the Hindu majority. Madni further asked, 'What would happen in case of breach of any of the mandatory safeguards? Would Pakistan intervene, by show of force, to save the Muslims from the tyranny and oppression of the Hindus?' (Faruqi 1963, 113). Although this argument carries some weight, its validity is diluted if one takes this line of argument further: how would the Muslim-majority regions (future Pakistan) be able to help the Muslims of Hindu-majority areas if India was to stay united (a situation supported by JUH)? In other words, the Deobandis expected the rulers of the Muslim-majority provinces in united India to be more effective than the rulers of independent Pakistan in helping the Muslim minorities living in Hindu-majority areas. Similarly, the Deobandi argument that Muslims would have strength in numbers in united India is not very sound because Muslims would be just one-fifth of the total population, even if India were to stay undivided. In fact, the DMM was depending on the promises of Gandhi and the Congress that the post-colonial united India would observe a form of secularism that would allow Muslims to preserve their Islamic cultural identity (Mian 1957, vol. 6, 93). Madni stressed this point in his presidential address to JUH's meeting in June 1940 by showing complete trust in the Congress's pledge to safeguard every religion, civilization, language and culture after independence (Mian 1957, vol. 6, 117).

In their campaign against the idea of Pakistan, the Deobandis were ready to put forward any rationale that could be employed to serve their cause. They argued that the Pakistan movement was creating antagonism between Hindus and Muslims, a situation that would hurt the peaceful missionary work of converting Hindus to Islam (Mian 1957, vol. 6, 271). Madni, the ideologue of JUH's anti-Pakistan campaign, stated that non-Muslims are the field of action for the *tabligh* (proselytizing) of Islam. The history and background of the DMM also betrayed this argument because *tabligh* had never been the forte of the movement; it had always been more concerned with the values and customs of Muslims than non-Muslims. Even Tablighi Jamaat (TJ), which was established by Deobandi *ulama* itself, had to face criticism from DMM leaders, like Ashraf Ali Thanvi, who did not approve of TJ's approach, which preferred a simplistic version of Islam as compared to the purified Deobandi Islam. It would also be pertinent to add here that even TJ's *tabligh* focused on Muslims rather than Hindus and as such that *tabligh* could be continued even after partition.

In yet another argument against partition, Madni tried to refer to the Truce of Hudaibiyah between the Muslims and Qureysh of Makkah, which despite being apparently unfavourable to Muslims, promoted mutual interaction between the two communities thus allowing more opportunities for Muslims to preach their religion to

Qureysh through peaceful *tabligh*. According to Madni, the truce was the precursor to the conquest of Makkah and later the whole of Arabia (Faruqi 1963, 114–15). Although it seems difficult to disregard Madni's argument, one counterargument might state that before the Truce of Hudaibiyah Muslims had migrated to Madinah and established an Islamic state there. The Muslims and the Qureysh went on to fight three big wars, and even the conquest of Makkah was made possible more through Muslim invasion than mere peaceful *tabligh*. Further, it is interesting to note that on the one hand the Deobandis condemned the Islam practiced by the majority of Indian Muslims, while on the other hand they were quite hopeful to convert Hindus to Islam and set up a united Muslim India on the pattern of conversion of the Qureysh of Makkah.

It may be noted that while referring to the treaties of Madinah and Hudaibiyah with regard to the relationship between the Hindus and Muslims of India, the Deobandis preferred to focus more on opposition to the demand of the majority of Indian Muslims for a separate state than on promoting their own future vision for united India. Instead of spending their energies on winning over Indian Muslims or at least convincing their Hindu allies in the Congress to support, if not sign, a treaty with Indian Muslims based on the above-mentioned treaties, the Deobandis were mostly busy condemning the idea of Pakistan and the leadership that represented mainstream Muslim society in India. As such, the Deobandi movement chose to define itself mainly by negation, by what it stood against than by what it supported.

The smorgasbord of Deobandi arguments against the demand for Pakistan on the one hand and their decision to disown an idea (i.e. of a Muslim state) upheld by their predecessors on the other, makes for a curious case. In this regard, the most common explanation for the DMM's opposition to the Pakistan movement is that the Deobandis believed that the AIML and its leaders were not capable of successfully building an Islamic state in Pakistan. The Deobandis conceived that neither the educational training nor the mental make-up of the league's leadership was suited to striving for such a high ideal (Faruqi 1963, 118). The Deobandis tried to undermine the Islamic credentials of the AIML leadership by pointing out that Jinnah and Raja of Mahmoodabad were Shias and Sir Zafrullah was a Qadiyani (Mian 1957, vol. 6, 108). Further, Jinnah, a popular leader who Indian Muslims called *Quaid-e-Azam*, was ridiculed by the Deobandis, who called him *Kafir-e-Azam* – the greatest infidel (Pirzada 2000, 38).

This capability issue was also showcased by JUH president Madni, who equated the AIML leaders with Turkey's Mustafa Kamal, whose secular and modernist approach was considered un-Islamic by the Indian *ulama*. He wrote to one of his disciples about the 'un-Islamic' behaviour of the league leadership and asked, 'Are the Leaguers not like Mustafa Kamal, Muslims only in name?' (Faruqi 1963, 118). Similarly, Madni was perhaps also indirectly referring to this 'incapability' when he declared in his presidential address to the 12th session of JUH at Jaunpur in 1940 that the idea of an Islamic government in future Pakistan 'cannot actualize under the present circumstances' (Mian 1957, vol. 6, 115).

However, it could be argued that if the capability of the AIML's leadership was the major issue, then it would have been more appropriate for the Deobandis to join hands with the AIML in the Pakistan movement and help them to build an Islamic state. Interestingly, many league leaders, like Nawab Ismail Khan, openly declared that Pakistan would be an Islamic state based on the principles of the Quran and the Sunnah. Even Jinnah occasionally referred to Islam, the Quran and the traditions of the Prophet while explaining the future state of Pakistan (Faruqi 1963, 119–20). Simultaneously, the AIML through its office secretary, Maulana Zafar Ahmad Ansari, also tried hard to convince the religious leadership of Indian Muslims to join the Pakistan movement. The spiritual leaders, *pirs* and *mashaikh*, of the Punjab and Sindh provinces had already joined the Pakistan movement soon after the 1940 resolution. Later, the Khaksar movement of Inayatullah Mashriqi as well as one faction of Farangi Mahall *ulama* in North India also announced its support for the idea of Pakistan. Most of the followers of the Barelwi movement either supported Pakistan or stayed neutral (Smith 1943, 322–40). Even the pro-Congress Ahrar party abandoned its once caustic denunciation of the AIML in the wake of the Pakistan movement and also dissociated itself from the JUH-dominated Azad Muslim Conference (Nagarkar 1975, 340).

Despite the above-mentioned successes, the AIML was not able to win over the Deobandi JUH. Another Muslim party which opposed the league's idea of a separate homeland was Maulana Maududi's Jamaat-e-Islami. Abul A'la Maududi (1903–79) was initially associated with JUH but 'he eventually parted ways with the pro-Congress *ulama* party and embarked upon a crusade to revive Islam as the sole apodictic answer to the Muslim communal predicament in India' (Nasr 1994, 3). Maududi opposed both the AIML and JUH and set up his own party, Jamaat-e-Islami, in 1941. He believed that Muslims 'should reject Hindu ascendancy and continue to lay claim to the whole of India' (Nasr 1994, 5). After 1947, Maududi accepted the partition and migrated to the new state of Pakistan, which he considered to be the would-be laboratory for practical experiments in the religio-political philosophy of Islam (Faruqi 1963, 119).

Coming back to the AIML's efforts to win the support of religious leaders for its cause, it had a breakthrough in 1945 when prominent Deobandi scholar Shabbir Ahmad Usmani set up a separate Deobandi party named Jamiat-ul-Ulama-e-Islam (JUI), which declared support for the Pakistan movement. Usmani (1887–1949) was a close aide of Mahmood Hassan. He wrote his speeches and even delivered them during the latter's illness. He served as the principal of Darul Ulum Deoband from 1935 to 1944. Usmani supported the idea of Pakistan because in it he saw the seed of an Islamic state that his predecessors had dreamed of. He hoped to strengthen through his party the capability of the AIML to make Pakistan an Islamic state, and expressed this objective by arguing that those who feared that Pakistan would be ruled by ungodly 'leaguers' should themselves join the AIML to ensure that Pakistan was run by true Muslims (Hardy 1971, 42–3).

Apart from Usmani's small group, the Deobandis continued to oppose the Pakistan movement with their heterogeneous arguments vis-à-vis the AIML, as mentioned earlier. In view of the divergence and contradiction in the Deobandi arguments against Pakistan, one would assume that it was not because of these arguments that they opposed Pakistan; rather, they seemed to have developed them because they opposed Pakistan. If this line of enquiry is taken further, then some other reason might be working behind the Deobandi opposition to Pakistan. That particular reason may be traced to the presence of countercultural currents in the DMM throughout its history and origins, going back to Shah Waliullah's movement.

Keeping in view the above discussion and looking from the countercultural perspective, one may argue that the Deobandis were not supposed to cooperate with the AIML, which represented mainstream Muslim society and whose values and customs the DMM had condemned for some time. The Deobandis criticized the appearance, habits, dress and overall customs and practices of the Muslim supporters of the AIML and declared that they had no idea about Islamic culture (Mian 1957, vol. 6, 196). They even ridiculed the majority of Muslim supporters of the AIML as 'totally illiterate, ignorant, uneducated and unwise people dominated by centuries-old superstitious customs' (Mian 1957, vol. 6, 81). The support of *pirs* and *mashaikhs*, the epitomes of folk Islam, for the AIML further reduced the possibility of any such cooperation. Mian (1957, vol. 6, 267) criticized this alliance in the following way: 'There is class of *maulvis* and *pirs* in India who have always been opposed to Deobandi *ulama*. They neither have an interest in politics nor a political sense. They are not even organized but the [Muslim] League needed them at this point to confront Jamiat-ul-Ulama-e-Hind.'

At the same time, it may also be argued that the DMM refused to join hands with the AIML because it found the idea of conceding a leading role to the League unacceptable. In this regard, Robinson (1974, 209) has suggested that the Deobandis refused to join Anjuman-e-Khuddam-e-Ka'bah in 1913 because they did not want to work under the leadership of Abdul Bari of Farangi Mahall, who represented folk Islam. Such behaviour fits more into countercultural pride than political opposition.

It may be recalled here that condemnation of Shia Islam was one of the three major targets of Deobandi counterculture, the other two being the opposition of *sufism* and popular customs of Muslim society. So, an additional reason for the DMM's countercultural condemnation of the Pakistan movement might be the presence of Shia Muslims among the top leadership of the AIML. In fact, Jinnah, the head of the AIML, as well as other important leaders such as Raja of Mahmoodabad and the prince of Pirpur, were Shias (Smith 1943, 330). The Deobandis referred to this issue when four million rupees of relief funds for the victims of communal riots in Bihar were channelled through Habib Bank. It was alleged that Jinnah had shown favour to the owner of the bank, who was a Shia friend of the League leader (Mian 1957, vol. 6, 407–8). Similarly, the Deobandi JUH, despite being a close ally of the Congress, strongly criticized the provincial government of the Congress in 1939 for imposing unnecessary restrictions on Sunni Muslims during the Shia–Sunni disputes in Lucknow (Nagarkar 1975, 292).

As the elections were announced in 1946, JUH allied with a few small regional Muslim parties to challenge the idea of Pakistan, but failed to impress the Indian Muslims, who overwhelmingly voted for the AIML candidates campaigning in the name of Pakistan. During the election campaign, the JUH president faced stiff resistance from ordinary Muslims who labelled him as traitor for going against what the vast majority of Indian Muslims were demanding. During his tour of Bengal, Madni was abused and physically assaulted several times by Muslims who wanted to stop him from addressing his election meetings. Although such attacks are usually attributed to the aggressive politics of the AIML against its opponents, a closer look at the origin and history of the DMM shows that similar attacks by ordinary Muslims had also been carried out against Shah Waliullah, his son Abdul Aziz and grandson Muhammad Ismail for opposing the values and practices of mainstream Muslim society. Madni was perhaps also the victim of the countercultural approach of the DMM in an apparently political scenario. Further, if the attacks on Madni during the 1946 campaign were simply an outcome of the AIML's aggressive political approach, then more such events would have occurred against other Muslim rivals of the AIML, like pro-Congress Abdul Ghaffar Khan in the NWFP and the Unionist Party leaders in the Punjab. However, no such aggressive resistance was reported in these regions.

The results of the 1946 elections in India under the British government allowed the AIML to boost its claim to be the representative of Indian Muslims. The AIML won the majority of the Muslim seats, while Congress candidates swept the general seats. JUH failed to make any mark in the elections. The colonial government, which had already been working on several schemes for the independence of India after World War II, was finally convinced about the partition of India on the basis of the election results. A partition plan was announced on 3 June 1947, according to which the new state of Pakistan was to consist of the Muslim majority areas of Western Punjab, Eastern Bengal, Sindh, Balochistan and the NWFP.

The Hindu–Muslim riots of 1946 had already left the two communities in a state of unrest, and when the partition plan was being finalized, communal tensions in India increased remarkably (Mian 1957, vol. 6, 421). When the plan was announced by the British government, the Deobandis expected their long-time ally, the Congress, to oppose it tooth and nail. When the Congress accepted the partition without much ado, JUH not only failed to condemn them but also ignored its arguments about signing a treaty with the Hindu community, like those of Hudaibiyah and Madinah. It seems quite strange that the Deobandis would be so passionate about these treaties when opposing the idea of Pakistan, but when the need arose to protect the Muslim minority in post-partition India, JUH made no effort to explore the possibility of any such treaty, perhaps knowing that their argument was more for public consumption than practice.

As the two independent states of Pakistan and India came into being at midnight between 14 and 15 August 1947, the minorities in both countries felt extremely insecure in the wake of the rising communal riots. The consequent mass migration of the minorities further aggravated the situation. While the two governments of the newly independent states took measures to rehabilitate the refugees and to establish law and order soon after independence, the Deobandis of India became introspective, evaluating their activist approach after World War I. Since the 1920s, their apparent strategy was to first win freedom for the united India through cooperation with the Hindu majority and then pursue their original goal of a Muslim state for Deobandi Islam. This strategy proved to be unsuccessful in the sense that they not only failed to keep India united but also lost the cooperation of the Congress when the latter decided to accept the partition plan. Confronted with an unenviable scenario whereby they had to face a huge majority of the Hindu community, the Deobandis of India decided to revert to their earlier ascetic approach and withdraw into their madaris to protect and preserve their version of Islam.

In the newly independent state of India, the DMM found itself facing a situation where the values and norms of Deobandi Islam were threatened by an aggressive Hindu majority on the one hand and the folk Islam of mainstream Muslim society on the other. Faced with an environment which threatened their values and norms, the Deobandis decided on 1 February 1948 in the Working Committee meeting of JUH to withdraw from the political field and restrict the role of JUH to religious, educational and cultural matters. In April 1948, Hussain Madni announced the new Deobandi approach to India in his presidential address to the general meeting of JUH. By emphasizing the need for the protection and survival of Islam in India (Mian 1957, vol. 6, 584), Madni ensured that the DMM adopted its original ascetic approach. To support this approach, he came up with new arguments, some of which actually contradicted his earlier arguments employed during the activist phase of the DMM. For example, he stated in 1948 that the future of a community did not depend on its population but on its character and conduct; whereas he had earlier opposed partition on the pretext of making Muslims a sizable minority that the majority could not ignore. Madni contradicted his argument in the same breath by reminding his party that during the previous Muslim rule, the total Muslim population of united India was even less than that of post-partition India (Mian 1957, vol. 6, 586).

While comparing the old and new arguments of Madni one may infer that if he had applied the new arguments to the earlier discussion over partition, the Deobandis might have supported the Pakistan movement wholeheartedly. In fact, in 1948 Madni himself advocated strong and friendly relations with Pakistan, a state which he opposed tooth and nail on the basis of an altogether different set of arguments that became irrelevant within six months of partition. This change in attitude of Indian Deobandis seems to reflect the change in their countercultural approach from activist to ascetic. Further, the change in attitude of Indian Deobandis vis-à-vis Pakistani Muslims was also due to the fact that from a countercultural perspective, the Indian DMM after independence was concerned with mainstream Muslim society in India only. As regards the countercultural scenario in Pakistan, the mainstream Muslim society of the new state was now the concern of the Pakistani Deobandis under the leadership of Shabbir Ahmed Usmani and Muhammad Shafi, who had migrated to the newly independent Muslim state.

The study of the Deobandi movement in post-partition India is beyond the scope of this book, which primarily focuses on the growth and evolution of the DMM in Pakistan, as shall be discussed in the next chapter.

Chapter 4

THE DMM IN PAKISTAN: COUNTERCULTURAL POLITICS AND EXTREMISM

A counterculture is in one sense a far more radical rejection of a given society than any political movement, even one bent on revolutionary change.

Kenneth Westhues, *Society's Shadow: Studies in the Sociology of Countercultures* (1972, 34)

This chapter discusses the history and evolution of the DMM in Pakistan while identifying different phases of the movement, marked by ascetic, activist and extremist trends. The chapter has been divided into four sections. The first section describes how a small group of Deobandis led by Allama Shabbir Ahmad Usmani actively campaigned to make Pakistan an Islamic state before being intercepted by the liberal and modernist leadership of the ruling Muslim League. After this initial failure, the DMM adopted an ascetic approach for some years before re-emerging in politics under new leadership. This section also highlights the role of the Deobandis in the Afghan *jihad* on the one hand and the DMM's growing links with the powerful military establishment of Pakistan on the other. The changing stances and strategies of the Deobandis in Pakistani politics are discussed in the second section. The third section elaborates the rise of extremism in the Deobandi movement after its involvement in Afghanistan. This section spotlights the links between the DMM and the Afghan Taliban as well as the countercultural nature of Deobandi militancy, which targeted *sufi* shrines as well as Shia Muslims in Pakistan. The final section sums up the countercultural tendencies of the Deobandi movement in Pakistan since 1947.

4.1 The Evolution of the DMM in Pakistan

After the creation of Pakistan, a small Deobandi faction that called itself All India Jamiat-ul-Ulama-e-Islam (AIJUI)) before partition organized itself in Karachi under the leadership of Allama Shabbir Ahmad Usmani in December 1947. Allama Usmani was supported by other Deobandi scholars such as Mufti Muhammad Shafi, Zafar Ahmed Usmani and Ehtishamul Haq Thanvi. This new party was named Markazi Jamiat-ul-Ulama-e-Islam (MJUI). This small group of Deobandis was very enthusiastic about turning Pakistan into a model Islamic state, which was their main reason to support the idea of Pakistan in the first place. Shabbir Usmani, through the support of the Muslim

League, also became a member of the Constituent Assembly of Pakistan (CAP), hoping to persuade the government that the new constitution should be based on Islamic principles.

During the Pakistan movement, slogans like Islamic government, Islamic state and Islamic constitution were raised by both the Muslim League and the Deobandis of JUI. However, neither the league politicians nor Deobandi *ulama* had any definite plan in this regard when independence came upon them (Binder 1961, 4–5). The modernist leadership of the Muslim League had in mind some mutation of European nationalist theory, but the Deobandis apparently had no clear plan about how to make Pakistan an Islamic state. Their first response was to pass a resolution on 13 January 1948 demanding that the government appoint a leading *alim* to the office of *shaikh ul Islam* with appropriate ministerial and executive power over the judiciary (Binder 1961, 98). The second Deobandi response came in the summer of 1948, when a meeting was held at the residence of Usmani to discuss a plan for a semi-independent Ministry of Religious Affairs. The proposed ministry was supposed not only to control and supervise the religious institutions, mosques, endowments and *qadhi* courts but also to act as general censor of all government activities and to exercise general supervision over the behaviour of all government servants (Binder 1961, 33).

Owing to their lack of clarity about the exact nature of an Islamic state in the modern era, the Deobandis were soon influenced by the ideas of Maulana Maududi of Jamaat-e-Islami, who became active in Pakistani politics in early 1948. He declared that the supreme sovereignty belonged to God and the state must administer the country as His agent. He demanded that *Shariah* should be the basic law of the land and all existing laws coming into conflict with *Shariah* should be repealed (Binder 1961, 103).

Usmani followed suit by demanding that the CAP should set up a committee of eminent *ulama* and thinkers to prepare a draft Islamic constitution (Binder 1961, 140–41). In March 1949, Prime Minister Liaqat Ali Khan moved to adopt the Objectives Resolution, which embodied fundamental Islamic principles for the future constitution of Pakistan.

The Objectives Resolution was merely an indication of good faith from the League Leadership, which seemed to have made up its mind to adopt a modern democratic nationalism in Pakistan. Although the resolution stated that sovereignty belonged to 'God Almighty alone, and the authority which He has delegated to the state of Pakistan through its people for being exercised within the limits prescribed by Him is sacred trust', the League government ensured that the word *Shariah* appeared nowhere in the resolution. However, the government simultaneously established a board of experts called the Board of Taleemat-e-Islamiyah (BTI), consisting of reputed scholars to advise on matters arising out of the Objectives Resolution when referred to them.

Deobandis carried great influence in the BTI through the membership of *ulama* like Mufti Shafi and Zafar Ansari as well as the support of Usmani as a member of the CAP. However, the recommendations of the BTI for an Islamic constitution showed that these *ulama* had no clear vision about an Islamic state – which they equated to a caliphate – in the modern era. They felt that the head of state should know and understand the laws of *Shariah* from the Quran and the Sunnah, and observe its rules – indicating the creation of a theocratic state. The founder of the nation, Muhammad Ali Jinnah, on the other hand, castigated the notion of a 'theocratic state to be ruled by the priests with a divine mission'. Similarly, Prime Minister Liaqat also opposed *mullaism* (i.e. a theocracy; Pirzada 2000, 15). Further, the *ulama* in the BTI intended to preserve their role (and reduce the power of the parliament) by proposing a committee of experts on *Shariah* to decide finally whether or not a particular law militates against the requirements of *Shariah* (Binder 1961, 169). The recommendations of the BTI were turned down not only by the Subcommittee on Constitution and Powers but also by the Basic Principles Committee of the Constituent Assembly. This negative response from the CAP to the BTI's recommendations and the death of Usmani on 13 December 1949 marked the parting of ways between the League government and the Deobandi MJUI.

The role of the Deobandis during the early years of Pakistan showed that their aim was 'to preserve, not to change; their method was through political recognition of their institution' as religious scholars (Binder 1961, 32–3). Lacking a clear vision about the modern Islamic state, the MJUI leadership soon allowed the religious issues to fall within the framework of the normal political process (Binder 1961, 237). After the death of its dynamic leader Usmani, MJUI became less active on the political front. Other reasons for MJUI's downturn included the withdrawal of government patronage as well as the lack of smooth adjustment to the new state by the Deobandi leaders, almost all of whom had migrated to Pakistan from different parts of India after independence (Binder 1961, 194). However, MJUI still played an important role in 1952 to set up the anti-Qadiyani Tehreek-e-Tahaffuz-e-Khatam-e-Nabuwwat (Movement for the protection of the finality of the Prophethood).

In the wake of MJUI's decline, in 1956 a group of Deobandi *ulama* comprising Mufti Mahmood, Ahmad Ali Lahori, Abdullah Darkhawasti and Ghulam Ghaus Hazarwi established a new party named Markazi Jamiat-ul-Ulama-e-Islam West Pakistan (MJUIWP). The party was dominated by Deobandis from the NWFP and the Punjab, as opposed to MJUI, whose leadership mostly belonged to Karachi. The major aims and objectives of the new party included an Islamic system of government, implementation of Islamic teachings in all walks of life, minority status for the Qadiyanis and separate electorates for non-Muslims (Pirzada 2000, 23). In 1958, Pakistan faced its first coup d'état, which was to establish the dominance of the military in Pakistani politics. When the military government of Ayub Khan banned party politics in 1959, MJUIWP organized itself as Nizamul Ulama Pakistan (System of religious scholars), a non-political organization whose objectives were mostly directed towards reorganizing Deobandi madaris. In 1962, when the official ban on political activities was lifted, the Deobandi leadership of MJUIWP emerged in the political arena under the name Jamiat-ul-Ulama-e-Islam Pakistan, generally known as JUI.

The military regime of Ayub Khan tried to modernize traditional Islamic activities. First, the *auqaf* (trusts) system, which provided support to madaris and shrines, was nationalized and later a move was launched to attach madaris to the formal system of education (Malik 1996, 123). Apart from that, Ayub's polemics against the religious leaders were already well-known. He thought that the *ulama* were not equipped to provide Islam with a modern-day orientation. He exhorted the *ulama* to acquaint themselves with the advancement of science, philosophy, economics and contemporary history (Pirzada 2000, 24). Ayub criticized the role and authority of the *ulama*, stating that they thought a 'constitution could be regarded as Islamic only if it were drafted by the *ulama* and conceded them the authority to judge and govern the people' (Khan 1967, 203–4). It was in this hostile scenario that the Deobandi madaris established their umbrella organization in 1959, called Wifaqul Madaris Al-Arabiyya (WMA).

In order to counter the government's move to interfere with the madrassah system, the Deobandi WMA included in its objectives reform of the curriculum through the inclusion of modern subjects. However, no practical initiative was ever taken by WMA. Malik (1996, 125) has stated that the failure of the *ulama* to reform the madaris provided their critics with sufficient grounds for considering them backward. However, it appears that it was less about their inability to reform than their ability to delay state intervention until the madaris could prepare themselves through integration with their umbrella organization. It may be recalled that the Deobandi model of madaris, from its very origin in 1866, was based on the policy of avoiding state intervention while receiving financial support through community donations (Rizwi 2005, vol. 1, 154–7).

As the overwhelming victory of Zulfiqar Ali Bhutto's Peoples Party in the 1970 elections gave rise to the idea that the clergy in Pakistan had vanished once and for all, the Bhutto regime at first did not try to engage the *ulama* or madaris (Malik 1996, 128–9). On the other hand, the madaris, which had acquired some confidence after thwarting Ayub Khan's reform attempts, were busy consolidating their power. In fact, they successfully resisted the Bhutto government's initiative to include madaris in its nationalization drive of the education sector (Riaz 2008, 197). During this period, the Deobandis convinced the government to recognize their board's higher degree, equivalent to a master's degree. However, the National Assembly of Pakistan added the condition of passing a bachelor-level English test for the proposed recognition. The Deobandis rejected the conditional support and the proposal petered out (Malik 1996, 129).

The growing confidence of the madaris and the relevant *ulama* during 1972–77 pressured Prime Minister Bhutto to announce in the 1970s several Islamization measures, which included declaring Qadiyanis non-Muslims and banning alcohol and gambling in the country. Ultimately, an anti-Bhutto alliance under the leadership of Deobandi scholar Mufti Mahmood launched an agitation for complete Islamization of Pakistan, with foot soldiers provided mainly by Deobandi madaris (Riaz 2008, 197–8). The backdrop to this movement was the military coup by General Zia-ul-Haq against the Bhutto government on 5 July 1977.

The Zia era (1977–88) marked a watershed in the history of madaris in Pakistan, especially Deobandi ones. Being a military dictator, General Zia lacked constitutional legitimacy. Therefore, immediately after usurping power, he launched an Islamization campaign to achieve credibility for his government among the *ulama*, who had led the movement against Bhutto with the slogan *Nizam-e-Mustafa* (System of the Prophet) for Pakistan. Apart from political expediency, Zia's Islamization project was also motivated by his ideological conviction (Riaz 2008, 198).

Zia came from a humble lower-middle-class background. From a young age, he was actively involved with the Tablighi Jamaat (TJ). After coming into power, he aspired to turn Pakistan into an ideological state ruled by a rigid interpretation of *Shariah*, thus empowering religious groups like Jamaat-e-Islami and the DMM, whose members were given jobs in the judiciary, the civil service and educational institutions. *Shariah* courts were established to try cases under Islamic laws, school textbooks were overhauled to ensure ideological purity, and books deemed un-Islamic were removed from syllabi and university libraries (Hussain 2007, 15–19).

Zia also tried to give a new Islamic orientation to the army, which had long been a secular organization in line with British traditions. He expanded the role of the army to defend the ideological frontiers of the country in addition to the geographical borders. Islamic teachings were introduced into the Pakistan Military Academy and Islamic training and philosophy were made part of the curriculum at the military's Command and Staff College. A Directorate of Religious Instruction was established to educate the officer corps on Islam, who were taught to be not just professional soldiers but soldiers of Islam. The army allowed the free flow of religious political literature in its training institutions. Graduates of Deobandi madaris were appointed to work among the troops as prayer leaders – a bridge for officers between the Westernized profession and the faith (Hussain 2007, 18–21). The Zia Islamization project led to critical implications, as shall be discussed later in this section.

In mid-1978, a delegation of *ulama* met General Zia and demanded greater autonomy for madaris. The government later set up the National Committee for Dini Madaris in January 1979 under the chairmanship of A. W. J. Halepota, who was largely responsible for the failed madrassah reforms of 1962 during Ayub Khan's era. In the meantime, Zia floated the idea unifying madaris of all denominations under one umbrella organization. However, the proposal was opposed by the Deobandi WMA. The 1979 reform proposals were not so different from those of 1962, especially with respect to the introduction of secular subjects and revision of curricula in madaris (Zaman 2007, 79). WMA immediately opposed the proposals of the 1979 committee, and interpreted the reforms as an attempt by the government to control madaris.

The Deobandis had, in fact, raised objections from the very beginning and had called for a boycott of the committee. Yusuf Ludhianvi of Jamia-tul-ulum-ul-Islamiyah in Binouri Town, Karachi, even questioned the mandate of the committee by saying that it was continuing the policies of the British government. Ludhianvi considered the mainstream system of education not worth striving for, and accused the committee of trying to subordinate traditional religious education to the modern sciences (Malik 1996, 136–7). Madaris of other denominations (except for Jamaat-e-Islami) also opposed the proposed reforms and General Zia was forced to postpone implementation.

The resistance of madaris to reform efforts gradually subsided as the military government recognized their degrees, made *zakat* (Islamic tax for the poor) funds available to them and offered job opportunities for their graduates in government organizations, both civil and military. By the early 1980s, the Barelwi and Ahle Hadith madaris had agreed to introduce 'secular' subjects, following the Jamaat-e-Islami (JI) madaris. The Barelwis offered as optional subjects English and mathematics only at the *Sanviya Aama* (equivalent to matric) level. Ahle Hadith madaris introduced Pakistan studies, science and social studies in addition to English and mathematics. For *Sanviya Khasa* and *Aliya* (equivalent to intermediate and bachelor levels respectively) students,

Ahle Hadith and JI madaris have since added more subjects like economics, political science, education and computer science (Khalid 2002, 388–405). On the other hand, the Deobandi WMA resisted such moves. However, WMA did allow many Deobandi madaris the option to prepare their selected students to appear as private candidates in mainstream examinations at matric, intermediate and bachelor levels in addition to their traditional *Dars-e-Nizami* studies. Although there was 'no essential alteration of the classic DM [Dini Madaris] course of instruction', the Zia regime secured, through this compromise, the 'acceptance of his leadership by the *ulama*' and 'an Islamic legitimation of his rule', whereas the madaris achieved 'social recognition' (Malik 1996, 172). The real rapprochement between the Zia regime and the madaris was to come in the wake of the region's changing political scenario after the Soviet occupation of Afghanistan in December 1979.

As Pakistan became an ally of the United States and a frontline state in the war in Afghanistan against the Soviet Union, an elaborate infrastructure under the guise of the madaris was built to provide training to *mujahideen* (holy warriors) from Afghanistan, Pakistan and various other Muslim countries (Riaz 2008, 200). Madaris from the Deobandi, Jamaat-e-Islami and Ahle Hadith denominations participated in this infrastructure, which was to receive money, training and weapons from the United States through Inter-services Intelligence (ISI) – Pakistan's premier spy agency (Riaz 2008, 105). Apart from Pakistan, radicals from other Muslim countries like Saudi Arabia and Egypt were also invited to participate in *jihad* against the Soviets. Between 1982 and 1992, some thirty-five thousand Muslim radicals from 43 Islamic countries in the Middle East, North and East Africa, Central Asia and the Far East joined the *mujahideen* in Afghanistan. In the Middle East, the Muslim Brotherhood (Ikhwan-ul-Muslimeen), the Saudi-based World Muslim League and Palestinian Islamic radicals organized the recruitment for this *jihad*. The centre for the Arab-Afghans was the offices of the World Muslim League and the Muslim Brotherhood in Peshawar, headed by Abdullah Azzam, a Jordan-based Palestinian whom Usama bin Laden first met at Jeddah University and came to revere as his leader (Rashid 2008, 130–31).

Pakistan's Afghan policy in the 1980s was conducted by ISI mainly with the help of Jamaat-e-Islami of Pakistan and Hizb-e-Islami under Afghan leader Gulbadin Hikmatyar. The Deobandi JUI and its allied *mujahideen* were not given a prominent role at the time, a policy that was to be reversed in the 1990s after the rise of the Taliban (Rashid 2008, 89). Olivier Roy described this war as 'a joint venture between the Saudis, the Muslim Brotherhood and the Jamaat-e-Islami, put together by the ISI' (Rashid 2008, 130).

Although Jamaat-e-Islami of Pakistan played a leading role in the war against the Soviets, the Deobandis were the most enthusiastic participants of this war, owing to their special historical connection with Afghanistan dating back to the movements of Shah Waliullah and Syed Ahmed as well as Mahmood Hassan's Silken Letters campaign. Further, most of the madaris involved in the Afghan *jihad* belonged to the Deobandi sect. From 1982 to 1988, around one thousand new Deobandi madaris were opened in Pakistan, mostly along the borders with Afghanistan in the NWFP and Balochistan. Their location in these provinces, 'which had close cultural, linguistic and sectarian affinities with Afghan Pashtuns, made it easier to motivate the pupils to fight for their brethren in distress' (Hussain 2007, 80).

The students in these madaris were taught specific books to encourage them to join the 'holy war'. Special textbooks were published in Dari and Pashto by the University of Nebraska through a USAID-funded project to promote jihadist values and militant training. Millions of these books were distributed at Afghan refugee camps and Pakistani madaris, where students were taught basic maths by counting dead Russians and Kalashnikov rifles. Recruits for the Afghan resistance were given training by the Pakistani military, particularly ISI, in the camps inside Afghanistan and Pakistan's tribal regions (Hussain 2007, 80).

As the Afghan *jihad* progressed, the *jihadi* madaris did not remain restricted to the remote border regions. Soon, several militant Deobandi seminaries began operating in Karachi, Pakistan's largest city and its financial centre. The largest among them was Jamia-tul-ulum-ul-Islamiyah in Binouri Town (also known as Jamia Binouria) under Mufti Nizamuddin Shamzai (1930–2004). This *jamia*, along with its eight affiliated madaris, enrolled more than ten thousand students from Pakistan as well as 30 other countries including Afghanistan, China, the Central Asian Republics, Chechnya, Malaysia, the Philippines and Britain. Many of the Afghan Taliban leaders also graduated from this seminary and took guidance from their former teachers (Hussain 2007, 83). Another such madrassah is Darul Ulum Haqqania in Akora Khattak near Peshawar, run by Maulana Samiul Haq, who heads his own faction of Jamiat-ul-Ulama-e-Islam (JUI). Known as the cradle of Afghan Taliban militia, this seminary has served since the 1980s as a recruiting centre for dozens of Pakistani militant groups fighting in Afghanistan and Kashmir (Hussain 2007, 77). It mainly attracted students from Afghanistan, Tajikistan, Uzbekistan and Turkmenistan. Similarly, Jamia Naumania of Dera Ismail Khan produced militants like Fazlur Rehman Khalil, leader of Harkat ul Ansar (HuA) and Harkat ul Mujahideen (HuM). These militant organizations have a long history of involvement in Afghanistan. Khalil ran Camp Badar near Khost on the Pak-Afghan border for the training and recruitment of jihadists to fight in Kashmir, Chechnya and Yugoslavia (Rashid 1998, 76). It was through this participation in the Afghan *jihad* as well as the presence of international students in its madaris that the DMM developed links with Muslim radicals in other Islamic countries (Rashid 2002, 44).

It may be noted that the official support and patronage provided by the Zia regime to madaris for their participation in active warfare is unprecedented. Never in the history of madaris had any Muslim state used these institutions as military academies to prepare soldiers for the battlefield. This extraordinary initiative by the Zia regime then led to equally extraordinary consequences, which have since been faced by the Pakistani state in the form of rising sectarianism, militancy and 'Talibanization', as shall be discussed later in this section.

When the Soviets withdrew from Afghanistan in 1989, the US government took no time to adopt a hands-off policy in the region, leaving Pakistan to deal with the aftermath of the decade-long *jihad*. After the death of General Zia in 1988, the weak civilian governments of Benazir Bhutto (1988–90 and 1993–96) and Nawaz Sharif (1990–93 and 1997–99) ignored the issue of the madaris. During the 1990s, Pakistan's military establishment continued to support the student militia, the Taliban, in Afghanistan as part of its strategic goal. Later on, militant madaris were also established in the southern part of the Punjab under the influence of Deobandis like Masood Azhar, a graduate of Jamia Binouria who later set up a jihadist outfit named Jaish-e-Muhammad (JeM) in 2000, reportedly at the behest of Pakistan's military establishment. In addition to guerrilla activities in Kashmir, JeM kept close ties with the Taliban as well as al-Qaeda in Afghanistan. JeM also promoted jihadi journalism through its Urdu weekly newspaper *Zarb-e-Momin*, which sold about a quarter of a million copies across Pakistan. The group also publishes the Urdu *Daily Islam*, with a nationwide circulation of more than one hundred thousand (Hussain 2007, 65–6). After the 9/11 attacks, the military government of General Pervez Musharraf banned several militant groups. When JeM was banned in 2002, Azhar set up a new group Khuddam-ul-Islam, which was also proscribed in 2003 (Mir 2004, 32). However, Azhar stayed a free man and patronized several madaris in South Punjab.

The Musharraf government also tried to reform madaris through the promulgation of the Pakistan Madrassah Education (Establishment and Affiliation of Model Dini Madaris) Board Ordinance (2001) and Madrassah Registration Ordinance (2002). Like previous such efforts, this reform initiative also failed to make any headway owing to sharp resistance, mostly from the DMM and the two provincial governments of the NWFP and Balochistan run by the Deobandi-led alliance of religious parties called Muttahida Majlis-e-Amal (MMA; Joint action group). The political role of the Deobandis and the MMA government is discussed in the next section.

4.2 The DMM's Shifting Stances in Politics

After their vain attempts for an Islamic constitution after 1947, the Deobandis seemed to have lost hope of making Pakistan an Islamic state. Soon, the Deobandi party, JUI, decided to join the electoral politics. Initially, it contested elections independently but its performance was quite disappointing. In the 1962 elections, JUI won just one National Assembly seat. In the 1965 elections, it failed to win even a single seat. However, the party kept on making its presence felt in politics through its stance on different social and political issues.

During Ayub Khan's era (1958–69), JUI opposed the Muslim Family Law Ordinance promulgated by President Ayub Khan in 1961 on the grounds that the restriction of seeking permission for a second marriage in the presence of an existing marriage was un-Islamic. The ordinance introduced registration of all marriages and maintenance of their records at the union council level. Further, the effect of the ordinance was to set up local arbitration councils whose business was to bring about, if possible, the resolution of disputes between couples or to process and document the divorce cases. According to the ordinance, no man was permitted to contract a further marriage so long as a previous marriage subsisted, except with the permission of the arbitrary council, to which an application had to be submitted stating whether the consent of the existing wife or wives had been obtained. The ordinance was in no way against polygamy, a practice allowed in Islam. Rather its purpose was to prevent its misuse by the weak, the vicious and the desperate.

President Ayub Khan tried to explain the spirit of the law to the Deobandi mufti Muhammad Shafi in a letter dated 11 June 1961, whereby he wrote that 'untold miseries and cruelties [...] are commonly perpetrated in our country under the cover of indiscriminate polygamy. This does not only result in embittering and ruining the lives of innumerable tongue-tied women and innocent children, but it also brings in its wake the social, moral, and economic collapse of thousands of families' (Feldman 1967, 144–8). However, the Deobandis and JUI continued to oppose the ordinance.

During the late 1960s, the DMM was divided on the issue of socialism. Initially, there was a consensus among the Deobandis that socialism was an apostasy and *kufr* (non-belief). In fact, one of the objectives of JUI declared in 1956 was to 'shield the citizens of Pakistan against the attacks of inhuman capitalism, atheistic communism, and socialism' (Pirzada 2000, 223). Later, when Deobandi politicians joined the movement against Ayub Khan, they came close to the Pakistan People's Party (PPP) of Zulfiqar Ali Bhutto and began to adopt a softer approach towards socialism, as the PPP was pro-socialist. At the time, the *nazim-e-aala* (chief organizer) of JUI, Ghulam Ghaus Hazarwi, was alleged to have lent support to the kind of socialism which he thought was not against Islamic principles. Similarly, a series of articles written by Zahidur Rashidi under the title 'Islamic Socialism of Bhutto' were published in the Deobandi monthly *Tabsira* (Commentary). Rashidi asserted in these articles that the term 'Islamic socialism' was not contrary to *Shariah*. Mufti Mahmood endorsed his view (Pirzada 2000, 30), but the non-political *ulama* of the DMM opposed this soft approach.

By 1970, the Deobandi movement in Pakistan was broadly divided, despite some overlapping, into Deobandi politicians and Deobandi *ulama*. The former focused on electoral politics, while the latter restricted themselves to the madaris and mosques. The former preferred a pragmatic approach over an ideological one in order to ally themselves with other political parties, whereas the latter centred their attention on the protection and preservation of their particular version of Islam through the network of madaris, mosques, print material (books, journals, magazines) and indirectly through the *tabligh* (proselytizing) missions which sojourned at the Deobandi mosques.

It is interesting that most *ulama* of the Deobandi madaris did not support the new interpretation presented by Deobandi politicians. A group of leading DMM *ulama* launched a strong criticism against JUI leadership when the party entered into an alliance with the pro-socialist Pakistan Labour Party (PLP). This campaign was led by renowned *ulama* like Mufti Shafi and Ehtishamul Haq Thanvi, who had initially joined politics under the leadership of Shabbir Usmani but later withdrew themselves to focus on their madaris. This 'socialism controversy' gradually died down as the politicians and *ulama* of the DMM settled back into their respective roles; the *ulama* seemed to have an edge owing to their authority to issue *fatawa* and rulings to provide support and legitimacy for Deobandi politics. This broad division gave the *ulama* a sense of superiority on the one hand and allowed Deobandi politicians more space to practice pragmatism and realpolitik on the other.

Since 1970, JUI has opted for political alliances in order to make an impression on mainstream politics. For example, for the 1970 elections, JUI joined the Muttahida Dini Mahaz (Joint religious front) – an alliance of 19 religious parties and minor organizations like the PLP. Seven candidates of JUI returned to the National Assembly in the 1970 elections. Inside the assembly, JUI became a component of the United Democratic Front (UDF) – an alliance which included old and hard rivals of JUI like the Barelwi Jamiat-ul-Ulama-e-Pakistan (JUP) and Maududi's Jamaat-e-Islami on the one hand and the secular, socialist and pro-Russia National Awami Party (NAP) on the other. At the provincial levels, JUI joined hands with NAP to form coalition governments in the NWFP and Balochistan. These governments lasted for less than ten months and JUI failed to make any impression on the people with regard to their declared commitment to *Shariah*.

For the 1977 elections, JUI joined an even broader alliance of nine parties named the Pakistan National Alliance. From 1988 to 1999, JUI under the leadership of Maulana Fazlur Rehman (after whom it is called JUI (F) to distinguish it from two smaller factions of JUI) adopted the strategy of joining or supporting the ruling coalitions. In the 2002 elections, JUI (F) allied with five religious parties under the name Muttahida Majlis-e-Amal (MMA). Other component parties included Jamaat-e-Islami, the Shia Tehreek-e-Jafria Pakistan (TJP, later renamed Islami Tehreek Pakistan), the Barelwi JUP, JUI (Samiul Haq) and Jamiat Ahle Hadith. The leaders of these parties were at the forefront of the anti-US demonstrations in Pakistan after 9/11. The MMA contested the elections with anti-US and anti-Musharraf slogans in the heated post-9/11 scenario. Public opinion in Pakistan about the United States was highly unfavourable after NATO forces invaded Afghanistan. According to a Pew Research Center report (2002, 53), the United States received its second-lowest favourable opinion rating (after Egypt) from Pakistan – just 10 per cent. This rating was more than 23 per cent in the Pew survey conducted a couple of years earlier (Pew 2012, 9). JUI successfully exploited these public sentiments against the United States in its favour, particularly in the two provinces contiguous to Afghanistan (i.e. the NWFP and Balochistan).

The elections of 2002 were the peak of JUI's electoral politics. In the National Assembly, the JUI-led MMA won 63 seats in the house out of 342. These seats were won mostly from the above-mentioned two provinces where the MMA was able to form governments. In the NWFP, the MMA had won a simple majority but in Balochistan it had to enter into a coalition with the pro-Musharraf Pakistan Muslim League (Quaid-e-Azam) which came to power in the centre and in two provinces (Punjab and Balochistan).

Although the MMA had promised during its election campaign to implement *Shariah*, it failed to make any serious effort in this regard either at the federal level, where it headed a sizeable opposition group, or in the two provinces where it was in power. This failure in the two provinces has generally been attributed to JUI's pragmatic approach, which prevented it from making any serious endeavour to implement *Shariah* in the face of a powerful liberal military dictator, General Pervez Musharraf. It was also alleged that the MMA had developed some understanding with General Musharraf, who was said to have tolerated the two provincial governments in return for the MMA's soft approach towards his military rule. In fact, the MMA supported the 17th amendment to the constitution, which provided indemnity to the extra-constitutional measures taken by the military government of Musharraf. Earlier in 2002, Musharraf's military regime had mobilized JUI and other religious parties to hold anti-US and anti-UN rallies, while his government continued to secretly support the Taliban (Rashid 2010, 218). It was amid these allegations that the MMA was satirically called the Mullah Military Alliance (Mir 2004, 185).

The provincial government of the MMA in the NWFP did not seriously demonstrate the means or the will to implement *Shariah*. However, it took some cosmetic measures to establish its Islamic credentials. These symbolic actions included: opening the sessions of the provincial assembly with the *adhan* (call to *salah* or prayer); banning alcohol, even for non-Muslim foreigners; prohibiting the playing of music and movies on public transport buses; and announcing a crackdown on 'pubs and gambling dens', despite the fact that there were no pubs in the province (White 2008, 52). Alongside these official moves came a rise in vigilante-style campaigns against 'obscenity' in the province. Other symbolic measures taken by the MMA government included the closing of video shops, prohibitions on traditional music and dance, obscuring women's faces on billboards, etc. Besides that, the MMA also discussed proposals to close down dance halls, music stores and cinemas as well as cable television in the province (*Daily Times* 2003).

Apart from the above-mentioned symbolic measures, the JUI-led MMA government set up the Nifaz-e-Shariat Council, a quasi-governmental recommendatory body of *ulama*, which debated the establishment of a 'vice-and-virtue ministry' within the provincial government, and issued suggestions on such matters as the proper colour of the *dupatta* (head covering) to be worn by schoolgirls (Ali and Khattak 2003). Almost without exception, the council's recommendations were announced with fanfare, featured prominently in the local press and then were promptly ignored (White 2008, 52). Under the guidance of the council, the MMA government prepared a blueprint for establishing an Islamic judicial system for the NWFP through the Hasba (Accountability) Bill, which was approved by the provincial assembly in 2005. This bill intended to equip the MMA with the means to oversee the implementation of *Shariah* through the appointment of hundreds of local ombudsmen. JUI hoped through these appointments to empower the Deobandi *ulama*, who were to be the main beneficiaries of this bill because of the traditional influence of the DMM in the province.

The ultimate objective behind the Hasba Bill was to establish a parallel judicial system under the *ulama*. The system was to work under a provincial *mohtasib* (ombudsman) with the powers of a high court judge; his office was to be supported by district and tehsil *mohtasibs*, who were to enjoy the powers of session and civil judges respectively. The *mohtasib* was given the authority to:

> (a) [Make] enquiries into the allegations of maladministration against any agency or its employees; (b) Protect/watch the Islamic values and etiquettes; (c) Watch the media established by Government or working under the administrative control of Government to ensure that its publications are useful to the purpose of upholding Islamic values; (d) Forbid persons, agencies and authorities working under the administrative control of government to act against *Shariah* and to guide them to good governance. (Hasba Bill, Section 10)

Apart from that, the *mohtasib* was equipped with extensive special powers under section 23. Some of these powers were either inspired by the countercultural tendencies of the

DMM or provided the platform for implementing Deobandi values through this bill. For example, the *mohtasib* was given the authority to: monitor adherence to the moral values of Islam in public places; discourage exhibitions of extravagance, particularly during marriages and other family functions; discourage entertainment shows; observe the decorum of Islam during *adhan* and other prayers; discourage un-Islamic and inhuman customs; and eradicate the practice of *taweez* (amulets), palmistry, magic, etc. In order to exercise his powers, the *mohtasib* was to be supported by a religious police force (section 26) that was not much different from that of the Taliban government in Afghanistan.

Section 25 (1) of the bill provided supra-judicial status to the *mohtasib* by stating that 'no court or authority shall be competent to question the legal status of the proceedings before a Mohtasib'. Section 14 granted the *mohtasib* powers equivalent to the high court regarding contempt of court in order to prevent any hindrance to the implementation of his orders. It was mainly because of these two sections that on 4 August 2005 the Supreme Court of Pakistan declared the Hasba Bill unconstitutional within one month of its approval by the provincial assembly of the NWFP (*Daily Times* 2005). The apex court observed that the provincial government could file an appeal after revising the controversial sections of the bill (Kamran 2007). The provincial assembly passed a fresh bill in November 2006. The federal government challenged it in the Supreme Court, which declared the bill partially unconstitutional by ruling that the *mohtasib* could not be given judicial powers to prosecute a person who disobeyed his orders and that a madrassah graduate could not be eligible for the post of *mohtasib* (Kamran 2007). The chief justice of Pakistan obliquely hinted towards the Deobandis when he remarked that one sect would not be allowed to impose itself on others through this bill. He observed that in the next stage this sect might dictate the size of one's beard, the length of one's *shalwar* (loose pants worn under a long shirt in Pakistan) and the procedure of offering prayers (*Daily Express* 2007). After that, JUI showed little resolve to further pursue the bill.

Before the 2008 elections, the MMA was practically dissolved when Jamaat-e-Islami decided to boycott the 2008 elections under the presidency of General Musharraf. So, JUI had to contest the elections without the support of its major allies. The performance of the party was quite dismal and it managed to win just 7 out of 342 seats of the National Assembly. Later, JUI joined the coalition government led by the PPP, which was being run by President Asif Ali Zardari after the assassination of his wife, Benazir Bhutto, in December 2007.

In 2013, JUI again contested the elections independently and slightly improved its overall tally in the National Assembly by winning 10 general seats. However, the share of JUI in the provincial assemblies of the NWFP and Balochistan has decreased since the 2008 elections. It would be pertinent to point out here that during the 2013 elections, JUI was unable to win a single national- or provincial-level seat in the provinces of Punjab and Sindh, which together make up more than 80 per cent of Pakistan's total population of 180 million. As for the smaller Deobandi groups like JUI (S), JUI (Nazariyati) and Ahle Sunnat wal Jamaat (ASWJ), these failed to win a single seat in any part of Pakistan in the 2013 elections when they joined a faction of Jamiat Ahle Hadith and a splinter group of the Barelwi JUP to form the Muttahida Dini Mahaz.

The above-mentioned three Deobandi groups share the same sectarian and ideological outlook with the main party JUI (F) and the DMM as a whole. However, it is the difference of approach and the leadership struggle that has separated them from JUI (F). Samiul Haq formed his own faction of JUI during the 1980s following his differences with the party head Fazlur Rehman. JUI (S) has always maintained a very close relationship with the military establishment of Pakistan and played an important role in recruiting *jihadis* for Afghanistan and Kashmir through its madrassah, Darul Ulum Haqqania. JUI (Nazariyati) was formed before the 2008 elections as a result of a leadership struggle in JUI (F)'s Balochistan chapter. As Fazlur Rehman tried to distance his party from the military establishment as well as the Afghan Taliban, the hardliners of his party in Balochistan rebelled under Maulana Asmatullah and challenged the leadership of the provincial head of JUI (F), Maulana Muhammad Khan Sherani. With the tacit support of the military establishment, Asmatullah set up JUI (N) and defeated Sherani in the National Assembly election. JUI (N) is a pro-*jihadi*, pro-establishment party that is restricted to the province of Balochistan. As regards ASWJ, it is generally considered a new name for Sipah-e-Sahaba Pakistan (SSP; Armies of the Prophet's companions), a banned militant Deobandi outfit. Its leader Muhammad Ahmed Ludhianvi contested the election from the traditional Deobandi stronghold of the Jhang district and was defeated by a narrow margin. Like SSP, the main objective of ASWJ is to make Pakistan into a Sunni Hanafi state and have Shias declared non-Muslims. These three minor groups of the DMM are part of the ISI-backed Defence of Pakistan Council, an umbrella organization of about forty small political and religious parties that advocate anti-US and anti-India policies. The main Deobandi political party, JUI (F), is not part of that alliance.

It is interesting to note that since 1970, Deobandi politicians, through JUI's various alliances, have shared political aspirations with a variety of political groups of every hue, including liberal, secular and regional parties. Pirzada (2000, 234–5) has concluded that JUI's approach is a veiled confession about the impossibility of establishing an Islamic state in Pakistan. Owing to such indiscriminate and conflicting alliances, Pirzada has termed JUI a 'munificent' Islamist party whose supporters gradually became disillusioned as the ideological basis of the party corroded. This disillusionment was reflected in JUI's electoral decline during the period 1970–97 (Pirzada 2000, 231–3). This trend was again shown in the 2008 and 2013 elections. The only exception was the 2002 elections, when JUI's alliance with other religious parties was able to significantly improve its electoral performance. In fact, it was not actually the alliance which worked for JUI. Rather it was the anti-US sentiment in Pakistan, which the MMA successfully exploited in its favour in the two provinces located on the Afghan border. Similarly, the alleged tacit support of the military also boosted the MMA's performance. Above all, it was the exile of the leaders of the two biggest parties, Nawaz Sharif of the Pakistan Muslim League (N) and Benazir Bhutto of the Pakistan Peoples Party, which created a great leadership vacuum helping JUI to improve its electoral fortunes.

It may be pertinent to add here that the little success JUI was able to manage in the 2013 elections was mostly restricted to the NWFP. The major factor that helped JUI to win seats there was the fact that two mainstream political parties, the Pakistan People's Party and the Awami National Party, were not able to campaign because of the threats and attacks by the extremist Deobandi groups operating in that province. The next section examines the extremist streaks in the Deobandi movement.

4.3 The Rise of Extremism in the Deobandi Movement

This section argues that extremism in the Deobandi movement was manifested at three levels in Pakistan. The first level was marked by assaults on Shias. The rise of local Taliban groups represented the second level. At the third level, Deobandi extremists started attacking the symbols of folk Islam, such as *sufi* shrines. The details of these three streaks of Deobandi extremism are given below.

After the Soviet withdrawal, many jihadists belonging to Deobandi madaris returned to Pakistan to support their brethren who were already involved in sectarian conflict with Shias. Actually, Zia's move to establish a Sunni Hanafi state to reflect the majority of Pakistani Muslims had created a sense of insecurity among the minority Shia community. Before the Zia era, the relationship between the Shias and the majority of Sunnis was generally peaceful (Murphy 2013, 27). As Zia promoted the Deobandi *ulama* by giving them high-level positions in the government and judiciary (Riaz 2008, 109), Shias became more anxious, knowing well the DMM's views about them. Until 1979, Pakistani Shias were a politically moderate community which supported secular political parties. But Zia's policy to enforce Hanafi laws on the one hand and the Iranian revolution on the other spurred the Shias into political activism. In 1980, tens of thousands of Shias protested in Islamabad against their marginalization by the Sunni majority. At around the same time, a Shia political party, Tehreek-e-Nifaz-e-Fiqh-e-Jafria (TNFJ; Movement for the implementation of Shia jurisprudence), was also set up under the leadership of Arif al-Hussaini, a student of Ayatollah Khomeini.

As post-revolution Iran became the centre of spiritual and political support for Pakistani Shias, the Zia regime and its Sunni allies perceived TNFJ as an Iranian conspiracy to export its revolution to Pakistan (Hussain 2007, 91–2). The spillover effect of the Shia revolution also worried many Arab rulers. The consequent Sunni reaction to Shia activism in Pakistan was launched with funding from Saudi Arabia and other Arab countries as well as tacit support from the military government of Zia. The first such reaction came from the Deobandis. Emboldened by their role in the Afghan *jihad* and facilitated by the weapons and funds, the Deobandis took a domestic initiative to wage *jihad* inside Pakistan. In 1985, they founded the Sawad-e-Azam Ahle Sunnat (Greater unity of the Sunnis), later institutionalized as Anjuman Sipah-e-Sahaba (Society of the Prophet's companions) with a one-point anti-Shia agenda under the leadership of fiery Deobandi cleric Haq Nawaz Jhangwi. A prayer leader at a mosque in the Jhang district of central Punjab, Jhangwi was reported to have close links with Pakistani intelligence agencies (Hussain 2007, 92). The only demand of Anjuman Sipah-e-Sahaba was to declare Pakistan a Sunni state and Shias non-Muslims. Against this backdrop, Manzoor Naumani, a renowned Deobandi scholar of India, issued a *fatwa* in December 1987 declaring Shias *kuffar* (non-believers). That *fatwa* was endorsed by hundreds of prominent Deobandi *ulama* in both India and Pakistan. Maulana Wali Hassan, Deobandi grand mufti of Pakistan, issued a separate *fatwa* in this regard whereby he wrote, 'Shias are *kafir*.

Their marriage with Muslims is *haram*. Muslims should not participate in the funeral prayers of Shias. An animal slaughtered by a Shia is not *halal* for Muslims. It is not permissible to bury Shias in the graveyards of Muslims. In short, Shias must be treated as non-Muslims' (Hassan 1988).

As Iran and Saudi Arabia supported their respected allies, Pakistan became a battlefield in an intra-Islam proxy war. In the meantime, Haq Nawaz Jhangwi had reorganized Anjuman Sipah-e-Sahaba as Sipah-e-Sahaba Pakistan (SSP). In February 1990, when he was killed by Shia militants, sectarian violence spiralled. The newly organized SSP unleashed a reign of terror with some five to six thousand well-trained militants backed by almost one million cardholding members. While blaming Iran for the murder of Jhangwi, SSP militants in December 1990 gunned down Sadiq Ganji, Iranian consul general in Lahore, as revenge. The situation worsened in 1991 when Shia militants killed the new leader of SSP, Isarul Qasmi, in retribution. After that, SSP was headed by Ziaur Rehman Farooqi until his death in 1997 in a sectarian attack. He was replaced by Azam Tariq, a fiery cleric who had served a two-year prison sentence for his involvement in several Shia murder cases. Tariq later turned towards electoral politics and was elected to the National Assembly four times from the Jhang district before he was killed by Shia militants in a revenge attack in 2003 (Hussain 2007, 92–100).

After Haq Nawaz Jhangwi's death in 1990, several of his diehard followers left SSP and formed their own groups with the aim of completing Jhangwi's mission. In this process, at least six groups were formed – namely, Jhangwi Tigers, Al Haq Tigers, Allah Akbar, Tanzeemul Haq, Al-Farooq and the Al-Badr Foundation. In 1996, the first three of these groups joined hands to launch Lashkar-e-Jhangwi (LeJ) with the consent of the SSP leadership (Mir 2004, 177). This new sectarian outfit made its mark as the most feared, violent outfit soon after its inception. LeJ believed in using terror tactics to force the government to accept its demands of declaring Shias non-Muslims. It also prepared female suicide bombers to attack Shia places of worship in Karachi (Mir 2004, 183). Head of LeJ Riaz Basra was a veteran of the Afghan *jihad* and was considered a dangerous terrorist, owing to his involvement in the murders of several high profile Shia leaders. He was arrested in 1994 for the murder of the Iranian consul general but escaped from the court and fled to Afghanistan to join the Taliban militia. After 1996, the Taliban government ignored several requests from the Pakistani authorities to extradite Basra, saying that he was a great *mujahid*. However, Basra regularly visited Pakistan secretly to motivate and organize attacks on Shia targets. During one such visit, he was killed in a shootout with the police near Multan in 2003 (Hussain 2007, 94–7). LeJ, despite being outlawed in 2001, continued to carry out attacks on the Shia community.

As regards the second level of Deobandi extremism, it was unveiled in the form of a phenomenon generally referred to as 'Talibanization'. The roots of that phenomenon can also be traced to the DMM's involvement in Afghanistan, as discussed below.

After the Soviet withdrawal from Afghanistan in 1988, various Afghan factions who had participated in *jihad* came to power. However, these factions soon started fighting among themselves. As this infighting grew more intense and merciless, the regional leadership of the warring factions in some provinces was virtually eliminated. One such province was Kandahar. The leadership gap in this province left the field free for the rise of a new Islamist group in 1994 – the Taliban, under the leadership of a local named Mullah Omar (Rashid 2008, 19).

This group chose for themselves the name Taliban (plural of *talib*, Islamic student) because most of them were part- or full-time students at madaris. Many of them had been born in Pakistani refugee camps, educated in Pakistan's Deobandi madaris and had learned their fighting skills from the *mujahideen* based in Pakistan (Rashid 2008, 22–3). Soon after 1994, thousands of young Afghan Pashtuns studying in the Deobandi madaris of Balochistan and the NWFP rushed to Kandahar to join the Taliban. They were then followed by Pakistani volunteers from Deobandi madaris, who were inspired by the new Islamic movement in Afghanistan (Rashid 2008, 29). This movement had in fact revived one of the dreams of Shah Waliullah's movement to set up an Islamic state under the Pashtuns.

Broadly speaking, the Taliban forces comprised of three categories. The first category consisted of the loyal members of the movement who were the students and graduates of the madaris operating in the rural areas of Afghanistan, where they had been taught a concise, official curriculum that mainly focused only on Quranic studies, the general principles of Islamic law and Arabic language. The second category included the students of Deobandi madaris as well as JUI activists from Pakistan, who catered to the administration and military ranks of the movement. The third category consisted of young Afghans studying in the refugee camps in Pakistan. This last category is further divided into two groups. The first group attended the madaris run by Afghan *mujahideen* who taught their national curriculum for religious schools. The second group in this category comprised of those Afghan students who attended Deobandi madaris in Pakistan and were taught a far more thorough curriculum than in Afghan madaris. This purely Deobandi group of Afghans later made up the core of the high-ranking leadership who ran the Taliban administration inside Afghanistan as well as managed their international affairs (Najomi 2002, 125–6). The influence of this group turned the Taliban into a predominantly Deobandi movement. Members of this influential group were trained at Pakistani madaris like Darul Ulum Haqqania, Jamia Binouria and Darul Ulum Karachi and occupied several vital positions such as the governor of Jalal Abad, Taliban's representative to the UN and their ambassador in Islamabad. In fact, three of the six members of the Taliban leadership council came from Jamia Binouria of Karachi (Najomi 2002, 120–21).

It may be pertinent to add here that owing to the Deobandi ideology they followed, the Taliban's behaviour became hard to interpret in academic terms. Some authors labelled the Taliban fundamentalists, others called them traditionalists, still others considered them totalitarians and terrorists. Former US ambassador to Pakistan Robert Oakley suggested that the Taliban represented the arrival of 'village' values and attitudes to the cities (Maley 1998, 16–22). This difference of opinion regarding the interpretation of the Taliban is not unlike the inconclusive debate about how to interpret the DMM, as discussed in Chapter 1.

As the Deobandi creed became the primary religious and ideological influence on the Taliban (Rashid 2008, 89), they developed their closest links with the leadership of the Deobandi madaris as well as the JUI of Pakistan, whose leader, Maulana Fazlur Rehman, had become a political ally of Prime Minister Benazir Bhutto. He had access to the government, the army and ISI, to whom he described this newly emerging force of the Taliban (Rashid 2008, 26). As head of the parliament's Foreign Relations Committee on Kashmir, Fazlur Rehman visited Washington, DC and several European capitals to lobby for the Taliban, and travelled to the Gulf and other Muslim states to enlist their support (Rashid 2008, 90). Pakistan's military establishment was also deeply involved in helping and guiding the Taliban in their battles against the Afghan Northern Alliance forces, which were being supported by Iran and Russia. Saudis later provided funds, fuel and vehicles for the successful Taliban attack on Kabul (Rashid 2008, 201). As a result of this moral, physical and financial support, the Taliban were able to control most of Afghanistan by 1996.

Pakistan played a pivotal role in bringing the Taliban into power. The prime objective of Pakistan's Afghanistan policy was to attain strategic depth against its old rival, India. This concept of 'strategic depth' was actually propagated by Pakistan's powerful military establishment. However, Eqbal Ahmad (1998) declared that in military terms this was a non-concept, unless one is referring to a hard-to-reach place where a defeated army might safely cocoon. In criticizing this concept, he wrote that a Taliban victory would likely augment Pakistan's political and strategic predicament. His analysis later proved to be prophetic, as discussed below.

Pakistan's military had assumed that the Taliban would recognize the Durand Line – the disputed boundary line between the two countries created by the British but never recognized by any Afghan regime, owing to their claims on some parts of the NWFP (renamed Khyber Pukhtun Khwah in 2010). The military also assumed that the Taliban would curb Pashtun nationalism in the NWFP and provide an outlet for Pakistan's Islamic radicals, thus forestalling an Islamic movement at home. In fact, just the opposite happened. The Taliban did not recognize the Durand Line and fostered Pashtun nationalism of an Islamic character, which led to the rise of the Pakistani Taliban in the NWFP and the Federally Administered Tribal Areas (FATA) of Pakistan. Further, the Taliban were to give sanctuary to the most violent Deobandi extremist groups involved in killing Pakistani Shias and advocating the overthrow of the ruling elite through an Islamic revolution. In short, the Taliban would not provide strategic depth to Pakistan; it would be the other way round (Rashid 2008, 187).

After the fall of the Taliban in the wake of NATO intervention in Afghanistan, the links between the DMM and the Taliban continued. In 2002, many Taliban members returned to their families who still lived in refugee camps in Pakistan, others returned to the Deobandi madaris in Pakistan from which they had been recruited. The JUI-led provincial governments in the NWFP and Balochistan, installed after the 2002 elections held under General Musharraf, provided considerable backing to the Taliban in raising funds and launching a campaign against the NATO forces in Afghanistan (Rashid 2010, 223). It was at this time that the Taliban started receiving help from al-Qaeda, who trained them about the use of improvised explosive devices (IEDs) and suicide attacks as well as sophisticated media outlets for producing DVDs and inspirational tapes against the NATO forces. After 2004, the number of suicide attacks by the Taliban markedly increased.

They also used websites, FM radio stations and e-mails, in sharp contrast to the Taliban of the 1990s, who abhorred the media. This newfound acumen actually came from al-Qaeda media outlet *as-Sahab* (Rashid 2010, 229–31). As the Taliban became more radicalized after their association with al-Qaeda, so did the Pakistani Deobandis fighting alongside the Taliban.

It was quite ironic that even after the fall of the Taliban government, Musharraf's military regime continued to provide clandestine support owing to the Pakistani army's fear that by backing the US invasion of Afghanistan, it had helped bring to power the Northern Alliance, whom the military loathed because they received support from Pakistan's regional rivals India, Iran and Russia (Rashid 2010, 224). However, it is also true that official patronage to the *jihad* in Kashmir and Afghanistan gradually decreased during that period and it had been reduced to a large extent by the time Musharraf resigned in 2008.

The outcome of this decrease in 'external *jihad*' in Afghanistan and Kashmir was a sharp increase in 'domestic *jihad*', marked by bombings and suicide attacks on security forces and non-combatant civilians in Pakistan. The real impact of the Taliban ideology was felt by the Pakistani state and society after 2001, when many Afghan Taliban fighters and commanders along with al-Qaeda activists escaped into FATA. With high mountains, rugged terrain, few roads and sparse populations, FATA made the ideal safe haven for the Taliban.

FATA is comprised of seven agencies (Khyber, Kurram, Orakzai, Mohmand, Bajaur and North and South Waziristan) with a population of about 4.5 million. FATA was established by the British in 1901 as a no man's land between Afghanistan and British India. Britain exercised indirect control over the agencies through its governor and political agents while allowing the tribal leaders to hold power over the local population. Pakistan has still maintained the system, which is now totally outdated. Efforts to introduce reforms in FATA were blocked on the one hand by the power-wielding tribal chiefs and on the other by the army, which used the region as a training ground for militants to be sent to Kashmir and Afghanistan (Rashid 2010, 236–8).

After 2001, at least two agencies, North and South Waziristan, were to become the training and recruiting grounds for the Afghan Taliban and their al-Qaeda allies for launching a guerrilla war against the US forces in Afghanistan. In the process, many activists from the outlawed Deobandi outfits of Pakistan like SSP, LeJ and JeM also gathered in FATA. Many locals also organized themselves into small groups or *lashkars* with the aim of protecting their guests as well as implementing the Deobandi version of Islam in the tribal areas.

Between 2001 and 2003, the military government of Musharraf made no effort to stop this activity in FATA and even denied the presence of the Afghan Taliban and al-Qaeda in Pakistan. However, after the two assassination attempts on Musharraf in December 2003, which were planned in South Waziristan, the army half-heartedly woke up to the threat. In March 2004, paramilitary troops of the Frontier Corps were sent to South Waziristan without any air cover, artillery or sufficient intelligence, and were badly mauled by the Wazir militants under Nek Mohammad. More than two hundred soldiers were killed and many more were captured and later executed.

On 24 April 2004, the army signed the first of several humiliating 'peace' deals with the Wazir militants in Shakai, pardoning Nek Mohammad and other Pakistani Taliban, offering compensation for their losses and freeing their prisoners on the condition that foreign militants would register with the authorities. However, in May 2004, Nek Mohammad objected to the process of registration and the fighting resumed. In June 2004, Nek Mohammad was killed in a drone attack by US forces (Pirzada 2013). The army signed further 'peace' deals in FATA while suffering even more setbacks and casualties, after which the militants were left in control of the territory they had already occupied. On 22 February 2005, a deal was signed with the militant group of Baitullah Mehsud in Sararogha, South Waziristan. Another deal was signed with the militants of North Waziristan on 5 September 2006. In 2007, yet another peace accord was signed with South Waziristan's militants, and on 21 June 2008 the army agreed to make a deal with the Afridi tribes and Lashkar-e-Islam of Mangal Bagh in the Khyber agency (Safi 2013). At the same time, these militant groups started setting up their own courts and administrations in FATA while killing more than three hundred tribal elders and chiefs who did not support them. Inspired by their Deobandi ideology, these militants banned TV, music and the Internet. They also destroyed schools for girls, while Deobandi madaris in the area multiplied (Rashid 2010, 238–9).

The impact of the FATA developments was soon felt in the settled areas of the NWFP. The Swat valley became the main centre for the local Taliban. Strategically located just 120 miles north of Islamabad and with a well-developed infrastructure, this valley provided access to the broad flatlands that extended into the Punjab, the largest province of Pakistan. In Swat, Mullah Fazlullah established an FM radio station in 2004 after setting up a madrassah. He began broadcasting inflammatory speeches against the United States and asked the locals to stop sending their girls to schools, avoid the evils of TV and music, and refuse polio vaccinations for their children to avoid infertility. He claimed to have burned TV sets, video equipment, computers and digital cameras worth 20 million rupees because 'these are the main sources of sin' (Khattak 2013). With the tacit support of the JUI-led provincial government, Fazlullah had set up a well-armed militia called Shaheen Force (Hussain 2013) and multiple FM radio stations when the army finally decided to intervene in 2007. The militants forced the army to withdraw, leaving Fazlullah in virtual control of the Swat valley.

On the other hand, the militant groups that had successfully resisted the army offensives for many years felt confident enough to launch their own movement in 2007 under the leadership of Baitullah Mehsud of South Waziristan. This movement was formed by two-dozen tribal militias and other groups from the Punjab and Kashmir and was named Tehreek-e-Taliban Pakistan (TTP; Movement of Pakistani Taliban). The aim of this loose umbrella organization of mostly Deobandi groups was to take over Pakistan and turn it into a *Shariah* state ruled by the Taliban. The TTP leadership declared Mullah Omar *ameerul momineen.* Mehsud, a close ally of the Afghan Taliban and Jalaluddin Haqqani, had fought for the Taliban in the 1990s. He was later charged with assassinating Benazir Bhutto in 2007 and was held responsible for dozens of suicide attacks in Pakistan (Rashid 2010, 236–40). He was killed in a drone attack in 2009 and replaced by another fellow tribesman from South Waziristan, Hakimullah Mehsud.

At around the same time, the rising extremism in the DMM was demonstrated at the Red Mosque (Lal Masjid) of Islamabad. In March 2007, radical Deobandis running a chain of madaris in Islamabad announced their intention of imposing *Shariah* in the capital. They closed a Chinese massage centre by force on the pretext of being un-Islamic and beat up a woman on the alleged charges of running a brothel. Later, they occupied a government building used as a children's library and announced that they would set up a female *madrassah* there. The Musharraf government was initially not willing to use force against these extremists in the hope of finding a peaceful solution. By the time the army was forced to attack the mosque in July 2007, hundreds of militants had already gathered there and tried to use the resident madrassah children as human shields. Many of these boarding students belonged to FATA and the NWFP. A three-day battle ensued in which about one hundred people including several children were killed. The militants who survived fled to FATA and were joined by the male relatives of the children killed in the mosque. They vowed revenge and became the core of a new group of suicide bombers for Baitullah Mehsud's TTP (Rashid 2010, 239–40). Many Deobandi activists from the Punjab also joined the TTP soon after its inception.

Meanwhile, Fazlullah merged his group with the TTP and was made head of its Swat chapter. The army again invaded Swat in 2008 but was defeated by the Taliban. The fighting forced a mass exodus and there were many civilian casualties. As the army withdrew, the Taliban swiftly imposed their interpretation of *Shariah*, including executions, floggings, the destruction of schools and homes, preventing women from leaving their homes and executing all those who had resisted their rule. In February 2009, the provincial government of the NWFP and the army signed a peace accord with the Taliban in Swat allowing *Shariah* courts to be set up in the province in return for the army's withdrawal and the Taliban's disarming. Without showing any willingness to disarm, the Taliban embarrassed the government by taking control of the local administration, police and education in the Swat valley. They also began expanding into other districts with the clear intention of trying to overthrow the Islamabad government. More than 2.5 million refugees fled from Swat and the adjoining districts of Buner and Dir. The army, impelled by international pressure and public opinion, finally attacked Swat in June 2009 with a much larger force than it had sent in before and drove the Taliban out of the valley. However, the entire leadership of Swati Taliban including some twenty commanders and Fazlullah managed to escape and later resumed sporadic attacks against the security forces in Swat (Rashid 2010, 240–41). In 2013, Fazlullah became the chief of the TTP after the death of Hakimullah Mehsud in a drone attack. By that time, the number of militant groups under the TTP had reportedly risen to 57, out of which 35 were under its direct control (Jawwad 2013).

Various groups attached to the TTP have been involved in hundreds of bombings and suicide attacks inside Pakistan since 2003. According to the South Asia Terrorism Portal (SATP), more than twenty-five thousand civilians and security personnel died in Pakistan between 2003 and 2012 during such attacks. According to a statement by the attorney of intelligence agencies before the Supreme Court of Pakistan in March 2013, the death toll in the terrorist attacks since 2001 had reached 49,000 (Raja 2013). The newest trend in these attacks has focused on targeting popular *sufi* shrines, which are visited by thousands of devotees daily, as the majority of the ordinary people in Pakistan express their religious sentiments through *sufism* (Jafferlot 2002, 232–4).

During recent years, the most revered shrines of *sufi* saints throughout Pakistan have been attacked by suicide bombers, killing hundreds of devotees. These and other suicide attacks have been categorically condemned by all sections of Pakistani society. However, the Deobandi response in this regard has generally been that of equivocation and tergiversation. The top Deobandi leadership in Pakistan has failed to condemn or stop such attacks and influential Deobandi *ulama* are reluctant to openly condemn or declare *fatwa* against them. In 2005, the Musharraf government tried unsuccessfully to convince the grand mufti of the Deobandis, Rafi Usmani, and the general secretary of Deobandi Wifaqul Madaris, Hanif Jallandhri, to issue a *fatwa* against suicide bombing (Jamal 2004). Another well-respected Deobandi scholar, Taqi Usmani, also refused cooperation with the government in this regard. According to a report in the *Daily Times*, the Interior Ministry believed that 'Taqi Usmani is a problem and a key man who can save a lot of lives by giving out one single statement [against suicide bombing]' (Chishti 2010). On the other hand, all the groups and religious leaders representing the majority Barelwi sect issue clear *fatawa* against such attacks from time to time. Even Ahle Hadith leader Hafiz Saeed opposed such attacks.

As regards the DMM, the only prominent Deobandi scholar who openly opposed the suicide attacks was Hassan Jan of Peshawar. To punish him for his opposition to what most Deobandi militant groups justify as a legitimate tactic, he was shot dead on 15 September 2007 (Gul 2009, 145). Some observers have also linked the murder of another influential Deobandi scholar, Mufti Nizamuddin Shamzai of Jamia Binouria, with his *fatwa* against suicide bombings (Nishapuri 2012). On 14 October 2008, the government managed to collect the signatures of a couple of less-important Deobandi *ulama* on a joint statement by all sects against suicide bombing inside Pakistan (*Daily Times* 2008). However, the Deobandi signatories at the same time ensured that their demand to stop the army operation against the local Taliban should be included in the joint statement, which was the outcome of the hectic efforts of a well-respected Barelwi scholar, Sarfraz Naeemi. On 12 June 2009, Naeemi was killed in a suicide attack reportedly carried out by the Deobandi militants.

Further, the Deobandi scholars have found it particularly hard to sympathize with the victims among shrine visitors. A Deobandi cleric and prayer leader at the Masjid Ahsanul Ulum in Gulshan-e-Iqbal, Karachi, bluntly refused to condemn the suicide attacks on *sufi* shrines (Chishti 2010). For the DMM, such practices are un-Islamic, and eliminating these activities is part of the 'practical tradition' they inherited from Waliullah's movement. The Ahle Hadith school of thought, whose origin can also be traced to Waliullah, also rejects these popular practices of folk Islam. However, Ahle Hadith holds little influence and following inside Pakistan as they represent less than 5 per cent of the population. It is the Deobandis, with their share of madaris exceeding 60 per cent and who enjoy the support of many political and militant groups, who seem to play a major role in challenging and influencing the values and customs of the mainstream Muslim society of Pakistan. More details of this third level of Deobandi extremism are given in the next section.

4.4 Countercultural Tendencies in the DMM since 1947

The DMM in Pakistan mostly behaved like an ascetic or mystic counterculture during the early years after partition. After failing to find a constitutional role for them, the founding fathers of Jamiat-ul-Ulama-e-Islam withdrew from the political arena and restricted themselves to the madaris. However, the second tier of Deobandi *ulama* continued their political activities without finding much success in terms of electoral representation.

As these two Deobandi streams gradually became disillusioned about the possibility of making Pakistan an Islamic state, the focus of the DMM became even narrower. The old Deobandi goal of forming an Islamic state was reduced to a distant dream. In this scenario, Deobandi politicians became more and more pragmatic in their approach through their motley alliances with secular, sectarian and liberal parties. Therefore, JUI, which was originally a party of Deobandi politicians, gradually became a party of politicians who happened to be Deobandis. Although JUI politicians took guidance from the *ulama* of Deobandi *madaris*, their politics was not much different from other political parties, which were either practising power politics or acting as pressure groups.

In the wake of JUI's pragmatic politics, the actual leadership of the DMM in Pakistan was retained by the *ulama* of Deobandi madaris. From the anti-Qadiyani movement of the 1950s to the socialism controversy of the 1960s, it was left to the Deobandi *ulama* to play the decisive role. These *ulama* also played the leading role by making JUI follow and defend its strategy of resistance against various madrassah reform initiatives taken by the state. After the 9/11 attacks, it was the Deobandi *ulama* like Mufti Shamzai of Jamia Binouria rather than the politicians of JUI who the government used to influence the Afghan Taliban for the ejection of Usama bin Laden from Afghanistan. Similarly, these *ulama* played a role in resolving the Lal Masjid crisis in Islamabad in 2007. Further, different Pakistani governments have been trying hard to stop suicide attacks by having the Deobandi *ulama* issue an explicit *fatwa* in this regard. In 2013, it was again the *ulama*, not the politicians of the DMM, who were requested by Prime Minister Nawaz Sharif's government to convince the TTP leadership to begin negotiations with the government. Despite all their influence and clout in the movement, the Deobandi *ulama*, not unlike their political counterparts, did not appear to be very optimistic about turning Pakistan into the Islamic state of their choice. Although these *ulama* frequently referred to the Islamization of Pakistan, they were not able to provide a roadmap or action plan for setting up an Islamic state. Still, through their writings and speeches they continued to provide guidance to Deobandi politicians of JUI through their interpretations of different political, religious, social and cultural issues.

For nearly three decades after the creation of Pakistan, the DMM was not able to establish itself in the arena of political Islam, which was mainly dominated by Jamaat-e-Islami. During those years, the DMM nurtured itself mainly as a movement that condemned and contradicted the popular customs and sociocultural as well as spiritual practices of mainstream Muslim society. Instead of producing religious scholars who could interpret the Quran and Hadith in the modern era, the output of the DMM in Pakistan was mostly restricted to sectarian scholars who specialized in condemning other Muslim sects and their practices. The target of these *ulama* was not just the folk

Islam that Barelwis claimed to represent, they also strongly condemned the followers of Shia Islam on the one hand and the *ghair muqallideen* belonging to Ahle Hadith as well as Jamaat-e-Islami on the other (see Appendix I). In other words, the DMM, like a typical counterculture, placed itself against the whole non-Deobandi Muslim society in Pakistan.

After having lost hope of setting up an Islamic state, the DMM's objectives were reduced to preservation and protection of their version of Islam and condemnation of the beliefs and practices of folk Sunni Islam, as well as censure of popular custom and castigation of Shia Islam. In this regard, the Deobandis in Pakistan, like their predecessors, employed two terms – *bidah* (innovation) and *shirk* (polytheism) – to denounce the beliefs and values of mainstream Muslim society. Although this was perfectly in line with the earlier tradition of Abdul Aziz and Rasheed Ahmed, the DMM leaders in Pakistan presented a more superficial and simplistic interpretation of the term *bidah* in order to make their message loud and clear to ordinary Muslims who did not hold a deeper knowledge of Islam. This approach largely followed the traditions of the Salafis (Wahhabis) of Arabia, who condemned and forcefully stopped all practices they considered *bidah* after they took power in the eighteenth century. Muhammad Ismail and Syed Ahmed also adopted a similar approach in the nineteenth century, but they simultaneously announced *jihad* against non-Muslims to gather the support of Indian Muslims in their favour. However, the situation of Pakistani Deobandis was quite different because they neither took power nor were they able to stir up *jihad* in Pakistan, where more than 95 per cent of people were Muslims. In this scenario, the DMM leaders in Pakistan adopted a countercultural approach that was more 'ascetic' and 'mystic' than 'activist'. Through the platform of Tablighi Jamaat, the Deobandis indirectly adopted a 'mystic' approach, whereby they had the opportunity to contact mainstream Muslims and ask them to join *tabligh* missions, during which they were not only taught about the basic tenets of Islam but also about the 'wrongful' and 'sinful' practices prevalent in mainstream Muslim society. The other platform the Deobandis employed was their mosques, where graduates of their madaris were given weekly opportunities to address ordinary Muslims during Friday prayers.

However, the DMM did not openly clash with mainstream society during the early years after independence. It was only after the involvement of the DMM in the Afghan *jihad* that it truly became active on the political front. However, by that time decades of training in the narrow sectarian and countercultural tradition had rendered the movement bereft of any broad vision about political Islam. Before that, the Deobandis did have an opportunity to head the provincial government in the NWFP after the 1970 elections. However, they failed to come up with concrete ideas for the implementation of *Shariah*.

When Mufti Mahmood of JUI became chief minister of the NWFP in 1972, Pakistan's Deobandis were given a great opportunity to establish a model for their original objective of turning Pakistan into an Islamic state. However, their vision about Islam had become so parochial by then that JUI could not present a viable road map for Islamization. Instead, they ended up announcing some symbolic initiatives: prohibiting alcohol and gambling; mandating observance of Ramadan (fasting); establishing an *ulama* advisory board; making reading of the Quran and study of Arabic compulsory for university admission; requiring women to be veiled in public; banning dowry; and making *shalwar-kamiz* (local dress comprising baggy cotton pants and a long shirt that extends to below the knees) mandatory for government servants (White 2008, 34). Ironically, these surface measures were to set the tone for JUI's future vision of Islamization in Pakistan.

At the same time, the DMM through mosques, madaris and *tabligh* missions had managed by the 1970s to make some impact on the urban middle class, who reckoned Deobandism as a middle ground between the Barelwis (whom the DMM portrayed as too lenient) and Ahle Hadith (whom they generally viewed as hardliners). This urban middle class supported the Deobandis through regular donations. Until that time, their activism was restricted to defending their madaris against any possible control or intervention by the government – a paranoid legacy of the colonial era (which still haunts the DMM). This situation continued until 1977, when JUI had the opportunity to adopt an activist approach. The JUI joined an alliance of nine political and religious parties (including the Barelwi JUP and Jamaat-e-Islami), which launched a successful mass movement against the populist prime minister Zulfiqar Ali Bhutto under the slogan *Nizam-e-Mustafa*. The movement led to a military coup by General Zia on 5 July 1977.

While pursuing its two-dimensional vision of political Islam, the DMM continued to beef up its sectarian and countercultural credentials. Therefore, when the DMM began to receive funds and patronage from domestic and foreign sources as well as opportunities to increase its influence in Pakistan in the 1980s, the movement was not able to rise above its countercultural and sectarian mindset. Resultantly, the DMM started behaving like an 'activist' counterculture. The major targets of this activist approach were the practices and beliefs of the Barelwis and Shias, who together represented around 75 per cent of Pakistani Muslims.

After the Soviet invasion of Afghanistan in 1979, when the intelligence agencies of the United States and Pakistan decided to use Pakistani madaris and their students to launch *jihad* against the Soviets, the Deobandis readily joined in. They saw in it the opportunity to revive Waliullah's vision of an Islamic state under the leadership of Pashtun Afghans. However, 1980s were a different time. The leadership of the DMM, unlike their predecessors, were not trained to uphold or revive the traditions of Waliullah or Abdul Aziz, or even Syed Ahmed. The Deobandi *ulama* of the 1980s fell far short of the genius of Waliullah and his eighteenth-century successors, whose traditions of intellectual synthesis and religious reform had long been disregarded by the DMM. Pakistan's Deobandis had limited themselves for about three decades to mere propagation of the basic tenets of Islam to ordinary Muslims, and criticism of the popular customs and sociocultural practices of the Muslim majority. The first generation of Deobandi leadership in Pakistan, who had some exposure to the traditions of political Islam, was already gone and the next generation merely represented a sect that was actually behaving like a counterculture vis-à-vis mainstream Muslim society.

When this countercultural leadership became involved in the Afghan war against the Soviets, they were not only exposed to funds and facilities provided by the United States and Saudi Arabia through ISI but also to Wahhabi Islam through their interaction with Arab *mujahideen*. This interaction with foreign radicals greatly contributed to the radicalization of the Deobandi activist counterculture (Rashid 2010, 238) and, gradually, it became more illiberal and rigid. This increasing inflexibility and intolerance led to the rise of a new kind of countercultural trend that not only condemned and anathematized the values and practices of Barelwis and Shias but also believed in physically eliminating these sects. This militant faction of Deobandis has not only been involved in killing thousands of Shia Muslims in Pakistan since the 1980s but has also been alleged to have supported the bombings of *sufi* shrines revered by the majority of Sunni Muslims.

The most esteemed shrines of *sufi* saints, such as Data Ganj Bakhsh in Lahore, Baba Farid in Pakpattan, Abdullah Ghazi in Karachi, Bari Imam in Islamabad, Rehman Baba in Peshawar and Sakhi Sarwar in Dera Ghazi Khan, have been attacked by suicide bombers in recent years, killing hundreds of devotees. This extremist approach does not fit any of Yinger's (1982) three types of counterculture – ascetic, mystic or activist. Neither can it be explained simply as terrorism, which is typically meant to hurt, directly or indirectly, some political authority against which the terrorists have grievances. As such, terrorism is the use of violence as a political weapon, generally targeted at a government or established order. Deobandi violence, on the other hand, is specifically directed against ordinary, powerless people. Therefore, one has to coin a separate term; this work suggests 'extremist counterculture'. It may be pointed out here that the recent attacks of the TTP against the security forces of Pakistan are more like typical terrorism because the TTP is trying to implement its vision of political Islam in Pakistan in the mould of the Taliban's rule in Afghanistan.

As regards the DMM's anti-Shia approach, the Deobandis have been involved in the killing of Shias since the inception of Sipah-e-Sahaba Pakistan (SSP). Later on, they founded Lashkar-e-Jhangwi (LeJ), a ferocious sectarian outfit that was even more ruthless and cold-blooded in its anti-Shia approach. Shias, in the meantime, also set up their own extremist organizations like Sipah-e-Muhammad to take revenge. Since the 1980s, thousands of Pakistanis have been killed during Shia–Sunni clashes, though in fact these are actually Shia–Deobandi clashes, because the majority (more than 60 per cent) of Sunnis in Pakistan belong to the Barelwi sect, which is not against Shia Islam. In these Shia–Deobandi clashes, the two sects have adopted two different approaches. While Shia groups have targeted the most influential Deobandi leaders campaigning against them, the Deobandis have indiscriminately killed Shias of every hue and class. For that reason, the number of Shias killed during such clashes is far more than the Deobandis.

Many Deobandi extremists took refuge in FATA and Afghanistan after 1998, when the Pakistani government launched an operation against the now-banned sectarian organizations. In FATA, SSP developed close links with the Taliban and other militants. After the fall of the Taliban government, many of these Deobandis returned to the NWFP and Balochistan in 2002. Since then, SSP and LeJ have been banned by the government. However, LeJ is still active in Karachi (Sindh), Quetta (Balochistan) and Gilgit-Baltistan (the Northern Areas). In Balochistan, they have targeted Shia Hazaras (Herald 2012, 55). The inspector general of that province categorically stated that LeJ and TTP were involved in the killing of Hazara communities in Quetta (Jamal 2012). Since 2001, more than six hundred Hazara Shias have been killed in about fifty attacks (*Dawn*, 11 January 2013). Disgruntled by such attacks, Hazaras are migrating from

Pakistan; around one hundred thousand of them have already migrated to Australia and other countries (Shahid 2012, 46–8).

After SSP was banned, it re-emerged as Ahle Sunnat wal Jamaat (ASWJ) under the leadership of Muhammad Ahmed Ludhianvi. Although ASWJ has apparently adopted a less aggressive stance, Ludhianvi has come up with a complicated formula for sectarian peace. He has declared that he would do 'anything and everything' for sectarian harmony as long as it does not compromise his party's 'avowed goals of turning Pakistan into a Sunni Islamic state and declaring Shias a religious minority', like the Qadiyanis in 1974 (Jamal 2002).

One may argue that Deobandi politics in Pakistan apparently did not behave like a typical counterculture. However, the *ulama* of Deobandi madaris apparently continued to follow the countercultural traditions of the DMM. These *ulama* had a great influence on Deobandi politicians and guided them on different issues in the light of Deobandi Islam. Their influence ensured that Deobandi politics remained countercultural in spirit, if not in form. That is why, given the chance to come into power (in the NWFP in 1970 and again in 2002), JUI's Islamization agenda was restricted mostly to announcing countercultural measures, which the Deobandis tried to explain in terms of *Shariah*, as was the case with Fazlullah's 'Islamic' rule in Swat from 2007 to 2009. As discussed in the previous section, Fazlullah's rule was known more for its anti-state and anti-society narratives than for its Islamic credentials.

While hailing the symbolic measures of the JUI governments as part of their Islamization agenda, the Deobandis have attributed their failure to impose *Shariah* during their stints in power to external factors. For example, in 1970, their government survived for less than ten months and their alliance with a secular party (NAP) hampered them. Similarly, they argue that after 2002 the secular president (Pervez Musharraf) and Supreme Court stopped them from imposing *Shariah* through their Hasba Bill. These arguments do carry some weight, and the Deobandis can be given the benefit of doubt in this regard. However, at the same time, the DMM can be criticized for not coming up with a clear, detailed roadmap for converting Pakistan into an Islamic state over the last 65 years. On the other hand, the DMM has simultaneously shown much clarity and commitment in condemning the social, cultural and spiritual values and practices of mainstream Muslim society in Pakistan, as shall be discussed in the next chapter.

Although the DMM was not given a free hand to rule in Pakistan, one may gather some idea about its vision of *Shariah* by reviewing the reign of the Deobandi Taliban in Afghanistan, where they enjoyed full power in all the provinces they occupied. As mentioned earlier, the Taliban's was primarily a Deobandi movement. Therefore, several measures taken by the Taliban to impose *Shariah* in Afghanistan highlight the countercultural complexion of the movement. For example, after coming into power, they immediately closed down girls' schools and restricted women to their homes, smashed TV sets, and forbade a whole array of entertainment and cultural activities including music, TV, Internet, videos, painting, playing cards, chess, kite flying, pigeon keeping and most sports and games (Rashid 2008, 2, 29, 219). The Taliban refused to recognize the very idea of culture. They banned Nawroz, the traditional Afghan new year celebrations, as well as Ashura processions by Shia Muslims. After coming into power, the Taliban also strongly condemned the instruments of mainstream politics and rejected the general elections because these were incompatible with *Shariah*. Further details about the Afghan Taliban's countercultural exposition are given in Appendix II.

The Taliban as rulers of Afghanistan implemented an extreme and narrow interpretation of *Shariah* that placed them in direct conflict with mainstream society: 'The Taliban were right, their interpretation of Islam was right and everything else was wrong and an expression of human weakness and a lack of piety' (Rashid 2008, 107). The Taliban interpretation divested Islam of all its legacies except theology, whereas Islamic philosophy, science, arts, aesthetics and mysticism were ignored (Rashid 2008, 211–12). This viewpoint can also be applied to the DMM as a whole.

Keeping in view the above discussion, the DMM hardly qualifies as a true religious or political movement. It may be added here that the Deobandi approach even about the theology of Islam was quite limited, narrow and superficial. Owing to its strict *taqlid* of Hanafi *madhab*, the DMM's contribution towards the theology of Islam had also become quite restricted. As mentioned earlier, the main focus of the DMM since its very inception has been to denounce the popular beliefs, social customs and practices of the subcontinent's Muslim population. Looking from another angle, the general approach and priorities of the present-day DMM might be to employ the theology of Islam to condemn these beliefs and practices. Instead of interpreting the religion with a broad canvas, the Deobandis have preferred to construe and excoriate the prevalent beliefs and practices of Muslim society in light of their own understanding of the theology of Islam. For example, when the Deobandis declared most of the popular customs and practices of Muslim society as *bidah*, they employed an especially narrow definition of that religious term, as shall be explained in the next chapter, which highlights the conflict between the Deobandi movement and folk Islam with respect to sociocultural and religious beliefs and practices.

Chapter 5

DEOBANDI ISLAM: COUNTERING FOLK ISLAM AND POPULAR CUSTOM

On the ideological level, a counterculture is a set of beliefs and values which radically reject the dominant culture of a society and prescribe a sectarian alternative. On the behavioural level, a counterculture is a group of people who, because they accept such beliefs and values, behave in [...] radically nonconformist ways.

Kenneth Westhues, *Society's Shadow: Studies in the Sociology of Countercultures* (1972, 9–10)

The objective of this chapter is to highlight the conflict between the DMM and the majority of Muslims in Pakistan. Unlike the previous chapters that identified the presence of countercultural tendencies in the history of the DMM, this chapter presents a direct comparison of the values and practices of folk Islam with those of Deobandi Islam. The chapter elaborates how the DMM has employed the theology of Islam to condemn and castigate the established religious and sociocultural beliefs and practices of mainstream Muslim society in Pakistan.

As mentioned in the introduction to this book, a large majority of Pakistani Muslims follow folk Islam – a charitable version of Islam broadly linked to spiritual and *sufi* traditions. For this work, folk Islam represents mainstream Muslim society, whereas the Deobandi sect, followed by about 20 per cent Pakistani Muslims, epitomizes a counterculture. The current chapter identifies the most prominent beliefs and practices of folk Islam as well as popular customs that have been condemned by the Deobandis. The chapter not only presents the arguments of Deobandi scholars in this regard but also compares their views with the perspectives of non-Deobandi *ulama*, mostly from the Barelwi sect that generally represents folk Islam in Pakistan. The latter viewpoint has been included to highlight the justification and continuation of these beliefs and practices by the majority of Pakistani Muslims.

For this discourse on the DMM's countercultural approach, the views and *fatawa* of three prominent Deobandi scholars – Ashraf Ali Thanvi (1863–1943), Abdul Haq (1912–88) and Yousaf Ludhianvi (1932–2000) – have been selected to represent the Deobandi persuasion. Thanvi is considered one of the most influential *ulama* of the DMM. He was the student and spiritual disciple of the DMM's founder Rasheed Ahmed and authored many books on varied subjects ranging from translation of the Quran to *tasawwuf* and from the role of women to reform of popular custom. Thanvi has a large following among Deobandis of both India and Pakistan. Two of his books are part of the *Dars-e-Nizami* syllabus in Deobandi madaris. These are *Jamal-ul-Quran* (Beauty of the

Quran) for male students and *Bahishti Zewar* (Heavenly ornaments) for female students (Khalid 2002, 388, 415).

The second Deobandi scholar, Abdul Haq, graduated from and taught at Darul Ulum Deoband before returning to his native town of Akora Khattak near Peshawar after the partition of India. Here he established his madrassah, Darul Ulum Haqqania, which played an active role in organizing the DMM in the newly established state of Pakistan. Apart from being a leading religious scholar, Haq participated in active politics through the platform of JUI and won three elections to become a member of the National Assembly. He played a pivotal role in recruiting madrassah students for the Afghan resistance against the Soviets and issued several *fatawa* to declare *jihad* in Afghanistan, Kashmir, Burma and Bosnia (Haq 2009, vol. 5, 288–94). His madrassah is presently run by his son, Samiul Haq, who heads his own faction of JUI and is known as 'the father of the Taliban' (*Dawn*, 22 January 2014). This chapter mainly takes excerpts from the compilation of Abdul Haq's religious edicts titled *Fatawa-e-Haqqania*.

The third Deobandi scholar, Yousaf Ludhianvi of Jamia Binouria, played an important role in organizing and strengthening the DMM in Pakistan. He was on the forefront of the Deobandi resistance to various madrassah reform initiatives taken by different governments in Pakistan. He actively participated in the anti-Qadiyani movement and also became involved in the anti-Shia drive of the DMM before he was murdered (allegedly by Shia militants) in 2000. He was a prolific writer and authored more than thirty books. He was editor of two monthly Deobandi journals and his weekly column on religious issues was published in Pakistan's largest-selling Urdu newspaper, *Jang*, for more than thirty years.

Before providing details of Deobandi criticism against dominant beliefs and practices, it would be pertinent to add here a brief discussion on *bidah* – a term repeatedly employed by the DMM to condemn folk Islam.

5.1 Different Interpretations of *Bidah*

The Deobandis in Pakistan, not unlike Ahle Hadith or the Salafis, have adopted an oversimplified definition of *bidah*. According to them, *bidah* is just the opposite of the Sunnah – the practice of the Prophet (Ludhianvi n.d., 90). The Deobandis have preferred to interpret *bidah* only as a negative term, as opposed to the majority of Islamic scholars, who declare that *bidah* can be good as well. The Deobandis perhaps thought that if the people accepted the positive aspect of *bidah*, the DMM would be deprived of its best weapon against the practices of the majority of Muslims. It is amazing that the Deobandis were so obsessed with the concept of *bidah* that they preached abandonment of all the practices followed by *ahle bidah* (those who practice *bidah*) – a term employed by the DMM to refer to the Barelwis and Shias who together represent around 75 per cent of Pakistani Muslims. The Deobandis have also declared that one should even avoid resemblance with the *ahle bidah* (Ludhianvi n.d., 120).

Ludhianvi (n.d., 92–4) has defined *bidah* as anything that was not in practice until the time of the Prophet, his *sahaba* (companions), *tabi'un* (followers, the generation of

Muslims who lived with the *sahaba*) and *tabi'ut tabi'een* (followers of the followers, i.e. those who lived with *tabi'un*).

Ludhianvi has identified two types of *bidah*; one is *bidat-e-aitqadi* (innovation in faith) and the other is *bidat-e-'amali* (innovation in acts). *Bidat-e-aitqadi* is said to occur when a person or a group of persons follows ideas that oppose the teachings of the Prophet and three generations of Muslims after him. This type of *bidah* can be divided into further categories, some of which can lead to outright *kufr* or non-belief (e.g. the Qadiyani faith, which questions the finality of the Prophethood of Muhammad, PBUH), while others are simply *dhalala* or misguidance. As for *bidat-e-'amali*, it does not involve any change in basic faith but is caused by pursuing acts and practices that were not followed by *salaf-as-saliheen* (pious predecessors) – a term generally used to refer to the first three generations after the Prophet.

The Deobandis have further expanded the scope of *bidah* by declaring that any practice which becomes a custom for the people needs to be condemned even if it is otherwise a good act in itself. Apart from the practices which the DMM have linked to *shirk* or *kufr*, the Deobandis have deplored most religious and sociocultural practices mainly on the grounds that these have become popular customs and cultural activities. This approach makes the DMM in Pakistan more of a countercultural movement than a religious reform movement.

Contrary to the simplistic approach of the Deobandis to divide *bidah* simply into two categories (i.e. *aitqadi* and *'amali*, both of which are condemned), most Islamic scholars have come up with a broader division of *bidah* into *bidat-e-hasanah* (good innovation) and *bidat-e-saiyyah* or *bidat-e-dhalala* (bad innovation), as detailed below.

The Deobandis have based their interpretation of *bidah* on the Hadith of Imam Muslim (2004, vol. 2, 335), in which the Prophet says that every innovation is a misguidance and every misguidance leads to hellfire. Ludhianvi (n.d., 97) has supported this viewpoint by quoting another Hadith in which the Prophet disapproves of those who change his Sunnah by turning back from the *deen* – the way of Islam (Mishkaat, n.d., vol. 1, 59).

While the Deobandis took these Ahadith (plural of Hadith) for their literal meanings, several imams and *muhadditheen* (experts of Hadith) have interpreted the above-mentioned Ahadith in a wider context. On the first Hadith, there is a widespread consensus among Islamic scholars that it is concerned only with wrongful innovation. In support of their argument they have quoted the second caliph Umar, who started the practice of *tarawih* (night-time prayers in congregation during Ramadan) and called it *ni'mal bidah* (good innovation). Further, Imam Shafi'i, Imam al Qartabi and Imam Mubarak al-Jazri have quoted the following Hadith of Imam Muslim to support the division of *bidah* into good and bad (Qadri 2005, 14): 'Whoever institutes a good practice in Islam has its reward and the reward of all those who practice it until the Day of Judgement without lessening the rewards of the latter. And whoever institutes a bad practice in Islam bears its onus and the onus of all those who practice it until the Day of Judgement without lessening the onus of the latter' (Muslim 2004, vol. 6, 265).

As regards the second Hadith quoted by Ludhianvi, different scholars have put forward different interpretations about the people who turned away from the Sunnah and *deen*. Abdullah bin Abbas, a companion of the Prophet, described them as *murtadeen* (plural of *murtad* – an apostate), who renounced Islam immediately after the

Prophet's death. The first caliph, Abu Bakr, fought against these *murtadeen* until they were killed or reverted back to Islam. Imam Tabari also interpreted those mentioned in the Hadith as *murtadeen*, while Imam Haakim and Hafiz ibn Abdul Barr have referred to them as they who were first involved in the murder of the third caliph, Usman, and then later fought against the fourth caliph, Ali, before being labelled as *khawarij* (Qadri 2010, 30–32). Imam Ibn-e-Hajr Asqalani is also of the same view (Raz 2004, vol. 6, 176).

Imam Shafi' has stated that those acts which are against the Quran, the practice of the Prophet and his *sahaba* as well as against the *ijma* (consensus) of the *ummah* (the Muslim community) are *bidat-e-dhalala*. On the other hand, those acts which are performed for the general good and don't contradict *Shariah* are *bidat-e-hasanah* (Qadri 2005, 17–18). Some scholars like Imam Ibn-e-Kathir and Imam Ibne Taiymiyah have divided *bidah* into *bidat-e-shariah* and *bidat-e-lughwia*; the former is considered wrong while the latter is generally considered good, depending on its objective (Qadri 2005, 45–7).

Apart from the above two interpretations, scholars like Imam Azzuddin Abdul Aziz bin Abd-us-Salam, Imam Shahabuddin al-Maliki, Imam An-Nawawi, Imam al-Qastalani (quoted in Qadri 2005, 29–67) have further divided *bidah* into the following five categories in line with the five principles of *fiqh*, i.e. *haram* (forbidden), *makruh* (detestable), *halal* (permissible), *mustahab* (recommended) and *mubah* (indeterminate and undefined). The first two of the following categories fall under bad innovation, while the last three come under good innovation (Qadri 2010, 49–51).

1. *Bidat-e-muharramah*

   This is an innovation which leads to conflict within Islam, e.g. establishing new religions like the Qadriyah, Jabriyah and Qadiyani religions. Opposition to such religions is compulsory for Muslims and that defiance is called *bidat-e-wajibah*, as mentioned below.

2. *Bidat-e-makruhah*

   This innovation causes abandonment of the Prophet's *Sunnah*, e.g. unnecessary adornment and embellishment of mosques or the Quran (although later *ulama* adopted a softer stance on these practices).

3. *Bidat-e-mubahah*

   This term is used for those practices which are not forbidden by *Shariah* and Muslims follow them without hoping to receive a reward (*sawab*) from God for such practices. Examples include handshaking after morning (*Fajr*) and evening (*Asr*) prayers as well as having lavish food and drinks.

4. *Bidat-e-mustahabah*

   This is a new act or practice which is neither declared forbidden nor compulsory, but Muslims do with the hope of *sawab*, e.g. the construction of madaris and free inns for travellers, *tarawih* prayers in Ramadan, social welfare and reform work, explanation of issues regarding *tasawwuf* or spiritual Islam.

5. *Bidat-e-wajibah*
   This is an innovation which becomes compulsory for the survival and growth of Islam, e.g. teaching and learning the principles of Arabic *nahw* (grammar) and *sarf* (morphology) for understanding the Quran and Hadith as well as developing doctrines and dogmas for *fiqh* and *Shariah*.

Taking lead from these interpretations of *bidah*, Qadri (2010, 36–8) has stated that the term *bidat-e-dhalala* would not include minor differences among Muslims but would rather be those crises of *fitnah* (evil trial), which would lead to: i) *irtadad* (apostasy), ii) contradiction of the fundamentals of Islam and the Prophet's Sunnah, or iii) *ikhtalaf-e-kaseer* (major difference), causing divisions and infighting among Muslims. Accordingly, Qadri has concluded that small and minor differences, as with Eid Milad-un-Nabi, *urs* and methods of *isal-e-sawab*, cannot be termed *bidat-e-dhalala* or misguidance because these neither lead to apostasy nor contradict the teachings of Islam or the Sunnah. He has simultaneously claimed that all such practices are linked to *Shariah* and have been derived from the practices of the *salaf-as-saliheen*.

Another Hadith of Imam Muslim (2004, vol. 4, 341) that is frequently quoted by the Deobandis to condemn the popular practices of Muslims says, 'Whosoever invents a new thing in our religion is rejected.' The Deobandis employ the literal and apparent meaning of this Hadith to generally conclude that any new practice for which there is no *nass* (a known or clear legal injunction) available from the Quran and Hadith is to be rejected as wrongful innovation. However, non-Deobandi *ulama* interpret this Hadith to apply to those who invent a new belief or those who invent a practice or action which is in contradiction with the Quran and Sunnah. According to Qadri (2007, 20–25), the simplistic Deobandi interpretation is wrong because if it is believed that any act which has not been mentioned in the Quran and Hadith is rejected or declared *haram*, then the established *Shariah* concept of *mubah* would become irrelevant and innumerable *mubah* acts in Islam would become *haram*. (*Mubah* is a term denoting an action as neither forbidden nor recommended while giving it a degree of approval.)

At another level, Qadri (2007, 160) has tried to reduce the *bidah* debate of the Deobandis to irrelevance by referring to another well-recognized principle of *Shariah* that has been approbated by Allama Shaami, Imam Asqalani, Imam Siyuti and Imam Sarkhasi. According to this principle, the reality of a thing is its legitimacy. Imam Asqalani has explained this principle by stating that anything which was not done by the Prophet is not illegitimate until it is proved *haram* by the established arguments of *Shariah*. Therefore, it has been concluded that everything is *mubah* until Allah and His Prophet declare it to be *haram* (Qadri 2007, 160).

5.2 The DMM and Dominant Beliefs and Practices in Pakistan

As mentioned above, the Deobandis have generally used the term *bidah* with a negative connotation, considering it wrongful innovation that is either *makruh* (detestable) or *haram* (forbidden). Various popular customs as well as dominant sociocultural and religious practices in Pakistan that have been consistently condemned by the DMM can be divided into three broad categories. The first two categories are directly related to folk Islam while the third concerns non-religious popular customs and cultural activities.

The first category includes those practices which can be termed *bidat-e-makruhah* (detestable innovation) from a Deobandi perspective. The second category covers those practices which the DMM consider *bidat-e-muharramah* (forbidden innovation) on the pretext that they lead to *shirk* and *kufr*. The third category includes those norms and practices which cannot be considered *bidah* in the sense that Pakistani Muslims do not link them to the religion. However, the Deobandis have condemned such practices and traditions using the same line of argument they employed against *bidah*.

A brief discussion of these three categories is given below.

5.2.1 Popular practices considered **makruh** *by the DMM*

The most important practice in this category is the celebration of the birth of the Prophet Muhammad (PBUH) on the 12th day of Rabi-ul-Awwal (the third month of the Islamic calendar). This day is popularly called Eid Milad-un-Nabi. The word Eid is otherwise used for two annual festive occasions for Muslims, one after the fasting month of Ramadan and the other in the month of *hajj* (pilgrimage). The name Eid has been given to the Prophet's birthday in order to highlight the happiness attached to this day, which is marked by large public processions as well as religious gatherings called *milad* in homes and mosques. At these meetings, speeches about the Prophet are made, *na'at* (poetry in the Prophet's honour) is recited and *durood-o-salam* (blessings and peace) for him is offered. Many Muslims distribute food among the poor as well as to friends and neighbours. Streets and market places are decorated with banners and buntings. At night, public buildings, market places and houses are decorated with colourful lighting. The Deobandis have condemned all these activities on different pretexts, as shall be explained later in this chapter.

Isal-e-sawab is another religious practice made controversial by the Deobandis. *Isal-e-sawab* is the Islamic practice of carrying out a good act and conveying its reward to some other Muslim. The Deobandis, like the majority of Pakistani Muslims, believe that the practice of *isal-e-sawab* is legitimate. However, they have simultaneously condemned this practice when it is carried out on a particular day or occasion (Ludhianvi n.d., 185–7). Their logic for this viewpoint is that Islam does not allow fixing a particular day for an act of goodness or elective (*nafl* or *nafila*) worship. On the basis of that interpretation, the DMM has deplored a lot of religious activities which are popular among Pakistani Muslims. These include the practices of *qul* or *teejah* (prayers and distribution of food for the deceased on the 3rd day after death), *chehlum* or *chaleeswan* (prayers and food distribution on the 40th day after death), *barsi* (death anniversary), *giyarhwin* (distribution of food and milk on the 11th day of every Islamic month for the *isal-e-sawab* of great saint Abdul Qadir Jilani) and *urs* (death anniversaries of saints), etc.

The Deobandis believe that if elective practices are performed on fixed and particular days, these gradually become obligatory (*fardh*), which is against the spirit of Islam. Apart from that, the Deobandis also condemn such practices for being extravagant and wasteful as well as resembling Hindu and Shia rituals. Abdul Haq (2009, vol. 2, 73–4) pronounced a *fatwa* that *isal-e-sawab* on death anniversaries is against *Shariah* and directed Muslims to avoid such nonsense and tawdry customs, saying that they were derived from Jews and Hindus.

Further, the Deobandis believe that *isal-e-sawab* is not done to convey rewards to a saint, rather people do it in the hope of winning favours or avoiding the saint's wrath (Ludhianvi n.d., 188–91). This Deobandi interpretation comes in the wake of the belief that saints, even after their death, are able to help their followers through their *tasarruf* or spiritual power (a concept denied by the Deobandis, who consider it *shirk*).

Haq (2009, vol. 2, 46) has declared in his *Fatawa-e-Haqqania* that although *isal-e-sawab* for the dead is permissible at any time, the practice of common Muslims to fix a particular day in this regard is forbidden. Thanvi (2002, 138–45) has castigated the *isal-e-sawab* practices after death on the grounds that these have gradually become routine social customs, which people feel bound to follow even when they do not have the resources to finance them. In order to give authenticity to this countercultural approach, Thanvi (2011, 15–18) has even declared, 'Whoever opposes the popular customs and practices is a saint and God's favourite person.'

Based on the above-mentioned line of argument, the DMM has opposed the following practices: distributing sweets after reciting the Quran in *tarawih* prayers during Ramadan; eating and distributing sweet vermicelli on Eid, and *halwa* (a dense sweet confection made of flour) on Shab-e-Barat (the 15th night of the Islamic month of Sha'ban); and distributing *haleem* and *khichrra* (salty dishes made from meat, rice and pulses) as well as sweet drinks on Ashura (the 10th day of Muharram).

However, these popular custom and practices have continued to be followed by the majority of Pakistani Muslims, who consider these to be acts of generosity or part of their culture and tradition. They hardly consider these practices to be an obligatory part of the religion, as has been portrayed by the DMM.

Some other religious practices which have been condemned by the DMM as wrongful innovations include kissing one's thumbs when the Prophet's name is mentioned during *adhan* (call for prayers), handshaking after congregational prayers and saying loud *dhikr* (short phrases recited in remembrance/invocation) after prayers. The DMM deplores these practices on the basis that they were not followed by the Prophet and the *salaf-as-saliheen*. Although these last two practices are not strictly followed by Pakistani Muslims as part of their religion, the Barelwi *ulama* consider these to be *mustahab*. These *ulama* have also traced the history of such acts in different Islamic traditions that the Deobandis disregard as weak or wrong. For example, Ibne Abbas stated in a Hadith that loud *dhikr* after prayers was a commonplace practice during the Prophet's time (Naeemi n.d., 183). This has also been reported in a Hadith by Imam Muslim (2004, vol. 2, 150). Further, the practice of kissing thumbs has been linked to a tradition mentioned in famous books on *fiqh* such as *Fatawa-e-Shami*, *Kitab-ul-Firdous*, *Fatawa-e-Sufia* and *Kanz-ul-Ibad*. Allama Ismail Haqqi has acknowledged in *Tafseer Rooh-ul-Bayan* that the tradition is weak. However, he has simultaneously mentioned the agreement among the *muhadditheen* that it is legitimate to accept and act upon a weak Hadith for the sake of creating love for Islam and fear of God (Al-Mustafa 2010, 285–9).

As for the practice of handshaking after congregational prayers, Deobandi Ashraf Ali Thanvi has forbidden it, whereas Abdul Haq (2009, vol. 2, 46) has declared that it is impermissible only when it is considered obligatory, though it should generally be avoided. In another *fatwa*, Haq (2009, vol. 2, 95) has declared this practice to be *bidah* and against *Shariah*. The Barelwi *ulama* have traced the origin of this practice to the writings of Imam Izzuddin Abdus-Salam, Imam al-Jazri, Imam al-Haitimi, Sheikh al-Khateeb and Mulla Ali Qari, who have declared this practice to be *bidat-e-mubahah* – neither forbidden nor recommended (Qadri 2005, 13, 32, 71).

According to Mulla Ali Qari, handshaking after morning (*Fajr*) and evening (*Asr*) prayers is considered to be *bidat-e-mubahah* in Shafi'i *madhab*, while it is considered *bidat-e-makruhah* (detestable innovation) by the Hanafi school (Qadri 2005, 73–4). This practice is generally followed in Barelwi mosques in Pakistan. However, they don't consider it to be a compulsory part of the religion. Further, this is also practised by Muslims in many other countries like Malaysia, Indonesia and Turkey. Although opposition to this practice can be explained in the light of different *fiqh*, the DMM has criticized this practice mainly in the light of their countercultural approach, otherwise the huge majority of Muslims in Pakistan, including Barelwis and Deobandis, belong to Hanafi *madhab*. The same is true about the DMM's approach towards widespread religious practices like loud *dhikr* and joint *dua* (supplication) after congregational prayers as well as *dua* after funeral prayers.

5.2.2 Beliefs and practices declared **haram** *by the DMM*

This category includes those beliefs and practices which have been castigated by the DMM far more aggressively than those included in the first category. The reason for this greater intensity is that, according to the Deobandis, the beliefs and practices included in this category lead to *shirk* and *kufr*.

The beliefs and practices covered in this category can be further divided into four subcategories. The first subcategory includes popular practices that are performed while visiting graves (*ziyarat-e-quboor*). For example, kissing, standing in respectful manner, or bowing or prostrating before graves; lighting lamps on shrines; laying flower wreaths or cloth sheets on graves; and offering *nadhr* or *mannat* on a shrine (like distribution of food, or sacrificing an animal on the fulfilment of some particular wish).

The second subcategory concerns the prevalent beliefs regarding the status and power of the Prophet. According to such beliefs, the Prophet is a *noor* or light of God (not a human being like us); he is *haazir* and *naazir* (i.e. he has the spiritual power to be present wherever he wants to as well as the power to listen and see); he is the knower of hidden knowledge (*ilm-ul-ghaib*); and he holds the power of *tasarruf* (ability to make things happen). The Deobandis have condemned these beliefs to be *shirk*.

The third subcategory includes the practices of calling for help (*istamdad*) from anyone other than God and praying to God to give something through the mediation (*wasilah*) of some saint or prophet. The DMM has also declared these practices *shirk*.

The fourth subcategory includes practices of Shia Muslims with respect to Ashura in the Islamic month of Muharram, when they commemorate the martyrdom of Imam

Hussain, through *taziyah* processions and mourning meetings. The DMM has declared these Shia activities *shirk* and *kufr*. In fact, many Deobandi scholars have declared Shia Muslims *kuffar* through different *fatawa*. The latest *fatwa* in this regard was issued in 1987 by the Deobandi *ulama* of India and Pakistan (Naumani 1988). Despite considering Shias non-Muslims, the Deobandis continue to condemn the practices of Ashura in order to influence the majority of Sunni Muslims who not only consider Shias to be Muslims but also tacitly approve the tradition of Ashura to mourn the martyrdom of Imam Hussain. Details are given in Section 5.3.

5.2.3 Sociocultural practices condemned by the DMM

This third category includes those customs and practices which are otherwise not considered part of the religion. As mentioned in the last chapter, the Deobandis applied the term *bidah* to practices which did not exist during the times of *salaf-as-saliheen* and which are considered religious or pious acts by the followers of such practices. Therefore, the Deobandi definition of *bidah* cannot as such be applied to the customs and practices included in this category. However, it is interesting to note that the approach and the intensity of Deobandi condemnation with respect to these practices are not much different from what they employed vis-à-vis the beliefs and practices declared *bidah*, *shirk* and *kufr*.

The most popular customs and practices that the DMM have condemned in this regard are the different ceremonies held at weddings. Thanvi (2002, 54–89) has described a total of 100 customs and ceremonies observed by Muslims during a typical wedding in North India in the twentieth century. Although most of these customs are not followed in Pakistan (and perhaps not even in modern-day North India), several of these marriage-related activities are still being performed in many parts of Pakistan. These include: *mayoon* (secluding the bride a few days before the marriage for her beautification through the use of special facial and body masks); *mehndi* (where the female guests colour their hands and feet with henna and sing songs); lighting and fireworks; *sehra bandi* (tying to the bridegroom a shiny golden-coloured headdress with garlands hanging over the face); displaying *jahez* (dowry from the bride's family) and *barri* (gifts from the groom's family); *joota chhupai* (in which the sisters and friends of the bride hide the groom's shoes); female relatives of the bride offering milk and sweets to the groom; and distributing dry dates among the guests after the *nikah* (marriage registration), etc.

Further, the Deobandis have also opposed popular sports and festivals as well as the practice of observing national and international days. They have also declared *haram* sports like chess, kite flying, pigeon keeping and the use of fireworks to mark a happy occasion. Details of the Deobandi viewpoint in this respect are given in Section 5.4.

5.3 The DMM against Folk Islam

This section focuses on those values and practices of folk Islam which the DMM has generally criticized as *makruh* or *haram*. A detailed discussion of these widespread practices is given below.

5.3.1 Eid Milad-un-Nabi (celebration of the Prophet's birth)

Haq (2009, vol. 2, 92) declared in his *Fatawa-e-Haqqania* that the practice of celebrating the birth anniversary of the Prophet Muhammad (PBUH) on the 12th day of Rabi-ul-Awwal was the worst kind of *bidah*. Ludhianvi (n.d., 76–90) also condemned this practice on the following grounds:

1. This practice was never followed by the early generations of Muslims for about six hundred years after the Prophet. It was actually introduced in the year AH 602 by Sultan Abu Saeed Muzaffar in Iraq.
2. The Prophet allowed only two Eid celebrations for Muslims, i.e. Eid-ul-Fitr (after the fasting month of Ramadan) and Eid-ul-Adha (during the month of *hajj* or pilgrimage). Further, the Prophet himself advised his companions not to make his grave an Eid. So this event cannot be called Eid because Eid is an Islamic term and applying it to the birth anniversary of the Prophet is *tahreef fid deen* (alteration in the religion).
3. A lot of money is spent on lighting and decoration on this occasion. This leads to prodigality, which is condemned by Islam.
4. Eid Milad-un-Nabi shows resemblance with Christianity, which celebrates the birth anniversary of Jesus Christ (PBUH) as Christmas on 25 December. Therefore, it is wrong because of *tashabbuh bil kuffar* (resemblance with the non-believers). The resemblance with Shias as well as Christians has been condemned in the light of a Hadith in which the Prophet says, 'He who imitates a people is from them' (Hanbal n.d., vol. 3, 165).
5. In Milad gatherings, unauthentic stories of the miracles of the Prophet are told and young men without beards recite poetry (*na'at*) in the Prophet's praise, which elevates him to an extent that violates the principles of *tawhid*.

Ashraf Thanvi (2002, 107–20) of the DMM has declared that Milad should not be celebrated in a particular manner and on a particular date. Thanvi derived this approach from the following two Ahadith narrated by Abdullah bin Abbas.

In the first Hadith, Abdullah advises the Muslims that 'it is binding on each of you not to leave any share for the Satan in your prayers. That share is there when you consider it obligatory to turn towards your right side after finishing the prayers. I saw the Prophet on many occasions turning towards his left side after completing his prayers' (Muslim 2004, vol. 2, 235). In the second Hadith, he says that the Prophet advised against making a particular practice of fasting on Fridays and worshipping on Friday nights (Thanvi 2002, 112–13).

Thanvi repeatedly employed these two Ahadith to condemn many popular customs and practices of Muslim society in the subcontinent. He argued that Islam does not allow the fixing of a date and time for carrying out a pious or good act that is otherwise not declared obligatory in *Shariah*. However, non-Deobandi scholars have disagreed with this approach by stating that it is impossible to survive in this world without timetables and schedules. They have quoted many Ahadith supporting the idea of affixing a particular time for a particular act. For example, according to a Hadith narrated by Abi Sa'ad, the Prophet fixed a particular day of the week for teaching Islam to women (Bukhari 2004, vol. 1, 250). Similarly, Abdullah bin Masood, a companion of the Prophet, used to hold a meeting every Thursday to give religious advice and guidance to Muslims (Niazi 2012, 47).

Coming to other counterarguments against the above-mentioned Deobandi objections, the proponents of Eid Milad-un-Nabi have declared that this event was celebrated by ordinary Muslims a long time before AH 602 and Sultan Abu Saeed Muzaffar only made it official, making it even more popular among Muslims. Imam Asqalani has stated that Muslims were holding Milad meetings even before that (Attari 2009, 229–31). Refuting the DMM's claim that Milad is *bidah*, followers of this practice have quoted the following Quranic verses and Ahadith to support their celebrations to mark the birth of the Prophet (Attari 2009, 226–9).

Quranic verses:

1. *And remember Allah's favour upon you.* (3:103)

Here the 'favour' is interpreted as the Prophet.

2. *Say you, only Allah's grace and only His mercy, on it therefore let them rejoice. That is better than all their wealth.* (10:58)

Here the Prophet is represented by Allah's grace and mercy, for which Muslims should rejoice and spend their wealth on this rejoicing. Al-Mustafa (2010, 28–9) has stated that such spending on Milad is superior to any other spending, thus refuting the DMM's objection regarding prodigality.

3. *Undoubtedly, Allah did a great favour to the Muslims that in them from among themselves sent a Messenger.* (3:164)

It has been inferred from this verse that Muslims should feel jubilant for this favour from Allah.

Ahadith:

1. After the death of Abu Lahab (the Prophet's uncle and an avowed enemy of Islam), some of his family members saw him in a dream in a very bad condition and asked him about his situation. He replied that he received no reward except for a supply of water from his finger, the same finger with which he had indicated to free his slave girl Sobia to celebrate the birth of his nephew, i.e. the Prophet. (Bukhari 2004, vol. 6, 593)

Abdul Haq Muhaddis Dehlwi has employed this Hadith to support Milad celebrations and expenditure in this regard. He has argued that if a *kafir* and enemy of Islam like Abu Lahab can be rewarded in this regard, then Muslims would be recompensed by God in a far more generous manner.

2. According to a Hadith by Imam Muslim (2004, vol. 3, 167), when the Prophet was asked about his practice of fasting on Mondays, he replied that he was born on that day and that the Quran was also revealed to him on the same day.

This Hadith has been used to show that the Prophet himself celebrated his birth by thanking God through fasting.

Many great imams and religious scholars have supported the practice of celebrating Milad. These include Imam Jazri, Imam Qastalani, Ismail Haqqi, Ibn-e-Hajr Haitimi, Imam Sakhawi, Imam Siyuti, Abdul Haqq Muhaddis Dehlwi and Mujaddid Alf Saani (Attari 2009, 231–8). It is interesting to note that Shah Waliullah also supported Milad and many other practices which were to be later condemned by the DMM (Jaaisi 2007, 5–6).

In challenging the Deobandi objection of *tahreef fid deen* to declaring the 12th day of Rabi-ul-Awwal Eid, the Barelwi *ulama* have appealed to the following Ahadith, which indicate that there are more than two Eids.

1. The Prophet said, 'verily Friday is the king of all days and its esteem is even superior to Eid-ul-Adha and Eid-ul-Fitr in the eyes of Allah. Adam was created, descended to the earth and then given death by God on Friday' (Amin 2010, 83).
2. When Ibne Abbas recited Quranic verse 5:3 ('This day I have perfected your religion for you and completed my favour upon you and have chosen Islam as the religion for you') in front of a Jew, the latter said that if this verse had been revealed to the Jews, they too would celebrate Eid. Ibne Abbas replied that this verse was revealed on a day when there were two Eids for Muslims as it was Friday as well as the Day of Arafa – the ninth day of the last month of the Islamic calendar and the most important day during *hajj* (Bukhari 2004, vol. 1, 223).
3. Once during the Prophet's time, Eid fell on a Friday. The Prophet told the Muslims that two Eids have come together for you (Bukhari 2004, vol. 7, 224–5).

Further, non-Deobandi scholars have also refuted the DMM's criticism regarding the resemblance of Milad celebrations to Christmas and Milad processions with Shia practices. They argue that the Deobandi interpretation and application of the Hadith 'He who imitates a people is from them' can hardly be considered accurate for two reasons. One, all the four *madhabs* consider Shias part of the Muslim community and any resemblance to Shias is not condemnable as such. Two, almost all modern-day *ulama* interpret said Hadith regarding resemblance to non-Muslims as applicable only when Muslims adopt a practice which is the hallmark of a particular non-Muslim community. If Muslims gradually adopt that practice to such an extent that it is no more considered symbolic of some other community, then the above-mentioned Hadith shall not apply in that scenario. For example, the practice of wearing Western-style trousers or jeans was once identified with Christians in the subcontinent and was execrated by the *ulama* as un-Islamic. However, when modern Muslims gradually adopted this style, religious scholars (except for the Deobandis) showed flexibility in their opinions. According to *ghair muqallid* scholar Waheed-uz-Zaman, there is no harm in *tashabbuh* (resemblance) until one actually intends to embrace resemblance with non-Muslims (Qadri 2005, 91).

Therefore, in case of Milad, the concept of *tashabbuh bil kuffar* hardly applies vis-à-vis Christians. Even if it is agreed for the sake of argument that Muslims took the idea of Milad celebration from Christians, the concept of *tashabbuh* became irrelevant once the practice became established and popular among Muslims.

Qadri (2008, 15–18) has further explained the Milad celebrations in the subcontinent from a cultural point of view, whereby processions on Eid Milad-un-Nabi are part of the culture. People there go to processions on occasions of joy, grief and protest. They even celebrate victories in sports by holding processions. Similarly, the lighting and decoration of buildings and mosques for celebrations has also been derived from the local culture. According to Qadri, standing up during *durood-o-salam* for the Prophet in Milad meetings is a sign of respect in that culture. On the other hand, the DMM's founder Muhammad Qasim and other Deobandis have condemned this last practice as it acknowledges the spiritual presence of the Prophet in Milad meetings (Amin 2008, 17–18). Hence, Deobandi scholar Abdul Haq (2009, vol. 2, 72) issued a *fatwa* that standing up to recite *durood* is against *Shariah*.

As regards the Deobandi approach of considering it un-Islamic to fix date and time for a particular event, non-Deobandi scholars have refuted it with the following Hadith: 'When the Prophet came to Madinah from Makkah, he observed that the Jews of Madinah fasted on the day of Ashura. When asked about this practice, the Jews replied that we fast on this day to thank God who delivered the Prophet Moses (PBUH) and drowned Pharaoh on this particular day'. The Prophet Muhammad (PBUH) then fasted and allowed his companions to follow this practice of fasting on that particular day to celebrate the victory of Prophet Moses (Bukhari 2004, vol. 4, 679).

5.3.2 The Prophet as **noor** *(light) or* **bashar** *(human being)*

Many great Islamic scholars and saints have supported the belief that the Prophet Muhammad (PBUH) was *noor*. These included Abdullah bin Abbas, Imam Razi, Imam Asqalani, Imam Nafsi, Imam Zarqani, Qadhi A'yadh Maliki, Imam Qastalani, Allama Alusi, Imam Abul Ahsan Ash'ari, Allama Khazin, Imam Siyuti, Imam Baithawi, Imam Ibn-Hajr Makki, Ismail Haqqi, Mullah Ali Qari, Abdul Haqq Muhaddis Dehlwi, Maulana Jalaluddin Rumi, Imam Buseeri, etc. (Attari 2009, 190–201). Interestingly, most of the early Deobandi *ulama* like Muhammad Ismail, Imdadullah, Rasheed Ahmed, Ashraf Thanvi, Hussain Madni and Shabbir Usmani also endorsed this popular belief (Attari 2009, 201–4). Rasheed Ahmed (n.d., 86) even stated that the Prophet had no shadow because he was light.

However, later Deobandi *ulama* declared that the Prophet was a human being like all of us. The Deobandis adopted this belief under the influence of Salafi (Wahhabi) Islam. According to this belief, the Prophet was *noor* in the symbolic manner as he served as a beacon of light for humanity (Ludhianvi n.d., 33). Therefore, Abdul Haq (2009, vol. 1, 161–2) stated in his *fatawa* that the Prophet could only metaphorically be described as *noor*. Otherwise he was created as a human being. Interestingly, this symbolic interpretation is incompatible with the DMM's approach of explicating the concept of *bidah* by taking the literal and apparent meaning of the Ahadith.

This viewpoint of the Deobandis stands in contrast to the belief of the overwhelming majority of Muslims in the subcontinent, who consider it contemptuous to call the Prophet a human being like any other. They generally believe that the Prophet is a light derived from the light of God and appeared in this world in the form of a human being. The Deobandis, however, condemn this belief due to its resemblance with that of Christians, who consider Jesus Christ (PBUH) to be God. Therefore, Deobandis have declared this belief *shirk* and *kufr* (Ludhianvi n.d., 34). Barelwi *ulama* have replied to these declarations by stating that the Prophet was created from God's light because God made him so. It does not mean at all that he was part of God's light as such or that God became part of him through His light. The Barelwis not only deplore the DMM's claims in this regard but have paid back in the same coin by declaring that such beliefs could lead to *shirk* and *kufr* (Attari 2009, 184).

Deobandi arguments in this regard have referred to those Quranic verses that declare past prophets brothers of their respective nations (e.g. 7:85 – 'And to Madyan We sent Shuaib from their brethren') and where the Prophet Muhammad (PBUH) calls himself a human being like others (e.g. 18:110 – 'Say you, "Apparently I am a human like you, I receive revelation that your God is one God"'). The Deobandis also quote a Hadith of Bukhari (2004, vol. 4, 717) in which the Prophet advises his followers not to praise him to the extent of Christians, who declare that Jesus is God and the son of God. He said that he was a slave and a prophet of God and he should be called just that (Ludhianvi n.d., 34–5).

In reply to such arguments, the Barelwis have referred to the following verses from the Quran.

1. Then the chiefs of the unbelievers of his people spoke, 'We see you a man like us, and we see not that anyone who has followed you but the meanest of us inadvertently, and we do not find in you any superiority over us; but rather we think you a liar.' (11:27)
2. And the chiefs of those people who disbelieved and belied the presence of the Hereafter and whom We gave comfort in the life of the world, said, 'He is not but a man like you, he eats of that what you eat and drinks of that what you drink. And if you obey a man like you, then necessarily you are in loss.' (23:33–4)
3. Then We sent Musa and his brother Haroon with Our signs and a clear authority. To Firawn [Pharaoh] and his courtiers, but they boasted and they were a people already possessed with dominance. Then they said, 'Shall we believe in two men like ourselves while their people are serving to us? (23:45–7)

Barelwi *ulama* have inferred from these verses that only God or the prophets themselves or the *kuffar* (non-believers) have referred to the prophets as human beings. Other than that, no one has called the Prophet a human being. Therefore, they believe that calling the Prophet a human being like ourselves is *kufr* and misguidance. Apart from quoting many miracles of the Prophet to prove that he was not a human like us, the Barelwis have interpreted that the word 'light' (*noor*) in the following verses in fact refers to the Prophet (Attari 2009, 209–24).

1. O people of the Book! Undoubtedly, Our Messenger has come to you who makes clear to you much of that which you had hidden in the Book and pardons much. Undoubtedly, there has come to you from Allah a *light* and a Book, luminous. (5:15).

2. They wish to put off the *light* of Allah with their mouths and Allah will not agree but to perfect His *light*, though the infidels may dislike it. (9:32)
3. They desire to extinguish the *light* of Allah with their mouths and Allah is to accomplish His *light*, even though the infidels may take it bad. (61:8)

It is interesting to note that the difference between the Deobandi and Barelwi *ulama* on this issue is more of a philosophical nature. This difference was not very sharp until the time of the early leaders of the DMM, who themselves believed that the Prophet was *noor* in actuality. However, as the scope of the Deobandi movement gradually narrowed and it adopted a typical countercultural character, they contradicted this otherwise undisputed belief.

5.3.3 The Prophet as **alim-ul-ghaib** *(knower of the hidden knowledge)*

This widespread belief that the Prophet had knowledge of the unknown (*ghaib*) has been supported by many great scholars (e.g. Imam Baithawi, Imam Qastalani, Imam Ibn-e-Hajr Makki, Imam Asqalani, Imam Ghazali, Qadhi A'yadh, Allama Zarqani, Abdul Haqq Muhaddis Dehlwi, Mulla Ali Qari, etc.), as well as the forefathers of the Deobandi movement (e.g., Abdul Aziz, Imdadullah and Muhammad Qasim; Attari 2009, 171–8). However, as the countercultural character of the DMM came to the fore and it was influenced more by the views of Muhammad bin Abdul Wahhab through Muhammad Ismail, the later Deobandi *ulama* began to challenge this widely accepted belief.

Rasheed Ahmed of Gangoh was the first Deobandi scholar to openly support the views of Muhammad bin Abdul Wahhab. In one of his *fatawa*, he praised Muhammad bin Abdul Wahhab as a good, pious person who practiced the Sunnah of the Prophet and prevented *bidah* and *shirk*. He defined a Wahhabi in his *fatwa* as a very religious person who follows the Sunnah (Nizami n.d., 72–3). He also issued the following *fatawa* regarding the Prophet's knowledge of the unknown.

1. Knowledge of the unknown is reserved for God alone and applying this to someone else through arguments is akin to *shirk*. (Gangohi n.d., vol. 3, 37)
2. Having the belief that the Prophet had knowledge of *ghaib* is a clear and obvious *shirk*. (Gangohi n.d., vol. 2, 10)

Later on, Ashraf Thanvi (n.d., 7), a disciple of Rasheed Ahmed, stated in his book *Hifz-ul-Iman* (Protection of faith) that the Prophet was not given whole knowledge of *ghaib*, and if he was given any knowledge then it is not particular to him; it is given to anybody, even a child or a deranged person. Thanvi's statement created an uproar among Indian Muslims, and the DMM had to face a barrage of criticism from the *ulama* of all schools of thought, who declared it to be contempt of the Prophet. A heated debate ensued and a campaign was launched against the Deobandi *ulama*, who employed different conflicting stances in order to defend their position against the belief system of mainstream Muslim society (Nizami n.d., 131–51). In recent years, Abdul Haq (2009, vol. 1, 159) has declared that Satan's knowledge was even more than that of the Prophet.

Presently, the Deobandis have adopted on this issue the same approach they employed to the belief regarding the Prophet's status as *noor*. According to Ludhianvi (n.d., 35–7), the Prophet was given more knowledge than all the prophets and angels put together. But his knowledge cannot be called knowledge of the unknown because it was revealed to him, and something that is already revealed cannot be called unknown. The Deobandis have presented the following verse of the Quran to support their view that the Prophet did not possess knowledge of *ghaib*: 'Say you, "Whosoever are in the Heavens and earth do not know themselves the unseen but Allah." And they do not know when they will be raised up' (27:65). They have also quoted the Hadith of the Prophet's wife Ayeshah, who stated that 'the one who says that the Prophet had knowledge of *ghaib* attributes falsehood towards God' (Mishkaat n.d., 501).

While conceding that no one can have any idea about the vastness of the Prophet's knowledge, the Deobandis simultaneously declare that neither is his knowledge equivalent to that of God nor is it permissible to call anyone *alim-ul-ghaib* except God. The Deobandis have defined knowledge of unknown (*ilm-ul-ghaib*) as something that cannot be proven through evidence or argument (*daleel*) and no creation is aware of it (Ludhianvi n.d., 37). So, they conclude that what is already known to the Prophet is technically not *ilm-ul-ghaib*.

On the other hand, Barelwi *ulama* have defined *ilm-ul-ghaib* as a hidden thing which cannot be known through the use of the five senses or the intellect. They have described two types of *ilm-ul-ghaib*: i) that which can be known through *daleel* – e.g. heaven, hell, angels, *jinn*, etc., which have been mentioned in the Quran; ii) that which cannot be deduced through *daleel* – e.g. knowledge about the Day of Judgement, time of death, good or bad fortune, etc. (Attari 2009, 155).

According to the Barelwi definition, the Prophet's knowledge was actually *ilm-ul-ghaib*, even when it was revealed to him by God. It was no longer *ilm-ul-ghaib* when he revealed it to the people. They believe that all prophets were given *ilm-ul-ghaib* but Prophet Muhammad (PBUH) was granted more than all of them. Barelwi *ulama* have quoted many Quranic verses and Ahadith to support their belief about prophets' *ilm-ul-ghaib*. A few of these are given below (Attari 2009, 157–71).

Quranic verses:

1. And Allah has sent down to you the Book and Wisdom and has taught to you what you did not know and great is the grace of Allah upon you. (4:113)
2. The Knower of the Unseen reveals not His secret to anyone. Except to His chosen Messengers. (72:26–7)
3. And he is not niggardly as to the disclosing of the unseen. (81:24)
4. These are the tidings of the unseen that We reveal to you in secret. (3:44).

Ahadith excerpts:

Non-Deobandi *ulama* have quoted dozens of Ahadith in which the Prophet perfectly foretells future events. Only three of these are mentioned here to give an idea of his *ilm-ul-ghaib*.

1. The Prophet once stood up and told of the birth of all creation and continued to explain until those who deserved heaven had reached there, while those who were to go to hell had reached their destination (Bukhari 2004, vol. 1, 453; Muslim 2004, vol. 5, 63).

2. The Prophet said that God rolled the whole earth for him to see it all from the East to the West (Muslim 2004, vol. 2, 390).
3. Umar said that the Prophet showed them one day before the Battle of Badr the exact places where the *mushrikeen* (disbelievers) were to be killed. He was correct in every case (Muslim 2004, vol. 2, 102).

In light of the above discussion, one can conclude that the difference between Deobandis and other Muslims is of an intellectual and philosophical nature and it should be treated as such. However, owing to its countercultural inclinations, the DMM interpreted this difference to condemn and contradict an established belief of mainstream Muslim society to the extent of declaring it *shirk*.

5.3.4 The Prophet as **haazir-o-naazir** *(he who is present and watching)*

The DMM has defined the concept of *haazir-o-naazir* in a manner that distinguishes them from the followers of folk Islam in Pakistan. The Deobandis think that the term *haazir-o-naazir* refers to someone whose presence is not restricted to one place, rather his presence covers the whole universe and he is able to see the beginning and the end of everything (Ludhianvi n.d., 37–8). In light of this definition, Ludhianvi has explained the Deobandi belief that the concept of *haazir-o-naazir* applies to God alone, while the Prophet's presence is restricted to his grave.

On the other hand, Barelwi *ulama* have stated that the concept of *haazir-o-naazir* is neither related to the physical body of the Prophet nor to his human existence, which is restricted to his grave. Rather, it is concerned with his *noor* and spirituality, which allow him to be present anywhere or everywhere. To support their views, the Barelwis have quoted the example of the Sun, which is present in the sky but its light reaches all over the earth (Abdul Hakeem Sharf Qadri quoted in Attari 2009, 59–60).

It may be added here that the forefathers and early leaders of the DMM agreed to the spiritual presence of the Prophet in this world even after his death. Waliullah stated in his book *Fuyuz-ul-Haramain* (n.d., 28) that the whole atmosphere is filled with the shining spirit of the Prophet. Abdul Aziz also agreed with this concept. Rasheed Ahmed (n.d., 10) was even more generous about the notion of *haazir-o-naazir* and conceded that the spirits of the saints are not restricted to one place and could reach their disciples when called upon.

As the DMM's approach gradually became more countercultural, they contradicted the concept of the Prophet's spiritual presence. Ludhianvi (n.d., 38–9) has not only refused to accept this explanation of *haazir-o-naazir* but has also propagated the later Deobandi belief according to which a person would become *kafir* if he believes that the spirits of the saints could make themselves present. This Deobandi belief contradicts the long-established beliefs of great Muslim scholars and spiritual leaders (Attari 2009, 67–70). A few examples in this regard are quoted below.

1. Imam Ghazali said, 'Whenever you enter a mosque, offer *salam* [peace greetings] to the Prophet. Undoubtedly, he is present in the mosque.' Ghazali also believed that the Prophet still has the authority to visit different parts of the world and many saints have seen him in actuality.

2. The Prophet's companion Alqama stated that whenever he entered a mosque he would say, 'O Prophet, peace and blessings on you.'
3. According to Imam Qastalani, there is no difference between the life and death of the Prophet. He watches his *ummah* and is aware of their state, their ambitions and intentions. Imam Siyuti has stated that it is still part of the Prophet's spiritual engagements to keep an eye on the actions of the *ummah*, to pray for Muslims, to visit different places and to join the funeral prayers of the most pious Muslims.

Following the lead of great Islamic scholars, Barelwi *ulama* have quoted dozens of Ahadith to defend the popular belief of *haazir-o-naazir* (Attari 2009, 62–7). Excerpts from a few of those Ahadith are given below.

1. The Prophet said, 'I am your predecessor and your witness to the promised place of Haudh-e-Kauthar [the Pond of Plenty] in the heavens. I am watching that place from here and I have been given the keys to the treasures of the earth' (Muslim 2004, vol. 2, 250).
2. When a Muslim is buried in his grave, two angels come and after indicating towards Muhammad (PBUH) ask the dead what he thinks about the Prophet. The believer replies that he is the slave and Prophet of God (Muslim 2004, vol. 1, 178). This Hadith has been interpreted to show that the Prophet visits the graves of believers.
3. According to a Hadith of Bukhari (2004, vol. 4, 446), the Prophet, while sitting in Madinah, informed his companions about the martyrdom of Zaid, Ja'far and Ibn Rawaha in the battle being fought at Mauta, about a thousand kilometres away from Madinah. He also informed them beforehand about Khalid bin Waleed taking the flag and winning the battle.

5.3.5 Calling **Ya Rasool Allah**

Another established belief of Pakistani Muslims that has been criticized by the DMM is that the Prophet listens to the call of Muslims when they directly address him by saying 'Ya Rasool Allah' (O Prophet of God). This belief has been derived from the above-mentioned belief of *haazir-o-naazir*. The Deobandis have condemned this belief and practice mostly on the grounds that the prophet is not *haazir-o-naazir* and hence cannot listen to the call of Muslims. Apart from that, the Deobandis have also opposed this practice because of its resemblance with a Shia practice of calling 'Ya Ali' to address the fourth caliph. (It is to be noted that the DMM consider any resemblance to Shia traditions as sinful as any non-Muslim practice.)

However, Ludhianvi (n.d., 43–5) has mentioned the following four exceptions in directly addressing the Prophet, with the condition that the caller does not believe that Prophet's spirit can actually be present everywhere.

1. When someone calls the Prophet in the manner poets imaginatively address mountains, trees and birds, knowing well that they cannot give an answer.
2. When someone says 'Ya Rasool Allah' out of the sheer pain and intensity of love.
3. When someone offers *durood-o-salam* to the Prophet with the hope that angels will take it to the grave of the Prophet. However, this should be avoided because this can lead to *fisaad* (transgression), wrongful beliefs and *shirk*.

4. When someone is actually present at the grave of the Prophet, he can directly address him and offer *durood-o-salam* because the Prophet can hear him. The Deobandis believe that all prophets are alive in their graves but are restricted to their tombs. Apart from the prophets, no one including the greatest of saints can hear when they are dead. This concept, called *nafi-e-sama-e-mauta* (negation of listening by the dead), is contrary to the popular belief among Muslims who offer *salam* (peace greetings) to the dead in graveyards and even call the spirits of the saints for *istamdad* (help) – a concept that will be discussed later in this section.

Deobandi scholar Abdul Haq allowed this practice of directly addressing the Prophet only for reciting *durood-o-salam* with the hope that angels will take it to the grave of the Prophet. However, he simultaneously declared that this practice is illegitimate in a gathering because it can be detrimental to the faith of ordinary Muslims. He also declared that addressing the Prophet directly in *durood* and believing that he can hear is *haram* and a cause of *shirk* and *kufr*. If not for *durood*, calling 'Ya Rasool Allah' has been altogether forbidden (Haq 2009, vol. 1, 162–73).

On the other hand, the belief and practice of directly addressing the Prophet has long been accepted by most Muslims. The following excerpts from Ahadith and writings of prominent Islamic scholars show the widespread acceptance and practice of this belief (Attari 2009, 117–26).

1. One of the companions of the Prophet addressed him at his grave by saying, 'Ya Rasool Allah! You are the abode of our hope, you were very kind to us and you were not harsh on us' (Zarqani alal Mawahib, vol. 8, 274).
2. The Prophet said that when Jesus would return to this world, 'he would visit my grave and say "Ya Muhammad" and I would answer him' (Tirmidhi; quoted in Attari 2009).
3. Imam Jazri stated that it was the practice of early Muslims to loudly raise the slogan 'Ya Muhammad' in war before launching an attack on the enemy. (Attari 2009).
4. After the death of Imam Hussain in Karbala, Zainab, granddaughter of the Prophet, called, 'Ya Muhammad! Ya Muhammad! This is Hussain, who is lying in blood among the enemies.' (Attari 2009).

It may be noted Shah Waliullah and his son Abdul Aziz agreed with the practice of directly addressing the Prophet. Similarly, Haji Imdadullah, the spiritual leader of the DMM founders, also recommended directly addressing the Prophet during spiritual exercises (Attari 2009, 117–26). However, as the countercultural approach gradually dominated the movement, the Deobandis declared that it was not legitimate to call 'Ya Muhammad', even as a mystic ritual (Ludhianvi n.d., 46–7).

5.3.6 **Tasarruf** *and* **ikhtiyar** *of the Prophet and the saints*

After condemning the established beliefs regarding *haazir-o-naazir* and 'Ya Rasool Allah', it was quite logical for the Deobandis to challenge the prevalent concept of *ikhtiyar* (authority) and *tasarruf* (power to make things happen through miracle or thaumaturgy) with regard to the Prophet and the saints. Abdul Haq (2009, vol. 1, 188–9) promulgated a *fatwa* stating that belief in the *ikhtiyar* of saints and prophets is explicit *shirk* that would lead to an eternal abode in hell. He also declared the belief in *tasarruf* to be overt *shirk*.

Ludhianvi (n.d., 39–42) has declared that the sovereignty and authority over the whole universe belongs to God alone and He has not shared this authority with the Prophet, as generally believed by Muslims who consider the Prophet to be *mukhtar-e-kul* (all powerful). By the same token, neither have saints been given any power or authority. Ludhianvi has stated that any miracle on the part of the Prophet or *karamat* (thaumaturgy) on the part of the saints is actually an act of God and that no prophet or saint has ever claimed for himself any such power or authority. Ludhianvi has quoted the following Hadith to support this Deobandi belief.

> The Prophet said to Ibne Abbas, 'O' boy! Take care of God's rights and He will take care of you. If you take care of His rights, you would find Him in front of you. If you need anything, ask from Him. If you need help, ask it from God. And have faith that if the whole nation gathers to benefit you, it cannot provide you any profit except for the one destined by God for you. And if the whole nation unites to hurt you, it cannot give you any harm except for the one preordained for you by God.' (Mishkaat n.d., 453)

On the other hand, Barelwi *ulama* have supported *ikhtiyar* and *tasarruf* for the prophets and saints. They believe that God has delegated a great deal of power and authority to Prophet Muhammad (PBUH), who could declare the same thing *halal* for one person and *haram* for another. Attari (2009, 78–94) has quoted many Quranic verses, Ahadith and famous Islamic scholars and jurists to support this belief. Some excerpts are given below.

Quranic verses:

1. 'And it is not befitting to a Muslim man or Muslim woman, when Allah and His Messenger have decreed something that they would have any choice in their matters, and whoever disobeys Allah and His Messenger, he undoubtedly, has strayed away manifestly' (33:36).
2. 'Then O beloved! By your Lord, they shall not be Muslims until they make you [Muhammad] judge in all disputes among themselves, then they find not any impediment in their hearts concerning whatever you decide, and accept from the eve of their hearts' (4:65).

Ahadith excerpts:

1. According to a Hadith of Bukhari (2004, vol. 4, 690), the Prophet said that when the angel of death came to Prophet Moses (PBUH), he slapped the angel, who then returned to God. This Hadith demonstrates the *ikhtiyar* of prophets.
2. According to a Hadith of Bukhari, the Prophet said that God gave him the option of either choosing to take what was in the world (life) or what was with God (death) (Attari 2009, 78–94).
3. When a delegation of the Saqeef tribe put up three conditions for accepting Islam (i.e. no *zakat*, no *salah* and no *jihad*), the Prophet allowed relaxation of *zakat* and *jihad* despite the fact that these were compulsory in Islam (Abu Dawood n.d., vol. 2, 72).

4. The Prophet said, 'Let it be known to you that the earth belongs to God and His Prophet' (Muslim 2004, vol. 2, 94).
5. The Prophet once asked his servant Rabee'a bin Ka'ab about his wishes. The latter said that he wanted to be a companion of the Prophet in the heavens. The Prophet assured him by saying that he should offer *nafl* (supernumerary prayers) more frequently (Muslim 2004, vol. 1, 193).

Views of scholars and saints (Attari 2009):

1. Imam Nawawi has declared that it is legitimate for the Prophet to amend the commands of *Shariah*. Similarly, Mulla Ali Qari has stated that it is the discretion of the Prophet to interpret and apply the commands of *Shariah* in whatever manner he deems right.
2. Allama Shatnufi stated that he saw four *mashaikh* (saints or spiritual leaders) who employed *tasarruf* from their graves just as they did when they were alive. These were Abdul Qadir Jilani, Maroof Karkhi, Aqeel Manji and Hayad bin Qais Hirani.
3. Shaikh Abdul Qadir Jilani, also known as Ghaus-e-Azam (the greatest of the helping saints) wrote that when saints reach their highest status, they are given the power of *takween* (derived from God's saying of *kun*, which means 'be', to make things happen). At this stage, whatever they want happens itself with God's permission.
4. Shah Waliullah declared that saints belonging to the Naqshbandi order have strange powers of *tasarruf*, which include healing illness, making people offer repentance, influencing the feelings and thoughts of the people and knowing what is in the hearts and minds of others.

5.3.7 **Istamdad** ***(asking for help and intervention)***

Istamdad (asking for help and intervention from anyone other than God) is a concept which is associated with the notions of *tasarruf* and *ikhtiyar*. The Deobandis have condemned this practice as *shirk* on the grounds that all power and authority belong to God and no one else can help except Him. Abdul Haq (2009, vol. 1, 188) in one of his *fatawa* declared the practice of *istamdad* to be *shirk*. In another *fatwa*, he declared the belief in *istamdad* to be *haram* and *kufr* (Haq 2009, vol. 1, 190).

For centuries Muslims have carried on the practice of *istamdad*, whereby help from prophets and saints is sought during their life as well as after their death. While the Deobandis have decried this practice after interpreting the call for help in its literal meaning, non-Deobandi scholars have explained it in a more philosophical and ideational manner. Allama Waqaruddin has stated that in every language an act is either referred towards the real actor or to the apparent actor (Attari 2009, 96). For example, it is said in Arabic, 'Ambat-ar-rabiyul baql' (the spring weather has grown the vegetable). Here, the weather is the apparent actor, while the real actor is God. Similarly, it is said in Urdu language, 'Dawa ne bimari door kar di' (the medicine healed the disease) or 'Doctor ne mareez ko achha kar diya' (the doctor cured the patient). Here the medicine and the doctor are the apparent actors. It is interesting that no one considers these sentences *shirk* or *kufr*; every Muslim believes that the actual and ultimate Healer is God – the rest are only reasons and resources.

Attari (2009, 96–7) has explained that such apparent references are mentioned even in the Quran. For example, the angel Gabriel tells Mary, 'I am only a messenger of your Lord. That I may give you a pure son' (19:19), whereas Muslims believe that it is only God who gives children. Similarly, it is stated in Surah Muhammad of the Quran, 'How then shall it be, when the angels will cause them to die, beating their faces and their backs?' (47:27). On the other hand, it is the firm faith of Muslims that God alone can give death to anyone.

It is in line with the above discussion that the Barelwi *ulama* have interpreted the concept of *istamdad* whereby help is sought from anyone other than God (*ghairullah*) through a source or mediation (*wasilah*), whereas the original belief is still there that the ultimate help comes from God alone (Attari 2009, 96–7). In light of this Barelwi interpretation, the Deobandis could have found a synthesis or common ground. However, the countercultural spirit of the DMM put the movement in direct conflict with the majority of Muslims, who were just following an established practice.

The following are some of the references from the Quran, Hadith and writings of many great Islamic scholars quoted by Barelwi *ulama* to support the concept of *istamdad* (Attari 2009, 98–107).

Quranic verses:

1. 'O Believers! Seek help with patience and prayer; no doubt, Allah is with the patients' (2:153).
2. 'Then undoubtedly, Allah is his helper, and Gabriel, and the righteous believers and after that the angels are his helpers' (66:4).
3. Then again when Isa [Jesus] found infidelity in them, he said, 'Who become my helpers towards Allah?' The disciples said, 'We are the helpers of the religion of God' (3:52).
4. 'And help each other in righteousness and piety, and help not one another in sin and transgression and remain fearing Allah' (5:2).

Ahadith excerpts (Attari 2009, 98–107):

1. The Prophet told his companions that if their riding animal runs away from them in an unknown place, then they should loudly say, 'O slaves of God! Stop it. There are certain (invisible) people on earth who would stop that' (Tafseer-e-Kabeer). Imam Shokani has categorized the narrators of this Hadith to be *siqah* (reliable).
2. Ibne Abbas stated that there are angels who write the number of leaves which fall from trees in the forest. Therefore, he told his companions that if they find themselves in some trouble during travel, they should say, 'O slaves of God! Help me, May god bless you' (Imam Ibn Abi Sheebah).
3. The Prophet said that if anyone of you loses something in an unknown place, he should say, 'O slaves of God! Help me. There are some creations of God we cannot see.' The Prophet added that it was his tested technique. (Tabarani)

Views of Islamic scholars (Attari 2009, 98–107):

1. Imam Ghazali has stated that the one who is called for *istamdad* in life can also be called for help after his death.
2. Imam Shafi'i has recommended the grave of Imam Moosa Kazim for the acceptance of supplication.

3. Imam Nawawi has mentioned that once while travelling the riding animal of one of his fellow travellers ran away. He repeated the words of the Hadith, 'O slaves of God, stop it', and the animal stopped. Mulla Ali Qari has explained that those words of the Hadith refer to angels as well as saints whom we cannot see.
4. Abdul Haqq Muhaddis Dehlwi has said that one of the *mashaikh* declared that *istamdad* by dead saints is stronger and more effective than that of living ones because the dead are stationed closer to God.

It may be noted that the forefathers and early leaders of the DMM also accepted and practiced *istamdad*. For example, Shah Waliullah wrote in his book *Fuyuz-ul-Haramain* (n.d., 28) that during his visit to the Prophet's grave, he appealed to the Prophet for help. The Prophet listened to his request and granted him many spiritual powers. Further, Waliullah recommended calling Ali for help to relieve grief and misery by saying 'Ya Ali, Ya Ali, Ya Ali'. Similarly, Shah Abdul Aziz declared that if someone asks for help from another person, as long as they believe that it would be ultimately coming from God through that person then it is permissible in *Shariah*. This type of *istamdad* is equivalent to help from the prophets and saints – it is actually help from God. Further, Muhammad Qasim, founder of the DMM, also addressed the Prophet in his poem by calling 'Ya Nabi' while asking for his help.

However, later Deobandi leaders like Rasheed Ahmed and Ashraf Ali Thanvi attached some conditions to the concept of *istamdad* to rule out any possibility of *shirk*. For example, Rasheed Ahmed declared that it is permissible to recite poetry (*na'at*) in which the Prophet is addressed directly and asked for help. However, he simultaneously stated that such poems should be recited out of love and in seclusion, hoping that God will place such requests before the Prophet. Later on, Mahmood Hassan adopted a more inflexible approach about *istamdad* and declared that it was forbidden to ask for help from anyone other than God. Ultimately, the DMM condemned the belief and practice of *istamdad* as *shirk*, *kufr* and *haram* (Haq 2009, 188–90).

5.3.8 **Tawassul** *(mediation) and* **wasilah** *(source of mediation)*

Tawassul refers to a practice whereby one prays to God to accept one's supplication through the intervention of a prophet or saint. This concept has been accepted and practiced by Muslims since the very early days of Islam. The forefathers of the DMM also shared this belief with all other Muslims of the subcontinent. However, as the movement began to exhibit its countercultural colours, it was natural for the Deobandis to distance themselves from mainstream Muslim society. Hence, the DMM disputed this concept and many shades of opinion gradually developed in the movement about *tawassul*. According to a *fatwa* by Abdul Haq (2009, vol. 1, 217), the belief that God will accept a supplication through the *tawassul* of saints goes beyond *Shariah*.

According to Ludhianvi (n.d., 47–8), some Deobandi *ulama* thought that *tawassul* of one's good acts was permissible, but considering a personality *wasilah* was *shirk*. Others declared that *tawassul* of a living person was allowed but that of a dead person was *shirk*. One group of Deobandi scholars allowed *tawassul* of not only some good deeds but also that of pious persons, both alive and dead. They justify this practice in the name of humility, submissiveness and fear of God because the one who refers to a *wasilah* in fact admits indirectly that he himself is not pious enough to directly pray for his own self.

While accepting the practice of *tawassul* in a direct prayer to God, the Deobandis identified two other types of *tawassul* practiced by Muslims of the subcontinent. These two types of *tawassul* have been declared wrongful *bidah*, which lead to misguidance and *shirk*, as discussed below.

As regards the first type, Ludhianvi (n.d., 49–59) explained that many Muslims who do not consider themselves pious enough to directly ask from God employ *tawassul* of the saints (both dead and alive) in their supplications. They believe that saints can mediate on their behalf for the acceptance of their prayers. The Deobandis, instead of giving the benefit of the doubt to such Muslims on the grounds of humility and fear of God, have declared their *tawassul* to be *shirk* for two reasons. First, these Muslims liken the Kingdom of God to a worldly kingdom, where people cannot directly access the king without a means of mediation. Applying this principle to God has been declared totally wrong because it equates a worldly king with God, who is not similar to anything or anyone. Second, these people believe that like worldly kings, who delegate power to their subordinates, God has delegated authority to prophets and saints. According to the Deobandis, the above-mentioned Muslims are making two grave mistakes here. Not only are they creating similarity between God and worldly kings, but through this similarity they are indirectly acknowledging that God has the same limitations as worldly rulers, who delegate powers because they are not able to know or perform all the activities of their countries. God not only knows each and everything but also holds the power to make everything happen without sharing his authority with anyone.

The second type of *tawassul* condemned by the DMM involves Muslims who simply request saints (both dead and alive) to pray to God on their behalf. The Deobandis have declared that making such requests to living saints is permissible. As regards requests made to saints who have passed away, there are two groups in the DMM. One group believes that deceased people cannot hear the voices of those who are alive; the only exception is the *tawassul* of prophets. The second group completely condemns this type of *tawassul*, with no exceptions.

This debate about addressing the dead at their graves has long been going on among Islamic scholars under the title of *sama-e-mauta* (listening by the dead). There was a small group among the early Deobandi *ulama* who believed that dead people do listen in their graves when someone addresses them. Ignoring this early belief, the DMM gradually adopted an inflexible stance on this category of *tawassul*. The later Deobandis also issued *fatawa* against *sama-e-mauta*, which were compiled into a book titled *Nafi-e-Sama-e-Mauta* (Negation of listening by the dead; Ibrahim 2011, 238–43).

On the contrary, Barelwi *ulama* have defended the practice of *tawassul* by declaring that *wasilah* of prophets as well as saints (both alive and dead) is permissible. Attari (2009, 132–47) has described several references from the Quran, Hadith and *salaf-as-saliheen* to prove that *tawassul* has always been practised by Muslims. Some of these references are given below.

Quranic verses:

1. 'O believers! Fear Allah and seek *wasilah* to Him and strive in His way haply you may get prosperity' (5:35).
2. 'And if when they do injustice unto their souls, then O beloved! They should come to you and then beg forgiveness of Allah and the messenger should *intercede* for them then surely, they would find Allah Most Relenting, Merciful' (4:64).
3. 'And before that they were asking for victory over the infidels *by means* of the same prophet' (2:89).

Ahadith excerpts:

1. Caliph Umar used to pray for rain through the *wasilah* of the Prophet. After the Prophet's death, he prayed to God through the *wasilah* of the Prophet's uncle Abbas and it rained (Bukhari 2004, vol. 1, 137).
2. Ibne Abbas narrated that once the Jews faced the tribe of Ghatfan in a battle, they prayed through the *wasilah* of the Prophet by saying, 'O God! We ask your help through the *wasilah* of your promised Prophet who would come near the end of times' (Tafseer Qartabi, vol. 2, 27–8).
3. A blind person asked the Prophet to pray for him so that he should have his eyesight restored. The Prophet asked him to offer *nafl salah* (optional prayers) and then say: 'O God! I ask of you and I turn to you through the *wasilah* of Muhammad. O Muhammad! I present to God my need through your *wasilah*. So please fulfil my need.' After that supplication, the eyes of the blind person became perfect (Tirmidhi, vol. 2, 197).

Views of salaf-as-saliheen:

1. Shaikh Abdul Qadir Jilani advised his followers that when they pray to God, they should ask Him through his *wasilah* (Bahjatul Asrar n.d., 23).
2. When Caliph Abu Jaffar Mansoor visited the Prophet's grave in Madinah, he asked Imam Malik whether he should turn towards Ka'bah or towards the Prophet to make a supplication. Imam Malik replied, 'How could you turn your face away from the Prophet when he has been declared a *wasilah* for you and even for the prophet Adam (PBUH). So you should turn your face towards the Prophet while making your supplication (Shifa n.d., vol. 2, 33).
3. During his sojourns to Baghdad, Imam Shafi'i would always visit the grave of Imam Abu Hanifa, where he offered *salam* (greetings) and made supplication to God through the *wasilah* of Abu Hanifa (Tareekh Khateeb-e-Baghdadi, vol. 1, 123).
4. Imam Hanbal who used to supplicate through the *wasilah* of Imam Shafi'i said that the personality of the latter was like sunlight for the people and like health for the body (Shawahid-ul-Haq, 166).

Interestingly, the ideologues and forefathers of the DMM themselves preached and practised *tawassul*. For example, Ibne Taiymiyah declared in one of his *fatawa* that it is correct to make a supplication to God through the *wasilah* of prophets, angels and pious people. Shah Abdul Aziz also declared that there is not an iota of *shirk* in *tawassul* of pious persons (both dead and alive). Similarly, Rasheed Ahmed declared that *tawassul* is permissible through dead and alive persons as well as through pious acts of one's own or of others (Attari 2009, 142–7).

However, as the movement became more countercultural with the passage of time, its followers adopted a narrow definition, declaring that one should not believe that any supplication without *tawassul* shall not be accepted by God or that a supplication with *tawassul* shall surely be accepted. Such restrictions allowed the DMM enough room to castigate all other Muslim groups and sects who practised *tawassul*. At present, most Deobandis believe in the concept in theory alone; in practice, they mostly try not to preach or employ it in their supplications. Although a small group of Deobandis do practice *tawassul*, it is restricted to the Prophet alone. *Tawassul* of saints is particularly avoided so as to separate the Deobandis from the majority of Pakistani Muslims.

5.3.9 Ziyarat-e-quboor *(visiting graves)*

The Deobandis allow the practice of *ziyarat-e-quboor* with the objectives of remembering one's own death as well as the hereafter, praying for the souls of the dead, and conveying the reward of good deeds to the dead (*isal-e-sawab*). However, they simultaneously condemn as *shirk* the following popular practices and rituals which many Muslims perform with regard to graves (Ludhianvi n.d., 59–76).

1. Constructing stone graves and erecting buildings over graves

Abdul Haq (2009, vol. 1, 185) declared in his *fatawa* that this practice is illegitimate and leads to *shirk*. In this regard, the Deobandis quote the Hadith of Jabir, who claims that the Prophet forbade his followers to construct graves with stones, to build domes or tombs, and to sit on graves (Mishkaat n.d., 148). Deobandi *ulama* have also referred to the *fatwa* of Imam Muhammad (a disciple of Imam Abu Hanifa), who declared it *haram* to construct graves and tombs with stones or bricks (Ludhianvi n.d., 63).

The Barelwis, on the other hand, have declared it permissible with regard to the graves of saints and Islamic scholars. Niazi (2012, 132–45) has argued that if such a construction was forbidden then the building in which the Prophet was buried should have been demolished. On the contrary, Caliph Umar built a brick wall around the Prophet's tomb. Later on, a wall was constructed with carved stones during the reign of Caliph Waleed. It has also been reported that when a wall of the Prophet's tomb fell down, the *sahaba* reconstructed it. Abdul Haqq Muhaddis Dehlwi has written in his book *Jazb-ul-Quloob* that in AH 550 (1155 CE), Jamaluddin Isphahani erected a netting of sandalwood around the wall in the presence of the *ulama* of that time. Then in AH 678 (1279 CE), Sultan Salihi built a green dome over the Prophet's grave. It may be noted that this construction is not an exception for the Prophet alone, as in the same building are the graves of two caliphs, Abu Bakr and Umar.

One of the arguments of non-Deobandi *ulama* to support construction on the graves of saints is that such buildings are meant to display the grandeur of Islam (*shaukat-e-Islam*). Allama Ismail Haqqi (d. 1725 CE) supported this practice in his *Tafseer Bayan-ul-Quran* when interpreting chapter 9, verse 18. He asserted that it was legitimate to establish buildings over the graves of scholars and saints with the object of enhancing their reverence among the people. Similarly, Abdul Haqq Muhaddis Dehlwi believed that the grandeur of such tombs helped in creating awe and obedience among non-Muslims (quoted in Niazi 2012, 134). Deobandi Ashraf Thanvi (2002, 22) also employed this *shaukat-e-Islam* argument to defend the practice of announcing rituals during *hajj* by firing a cannon, as shall be discussed in Section 5.4.2. However, the Deobandis are not willing to accept the same argument for building shrines.

Many other scholars like Imam Shami, Allama Haskafi, Imam Shi'rani and Abu Hanifa have allowed the practice of constructing tombs. Imam Shami declared that it is not *makruh* to erect a building over the graves of saints and *ulama*, whereas Allama Haskafi wrote in *Durr-e-Mukhtar* that there is no harm in constructing a building over a grave. (Niazi 2012, 134–5).

As regards the above Hadith of Jabir, many non-Deobandi *ulama* have interpreted the prohibition of using stone to be applicable to only those graves that are: made from stone inside and outside; meant for ordinary Muslims; or constructed with the intentions of decoration and pride. In one Hadith of Mishkaat, it is stated that the Prophet affixed a stone to the head side of the grave of Usman bin Madh'un and said to his followers that it would mark the grave of their brother and that they would bury their family members around the grave. Further, the Quranic story of the People of the Cave (known in the Christian world as the Seven Sleepers) includes a verse which refers to the construction of their mausoleum. It states, 'Build over their cave any building or mosque' (18:21). This verse has also been quoted by non-Deobandi scholars to justify the practice of building shrines and tombs (Niazi 2012, 137–8).

Mufti Ahmad Yar Naeemi has mentioned in his book *Jaa'al-Haqq* (n.d., 148–50) that the practice of building tombs was followed in the times of the *sahaba*. For example, Caliph Umar constructed a dome over the grave of Zainab bint-e-Jahash, wife of the Prophet. Similarly, Muhammad Ibn Hanfia constructed a building over the grave of Abdullah bin Abbas and the Prophet's wife Ayeshah had a dome built over the grave of his brother Abdur Rehman bin Abu Bakr. The wife of Imam Zain-ul-Abideen also had a building constructed over his husband's grave. The covered area was meant for those who visited the grave to pray for the imam and recite the Quran for *isal-e-sawab*.

2. *Putting sheets of cloth on graves*

The DMM has also declared this practice to be *haram* on the basis that it was not followed by the *salaf-as-saliheen*. They refer to Imam Shami's *fatwa* in *Radd-ul-Mukhtar* which declared this practice to be *makruh* (Ludhianvi n.d., 64). On the other hand, the non-Deobandi writer Niazi (2012, 83–8) has stated that this practice is unnecessary vis-à-vis the graves of ordinary Muslims. However, it is permissible in case of saints because such practices increase the respect of the saint in the eyes of visitors. Many Barelwi *ulama* have referred to another of Imam Shaami's *fatawa* in which he allowed this practice with the intention of creating respect and awe of the saint in the hearts of ordinary people who visited shrines. Some *ulama* have linked this practice to the tradition of placing a cloth cover over *ka'bah* as a mark of respect (Niazi 2012, 83–8).

3. *Lighting lamps on and prostration before graves*

While declaring the practice of lighting lamps on graves as wicked and illegitimate in his *fatawa*, Deobandi scholar Abdul Haq (2009, vol. 1, 183–5) pronounced that prostration before graves is *haram* and *shirk*. The Deobandis have quoted the following Ahadith to support their viewpoint (Ludhianvi n.d., 65–7).

1. Abdullah bin Abbas says that the Prophet condemned those women who visited graves as well as those people who prostrate before graves and burn lamps there (Mishkaat n.d., 71).
2. Ayeshah says that the Prophet condemned Jews and Christians because they had made their prophets' graves into places of prostration (Mishkaat n.d., 69).
3. The Prophet prayed to God, 'Don't make my grave like an idol which is worshipped' (Mishkaat n.d., 172).

Furthermore, the Deobandi *ulama* have referred to the writings of Shah Waliullah in his book *Al-Fauz-ul-Kabeer* (The great success), where he says that the acts of ignorant and ordinary people on graves actually reflect the beliefs and acts of *mushrikeen* (Ludhianvi n.d., 68). Apart from that, the Deobandis have condemned as wrongful *bidah* the touching and kissing of saints' graves to receive blessings. Haq (2009, vol. 2, 78) promulgated a *fatwa* stating that the act of kissing graves is impermissible and *haram*. According to a *fatwa* by Abdul Haq (2009, vol. 1, 186), the act of kissing graves out of respect is *kufr* and misguidance, while doing the same without any intention of respect is a great sin and *haram*.

On the other hand, the Barelwi *ulama* have declared that burning lamps on the graves of ordinary Muslims without any need is forbidden. However, this is allowed for the graves and shrines of saints (Naeemi n.d., 160). The Barelwi *ulama* have further argued that bowing before a saint's grave out of respect cannot be termed prostration because the objective of prostration is worship, whereas Muslims never intend to worship graves when they bow before them. Similarly, kissing the grave is out of respect and not a mark of worship. This difference between respect and worship is also manifested in the established practices of kissing the Black Stone (Hajr-e-Aswad) at Ka'bah as well as kissing the Quran and books of Hadith. Imam Hanbal allowed kissing of the Prophet's *minbar* (pulpit) as well as his grave. In fact, caliph Umar used to touch the Prophet's *minbar* with his hand and then kiss that hand. Imam Siyuti stated that the practice of kissing graves is derived from the kissing of the Black Stone (Niazi 2012, 88–95). Interestingly, the DMM has condemned the kissing of graves even as a mark of respect.

Imam Hanbal also said that Abu Ayub Ansari, a *sahabi*, once placed his face on the grave of the Prophet. When the governor of Madinah, Marwan, tried to stop him, Ansari replied that he knew what he was doing. He said, 'I have not come to the clay and stone. I am present in the court of the Prophet' (Niazi 2012, 96–7).

4. Placing flowers on graves

The Deobandis have also forbidden the popular practice of placing flower petals and wreaths on the graves because it was never followed by the *salaf-as-saliheen*. Contrarily, many Sunni *ulama* have allowed this practice in light of an authentic Hadith which states that the Prophet once placed the green twigs of a palm tree on two graves and said that until those twigs dried up, the punishment of the dead in those graves would hopefully be lessened (Bukhari 2004, vol. 7, 458).

The Deobandis, however, have interpreted this Hadith from a different angle to oppose the practice. Abdul Haq is one notable exception who agreed that placing flowers and green leaves and twigs on graves with the intention that it will benefit the dead is allowed in *Shariah*. However, he simultaneously pronounced that in the modern era of corruption, evil and strife, people's intentions are mostly vitiated; therefore, *ulama* have declared it against *Shariah* to place flower wreaths on graves (Haq 2009, vol. 2, 77).

The DMM has generally opposed the practice of placing green plants or flowers on graves on the following grounds (Ludhianvi n.d., 198–211).

1. It was not a regular practice of the Prophet and he did it only two or three times. Non-Deobandi scholars have argued that the Prophet might not have done it regularly because it would have become a binding Sunnah or obligation for Muslims. According to the Hadith (Muslim 2004, vol. 2, 239–40), the Prophet avoided many practices he liked so that they would not become obligatory for his followers.
2. The reduction in punishment was due to the blessing and miracle of the Prophet's hand. Non-Deobandis have stated that green plants are living things and every living thing praises God, as mentioned in Quran (17:44). So due to that praise the punishment is reduced. Fresh flowers and leaves are also living things.
3. If it is accepted that the reduction in punishment was due to the green twigs, then it would be better to place green twigs rather than flowers. The exact Sunnah should be to use palm twigs. According to non-Deobandi scholars, the spirit of the practice was to use any fresh parts of a plant or flower and sheaths of flowers also include green twigs and leaves. As flowers also reflect beauty, this practice gradually became more popular. Further, the Prophet used a palm tree because it is more common in Arabia (Niazi 2012, 83).
4. Nowadays, this practice is no more followed in light of said Hadith. Rather, the objective of this practice is to show respect to the graves or to receive favours and blessings from the dead saints, both of which are *bidah* and *shirk*. According to the non-Deobandi viewpoint, if Muslims are doing it to show respect to dead relatives, saints or national leaders, then this practice cannot be termed wrongful *bidah* because most people do not consider it to be a part of the religion. As regards receiving favours from the saints, that comes under the concept of *istamdad*, as discussed in Section 5.3.7.
5. If the explanation of reduction in punishment is accepted, then this practice should not apply to saints, being pious persons and friends of God (*aulia Allah*). Looking from that perspective, this practice actually shows them contempt. From the non-Deobandi perspective, this is an even weaker argument; if this line of reasoning is accepted, then the practice of *istaghfar* (the act of seeking forgiveness from God for one's sins) by the Prophet could be interpreted in a far more contemptuous manner. Similarly, rendering *durood-o-salam* to the Prophet (a highly revered practice followed by all Muslims) would also lead to scornful interpretations. Likewise, the concept of *isal-e-sawab* for prophets and saints would become redundant, whereas the DMM has approved it with the condition of not fixing a date for it. The truth of the matter is that the reward of good acts conveyed through *isal-e-sawab* helps sinful persons in reducing their punishment, whereas it leads to the elevation in status of pious and innocent people (Niazi 2012, 81–2). Further, if a Muslim performs a good act to be transferred to a saint, then that act would not only benefit the latter but would also be helpful for the former through the blessings returned by the saint.

5.3.10 Nadhr *or* mannat *vis-à-vis shrines*

A *nadhr* or *mannat* is one's vow to carry out a good act for the sake of God if a particular supplication or wish comes true. The scope of such good acts in return for the fulfilment of a wish is quite broad. For example, these include offering *nafl* (supernumerary) prayers, fasting, and distributing money or food among the poor, etc. In the subcontinent, the most popular acts for *nadhr* include distributing food and sweets on the shrine of a particular saint or placing a cloth sheet or flowers on their grave.

Mannat or *nadhr* is a widespread practice among Muslims all over the world. God has permitted this practice by stating in the Quran, 'And whatsoever you spend or vow Allah knows it and the unjust have no helpers' (2:270). As such, the Deobandis have interpreted this practice to be an act of worship allowed by God. However, they have simultaneously declared that an act of worship cannot be performed for the sake of a saint. Through this interpretation of *nadhr*, the Deobandis have declared this popular and religiously legitimate practice to be *haram*.

The Deobandis have agreed in principle that if someone practices *nadhr* purely for God and his act of distributing food among the poor is just for the sake of *isal-e-sawab* or for helping the poor, then such *nadhr* or *mannat* cannot be called *haram* or *shirk*. However, in practice, they don't even allow such a pure and legitimate *nadhr* on the grounds that common Muslims are not able to keep this delicate balance between worship and *shirk*. Ludhianvi (n.d., 74) has observed that although people who practice *nadhr* involving shrines and saints declare that they are doing it for the sake of God and *isal-e-sawab* of the saints, they are only deceiving themselves because their ulterior motive is to receive blessings through *istamdad* and *tasarruf*, which lead to *shirk* and *kufr*. Therefore, Abdul Haq (2009, vol. 1, 230) issued a *fatwa* declaring *nadhr* at the shrines *haram* and *shirk*.

It is interesting that on the one hand the Deobandis opposed the above-mentioned practices because they involved showing respect to the graves, whereas on the other hand they themselves displayed extraordinary veneration for the graves of their elders. For example, Deobandi *ulama* fervidly protested in 2006 when militant Hindus damaged the grave of Ashraf Ali Thanvi in a cemetery called Ashraf-ul-Maqabir (Best of the graves) in India. The graveyard is highly revered by Deobandis because many DMM leaders are buried there. Zafar Usmani, a renowned Deobandi leader, wrote of the graveyard: 'This place is like heaven because of God's blessings, and who was buried here became purified. Whoever wants to spend a night in the Garden of Heaven must come here because this is a perfumed garden' (Tirmazi 2007, 34–9).

5.4 Deobandi Opposition to Non-religious Sociocultural Practices

The discussion in this section mostly includes those customs which have been condemned by Ashraf Ali Thanvi in his book *Islah-ur-Rusoom* (Reform of the customs). This is a short book, written for common Muslims with the intention of condemning their beliefs and customs. In this book, he employs the instruments of Quran and Hadith to strengthen his arguments against the sociocultural practices prevalent among North Indian Muslims at the start of the twentieth century. He uses plain language and avoids complex religious terms to attract wide readership among ordinary Muslims. Even references are not given to distinguish *sahih* (authentic) Ahadith from the *dhaeef* (weak) ones. Apart from *Islah-ur-Rusoom*, a few *fatawa* of Abdul Haq have also been included in the relevant sections.

Some popular sociocultural practices condemned by the DMM are discussed below.

5.4.1 Celebration of matrimonial events

Although marriage-related customs and practices vary in different parts of Pakistan depending on geography, history and culture, the DMM has condemned all these customs on one pretext or the other. For example, Abdul Haq (2009, vol. 2, 73–4) issued a *fatwa* that wearing of *sehra* by the bridegroom is a Hindu custom that must compulsorily be avoided and insistence on following this custom is sinful. Thanvi (2002, 54–89) has given several reasons for castigating different ceremonies practised during matrimonial events. These reasons include: prodigality, pride and exhibition of wealth; non-observance of *purdah* (physical segregation and proper covering of bodies by women) during these ceremonies; *tashabbuh bil kuffar*; taking loans for these events even on interest (*riba*); supporting sinful activities like interaction between men and women; singing and dancing that is *haram*; backbiting and jealousy among women who compete with one another in dresses and make-up; ignoring or delaying obligatory prayers during the ceremonies, etc. Above all, Thanvi has included in this list the committing of *shirk*, the DMM's favourite weapon of condemnation.

It may not be out of place to add here that the exaggerated emphasis of Deobandis to declare the customs and practices of the majority of Muslims as *shirk* is in conflict with the authentic Hadith in which the Prophet swore on God that he was not afraid that Muslims would commit *shirk* after him and that his only fear in this regard was that they would dispute among themselves for worldly gains (Bukhari 2004, vol. 8, 55).

Coming back to marriage rites, Thanvi has also pilloried some marriage-related customs that are considered good omens for the new couple, e.g. distributing money after waving it around the head of the bride or groom in order to ward off evil. Similarly, special foods are prepared for particular ceremonies as a good omen and absence of such foods is considered a bad omen. It is worth noting that while declaring the concept of good or bad omens *haram*, Thanvi ignored an authentic Hadith whereby the Prophet says that there is nothing wrong with taking a good omen (Bukhari 2004, vol. 7, 317–18).

According to Thanvi (1992, 7–15), 'Many customs of marriage are *bidah* [while] several of these are *shirk*.' In fact, he has declared, directly or indirectly, almost all the matrimonial customs and practices to be *bidah*, *haram* or *shirk*. In this regard, he has quoted (albeit without references) the following Quranic verses and Ahadith:

Quranic verses:

1. 'O children of Adam! Take your adornment whenever you go to mosque and eat and drink and do not cross the limit. Undoubtedly, the persons crossing the limit are not liked by Him' (7:31).

2. 'And give kinsmen their right and to the needy and the traveller and spend not extravagantly. No doubt, the extravagant are the brothers of the devil [Satan]. And the devil is very ungrateful to his Lord' (17:26–7).

Ahadith excerpts:

1. The Prophet said that the one who follows affectation and pretension shall be humiliated by God.
2. The Prophet condemned *riba* (interest) and discouraged the practice of taking loans.
3. The Prophet said that God detests those who follow the practices of *jahiliyyah* (the state of ignorance of divine guidance) even after embracing Islam.
4. The marriage banquet (*walima*) by the groom, if done with pomp and pride, was called an evil food by the Prophet (otherwise, *walima* is a Sunnah).
5. The Prophet condemned the woman who goes outside her home wearing a strong perfume.
6. The Prophet declared that there is a Satan with every musical instrument.

Despite all the condemnation of the DMM, the above-mentioned customs and practices are still very popular among the majority of Pakistani Muslims who consider these part of the culture and norms of society. It is pertinent to mention here that the holding of different ceremonies at weddings was common practice during the Prophet's time. According to an authentic Hadith, the Prophet's wife Ayeshah once led a bride to the bridegroom in a group. When she reported the ceremony to the Prophet, he suggested that someone with a tambourine (*duff* or *riq*) should have also accompanied the women to support their songs (Bukhari 2004, vol. 6, 631).

5.4.2 Sports and recreational activities

The Deobandis generally deplore popular cultural events such as festivals and fairs as well as sporting events. Thanvi (2002, 106) has strongly condemned attending horse races, wrestling matches, exhibitions, fairs and theatres for entertainment. He has denounced such events on the grounds that many un-Islamic things happen at these gatherings e.g. music, interaction between men and women, gambling, wrongful sportswear (e.g. athletes whose thighs are uncovered), etc. The Deobandi Taliban also banned in Afghanistan the wearing of shorts by men in sporting events.

Thanvi declared that going to such events was akin to accepting and promoting all these sinful acts and hence helping increase the congregations of *fisq* (open disobedience of God) and *kufr*. To strengthen this last argument, he has quoted a Hadith whereby the Prophet states that he who helps increase the gathering of a group or nation belongs to that group. Further, Thanvi has tried to link the issue to another Hadith in which the Prophet forbade his companions to sit on the roadside. However, Thanvi failed to mention the whole Hadith, which states that when his companions explained their custom of sitting on the roadside, the Prophet allowed them to do so while avoiding immoral behaviour (Bukhari 2004, vol. 3, 585).

The Deobandis have also condemned sports and recreational activities like pigeon keeping, kite flying, fireworks and chess, as discussed below.

Thanvi (2002, 17–18) has declared pigeon keeping *haram* on two presumptions: one, it can lead to gambling; two, sometimes the person involved in this sport ignores his obligatory prayers as well as his duties towards his family, and avoiding an obligatory act is considered *haram*. Since pigeon keeping can lead to something that is *haram*, the sport is also *haram* because anything that leads to *haram* is itself *haram*. Apart from these convoluted arguments, Thanvi has also quoted an unauthentic Hadith in which Abu Hurairah says that when the Prophet saw a person running after a flying pigeon, he said, 'One Satan is chasing another Satan.' For the same reasons, Thanvi has also forbidden other hobbies like raising cocks and quails for bird fighting.

Although these sports are not very popular these days, the majority of Pakistanis do not consider them to be *haram* or sinful. The Deobandis on the other hand continue to condemn them. It is interesting that when the Deobandi Taliban established their rule in Kabul in 1996, one of the decrees announced by their religious police stated: 'To prevent keeping pigeons and playing with birds: Within ten days this habit/hobby should stop. After ten days, this should be monitored and the pigeons and any other playing birds should be killed' (Rashid 2008, 219).

As for kite flying, Thanvi (2002, 18–20) has deplored it on almost the same grounds as pigeon keeping. However, his presumptions here are even more far-fetched, as shown below.

1. Running after a kite is like running after a pigeon and the latter has been condemned by the Prophet.
2. Catching a free kite is *haram* because it belongs to someone else. Looting another person's belongings is *haram* and the Prophet has apparently declared that a looter shall lose his *iman* (faith). The same principle applies to the looting of strings after a kite is cut by another kite.
3. Everyone participating in this sport intends to cut the kites of others. This is akin to harming other Muslims, which is *haram*. And so, because of this intention, all kite flyers become sinners.
4. The sport can lead to one forgetting and missing obligatory prayers. Since God has forbidden gambling and alcohol as *haram* on the grounds that these evils lead to one ignoring prayers, kite flying also falls into the same category of sins.
5. A kite is made of paper, which is an instrument for spreading knowledge. Therefore, kite flying shows disrespect of knowledge. Similarly, a paste of wheat flour is generally used to make kites, a practice that is disrespectful of a food item. Thanvi has linked it to a Hadith in which the Prophet advised his wife Ayeshah to respect bread (i.e. food).
6. A lot of money is wasted on these sports and extravagance is *haram*.

It was perhaps in line with the above arguments that the Deobandi Taliban in Kabul issued a decree against kite flying and closed all kite shops (Rashid 2008, 219). Abdul Haq (2009, vol. 2, 111–12), also issued a *fatwa* declaring that Basant (an annual kite-flying festival) is a Hindu custom and therefore impermissible because of *tashabbuh bil kuffar*. Despite all these arguments, the DMM has not been very successful in convincing Pakistani Muslims in this regard, despite using religious arguments. The majority of Pakistanis still believe that kite flying is just a hobby or entertainment activity. Basant in Lahore was a big national event until very recently, when the courts banned it after several persons were injured by extra-sharp strings. The event is set to return in the near future with restrictions on the use of dangerous strings.

As regards fireworks, this practice is very popular in Pakistan and is generally associated with occasions of happiness. People use fireworks not only to mark weddings, festivals and Independence Day, but also to celebrate victory in sports or elections. In small towns and villages, people also use fireworks and crackers to announce the return of a friend or relative from *hajj*. Fireworks are also displayed on other religious occasions like Eid Milad-un-Nabi and Shab-e-Barat on the 15th night of the Islamic month of Sha'ban.

Thanvi (2002, 21–2) has declared this practice *haram*. Here again, he has made extra effort to add weight to his declaration through indirect references to the Quran and some Ahadith. Some of his old arguments regarding the waste of money and paper in making fire crackers have also been repeated here. Besides that, he has used the following arguments to castigate this popular practice.

1. The Prophet directed in one Hadith that one should avoid unnecessary use of fire and that one should put out any fire or lamp before going to bed. Therefore, fireworks should also be avoided because these are unnecessary, and can be harmful to life.
2. Islam has ordered that children should focus on religious knowledge and teachings. When children are encouraged to watch fireworks, it means their initial learning becomes sinful. This is in contradiction and opposition to the Islamic order.
3. Fireworks, which go straight upwards, are *haram* because they resemble the actions of Yog and Magog (two evil nations which shall rise near the Day of Resurrection or *Qiyamah*), who shall, according to the Hadith, throw their arrows straight upwards into the sky. Since Yog and Magog shall be non-Muslims and resemblance with non-Muslims is *haram*, so the fireworks are also *haram*.

Interestingly, Thanvi has defended the practice of using cannon fire (which is also directed upwards) during the *hajj* to announce the beginning or end of some ritual (e.g. the end of stay at the plain of Arafa and beginning of the journey towards Muzdalifah). Thanvi has allowed this cannon fire in the name of necessity (i.e. the necessity of making a religious announcement) and showing the grandeur of Islam (*shaukat-e-Islam*) as well as respect for its religious places. It is remarkable that the last two arguments have been disregarded by the Deobandis when the Barelwi *ulama* have employed the same to defend the practice of building shrines and tombs for saints, as discussed in Section 5.3.9.

The Deobandis have also prohibited the playing of chess. Abdul Haq (2009, vol. 2, 434) pronounced a *fatwa* that one should avoid playing chess because it is a waste of time and leads to compulsive craving. Thanvi (2002, 15–17) has quoted the following Ahadith in order to declare chess playing *haram*. These Ahadith were not authentic enough to be included in the most reliable Hadith books by Imam Bukhari and Imam Muslim.

1. The Prophet said that he who plays chess and then goes directly from there to offer his prayers is like a person who does *wudhu* (ablution) with the pus and blood of swine before saying his prayers.

2. Caliph Ali declared chess to be the "gambling of non-Arabs".
3. Abu Moosa Ash'ari said that chess is not played by anyone but the sinful.

It may be added here that playing chess has been declared permissible by Imam Shafi'i. However, Thanvi, who is a Hanafi, has stated that Imam Shafi'i allowed it only in his earlier writings.

Apart from the aforementioned customs and sociocultural practices, the DMM has also criticized many other norms of mainstream Muslim society. Actually, this has been a continuous and ongoing process through which the DMM has kept itself distinctly apart from the majority of Pakistani Muslims by contradicting their norms and values. As the scope of the DMM narrowed down over time to make it more of a countercultural than a political or religious movement, the range of mainstream customs and practices condemned by the DMM was broadened. For example, the DMM in later years condemned other practices such as celebrating anniversaries like birthdays, exchanging greeting cards on occasions like Eid or New Year's Eve, and wearing trouser pants and jeans.

The DMM has also opposed watching television on the grounds that pictures are *haram*. The Internet is generally opposed because of the use of pictures as well as for its potential use for obscenity. As a matter of fact, the DMM has condemned all such popular customs and practices by declaring them un-Islamic on one pretext or the other (e.g. *bidah*, *shirk*, *tashabbuh bil kuffar*, forbiddance of fixing dates and rituals to mark some event, etc.). The use of religious rulings against the norms and practices of mainstream society apparently makes the DMM look like a religious movement while pushing to the background its true countercultural spirit. It may be reiterated here that the Deobandis have not contradicted the values and practices of only the popular folk Islam generally represented by Barelwis. They have, in fact, also condemned all other Muslim sects and groups present in Pakistan (i.e. Ahle Hadith, Shias and Jamaat-e-Islami). A brief description of the Deobandi condemnation of these Muslim groups is given in Appendix I.

The Deobandis also deplore officially recognized national days of celebration like Independence Day, Pakistan Day, May Day, Defence Day, Quaid-e-Azam Day (for the founding father of Pakistan), Iqbal Day (after the national poet), etc. This opposition by the DMM is an indirect subversion of the state. Similarly, the Deobandis have contradicted the established practices of flying the national flag at half-mast to mourn a tragic event or observing silence to remember the dead. This condemnation is again based on *tashabbuh bil kuffar* – a concept which the Deobandis employ almost invariably to decry the worldly norms of Muslim society just like they apply the concept of *bidah* to denounce its religious norms. Recently, the Deobandis have also condemned hunger strike as a political tool by declaring it impermissible (Sahibzada 2008, 33–5). Abdul Haq issued a *fatwa* that if there is a risk of losing one's life in hunger strike then it would be akin to suicide and hence *haram* (Haq 2009, vol. 2, 358). However, it is interesting to note that the Deobandi leadership of JUH supported Gandhi's *maran barat* (hunger strike until death) at the time of partition in 1947. In that sense, the DMM appeared to be more cooperative towards *kuffar* (non-believers) than towards those who allegedly embraced *tashabbuh bil kuffar*. This 'intra-society' nature of the DMM's opposition underlies its countercultural inclinations.

It has also been observed that as the countercultural character of the DMM gradually dominated the movement, the Deobandis began to criticize the mainstream institutions and policies of the state. In this regard, they particularly opposed the mainstream educational system mainly in order to defend their madaris. Many Deobandi *ulama* have also criticized democracy as an un-Islamic system of governance. Despite that, the Deobandi party JUI has continued to participate in the electoral process without disowning the countercultural views of the movement. Recently, the Deobandi Taliban of Pakistan represented by Tehreek-e-Taliban Pakistan (TTP) openly declared democracy un-Islamic (*Dawn*, 29 December 2012). The TTP has not only killed those politicians who disagreed with its values but has also targeted the powerful military establishment because of its operation against the Taliban in Pakistan's tribal areas, where it has established its hideouts.

Furthermore, the Deobandis openly deplore the state's policies vis-à-vis the role of women in mainstream society. The DMM, just like the Afghan Taliban, wants women to be restricted to the boundaries of their homes. Similarly, the movement has tacitly opposed the state and society at large, which treat Shias as Muslims. Killings of Shias in Pakistan at the hands of banned Deobandi organizations like Sipah-e-Sahaba Pakistan and Lashkar-e-Jhangwi reflect the extremist nature of the DMM's countercultural course. Some reports have also linked the recent spate of attacks on *sufi* shrines to extremist Deobandi organizations.

To sum up, the Deobandis' condemnation of the norms and practices of mainstream society on the one hand and their use of force to impose the movement's own sociocultural and political values on the other, point towards the anti-society as well as anti-state nature of the DMM's countercultural tendencies. The next chapter analyses the viewpoint of Deobandi journals as well as madrassah students to further highlight the current countercultural approach of the DMM vis-à-vis the established sociocultural and political norms and practices prevalent in present-day Pakistan.

Chapter 6

THE DMM VERSUS MAINSTREAM SOCIETY: VIEWPOINTS OF DEOBANDI JOURNALS AND STUDENTS

It is an entirely new and different reality that members of a counterculture bear in their minds and seek to embody in social islands that exist in the midst of the rationality of the dominant order.

Kenneth Westhues, *Society's Shadow: Studies in the Sociology of Countercultures* (1972, 34)

This chapter is the outcome of fieldwork in Pakistan that was conducted in two stages. The first stage reviewed the recent Deobandi literature published by different madaris, while the second stage compared the views of students from Deobandi madaris and mainstream educational institutions. Accordingly, the chapter is divided into two parts. Both stages of fieldwork focused on four themes: popular customs and practices, politics, education and the role of women in society. Findings of the fieldwork are discussed below.

Part One: Review of Deobandi Journals

This part of the chapter explores the extent to which the trends identified in the previous chapters are manifest in the journals published by the DMM in Pakistan. The objective of this journals review is to look for countercultural trends vis-à-vis mainstream Muslim society in Pakistan during the last two decades. For this review, the following three prominent monthly journals published by major madaris were selected to represent three of the four provinces of Pakistan (no well-recognized journal from Balochistan has been published long enough for inclusion in this research).

i. *Al-Qasim* (named after one of the founders of the DMM, Muhammad Qasim)
   Published by Jamia Abu Hurairah, Nowshehra, Khyber Pukhtunkhwah Province
ii. *As-Sayyanah* (The protection)
   Published by Jamia Ashrafia, Lahore, Punjab Province
iii. *Bayyinat* (The clear proofs, named after Chapter 98 of the Quran, Al-Bayyinah)
   Published by Jamia-tul-ulum-ul-Islamiyah, Karachi, Sindh Province

As regards the publishing madaris, Jamia Abu Hurairah is located in the small town of Khaliqabad in the district of Nowshehra. It is managed by Abdul Qayyum Haqqani, a renowned Deobandi scholar who graduated from Jamia Haqqania of Akora Khattak in the same district. Following the footsteps of his alma mater,

Haqqani's madrassah kept close links with Pakistan's military establishment in connection with the *jihad* in Afghanistan. *Al-Qasim*, the journal of this madrassah, edited by Haqqani himself, published pro-*jihad* articles especially in favour of the Taliban. When the Taliban came into power in Afghanistan, this journal preached for a Taliban-style government in Pakistan and developed a large readership among Deobandis all over Pakistan. Presently, the circulation of *Al-Qasim* is about seven thousand copies per month. Jamia Abu Hurairah has also been linked to extremist Deobandi organizations. In 2003, when the Musharraf government banned militant organizations, the police conducted a raid on this madrassah in search of Deobandi extremists. Since then, it seems to have lost the support of the military establishment and its journal took an aggressive stance against the Musharraf regime after the incident. Otherwise, Jamia Abu Hurairah had earlier opted to affiliate itself with the Musharraf government's Madrassah Education Board established in 2001, with the objective of ensuring registration of all madaris as well as prescribing a syllabus for worldly subjects (Candland 2008, 105–7).

Jamia Ashrafia of Lahore, on the other hand, is a relatively moderate Deobandi madrassah in the sense that it has never been linked to any militant or *jihadi* organization. Named after Ashraf Ali Thanvi (1863–943), this madrassah was established in 1947 by Mufti Muhammad Hassan, a disciple of Thanvi. Since Hassan's death in 1961, it is being headed by his son Mufti Obaidullah. There are ten branches of this madrassah in Lahore with an enrolment of about four and a half thousand. According to the website of Jamia Ashrafia, a four-year religious course has also been launched for graduates of mainstream educational institutions with the objective of bridging 'the gap between the secular and Islamic streams of education' (2013). The journal of this *madrassah*, *As-Sayyanah* is edited by Wakil Ahmad Sherwani and its monthly circulation is around two thousand. This journal takes inspiration from the teachings of Ashraf Thanvi, whose writings it regularly publishes on topics like the role of women, reform of custom and education. As compared to the other two selected journals, *As-Sayyanah* publishes articles on political issues infrequently.

Jamia-tul-ulum-ul-Islamiyah in Binouri Town, Karachi, is one of the biggest Deobandi madaris in Pakistan with 13 branches in the city. According to the website of this *madrassah*, total enrolment is about 12,000 and students from more than sixty countries have so far studied at this *jamia* since its inception in 1954. Jamia-tul-ulum-ul-Islamiyah was established by Maulana Yousaf Binouri (1908–77), a graduate of Darul Ulum Deoband. Several prominent Deobandi scholars were associated with this madrassah including Mufti Rasheed Ahmed (1928–2002), Yousaf Ludhianvi (1932–2000) and Nizamuddin Shamzai (1930–2004). Until the 1970s, it was mostly associated with the anti-Qadyani movement. During the 1980s, it became involved in the anti-Shia campaign as well as the *jihad* in Afghanistan. It was also associated with extremist and militant Deobandi organizations like SSP, LeJ and JeM (whose leader, Azhar Masood, is an alumnus). The seminary also enjoyed close links with the military establishment of Pakistan as well as the Afghan Taliban until 2003, when the Musharraf government distanced itself from militants by proscribing several Deobandi extremist groups (Hussain 2007, 65–83). The journal of this madrassah,

Bayyinat, is edited by Maulana Abdur Razzaq Sikander and its monthly circulation is about four thousand. It is also published in Arabic under the title *Al-Bayyinat*. Apart from glorifying the *ulama* of its parent madrassah, the journal has published articles against Shias and Qadyanis on the one hand and against the mainstream customs, education and politics of Pakistan on the other.

Based on a thorough review of the above-mentioned three journals for the period 1993–2012, the coverage of topics can broadly be divided into three categories: i) preaching of Hanafi Islam through articles on interpretation of the Quran, Hadith and *fiqh*; ii) promotion of the DMM through essays on the performance of Deobandi madaris, achievements of Deobandi *ulama* and rise of the Deobandi Taliban in Afghanistan; and iii) opposition of mainstream society with respect to folk Islam, popular customs and practices, education, politics and the role of women. This part of the chapter shall discuss only those writings that are concerned with the third category, presented primarily through an *ad verbum* approach. The objective of this discussion is to highlight and understand the current countercultural mindset of the Pakistani Deobandis in light of their own words.

6.1 The DMM versus Popular Customs and Practices

Although there was a consensus among the three selected journals with regard to condemnation of various popular custom and practices, *As-Sayyanah* covered these issues more than the other two journals, mainly owing to its strict adherence to the teachings of Ashraf Thanvi, whose views in this regard have already been discussed in the previous chapter. The following discussion taken from said journals reiterates the countercultural tendencies of the DMM identified in the previous chapters.

6.1.1 On Milad-un-Nabi (the Prophet's birth celebrations)

Every year during or before Rabiul Awwal, the Islamic month during which the Prophet was born, the selected journals publish articles opposing this popular practice of folk Islam. Occasionally, the same articles are repeatedly published to voice Deobandi disapproval of various activities associated with Milad events. The general approach is to condemn Milad in light of the writings of past Deobandi scholars. Sometimes, original writings are simply reprinted. For example, Ashraf Thanvi's views are regularly published in *As-Sayyanah* on various subjects including Milad.

The selected journals criticize the practice of *Milad* on various grounds. For instance, the ordinary Muslims who participate in *Milad* meetings are condemned for their lack of commitment to Islam. Their love for the Prophet is also brought into question. One article states:

> We have seen most of the *Milad* meetings to be completely devoid of love [for the Prophet]. The worshippers of *Milad* are seen raising bamboo shoots and placing cloth over these and providing light and electricity [for *Milad* meetings], while in the

> meantime they ignore the obligatory prayers. And they also don't support beards. May I ask gentlemen! is it the appearance and condition of a lover of the Prophet? (Thanvi 2001b, 20–24)

Another article questions:

> Is the distribution of sweetmeat worth a few rupees the only right of the Prophet [on us]? […] Do you consider the Prophet to be a professional *pirzadah* [son of a spiritual leader] who would become happy over a little sweetmeat and be satisfied with a little amount of *nadhr* [gift]? Let's ask for forgiveness and protection from God. Remember! The Prophet is not happy with such lovers. (Thanvi 2011, 12–24)

The practice of celebrating the Prophet's birthday is also linked to Hindus, Christians and even Shias. According to Thanvi (2003, 14–21): 'To observe a particular day for a prophet or a saint is a custom derived from the Hindus and *mushriks* [polytheists]. […] There is no origin [in Islam] of remembering or observing a day. […] This is a mere custom taken from the Hindus and the Christians and it is *haram* due to resemblance with them.' Muawiyah (2003, 30–32) observes, 'Holding processions on [the Prophet's birthday] has no origin in Islam. Rather, this practice resembles with that of Shias [who hold processions in Muharram].'

6.1.2 On celebration of Eid

There are two Eids celebrated by Muslims every year. One at the end of the fasting month, Ramadan, called Eid-ul-Fitr and the other in the month of *hajj* (pilgrimage) called Eid-ul-Adha. The former is celebrated as a reward and thanksgiving for the fasting, while the latter commemorate the sacrifice of Prophet Abraham (PBUH), who surrendered to God's command to slaughter his son. Before he could act, God replaced his son with a lamb. Muslims mark that event by slaughtering animals and distributing meat among friends, relatives and the poor on the 10th day of Dhul Hijjah (the 12th month of the Islamic calendar). In Pakistan, the two Eids are also marked by activities like exchanging greeting cards and gifts, wearing new clothes, meeting friends and family, and cooking and distributing special dishes among friends and neighbours.

The selected Deobandi journals consistently condemn these Pakistani practices every year before the arrival of these occasions. In one essay, the traditional practice of cooking sweet vermicelli (*siwayyan*) is denounced just because it has become a custom. According to Thanvi (2012, 18–36):

> On the day of Eid-ul-Fitr, preparing [sweet] vermicelli has become a stipulated practice. One justification for the origin of this practice is that it does not take a lot of effort to cook and hence allows enough time for other chores on Eid day. [However], later on, it became a custom to send this sweet dish to friends. This has been justified in the light of the Hadith, which encourages giving away gifts on happy occasions. […] Although such

a gift on a happy occasion in itself increases love among people, by God sending such a gift as custom increases malevolence. [...] A gift sent as part of a custom is impermissible.

Other practices related to Eid like sending greeting cards and wearing new clothes are also condemned. Rauf (2011, 44–53) observes:

Undoubtedly, God has declared Eid to be a day of happiness for Muslims. It is also supported by *Shariah* that one should wear the best available dress on this day. However, numerous activities of extravagance and prodigality [like buying new clothes, new shoes, new household things, costly greeting cards, etc.] which are considered a customary part of Eid have nothing to do with religion and *Shariah*.

The exchange of Eid greeting cards is particularly declared un-Islamic because it has become a custom, it leads to wasting money and many cards carry pictures that are *haram*. According to Rauf (2000, 26–31), 'Eid cards invoke so many wrongs and sins that Muslims must avoid buying and sending these cards.'

It may be added here that the Deobandi journals also disapprove of celebrating completion of the Quran during the last nights of Ramadan before Eid-ul-Fitr. According to one essay by Thanvi (1994, 7–18), 'To light lamps on the day of completion of the Quran in Ramadan is a *bidah*. People say that this practice shows the grandeur of Islam. We say, why it is necessary to show grandeur of Islam only in Ramadan? You should rather always light numerous lamps in other months as well.' He further declares that 'if sweetmeat [on completion of the Quran in Ramadan] is purchased from one man's money, then its objective is pretentiousness, prominence, popularity and pride. If it is purchased by collecting donations from many people, they must have been coerced [by shaming or daring] to donate.' It is interesting to note here that the Deobandis themselves run their madaris through public donations.

6.1.3 On events related to marriage and death

The Deobandis oppose such events not only for being un-Islamic but also for the extravagance associated with them. One article states:

The real reason behind the present disarray in [Pakistani] society is its remoteness from religion and strict following of [un-Islamic] customs and sociocultural practices. [...] Simplicity is absent [these days] in marriage ceremonies. [...] As for the customs and practices regarding the death, it has been observed that people have to even borrow to carry out those rituals [of death]. And there are all kinds of absurd practices going around. We have made marriage a source of [financial] destruction rather than construction [of a new family]. [Similarly], death of a person leads to the [financial] death of the whole family. (Kafeel 2000, 52–4)

Another article even questions the pious intentions of those who hold various activities for *isal-e-sawab* (transfer of merit) for their dead. Qadir (2012, 34–8) observes that on the occasion of *qul* or the third day of death, 'it is pretended that all the activities [like reciting the Quran, supplication, offering food, etc.] are being carried out for the *isal-e-sawab* of the dead. However, the reality is contrary, because all this is done [as a custom] to avoid criticism and rebuke from other people as well as to display pharisaic pretentiousness.'

The Deobandis also denounce many other widespread practices observed to display sorrow and grief. For example, Agha (2009, 41–3) declares, 'There is no place in Islam for the modern-day anti-*Shariah* and customary observance of grief over death like declaring a black day, observing silence, wearing black armbands and placing flags at half-mast, etc. This is, in fact, a *taqlid* of Western civilization by the Muslims. All these practices are impermissible and against *Shariah*.'

As for the popular practices regarding shrine visiting, Bhatti (2010, 35–41) maintains that showing respect to graves by 'kissing them and bowing before them is absolutely *haram*. Similarly, the objective of constructing grand buildings for the shrines of saints is also about showing respect to graves. This type of respect for the saints is *haram* in *Shariah*.'

6.1.4 On sports and entertainment

For sports activities, *Al-Qasim* adopts the most aggressive approach among the three selected journals. Its criticism was mostly published against the backdrop of the Taliban's rise in Afghanistan. At that time, hard-line Deobandis apparently tried to wean off the Pakistani youth from sports to *jihad*. An editorial in *Al-Qasim* claims,

> Ninety per cent of Pakistanis are busy in sports matches. It is a waste of time and money. […] It is time for *jihad*. […] Make this nation a *mujahid* nation. Don't engage them in cricket, football and hockey. […] Make the daughters of the nation aware of the need for *jihad*. Don't teach them the lessons of obscenity and vulgarity by involving them in sports. […] When they [girls] move their feet and hands in the sports arena to play cricket, football, hockey and volleyball, the exhibition of their body parts creates an uncontrollable sexual desire in young men. (Haqqani 1999a, 2–4)

At around the same time, the Pakistani youth were also criticized for their involvement in other entertainment activities. Khan (1999, 38–41) observes, 'If you want to find our young man, find him in parks and sports grounds, in cinema halls and theatre, in VCR centres and video game clubs. Find him in markets and restaurants. […] He is totally unaware of the basic tenets of Islam. He can never disengage himself from these futile activities to offer five obligatory daily prayers.'

As regards music, all three journals frequently castigate it as un-Islamic. It may be pointed out here that many different types of music are popular among Pakistanis. The youth mostly listen to Bollywood and pop songs. Folk music comprised of classic poetry in local languages is part of the rural culture. Further, folk Islam allows *sufi* music in the form of *qawwali*, which is frequently performed on the shrines of several great saints.

However, Deobandi Islam declares music of every type to be strictly *haram* and even *kufr*. One article in *Bayyinat* pronounces,

> These days, songs are broadcast from radio, TV, etc. It is impermissible and *haram* to listen to such music. Because of that [music], every person has some kind of hypocrisy; faith is no more there in the hearts of the people; and modesty and demureness have gone missing. There is no worth for others' respect and regard. Fear of God has vanished. [...] Listening to music is *haram* and sinful, sitting for it is *fisq* [open disobedience of God] and enjoying it is a kind of *kufr*. (Mukhtar 1995, 11–15)

Another article in *As-Sayyanah* adopts an even stricter approach by declaring that 'if the listeners [of music] enjoy the songs, they reach the level of *kufr*. If a listener is married, his *nikah* [marriage registration] becomes invalid and it becomes obligatory for him to renew his *nikah*. [...] If you want to free yourself from the satanic trap of the non-believers, then cleanse yourself from the curse of songs [music]' (Saeed 2002, 26–30). It may be relevant to add here that Deobandi Abdul Haq (2009, vol. 1, 194) issued a *fatwa* declaring that if a Muslim considers music and dance to be legitimate and *halal* then he will be excommunicated from Islam.

Furthermore, all three journals frequently publish articles against pictures, TV and the Internet, which are part and parcel of Pakistani society. Pictures and photography are opposed mainly on the grounds that these resemble the idolatrous practices of the pre-Islamic era. According to Aslam (2008, 41–4), 'There is only a difference of time [era] between photography and sculpture. At one time, it was idol making. Today, it is the era of photography. There is only one single declaration about these two practices: both are *haram*.' Similarly, Darkhawasti (2012, 59–61), declares that 'a picture, whether hand painted or made with a camera or some other equipment, is like an idol. Drawing a portrait of others or getting one's own portrait drawn, photographing others or getting oneself photographed, keeping a picture at home or in the pocket, all are declared *haram* by consensus in our pure *Shariah*.'

Pictures are also castigated for being part of Western culture. Hussaini observes,

> Western culture is totally a culture of pictures. Our interest in photography and its worth and respect among us is because we have been cowed by Western civilization. Painting, etching and sculptor in Hindu, Buddhist and all other old *jahiliyyah* [ignorant of divine guidance] civilizations have been closely associated with *shirk* and idol worship on the one hand and sin and obscenity on the other. (1993, 47–9)

Ahmed (2008, 37–43) considers the use of photographs forbidden, even for the propagation of Islam:

> We are bound to propagate and disseminate Islam via those methods and sources through which Islam reached us. One popular method and source is *tabligh* [proselytizing] and teaching. Another method is writing and publishing. Many instruments and resources have been used for both these methods. However, there is not a single instance to

> show that a picture has been seen or shown with regard to the defence and survival of Islam. [...] Television and other visual [picture-based] instruments are themselves a collection of wrongs. Using a wrong to eradicate another wrong is not permissible at all.

Television is declared a curse and evil for society. One article proclaims that 'watching TV and VCR, etc. is an evil sighting. [Our] elders have declared that keeping a TV in the house is worse than raising 70 pigs [forbidden animals for Muslims]' (Rehman 2001, 49–52). Another article concludes that 'every television play ends up focusing on a love affair, with the [underlying] message for young boys and girls that they should not waste their time in suffocation [i.e. social and religious restrictions] and go ahead with full expression of their pent up emotions' (Muawiyah 2000, 29–30).

President of the Deobandi Wifaqul Madaris Al-Arabiyya Salimullah Khan (2008, 17–25) writes,

> I want to invite your attention to the *fitnah* [evil trial] of modernism [i.e. TV] because of which we are turning away from the path of our forefathers. For example, [...] Mufti Rasheed Ahmed [a Deobandi scholar] launched a movement against television. As a result of that, numerous people broke their TV sets, [...] but now his followers are turning away from the path of their antecessors and a [sinful] demand is being made that TV channels may be launched to condemn the *kufr*.

Similarly, Naseem (2009, 60–63) declares that watching 'TV, dish [satellite TV], etc. even for a good and religious purpose is not permissible in *Shariah*'.

Rauf (2011, 44–53) believes that 'TV is a collection of many malefactions and sins. That is why it is not permissible to watch television even for a religious or educational programme.' A Deobandi *fatwa* in this regard declares that 'propagation of Islam through wrongful and forbidden means [TV, video, etc.] is impermissible. [...] Further, a Quranic lesson, religious speech or some other religious scene recorded onto a video cassette shall after all be shown on the same television [channel] where prostitutes and dancers are prancing and corrupted impersonators are disseminating obscenity [at the same time]' (Haq 1996, 57–63).

The Deobandis believe that the state is responsible for spreading these 'evils' in society. Ludhianvi (1994, 3–19) laments that

> the religion and ethics of the nation are being spoiled under the guardianship of the government. Earlier, movie songs of the radio and other sources of obscenity were operating under government protection. Then, the curse of television was imposed on the country and each and every home was converted into a cinema house. Later, VCR was promoted. Now, a fourth step has been taken and the floodgate to the obscenity of the whole media has been opened through satellite dishes.

The Internet has also been criticized but with far less frequency and intensity than television. The reason might be that many Deobandi madaris and their umbrella organization Wifaqul Madaris Al-Arabiyya run their own websites. The main criticism of Internet concerns its potential to spread obscenity among the youth. Qasmi (2007, 31–5) observes that 'a flood of vulgarity and obscenity has arisen [through the Internet] and the youth is especially at risk'.

6.1.5 On other customs and practices

Deobandi journals disapprove many prevalent practices in Pakistan by linking them with Western culture. For example, the use of the Gregorian calendar is rejected in an article published in *Al-Qasim* which declares that 'the names of the days of the week in the Western calendar, which are commonly used in Pakistan, represent *shirk* and *kufr* [owing to their Greek and Roman origins, and] have no justification in Islam' (Bukhari 1999, 23–5). Similarly, Soomro (2005, 46–7) castigates New Year's Eve celebrations by stating that 'the new year of the Muslims does not start on the first of January but on the first day of Muharram [the first Islamic month]. [...] Alas, Muslims also follow the footprints of the Christians and invite the wrath of God due to this *taqlid* of the West.'

The Deobandis have also criticized the prevailing practices regarding men's clothing. In Pakistan, men in rural areas and small towns mostly wear *shalwar kamiz*, while in big cities Western dress like pants, shirts, coats, neckties as well as jeans are also popular. The DMM has opposed Western dress by linking it with Christianity. For example, Bukhari (2002, 21–2) declares that 'wearing a neck-tie is *haram*. [...] Christians wear ties as a symbol of the cross around their neck. They [thus] approve of Christianity and oppose Islam.' Even in *shalwar kamiz*, the Deobandis oppose having collars and cuffs on the *kamiz* (long shirt) on the basis that these originated in the West. Renowned Deobandi scholar Taqi Usmani (2002, 37–40) writes in *As-Sayyanah*, 'Our [Deobandi] elders used to wear *kurta* [long shirt] without cuffs. It is appropriate for a man to dress like his elders. And thank God it is my routine to wear such *kurta* [without cuffs]. However, wearing a shirt with cuffs is not against Sunnah because the Prophet did wear a shirt with tight sleeves.' It is interesting that the Deobandis have preferred their own norms and customs despite having a different precedent in the Sunnah.

Further, the Deobandis have opposed the huge majority of Pakistani Muslims for not using a cap or turban to cover their heads. Mufti Abdul Qawi (2011, 27–32) writes in *Al-Qasim*, 'Nowadays, wearing a cap [by men] is considered by the modern educated class as bizarre as bare-headedness was considered some years ago. This is the result of the efforts of modern civilization, i.e. the sole Jewish civilization of the world called globalization. Therefore, it is proved that this modern-day fashion [of not covering one's head] is un-Islamic and despicable'.

While criticizing the lifestyle of modern-day Pakistanis, one article in *Bayyinat* concludes that 'Western culture means *taqlid* of Western nations and their lifestyle [including] fashion, dress, eating, drinking, moving around, meetings, greetings and [forms of] addressing [one another]. [...] *Ulama* should highlight Islamic culture and lifestyle and adopt the golden rules of their ancestors' (Muhammad 2009, 41–9). Yousaf Binouri tries to explain Islamic culture as follows:

> Islamic diction is a stranger to the word *saqafat* [culture], which is not at all mentioned in the Quran, Hadith and other repertoire of Islamic knowledge. [...] In English, the

> word culture was employed to refer to civilization and lifestyle. Our literati translated it as *saqafat* and since then this ambiguous word has been used without any clear interpretation and meaning. Everyone has tried to define its meaning according to his own taste. These days, it is generally used to refer to the scenarios associated with dance, vulgarity and obscenity. [...] If this is an Islamic country and its citizens are Muslims, then there can be only one culture for all of them, i.e. the teachings of the Quran and the pious path of the Prophet. (2012, 3–12)

It may be recalled here that the mainstream society of Pakistan is quite tolerant and flexible about the West. According to a survey report by the University of Michigan's Centre for Social Research (2013), only 30 per cent of Pakistanis are worried about the Western cultural invasion. On the contrary, 26 per cent agree on the desirability of the Western political model and 89 per cent believe that their country would be better placed if it had Western technology. Similarly, the report declares that Pakistan shows the highest level of religious tolerance among the seven Muslim-majority nations included in the survey (the others being Egypt, Iraq, Lebanon, Saudi Arabia, Tunisia and Turkey). According to the survey, 99 per cent of Pakistanis disapprove of any attacks on US citizens working in Islamic countries and 97 per cent disagree with the idea of prohibiting non-Muslims from practising their religion. An overwhelming majority of Pakistanis (90 per cent) actually believe that non-Muslims should enjoy equal rights with Muslims.

Apart from the above-mentioned popular customs and practices, the Deobandi journals also very strongly condemn the Shia practice of mourning the death of Imam Hussain. This practice is otherwise well respected by followers of folk Islam, who themselves observe the 10th of Muharram as a day of mourning. However, the writings in the selected journals declare the practices of Shia Muslims in the month of Muharram as *bidah* and *shirk*, as shown by the following excerpts.

i. There is no recognition in *Shariah* of doing *matam* [Shia practice of hitting oneself to feel the pain of the martyrs of Karbala] even in Shia *madhab*. These are neither *fardh* [obligatory] nor *wajib* [necessary], neither Sunnah nor *mustahab* [recommended]. [...] Even if it is worship for them [Shias], can't this worship be carried out individually? Is it a condition to do it in congregation? [...] If *matam* and mourning [by Shias] are restricted to the boundary walls of their places of worship, then the country would be saved from many difficulties. Several problems including traffic [blockades] shall be solved and the protection of the life and property of citizens shall be ensured. (Haidri 2009, 46–9)
ii. Narrating the martyrdom of Imam Hussain is in itself true and right. But since it has been associated with the first ten days of Muharram, since its objective is also to enhance grief [which is impermissible in *Shariah*], and since it is the practice of *ahle bidah* [those who follow wrongful innovation] to hold a meeting exclusively for Imam Hussain, it is therefore obligatory to avoid participation in such meetings because of resemblance to Shias. Otherwise, it would be considered a great sin. (Quddus 1991, 23–7)
iii. The way *taziyah* [Shia mourning procession carrying replicas of monuments of martyrs of Karbala] is observed (in the subcontinent) is unprecedented. Even in Iran, which is a special home for Shias, it [*taziyah*] is not observed. [...] *Taziyah* is *bidah*. [...] *Taziyah* is *shirk*. (Karim 1998, 33–42)

iv. All [...] *bidah* practices in the month of Muharram are either impermissible, *haram* or big sins. [...] We should seek forgiveness [and protection] from these and should endeavour with our lives to eradicate all such *bidah*, customs and absurd practices. (Halim 1998, 51–7)

The vision of the DMM in this regard is discernible in an article by Haqqani (1998a, 32–4), who reports that 'Shias in Afghanistan shall not be allowed [by the Taliban] to openly carry out [their] customs, practices and mourning meetings and processions'.

To conclude this section, one may infer that the opposition of the Deobandis to several popular customs and practices of mainstream Muslim society in Pakistan, as mentioned in the selected journals, clearly indicate towards the countercultural nature of Deobandi Islam. Further, it is not only the frequency of the coverage of such topics but also the intensity of the views in this regard which emphasizes the countercultural character of the DMM. For the Deobandis, 'It is obligatory for each Muslim, man and woman, to prepare for the eradication of weird customs and practices and make an effort from both heart and body to ensure that not a single custom survives. [...] The one who opposes these customs and practices is a saint and a favourite slave of God' (Thanvi 2001a, 15–18).

6.2 The DMM versus the Mainstream Political System

As mentioned in previous chapters, the Deobandis have long dreamt of establishing an Islamic state which can be governed under their own version of Islam. However, with the passage of time the political vision of the DMM has been dominated by its countercultural vision, which is more concerned with opposing the beliefs and practices of the Muslims of the subcontinent than establishing a separate Islamic state. By the time of partition, the DMM was already grappling with its countercultural vision and the Deobandi Jamiat Ulama-e-Hind opposed the creation of Pakistan despite the fact that it was an opportunity for the Deobandis to revive their old political vision.

After the creation of Pakistan, the small group of Deobandis who had belatedly supported partition tried to resurrect their political vision by looking for a place for themselves in the politics of the new country. However, they were soon pushed aside by the mainstream political parties, which promote the idea of a democratic Pakistan. Presently, there is overwhelming support for democracy in Pakistan. According to the aforementioned survey of the University of Michigan (2013), Pakistanis prefer a stable, non-military, non-religious government, while simultaneously showing support for *Shariah*. Despite being socially conservative and having a strong attachment to religious norms, their political preference is decidedly democratic. The survey reports that 88 per cent Pakistanis believe that democracy is an ideal form of government and 90 per cent support a democratic political system for their country. On the other hand, only 33 per cent thought that it was good to have an Islamic government and only 18 per cent agreed with the idea of a strong head of government who does not bother with parliament or elections.

The review of the selected journals shows that the Deobandis in Pakistan have little respect for the mainstream political system and its leadership. In fact, they generally show a kind of disdain and derision towards democracy as well as the political leaders of Pakistan. It is quite remarkable to note that the father of the nation, Muhammad Ali Jinnah, who is always referred to by Pakistanis as Quaid-e-Azam (the greatest leader), is simply referred to as Jinnah or Jinnah Saheb by Deobandi writers.

The following discussion about the views expressed in the three Deobandi journals gives a glimpse of the countercultural vision of the DMM with respect to the mainstream political system of Pakistan.

6.2.1 On democracy

Despite the fact that the Deobandi JUI has long been participating in the electoral politics of Pakistan, DMM scholars writing in the selected journals rarely support the concept of democracy. On the other hand, most of them consider democracy to be contradictory to Islam. Ashraf Ali Ṭhanvi is quoted in *As-Sayyanah* as saying:

> There is no such thing as democratic government. Islam only teaches about an individual's government. [It is true] that the faults in governance for which democracy was introduced are of course likely to occur in an individual's government as well. But these [faults] could certainly occur in a democracy [because] if the opinion of an individual can be wrong then the opinion of a group of people can also be wrong. [...] Therefore the principle of making a decision by the majority voting is totally wrong. (Zafar 2003, 50–52)

Similarly, Qasmi (2002, 14–17) observes in *Al-Qasim*:

> In actuality, democracy means severing the values, lifestyles, circumstances, civilization and culture of the people from their faith and religion and thus making them secular instead of regular [with *Shariah*] in the name of societal discipline and people's government. The purpose of this democracy is to set up a common system behind which the wily of the world could establish their dictatorship all over the planet. A system with such ideology and goals shall definitely come into conflict with the system of God, ultimately leading to a battle.

Further, the president of the Wifaqul Madaris is quoted as declaring that 'democracy is against *Shariah*' (Zahid 2007, 4–9).

This lack of faith in democracy is aptly reflected in another article published in *Al-Qasim* which condemns the democratic system in a very harsh manner. It states,

> He who fits the die-casting of democracy shall turn out to be two-faced in personality and character, duplicitous in views and vision, double-dealing in social and societal attitudes, Janus-faced in ethics and actions, deceitful in intentions and promises and a confirmed hypocrite in his words and promises. [...] On the chessboard of our country, our political leaders have changed their colours like chameleons owing to their cunning, duplicity and guile. Whenever they came into power, they promoted dictatorship and

> fascism in the name of democracy. [...] The system of democracy is ideal for their stratagem. (Athar 2000, 7–10).

One essay by renowned Deobandi scholar Mufti Shafi in *As-Sayyanah* denounces the concept of electoral politics as:

> a game which is played in elections in the name of democracy, whereby this short-lived ambiguous honour [election success] is achieved through the use of all the evil resources of aggression and physical force. [...] The better way for this [election] is that no one should declare himself a candidate. Rather, a group of Muslims should nominate a person who is considered to be commensurate with the job. (Shafi 2007, 5–10)

Another editorial of *Al-Qasim* condemned the electoral process in the following way:

> We neither feel happy about the holding of elections nor do we feel the need to mourn their delay because we already know the final [ruinous] fruit of this garden [elections and democracy]. [...] We shall request our readers and political leaders that before entering this election [in 2008], they should think of coming out of it [i.e. boycotting it]. (Haqqani 2008a, 3–5).

As they declare democracy un-Islamic, the Deobandi scholars believe that an Islamic system could only be implemented after removing democracy altogether. As Muawiyah (2008, 42–5) observes in *Bayyinat*:

> Since 14 August 1947 [Independence Day in Pakistan], democracy is the reason for the lack of implementation of an Islamic system in the state, which was achieved in the name of Islam. Until we get rid of democracy, the rich will continue to become richer and the poor poorer. [...] As Mufti Shafi said, it is an out-and-out requirement of the natural system of the universe that the responsibility of the system of government should lie with a single authoritative person who can actually be called *ameer* [commander]. And the *hall-o-aqd* [loosening and fastening] of government affairs should belong to him and his obedience should be binding on all the people [...]. [In democracy], there is no authority of the *ameer* and other opinion leaders and experienced persons vis-à-vis the majority's opinion. That is one fault [of democracy], which in itself holds hundreds of other faults.

It may be added here that while the Deobandis have given the power of *hall-o-aqd* to the *ameer*, the term *ahl al-hall wal-aqd* is generally used to refer to those qualified to elect or depose a caliph on behalf of the Muslim community. In modern Islamic political thought, this term is commonly equated with parliament.

6.2.2 On political leadership

Al-Qasim criticizes the mainstream political leadership far more aggressively than the other two journals, which prefer to condemn the policies rather than the personalities of the rulers. Hoping for a Taliban-style government in Pakistan, the editor of *Al-Qasim* writes,

> Why have we supposed that our land has become infertile and that no righteous and just leader can be born here? Why have we concluded that only someone returning from Harvard and Cambridge can change our fate? [...] There are numerous pearls under the depth of *ummah*'s ocean [i.e. *ulama*]. They just need a little time before being pushed to the shore. (Haqqani 2009b, 3–8)

The editor of *Al-Qasim* tries to discredit all politicians by stating that

> Pervez Musharraf, Zardari, Leghari, Nawaz Sharif, Chaudhry Shujaat, Jamali, Pervez Elahi, Sheikh Rasheed, Sher Afgan, Asfandyar, Shaukat Aziz [the whole top political leadership except religious leaders] fall into same category as far as the ideological foundation of the country is concerned. Expecting loyalty and hope from such people is the contempt of hope itself. We don't know the criteria on which the people elect such leaders, who own bungalows at every health resort and for whom New York is only at a distance of two arms. (Haqqani 2008b, 3–6)

The Deobandi vision for change is also very different from that of mainstream society, which looks for changes to strengthen the democratic system. One article observes, 'You say that the system should be changed. We also say that the system should be changed. Then what is the hurdle? In your view, there are technical and legal hurdles, but for us there are individual and personal hurdles [i.e. politicians]' (Haqqani 2009a, 3–6). Another article concludes, 'Don't just change the *nizam* [system]; change the *imam* [leader] as well. A system is just a reflection of the leader' (Haqqani 2008c, 3–6).

6.2.3 On the Taliban

All three journals present the Afghan Taliban in a positive light, mainly because the latter follow Deobandi Islam. Further, the madaris publishing *Al-Qasim* and *Bayyinat* maintain close ties with the Taliban through teaching Afghan students and providing recruits for the Afghan *jihad*. Owing to this connection, these journals give far more coverage to the Taliban than *As-Sayyanah*, whose madrassah maintains no links with them. Despite that, articles in the latter journal are still supportive of their fellow Deobandis in Afghanistan. For example, one article in *As-Sayyanah* shows optimism about the Taliban's success in imposing *Shariah* in Afghanistan:

> The Taliban have always kept their objectives focused on two things: one, establishing peace, and two, imposition of *Shariah*. As far as peace is concerned, no one disagrees with the opinion that the Taliban have succeeded in establishing an exemplary peace. [...] As for the imposition of *Shariah*, the Taliban are distinct from different other groups that have ruled Kabul in the sense that they entered Kabul using their own power rather than through some power-sharing mechanism. That is why they are free

> to make their own decisions and, thank God, they possess the true spirit and fervour to do that. (Abbasi 2001, 42–55)

Articles in the other two journals, particularly *Al-Qasim*, are quite upbeat about the Taliban – giving credit to Deobandi madaris for training them – and hope for the replication of their system in Pakistan. One article claims:

> Madaris are the garrisons of the Taliban. These are the training centres of the Taliban. These are the factories of the Taliban where the latter are manufactured. From there, they leave, holding the flag of *Shariah*, to fight a great battle against the enemy. [...] If [the Pakistani leadership] wanted to solve the Kargil dispute [with India], they should not have gone to [President] Clinton. If they had [simply] placed the dirt of Mullah Omar's feet in their eyes as *kohl*, then by God the problem would have been solved [an attempt to give Mullah Omar holy status as well as suggest following in his footsteps]. (Athar 1999, 7–9)

Another article states:

> Islamic revolution in Afghanistan is the discernible outcome of madaris. [...] The movement for the protection of Islamic prophetic knowledge launched by Darul Ulum Deoband a century ago has now come to the fore in Afghanistan in the form of the domination of Islam, the implementation of *Shariah* and the establishment of peace. Before the Taliban, Kabul and Mazar-e-Sharif were the centres of vulgarity, nudity and obscenity. But these [same] cities looked like a gathering of proselytizers as soon as they were conquered [by the Taliban]. (Haqqani 1998c, 11–12)

As the Taliban took control of Afghanistan, the role of madaris was reinterpreted. In the wake of deteriorating law and order in Karachi, the editorial of *Al-Qasim* suggested that 'the Taliban (students) of Karachi's madaris can establish peace in the city. [...] May God enable us to follow the Taliban of Afghanistan' (Haqqani 1998b, 2–4). Similarly, the TTP was expected to play a bigger role in implementing the Afghan Taliban's system in Pakistan. One article claimed as early as 1998, 'Now, Tehreek-e-Taliban [Pakistan] shall not be restricted to Waziristan [the tribal area] alone. It shall be introduced throughout the country. We have before us the ideal of Afghanistan's Taliban. [...] Immediate steps have been taken against VCRs, vulgar movies, video cassettes, video games as well as against obscenity [in Waziristan]' (Haq 1998, 6–8).

6.2.4 On foreign policy

Almost all the articles of the selected journals in this regard focus on condemnation of the United States. Afghanistan is treated as a domestic issue and the US invasion of that country is opposed as if it were an intervention in Pakistan. On the other hand, there is hardly any criticism of India, Pakistan's traditional rival, despite the fact that the two countries have fought four wars since independence in 1947. This soft approach towards India can be understood in the context of the DMM's origins and continuing presence in that country. It is perhaps because of this soft approach that Pakistan's military establishment preferred Ahle Hadith Lashkar-e-Taiba (LeT) over the Deobandis in its proxy war against India. The Deobandi militants, on the other hand, were mostly diverted towards Afghanistan.

As for the anti-US stance of the Deobandi journals, this approach was adopted well before the rise of the Afghan Taliban. In 1995, an article in *Bayyinat* expressed the following:

> In fact, the standard of good and bad in Pakistan at the official level is that what is considered right by America is good and what is declared bad by America is bad and that's all! America and its protégé lobby is afraid of that 'atomic bomb' [*mujahideen*] manufactured in madaris that has written a golden chapter in history by fighting with their lives as a frontline force in the Afghan *jihad*. Now, the danger for the United States is that the same 'atomic bomb' may pulverize America just like [it did] the Soviet Union. (Khalid 1995, 51–5)

Deobandi criticism against the United States became extremely aggressive after the fall of the Taliban government in 2001. A *fatwa* in this regard was signed by 88 *ulama* and was published in *As-Sayyanah* (November 2001, 61–2), which proclaimed that 'it is obligatory for each Muslim that he should provide as much support as possible to this *jihad* against the United States in Afghanistan'. Since then, the Deobandi journals have consistently castigated Pakistan's support to NATO forces in Afghanistan. Ajiz (2010, 19–22) writes in *Al-Qasim* that Pakistan 'must immediately come out of America's war [in Afghanistan] and must stop the logistic support for the United States. Furthermore, talks should be held with the people of Waziristan in order to put out the fire started by America.'

The anti-US approach of the DMM is so strong that the Deobandis might be ready to review their soft approach towards India if the United States would play some role in improving Pak-India relations. For example, the editorial of *As-Sayyanah* after the Kargil War between Pakistan and India in 1999 opined:

> Although Pakistan might have suffered a lot because of its traditional clash with India, there have been some benefits as well. Acquiring of nuclear capability is, in fact, the outcome of that tussle [with India]. Now, instead of solving the real problems of the two countries, the United States is tightening its noose around us by giving an impression of friendship or at least normalization of relations [between India and Pakistan] by referring to the evanescence of the justification for our defence programmes. That is why America has shown the utmost anxiety and haste for a truce between the two countries [after Kargil]. (Zahid 1999, 3–6)

In short, the foreign policy vision of the DMM can be summarized in the words of an excerpt from the editorial of *Al-Qasim*, which states that 'while guiding His Muslim slaves on foreign policies, God has forbidden them in the Quran from holding friendship and relations with non-Muslims. [But] in this regard, we are still taking steps and making decisions in the light of the information and directions given by the United States' (Haqqani 2002, 3–4). However, it may be pointed out here that the DMM is so obsessed with its anti-US approach that there are hardly any articles in the Deobandi journals to emphasize Pakistan's friendly relations with Muslim countries.

6.2.5 On Pakistan's origins

It is a historical fact that the DMM and its political party JUH opposed the idea of Pakistan. Only a small faction of Deobandi *ulama* under the leadership of Shabbir Ahmad Usmani supported the creation of a new country for Indian Muslims. Usmani was a disciple of Ashraf Ali Thanvi, who remained aloof from politics. It may be noted that Usmani openly supported the Pakistan Movement at its peak in 1945, while Thanvi died in 1943 well before the movement had gained momentum. However, the Deobandi journals, *As-Sayyanah*, which follows the teachings of Thanvi, tried to create the impression that Thanvi was the ideologue of Pakistan movement. In an attempt to confound history, one article claimed that 'before getting a nod of approval from Thanvi, the [All-India] Muslim League was just a body without a soul. It had no voice among the masses. [...] The credit for the success of the Muslim League as well as the establishment of Pakistan goes to these people [the *ulama*].' The article further twisted the history for the image building of the DMM:

> It is a common understanding that the idea of Pakistan was first presented by Allama Muhammad Iqbal in 1930 [...]. However, if one looks closely [at history], this idea was first of all revealed by God on the blessed heart of the fourteenth-century *mujaddid* [reviver] of this *ummah*, Ashraf Ali Thanvi. [...] He once said in 1928, 'My heart yearns that there should be a piece of land with a pure Islamic government where all laws and rules, etc. should be issued in line with the orders of *Shariah*.' [...] In the present turbulent times, it is not expected from the people who control the media that they would unveil the real reasons and motivations behind the establishment of Pakistan. (Thanvi 2001, 11–25)

As-Sayyanah would regularly publish such misleading articles every year on Pakistan Day (23 March) and Independence Day (14 August) to obscure the historical truth regarding the overall Deobandi opposition to the creation of Pakistan. It is interesting to note that one prominent Deobandi scholar of the Thanvi family, Tanvirul Haq Thanvi (2013), wrote an essay in Urdu daily *Jang* in which he clearly stated that Ashraf Thanvi did not have even a distant connection with the Pakistan Movement.

As regards the other two journals, they at least did not try to take credit for the creation of Pakistan. However, some articles tried to distort history by defining the objectives of Pakistan from the Deobandi perspective. For example, in an article in *Bayyinat*, the founder of Jamia Binouria declares:

> The actual objectives of Pakistan's foundation were: the implementation of Islamic law in this country; the establishment of a pious society; the elimination of evil acts

> and obscenity; protection from the flood of vulgarity and nudity coming from Godless countries; the eradication of aggression and enmity, ensuring for each person a life of satisfaction and contentment under the Islamic system of justice and equity; and taking care of the destitute. (Binouri 1997, 3–5)

Similarly, an editorial of *Al-Qasim* observes that 'Pakistan is an ideological state. There is *kalama-e-tawhid* [Islamic declaration of monotheism] in its foundation and its status is like a mosque' (Haqqani 1999b. 53–6).

6.2.6 On the vision for Pakistan

All three journals express the opinion that an Islamic system should be implemented in Pakistan. However, hardly any of the articles published in this regard are able to give the contours and details of that system. After the rise of the Taliban in Afghanistan, there were some suggestions for an Islamic revolution through *jihad* to impose Taliban-style rule. For example, one article in *Al-Qasim* proposes that '*jihad* is the spirit of the Islamic domination as well as the need of the hour. Jamia Abu Hurairah [Nowshehra] shall also become a military garrison just like Darul Ulum Deoband' (Farooq 1998, 44–5). Another article declares that 'armed *jihad* has become inevitable for Islamic revolution [in Pakistan]' (Rehman 1999, 36–7).

After the fall of Taliban rule, the caliphate system was recommended for Pakistan. As Iqbal (2007, 59–60) observes in *Bayyinat*:

> The only reason behind all our [social and political] ills, is the lack of a caliphate system. [...] We are already aware of the [bitter] fruits of the democratic efforts. That road leads to somewhere else [...]. In a caliphate, all efforts are made under [the guidance] of a caliph and there is a singular common direction of the endeavours of the whole *ummah*. [Unlike the present scenario] it is not that some people are sacrificing their lives through suicide attacks while a huge majority is living a comfortable, carefree and luxurious life that is far removed from religious thought and objectives.

Almost all the suggestions for an Islamic system are put forward in the context of condemnation of the existing political system. Hussain Madni of the DMM vehemently opposed the creation of Pakistan and condemned it to be an *istadraj* – a term used for a situation when God gives fortunes to some disobedient people despite being displeased with them. With this in mind, an article in *As-Sayyanah* concludes: 'In [our] dear country Pakistan, Islam has never been implemented. Rather, every new ruler has been propagating the adoption of an irreligious and secular lifestyle. [...] Today circumstances have proven that the doubts expressed by that *qalandar* [ascetic saint, i.e. Madni] at the time of Pakistan's creation were correct' (Ali 2005, 26–33). Another editorial in *As-Sayyanah* declares:

> The war has not ended after the establishment of Pakistan. Rather, there has been a change of battleground. Earlier our war was with the Hindus and the British, who did

> not want a state to be established in the name of Islam. After winning that battle, the second stage of the war started whereby we have to fight with those people who do not want implementation of Islam in this country. (Zahid 1994, 40–53)

It may be added here that this is again a distortion of history because in actuality the Deobandis and their party, JUH, had joined the Hindus to oppose the creation of Pakistan.

Although the selected journals do not put forward any explicit idea about their vision for Pakistan as an Islamic state, one can still infer that such a state would be far removed from a modern democratic country. According to an article in *Bayyinat*, JUI leader Mufti Mahmood (1919–80) once declared:

> Jamiat-ul-Ulama-e-Islam believes that the inclusion of non-Muslims in the structure and composition of Islamic legislation is interference in religion and a joke with Islam. Such composition of legislature, which includes non-Muslims as members, cannot be called an Islamic legislature at all and a constitution that allows it cannot, in any case, be called an Islamic constitution. (Karim 1993, 17–31)

In view of the consistent support and praise for the Taliban, it appears that the DMM's vision for Pakistan is not much different from Afghanistan. Further, the DMM hopes to lead this Taliban-style system in Pakistan through its own *ulama*, as implied in an editorial in *Al-Qasim*: 'It is our hearty desire that the leadership of this purified country should be held by those who deserve it because of their piety, devoutness and other such qualities' (Haqqani 1999b. 53–6).

6.3 The DMM versus the Mainstream Educational System

The DMM, since its inception, has been obsessed with the protection of their madaris against intervention by the state. The Deobandi obsession in this regard has consistently been touching the boundaries of paranoia. However, the DMM did not challenge the mainstream educational system until after the 1980s – a period that saw a surge in Deobandi madaris in the wake of the Afghan *jihad*. As the number of Deobandi madaris and students increased remarkably, so did their self-confidence and pride. This not only allowed them to successfully resist state intervention but also criticize the mainstream educational system vis-à-vis their own madaris.

As mentioned earlier, as the scope of the DMM had gradually narrowed down to the point that it behaved like a countercultural movement, the canvas of its conflict with mainstream society broadened. Soon, it was not just the popular customs and sociocultural and spiritual practices of Muslim society that were castigated by the DMM. In fact, with the passage of time, the Deobandis also started to condemn the mainstream political and educational systems of Pakistan. The following discussion on the views of Deobandi journals spotlights the countercultural mindset of the DMM vis-à-vis the mainstream education pursued by Pakistani society. It may be added here that there is a complete consensus among the selected journals in this regard.

6.3.1 On the status of madaris

The Deobandis consider their madaris to be superior to mainstream educational institutions and even declared them the direct descendants of the Prophet's tradition. One article in *Bayyinat* states that

> a madrassah is a true successor and a caliph of the Prophet which is working for the proselytizing and education of your religion. Therefore, anyone who holds even very little true love for the Prophet must have love and interest for these madaris too. Every person who wants to gauge his love for the Prophet can estimate it by measuring his love for madaris [...] because these madaris are the deputies of the Prophet and according to the sages a deputy and his boss are to be treated in the same manner. (Ambethvi 1995, 17–18)

Another source of that pride is their belief that worldly knowledge is inferior to religious education. An editorial of *Al-Qasim* declares:

> Some intellectuals of the nation are directing to accept social sciences as a replacement of traditional sciences [*ulum-e-naqlia*]. They have forgotten that traditional sciences are permanent. Islamic sciences cannot change until *Qiyamah* [the Day of Resurrection]. The original source of knowledge is the revelation from God and the Beloved of God [i.e. the Prophet]. The Quran and Sunnah cannot be validated through the Western knowledge of science and arts. (Haqqani 2005, 8–11)

The Deobandis also maintained that madaris were the reason for the survival of Islam in Pakistan. Kashmiri (2004, 31–5) writes in *Al-Qasim*:

> If the Islamic identity of Pakistan is still intact and if the religious prudency and vitality is still present among the people [of Pakistan], it is just because of the madaris. If the madaris were not there, the powers of *kufr* would have taken this country far away from Islam. [...] *Jihad* in Afghanistan happened because of madaris and [consequently] the Soviet Union was destroyed. It is because of the madaris that our ideological frontiers are being protected and defended.

Similarly, Abbasi (2001, 42–55) writes in *As-Sayyanah*:

> If this system of madaris and mosques was not there, Islam and Islamic values in the subcontinent, just like in Spain, would have become a story of the past. [Likewise] the two-nation theory on whose basis the movement for Pakistan was launched and progressed would have become obsolete. The foundation of the God-given country of Pakistan was provided by this same educational system of madaris and this state of Pakistan still exists on that theory. An effort to change this system of madaris is like destroying the two-nation theory as well as the foundation of Pakistan.

It is an interesting line of argument by a Deobandi scholar in view of the fact that the DMM actually opposed the two-nation theory and allied with the Hindu-dominated Congress Party before partition and propagated united Indian nationalism, as was discussed in Chapter 3.

The rise to power of the Afghan Taliban provided an extraordinary boost to this sense of superiority among the Deobandi madaris:

> Some time ago, people used to consider the students and *ulama* of madaris as suspended organs of society. People used to make fun [by saying] that madaris were centres of mere eating and drinking [for free]. Now, when the situation is different, reality has been unearthed [before the people]. The students and teachers of madaris have very recently provided a model of the best peaceful system of government in Afghanistan. By establishing a comprehensive Islamic system in Afghanistan, the Taliban have shown a model of governance to those people who believed that students and *ulama* were not worth anything and that their job was restricted to just mosque and madrassah. (Haq 2004, 38–47)

This peculiar sense of self-pride has not only led the DMM to declare its madaris to be forts of Islam but has given the movement faith in the survival of its madaris because of society's dependence on them for guidance. In *Al-Qasim*, Maulana Zahid-ur-Rashdi explains this symbiotic relationship between society and madaris in an interesting manner:

> Madrassah is not a name given to a building or to stools and mats. Madrassah is [actually] about the connection between the *maulvi* [cleric] and society. We *maulvis* give something to society and also take something [back from it]. If there is a doubt [in society] about prayer [fasting, *zakat*, *hajj*, marriage, *halal*, *haram*, etc.], that shall be removed by the cleric. This [aspect of] connection with society is about 'giving'. Another connection is about 'taking', [e.g.] if a person is facing some adversity in the family, he is told to offer some *sadaqah* [i.e. voluntary charity for the poor to ward off that adversity]. He would go to the market and buy a goat for *sadaqah* [and present that goat to a madrassah for poor students]. We don't need to worry. It is settled that we have to explain to them the *mas'ala* [religious solution] and we have to eat the goat as well. Until that connection between us and society exists [...] madaris cannot be closed even if America hangs itself upside down. (Rashdi 2009, 11–13)

6.3.2 On the practices of mainstream educational institutions

One of the consequences of the DMM's pride in its madaris is that it looks down upon all other educational institutions, where more than 95 per cent of Pakistani children and youths are studying. The review of the Deobandi journals showed that the DMM considers mainstream education in Pakistan to be un-Islamic as well as anti-Islamic. Various articles not only condemn the text but also the context of mainstream education. Shakir (2002, 22–3) observes that 'the majority of experts in modern education are ignorant of their religion, oblivious to the love and obedience of their Prophet, uninstructed about issues like cleanliness, etc. given in their book, the Quran, unaware of their responsibilities and rights vis-à-vis parents and progenies'.

Similarly, Yousaf Ludhianvi presents a very negative picture of the modern educational system, including girls' education:

> Two benighted practices have become very popular in this era; one is girls' education and the other is the overall dissemination of [modern] education. If your [modern] education had inculcated ethics in the nation, I would have acknowledged that this education is a good thing. [...] However, [I observe] that the higher the level of education of a person, the worse are [his] ethics. [...] What else do you teach except maligning teachers, harassing women and having love affairs with girls belonging to noble families? Tell me, what else do your colleges and universities teach apart from that? (Ludhianvi 2009, 14–23)

The Deobandis also declare the uniforms of children in some mainstream schools un-Islamic. Rehman (2003, 34–8) states, 'The necktie is a religious symbol of the Christians. [...] We have begun the compulsory use of neckties for junior and senior children in both government and private schools. [...] And they have been forced to wear pants instead of Eastern dress, *shalwar*.' The mainstream system has been castigated for employing co-education and holding recreational events in educational institutions. One article in *Bayyinat* demands:

> Every kind of music, dance and recreation activity should be banned in all public and private [educational] institutions, [i.e.] schools, colleges and universities. The existing co-education system should be abolished. Every kind of vulgarity, obscenity and non-observance of *purdah* should be eliminated from educational institutions and all the resources and reasons for these [wrongs] should specifically be eradicated. (Binouri 2012, 3–12)

6.3.3 On the impact of modern education

The views presented in this subsection are linked to the DMM's sense of superiority about its madaris. However, the Deobandi criticism of mainstream education discussed here at the same time appears to be an indirect defence of the existence and continuation of the madrassah system in the wake of various reform efforts by the state. In their aggressive approach against the mainstream education system, the Deobandi journals have employed a variety of arguments. One article in *Bayyinat* declares that mainstream education promotes Western culture:

> The biggest defect in this [mainstream] education is that its followers [ultimately] become strangers to their traditions and civilization, their code of ethics as well as their history. All those things which are the foundations of nationality appear inferior in their eyes. They are submerged in Western civilization and customs. Their greatest skill is to imitate the West. Nowadays, they have turned into a sect, which is extremely threatening for the [overall] system of the nation. (Akhtar 2009, 42–7)

Another article even alleges that modern education promotes Christianity. According to Muhammad (2009, 41–9):

> Modern sciences, which are concerned purely with worldly affairs, were first introduced by Lord Macaulay [in the subcontinent]. [...] Someone trained in these modern sciences does not remain a Muslim of any worth, even if he does not become a Christian. [...] The root cause of all ills is this modern education. Therefore, it is the responsibility of the *ulama* that they should provide the right guidance to Muslims and make an effort to protect the children of Muslims from this flood of apostasy [i.e. mainstream education].

Mainstream education has also been discredited by exaggerating some institutional weaknesses and governance issues. For example, Khalid (1995, 51–5) proclaims:

> There is no such thing as education left now in these government-supported [educational] institutions. From teachers to students, the whole machinery is involved in stark wrongdoings. Honesty and integrity are absent. They are proud to be phony Muslims. Due to their blind following of the West in [practising] co-education, the new generation is falling into the dreadful ditch of obscenity and vulgarity. [...] Now, the success in examinations depends upon wrongful recommendation, cheating in examination and nepotism.

At the same time, mainstream education is presented as a threat to the Islam of the Pakistani youth:

> Modern [educational] institutions like schools, colleges and universities, where worldly knowledge and skills [...] are imparted, have become almost like slaughterhouses for the religion, faith, ethics and character of the youth. Islam has vanished from every aspect of life including their presentation and demeanour, appearance and grooming, dress and outfitting, lifestyle and civilization, as well as socializing and ethics, etc. (Ismail 1993, 31–6)

By creating a situation of 'Islam in danger', the Deobandis present their madaris as the final solution. As Khan (1999, 38–41) opines in *Al-Qasim*, 'In my view, the biggest reason for the destruction of the youth is the present archaic, useless, poisonous and slavish educational system. [...] The only solution for this is the Islamic educational system [of madaris].'

6.3.4 On comparisons between madaris and modern education

Most of the articles comparing the madrassah system and modern education were written against the backdrop of the government's reform efforts. The major objective of these articles is to overemphasize the strengths of madaris while simultaneously undermining mainstream education. Several of these articles employ overgeneralization and exaggeration to present a pro-madaris scenario. The following excerpts from an editorial in *As-Sayyanah* is typical of such comparisons.

> Nowadays, these public sector [educational] institutions have become centres of political dispute and places of murder. One section of students is holding Kalashnikovs in their hands in place of books. On the contrary, thank God, the madaris stay clear of such a destructive atmosphere. Here, the majority of the students are busy in their studies and present a picture of decency. Most of the madaris are far ahead of the government institutions in terms of observing discipline and other great Islamic and Eastern traditions like respect for elders, especially teachers. Madaris fundamentally function in the spirit of 'knowledge for service', whereas government institutions promote the concept of 'knowledge for employment. [...] That is why a madrassah graduate generally will not become the victim of extreme disappointment due to economic hardships, whereas incidents of even suicide have been occurring among the highly qualified youth of government institutions just because of unemployment. (Zahid 2002, 3–10)

As regards examinations, the Deobandis boast of the transparency of their system while accusing mainstream education of corruption and dishonesty. According to Zahid (2002, 3–10), 'Examinations are held regularly both in the government [educational] institutions as well as in madaris. [...] These examinations under Wifaq [the Deobandi board] are held in an extremely organized manner. There are no wrongdoings like bribery, cheating and coercion in madaris.' It may be pointed out here that the examination and testing system for the DMM is managed by a board of *ulama* who are not only Deobandis but also run their own madaris. The same is the case with the madaris of other denominations, which run their own boards. All of them have resisted efforts by the government to remove this conflict of interest in order to improve the quality of religious education. The government fears that if the board of a particular denomination administers the examinations of its own students, it may be more lenient in assessing their performance (Fair 2009, 85).

The Deobandis oppose the mainstream practice of commemorating and celebrating special days and events. An article in this regard tries to present this approach as a strength of the madaris. Rehman (2003, 34–8) states in *Al-Qasim*, 'In madaris, no "day" [i.e. anniversary] is observed. Rather, students are given extra work on such "days" to keep them busy [and to ignore the "day"].'

Further, modern education and mainstream society is identified with evil, while madaris are portrayed as saviours of humanity. Ansari (2006, 34–43) writes in *Bayyinat*:

> No one can better accomplish the task of turning humans into animals than schools, colleges, universities, television, newspapers, digests, movies, VCRs, cable, satellite dishes and computers, etc. [...] [This shows] that the genie which converts humans into animals has come out of the bottle. [...] If madaris were closed or even if they ignored their duties, it would not take long before the *Qiyamah* arrives. Then, [God] shall Himself push this genie back into the bottle.

Apart from this indirect defence of their madaris, the selected journals regularly publish articles by renowned Deobandi *ulama* to condemn efforts by the government to reform or even monitor their madaris. The language used in some of these articles is quite threatening. For example, Yousaf Ludhianvi wrote an editorial in *Bayyinat* in 1998 to warn the then prime minister Nawaz Sharif: 'The government should think of taking any steps against these madaris only if it has decided to meet its own downfall. We hope that the people in power shall behave sensibly and allow the madaris to keep defending the ideological frontiers of the country in order to ensure the survival of the country and the continuation of their government' (Ludhianvi 1998, 3–9).

Similarly, another article in *Bayyinat* challenged the government by stating that 'these senseless rulers, who have been deceived by their temporary authority in power, should not clash with that greatest of powers [God] and His great angels [the people of madaris] because a conflict with these bastions of Islam is akin to a clash with [God]. And fighting a war with [God] brings humiliation and loss in this world and the hereafter' (Muhammad 1998, 51–4).

6.4 The DMM versus Women's Role in Society

The DMM deplores the prevalent values and practices regarding the role of women in Pakistani society. There is a complete consensus in Pakistan about the need for providing modern education to girls, whereas the Deobandi journals categorically oppose it. According to the aforementioned University of Michigan's survey, the majority of Pakistanis even support university-level education for girls despite the fact that universities follow a co-education system. Similarly, Pakistani women in both urban and rural areas are increasingly working outside their homes along with men. On the other hand, the DMM has propagated the complete segregation and seclusion of women from the world outside their homes. Further, the Deobandi writings discriminate against women on the basis of gender and condemn the practice of allowing women any leadership roles in society.

The following discussions on excerpts from the three selected Deobandi journals exhibit the countercultural approach of the DMM vis-à-vis the role of women in mainstream Pakistani society.

6.4.1 On women's education

The Deobandi journals very aggressively oppose modern education for women. *As-Sayyanah* publishes a regular section titled 'Islah-e-Khawateen' (Reform of women), which includes the views of Ashraf Ali Thanvi regarding the role of women. 'Modern education is not about learning', observes Thanvi.

> It is ignorance in itself and is particularly harmful for women. This education is even worse than ignorance. Ignorance carries fewer evils than those of this [modern] education. [...] Girls are like a soft and weak wood, which when moulded and dried in a particular shape, will always stay that way. [Similarly], when modern education is

> provided [to girls] and they are taught new ethics, new styles and manners, that new way of life sticks to their minds and they internalize it. Later, when they are grown-ups, it is impossible to reform them. […] This knowledge, which is called modern education, is not at all appropriate for women. (2003a, 11–17)

In another essay, Thanvi (2003b, 17–21) goes on to declare:

> It is only ignorance that is appropriate for women. They should not be aware of the world and its evils. Only this [ignorance] is better for women and their safety lies in it. […] The true perfection of a woman lies in the fact that she should be ignorant of the whole world except for her husband and home. […] Therefore, teach religion to women, but don't teach geography, philosophy, [etc.]. As regards newspapers and novels, these are a killer poison for women.

Thanvi was not only against girls' schools but also opposed madaris for women. He was of the view that girls should be taught at their homes:

> The present-day practice of educating females through girls' schools or women's madaris is like a deadly poison. I do not like madaris for women even when these are managed by religious scholars. I can say in light of my experience that [you should] never ever allow it. Otherwise, if you did not obey me, you will repent later on. So, abandon the [female] schools and madaris. Teach women inside their homes. It is better if you teach in Arabic, otherwise teach in Urdu. […] School education is extremely harmful for women. It creates among them the ideas of freedom, obscenity and hatred with *purdah*. (Thanvi 2008a, 13–15)

According to Thanvi, girls should be selectively allowed to learn writing even when they are taught at their homes:

> As regards [learning] how to write, that is neither obligatory nor *haram*. This should be recommended according to the nature of girls. If a girl is not apparently bold and has modesty and prudency, she may be taught how to write. There is no harm in it, as it is required to meet the necessities of life. As for a girl who shows boldness and independence and if there is likelihood of some wrongdoing [on her part], she should not be taught how to write. It is better to avoid a wrongdoing than allow something which is not obligatory. In such a scenario, she should neither be taught nor allowed to write. (Thanvi 2008b, 13–16)

The Deobandi journals also appear to defend the Afghan Taliban's decision to close girls' schools. An editorial in *As-Sayyanah* observes,

> The Taliban have been alleged to stop women from acquiring knowledge [education]. First of all, these are just allegations, which have nothing to do with reality. Then, the question arises: which knowledge? That is an extremely important question which

> needs comprehensive attention. Alas, the people who adopt and propagate this Western concept [of women's education] are present even among us. They are looking to acquire the type of freedom that has brought down the human status of a woman by making her a sex symbol or sex worker. We have forgotten the status of a woman, which was granted to her by the God. That status holds the true bliss not only in society but also in the hereafter. [...] Do we need that kind of so-called [Western] freedom, which would completely destroy the remaining values of society and deprive us of all that distinguishes us from other civilizations? No sensible person can reply to this question in affirmative. (Zahid 2001, 3–6)

Although the DMM still follows the views of Thanvi regarding modern education for women, the movement has gradually accepted the concept of madaris for girls. However, unlike their male counterparts, residential madaris for girls are still not permitted. A *fatwa* in this regard was published in *Bayyinat*:

> The majority of the *ulama* have agreed that in modern times there is an intense need for local [i.e. neighbourhood] and non-residential female madaris. The reason for that need is that those important benefits that could be achieved through their [i.e. women] education are being wasted just because of their ignorance [about Islam]. [...] A minority of the *ulama* are against it. Their opposition is based on their cautious approach. [...] As regards residential madaris where a *mahram* [an unmarriageable kin of the opposite sex] cannot accompany the female students and non-residential madaris that girls must travel to by public transport, as well as madaris where arrangements for *purdah* are not possible – all such madaris are illegitimate and impermissible because they are sinful as well as violative of *Shariah* and religious traditions. (*Fatwa* by Qadir, Dinpuri and Haq 1998, 49–58)

6.4.2 On purdah

Purdah is a Persian word which takes two forms: physical segregation of the sexes and the requirement that a woman should cover her body properly. This section focuses on the latter form, which defines an Islamic dress code for women. There are some differences about the definition of *purdah*. The Deobandis follow a strict definition of *purdah* which requires women to cover their bodies from head to toe in the presence of those men who are not *mahram*. This definition is derived from a strict interpretation of *satr* or *awrah* (body parts that must be covered in public). According to this definition, the whole of a woman's body including her face, hands and feet should be considered *satr*. An article in *As-Sayyanah* declares, 'For a woman, *satr* starts from the hair of the head and goes down to her ankles. It is not allowed to expose any body part included in *satr* in front of a person who is not *mahram*. Even she is not allowed to uncover *satr* when she is alone' (Barkat 2001, 25–8). On the other hand, the majority of Pakistani Muslims accept a less strict interpretation of *satr* that includes the whole body except the face, hands and feet. The latter viewpoint is supported by a Hadith of Abu Daud wherein the Prophet says that when a woman becomes an adult, no part of her body should be seen except her face and ankles (Tariq 1998).

Justifying the inclusion of the face in *purdah* and *satr*, a Deobandi *fatwa* in *Bayyinat* declares,

> Observing complete *purdah* by a woman in line with *Shariah* by covering her face before going outside her home is in exact accordance with the teachings of Islam. [...] This [practice] in actuality presents before the world the responsibility of Islam for the protection of the modesty and chastity [of women]. On the contrary, the practice of exposing the face to invite male strangers to have a look [at it] contradicts the Islamic teachings and philosophy about modesty. This [practice] is not true Islam. Rather, it is the revival of the *jahiliyyah* [pre-Islamic era]. (Arif, Ali and Dinpuri 2010, 53–64)

Qureshi (2008, 45–8) explains that 'the aim and objective of the Islamic commands on *purdah* is that Islam wants its followers to be protected from misguidance, obscenity, vulgarity and sexual anarchy. And those secret sexual desires [of men] that can be ignited by non-observance of *purdah* by women should not be allowed to run amok.'

The Deobandis believe that women should not leave their homes except in unavoidable circumstances. An article in *As-Sayyanah* declares, 'It is a command for a woman that if she has to go outside her home due to some extraordinary need, then she has to cover her whole body from head to toe with a big shawl or *burqa*. Some part of that shawl should also cover the face so that men may know that she is a noble and pious woman and hence they may lower their gaze out of chastity' (Barkat 2001, 25–8).

The Deobandis also hold a strict view with regard to the age at which girls should start observing *purdah*. According to Thanvi (2007, 14–19), a girl has to observe *purdah* 'from non-*mahram* male kin from the age of seven and in the case of strangers even before the age of seven. [...] It is *haram* to expose the head, arms and lower legs, etc. in the presence of non-*mahram*.' On the other hand, Muslims generally believe that *purdah* is to be observed by girls at puberty. It would be pertinent to add here that the mainstream Muslim society of Pakistan does not support the *purdah* definition of the DMM. According to the 2013 University of Michigan survey, only 3 per cent of Pakistanis approve the Deobandi dress code for *purdah* that was imposed by the Taliban in Afghanistan. About two-thirds of Pakistanis support a dress code for women that allows them to show their faces. In fact, 22 per cent think that it is up to a woman to dress as she chooses.

6.4.3 On equality for women

The Deobandi journals envisage a limited role for women in society by restricting them to the boundary of their homes. According to Rehman (2003, 23–33), 'A woman has just a few important jobs to perform, i.e. pregnancy, childbirth, breastfeeding and the training of kids. God created woman so that through her the number of *mujahideen* of Islam, *huffaz* [plural of *hafiz* – one who learns the Quran by heart] and *ulama* is increased'.

The journals declare gender equality to be an evil concept. One article in *Al-Qasim* states, 'These days, a new *fitnah* [evil trial] has arisen. People are bringing forward women to stand shoulder to shoulder with men' (Rehman 2003, 23–33). An essay by Ashraf

Ali Thanvi in *As-Sayyanah* pronounces that women are both physically and intellectually inferior to men:

> There is a natural difference between men and women. Women can never gain equality with men [because]: they are inferior intellectually; they have less tolerance; their physique and organs are weak and that is why they get weaker and older far earlier than men. [...] A woman possesses less intelligence and the one who is less intelligent is liable to make mistakes in everything she does. Therefore, it is safer to place her under someone who is more intelligent [i.e. a man]. (Thanvi 2005, 15–19)

6.4.4 On women leadership

Since women are considered inferior to men, the DMM consequently opposes any leadership role for women in society, and the Deobandi journals strongly criticize the appointment of women as judges and police officers. Rehman declares this increasing participation of women in Pakistani society *fitnah*. He observes, 'If men are police, women are also acting as police officers. Men are farming and so are women. Men and women are both acting as judges. Islam has given to women a great status but Westernized people are not aware of it' (Rehman 2003, 23–33).

There is consensus among the three journals under study that a woman cannot be the ruler of a Muslim country. Many articles and *fatawa* have been published in this regard. One such *fatwa* was issued by Abdul Haq (2009, vol. 2, 296–7), who declares that Islam does not allow a woman to become a ruler and a female head of state is akin to punishment from God. However, the mainstream Muslim society of Pakistan still elected Benazir Bhutto twice, in 1988 and 1993, to be prime minister of Pakistan. In this regard, Yousaf Ludhianvi (1997, 3–7) declares in *Bayyinat* that 'the rule by a woman is not correct either in the light of religion or of logic. However, when people do evil things, God condemn them by imposing on them a woman ruler [i.e. Benazir Bhutto in 1988]. In fact, God removed that woman ruler once and then imposed her on them again [in 1993], and then cast on them such a terrible suffering that was unprecedented in this country.'

To conclude this section, the above review of the three well-recognized Deobandi journals clearly highlights the countercultural mindset of the DMM. This review also indicates that the DMM has not only contradicted the values and practices of mainstream society but has also challenged some of the mainstream institutions and systems of the state. Keeping in view the historical perspective discussed in previous chapters, one may infer that the countercultural tradition of the DMM has stiffened during recent years.

The next part of the chapter compares the values and attitudes of students from Deobandi madaris with those of students from mainstream educational institutions.

Part Two: Findings of the Interviews

This part of the chapter is the outcome of the second stage of the fieldwork, which involved interviews with students from Deobandi madaris and mainstream educational institutions.

The objective of this stage of the fieldwork was to corroborate the findings of the first stage entailing the review of Deobandi journals. Therefore, the interviews at this stage mainly focused on the same four themes covered in the first part – i.e. popular customs and practices, politics, education and the role of women in Pakistani society. These interviews were semi-structured qualitative interviews and involved 40 male students – 20 each from one Deobandi madrassah and a public sector postgraduate college in the town of Burewala, located in the southern district of Vehari in Pakistan's Punjab province. The students of the Deobandi madrassah who were selected for the interviews were in the final year of their course (i.e. *Dars-e-Nizami*). The selected madrassah was a moderate Deobandi institution, which encouraged its students to study a mainstream education syllabus alongside the *Dars-e-Nizami*. The respondents from Government Postgraduate College Burewala were also in the final year of their course. The purpose of selecting Deobandi students who were about to graduate was to form some idea about the future leadership and vision of the DMM. Further, the respondents from both the madrassah and the college were residential students belonging to the small towns and villages surrounding the town of Burewala. These interviews were conducted during 2012. The ages of the respondents ranged between 20 and 24 years. An interview guide reflecting the aforementioned themes can be found in Appendix III.

Before moving to the findings of the interviews, it would be pertinent here to have a brief overview of Pakistan's education system. Education in Pakistan can be divided into two categories: mainstream and religious. Mainstream education is imparted through both public and private institutions, which operate at three levels: school, college and university. Schools mostly provide education up to matriculation or secondary level (some schools go up to intermediate or higher secondary levels). Colleges generally provide education up to graduation level but some larger colleges also offer postgraduate courses. At the universities, bachelors, masters and PhD courses are on offer. On the other hand, religious education is imparted only through madaris of various religious denominations where the *Dars-e-Nizami* course is taught, with some variations in the textbooks selected by each denomination. The *Aliya* and *Alamiya* degrees of these madaris are considered equivalent to the bachelor's and master's degrees of mainstream education respectively. It may also be added here that mainstream education in Pakistan cannot be considered secular because Islamic studies is taught as a compulsory course up to bachelor level.

As far as enrolment is concerned, there are about two million students in madaris (Candland 2008, 103), which makes up around 4 per cent of total enrolment at school level. According to a 2003 report by the Social Policy and Development Centre, a Karachi-based research institute, about 73 per cent students are enrolled at public schools, which are also known as government or 'Urdu medium' schools. Others are enrolled at private schools, which are referred to as 'English medium' schools, even though not all of them truly use English as the medium of instruction. Although private schools are generally considered elitist, costly and urban based, many of them are non-elitist and affordable, while more than one-third of them are situated in rural areas (Fair 2009, 15–30). The elitist private schools are those based in the few large cities of Pakistan.

As for enrolment trends by socio-economic status, the Social Policy and Development Centre (2003) suggests that children belonging to the poorest families (with an annual income of less than Rs 50,000) mostly attend madaris (43 per cent) and public schools (40 per cent). Only about 18 per cent of them go to non-elitist private schools. For the lower middle classes (income Rs 50–100,000), the share is almost equally divided between madaris (30 per cent), public schools (38 per cent) and non-elitist private schools (30 per cent). For upper middle classes (income Rs 100–250,000), only 15 per cent and 18 per cent respectively attend madaris and public schools, while 36 per cent attend non-elitist private schools and 32 per cent elitist private schools. As regards the upper classes (income more than Rs 250,000), elitist private schools are the first choice (66 per cent), far above their second and third choices i.e. madaris (12 per cent) and non-elitist private schools (10 per cent). Public schools are given the least priority by this class, with only 3 per cent enrolment.

6.5 A Comparison of Madrassah and Mainstream Students

A brief comparative analysis of the values and attitudes of madrassah and mainstream students showing the countercultural character of the DMM is given below.

6.5.1 Popular customs, values and practices

There was a cognizable difference between the students of the Deobandi madrassah and the college with respect to the popular customs and practices of Pakistani society. As expected, all the madrassah students opposed the popular customs and beliefs as well as sociocultural and religious practices mentioned in the previous two chapters. On the other hand, all the college students more or less supported those customs and practices. Only one college student, whose family belonged to Ahle Hadith sect, disagreed about the practice of *chehlum* (prayers for the dead on the 40th day after death). Otherwise, he acknowledged that all other popular customs and practices related to marriage and death (including *qul* prayers for the dead) and even shrine visits were followed by his family.

As regards the spiritual practices of folk Islam, one remarkable finding was that while all the madrassah students except one had taken *bay'ah* to the *ulama* belonging to Qadri, Naqshbandi and Chishti orders, none of them believed in the common spiritual practices of folk Islam in Pakistan. On the contrary, only two of the college students had taken *bay'ah* in some *sufi* order, but all of them agreed with the popular spiritual practices of folk Islam discussed in Chapter 5.

As for identifying the differences between various religious sects in Pakistan, the madrassah students were quite clear in this regard and criticized all sects except for their own. One student proclaimed, 'The true and complete religion that has been followed since the Prophet's time is represented by Deobandi Islam.'

The Madrassah respondents believed that the Deobandi sect was a moderate, middle-of-the-road sect as compared to the Barelwi and Ahle Hadith sects, which were considered too permissive and too bigoted respectively. According to one student, 'Deobandi Islam is a complete code of life. It is on the virtuous path [*siratul mustaqeem*]. It adopts a moderate approach. It neither exceeds nor restricts the limits [of religion].'

There was general agreement among the madrassah respondents that their major differences with the Barelwis were because of their *bidah* and *shirk* practices, especially with reference to shrine visiting and the deification of saints. However, they did not support the use of violence to stop such practices. One student proposed that 'this should not be done by force. The *ulama* should stop it by convincing the managers of the shrines to stop *shirk* practices or the government should ban such practices [...] in the mould of Saudi Arabia.'

Another madrassah student suggested a more radical approach by proposing the closure of the most famous shrines to stop *shirk* in society. As for the Ahle Hadith sect, the major difference with the former was that they did not recognize *ijma* (consensus) or *qiyas* (deductive analogy) as the sources of Islamic jurisprudence.

The views of the Deobandi respondents about Shia Islam were quite belligerent. All of them said that Shias were outside the pale of Islam for showing disrespect to the Prophet's companions, especially the first three caliphs. 'The faith of Shias is not correct. Therefore, they deserve to be declared *kafir*', maintained one Deobandi respondent. There was a consensus among them on this.

Conversely, the college students were not clear about the differences between the various sects and none of them actually considered Shias to be outside the pale of Islam, despite the fact that some of them agreed that Shias were disrespectful to the Prophet's companions. A couple of them also mentioned that Shias were different and that their faith was not complete because of this disrespect. However, on the whole, the college students did not actually condemn any of the sects. They believed that there were minor differences among various sects including Shias. Their viewpoint can be summed up by the following words of one of the students: 'There is not much difference [among sects]. All are Muslims. The spirit [of Islam] is the submission to God and prostration before Him.'

As for celebrating and observing 'days' and anniversaries like Mother's Day, Father's Day, Teachers' Day, Valentine's Day and birthdays, etc., the madrassah students, in line with their Deobandi tradition, categorically opposed all such practices. It may be added here that according to a DMM *fatwa*, birthday celebration is an English custom and hence impermissible in *Shariah* (Haq 2009, vol. 2, 74–5). On the other hand, the college students did not find any harm in celebrating such days. Only a couple of them opposed the idea of Father's Day and Mother's Day on the grounds that for Muslims every day should be dedicated to one's parents. However, none of them agreed with the idea of Valentine's Day because for them it was un-Islamic since it mostly focuses on relationships between unmarried boys and girls, which is not permissible. However, they had no problem with the idea if it was practised by married couples. As for celebrating birthdays, there was a general observation by the college students that this practice is not followed in rural areas. In their view, the reason was most probably poverty rather than any conflict with the idea of celebrating birthdays.

As far as TV and the Internet were concerned, all the Deobandi respondents opposed the use of these media by emphasizing their potential to disseminate evil in society. A couple of Deobandi respondents agreed that 'TV can be watched for getting useful information and news'. However, they simultaneously contradicted themselves by saying that 'if female newscasters don't observe *purdah*, then TV watching is not permissible'. It is interesting to note that if the Deobandi definition of *purdah* is observed, then it would be impossible for women to appear on TV. Some Deobandi students also proposed censorship on TV to ban obscene and vulgar programmes.

It was observed that none of the Deobandi respondents used TV or the Internet and only one of them reported that his family owned a TV set. On the other hand, the families of all the college students not only owned a TV set but almost all of them had used the Internet at one time or another, mostly for entertainment (music and movies, etc.). Further, all the college students regularly listened to music, which is considered *haram* by Deobandis.

The madrassah and college students also held contrasting views about dress codes for men. All the college students said that they occasionally wore jeans, pants and shirts and thought there was nothing un-Islamic in that dress. However, some of them said that they did not wear pants in their villages because it was still not popular in the rural areas. Conversely, Deobandi respondents thought that only *shalwar kamiz* (national dress comprising of a long shirt and loose baggy trousers) was suitable Islamic dress. All of them condemned pants and jeans as un-Islamic. Their justification for this criticism was that pants or jeans evince the shape of the body parts because they are tightly attached to the skin. A similar argument was employed to condemn shirts. However, when asked if loose pants or a shirt could be Islamic dress, the madrassah students were still reluctant to consider it permissible. Their overall viewpoint about pants is best represented by the following statement of a Deobandi respondent: 'If body parts become prominent in some dress, then it would be considered un-Islamic. Otherwise, it can be allowed. However, it should still be avoided because of resemblance with Western people.'

6.5.2 The political system

The interviews mainly focused on three areas: the system of government, foreign policy and the challenges faced by Pakistan. As for the system of government, the madrassah students showed tergiversation about establishing a democratic system in Pakistan. None of them unmistakably supported democracy. Some of them rather condemned it. One Deobandi student declared, 'Democracy is not good. If one person [out of hundred] is right and 99 per cent are wrong then the wrong would prevail over the right, which is not a correct system.' Some of the madrassah students even advocated a caliphate system without knowing much about its implementation and functioning. 'I think *khilafat* is a good system, whereas democracy has many ills' pronounced one Deobandi student. However, he simultaneously remarked that circumstances and 'resources are not apparently available to introduce *khilafat* here'. Another Deobandi student supported the caliphate system while castigating democracy on grounds of human rights violations (which occur under Pakistan's weak democracy). He proclaimed, 'Democracy is not correct because human rights are not fulfilled under that system. *Khilafat* is right because it provides equality to all, small and big as well as white and black. The [political] leaders should be persuaded to introduce *khilafat*. But it should not be implemented by force.'

All the Deobandi respondents emphatically endorsed a Taliban-style system in Pakistan. 'The Taliban system was the best. They have one caliph, Mullah Omar', commented one Deobandi student. 'They established an Islamic system. I have not gone there but heard from our *ulama* who went there [in Afghanistan] and saw the system themselves.' One of the *ulama* who the students quoted in praise of the Taliban system included Commander Abdul Jabbar, leader of the Deobandi militant organization Jaish-e-Muhammad, which has also developed close connections with the Tehreek-e-Taliban Pakistan (TTP). It may be added here that Jabbar had set up his own *jihadi* group named Jamaat-ul-Furqan, which was involved in the 2002 suicide bombings in Islamabad, Karachi, Murree, Taxila and Bahawalpur. He was arrested in 2003 for masterminding these attacks and his group was banned (Mir 2004, 33).

Conversely, all the college students supported a democratic system for Pakistan while simultaneously criticizing the shortcomings of the existing democratic set-up. They were also optimistic that things would improve with the passage of time. Therefore, they thought that democracy should be allowed to continue. However, at the same time, the majority of the college students believed that they needed Islam alongside the democracy in Pakistan. Further, none of the college students supported a Taliban-style government in Pakistan. One of the students stated that 'all the Taliban are the products of madaris. They go abroad for *jihad* and are also involved in terrorism. I consider the Taliban-style government to be an extremist system.' A couple of them stated they had no idea about the Taliban government in Afghanistan.

On *jihad*, all the Deobandi students were convinced that it is a religious obligation for Muslims. On the whole, they agreed that *jihad* was to be launched against non-Muslims and that the activities of the militant organizations inside Pakistan could not be termed *jihad*. They also opposed suicide attacks in Pakistan but simultaneously supported such attacks in Afghanistan against the Americans. Despite opposing them inside Pakistan, some of the Deobandi students tried to justify suicide attacks by the Taliban against the security forces of Pakistan. One student observed, 'If you interfere with some institution or group, that group has a right to defend itself. We joined America to uproot the Taliban despite the fact that they were our supporters. We ignored the Quran, which tells us that Christians and Jews shall never be happy with you unless you adopt their religion.' He also opposed the army operations against the local Taliban in northern Pakistan and stated that 'the people whose family members were killed took up arms against our own army. They are now also carrying out suicide attacks in desperation.'

For the madrassah students, *jihad* was currently going on in Afghanistan and Kashmir. When asked if Pakistani Muslims should participate in the *jihad*, their overall response was rather equivocal. Apart from a couple of them who readily agreed to the idea, others linked the *jihad* with the approval of religious leaders or the consent of the government. As for the terrorist attacks inside Pakistan, most of the Deobandi students believed that Pakistan's enemies like the United States and India were behind them. Contrarily, the college students generally believed that such attacks were being carried out by Pakistani militants who had links with madaris on the one hand and with Afghanistan on the other. They also thought, not unlike the Deobandi students, that *jihad* was currently going on in Afghanistan and Kashmir. However, they opposed the idea that Pakistanis should participate.

On foreign policy issues, all the Deobandi students thought that Pakistan had no foreign policy of its own and was just following the dictates of the United States. One student opined, 'We are not making our foreign policy ourselves. Our decisions are being made outside the country [...] in America.' The madrassah students were of the opinion that Pakistan should set itself free from the extraordinary influence of the United States and should take its decisions independently. In fact, most of them suggested that Pakistan should take an aggressive stance and sever its ties with the United States.

However, the Deobandi students interestingly showed a relatively soft stance vis-à-vis Pakistan's long-time rival India. They opined that instead of going to war, Pakistan should solve all its problems with India including Kashmir through dialogue. They also suggested that Pakistan's foreign policy should give priority to the Muslim states over Western countries. Most of them were opposed to friendly relations with non-Muslim countries because according to them, 'the Quran and Hadith do not allow such relations'. However, some of them agreed to have diplomatic ties with non-Muslim states with the intention of spreading Islam to those countries. One student declared:

> First of all, Islam should be offered to non-Muslims. Those who agree shall embrace Islam. Those who disagree shall be asked to live under our Islamic rule because this world is meant for the Muslims. Non-Muslims must be told that they are to be ruled by us and either they should embrace Islam or prepare themselves to fight us. If they cannot fight, then they should accept our rule and pay *jizya* [a nominal tax for non-Muslims living under Islamic rule] as prescribed by Islam. We have to become strong enough to say all this to the non-Muslims [of the world].

As regards the college students, they were not particularly critical of the United States. However, they believed that Pakistan should have a balanced foreign policy and hold friendly ties with all countries including India and the United States. Interestingly, none of them declared the United States to be their enemy, an attitude that was in stark contrast to the findings of the Pew Global Attitudes Project, which reported that 74 per cent of Pakistanis considered the United States to be an enemy (Pew 2012, 1).

One interesting comparison between the madrassah and college students concerns their image of and vision for Pakistan. When asked about the three biggest problems faced by Pakistan, almost all the madrassah students identified the energy crisis as the number one problem, in view of the long hours of electricity load shedding during the summer of 2012 when the interviews were conducted. Apart from that, they were able to identify other problems such as unemployment, inflation, corruption, illiteracy and nepotism. A couple of them mentioned the spread of obscenity and evil as well as irreligious attitudes in society.

As for the college students, they identified a large variety of problems in this regard. However, the most common problem was terrorism and bad governance (especially of the then government led by President Zardari). Their list of problems was quite exhaustive. It included the decline of the education system, sectarianism, poverty, illiteracy, corruption, poor law and order, unemployment, injustice, the leadership crisis, the lack of true democracy, civil–military conflict, the energy crisis, inflation, the lack of meritocracy, poor health infrastructure and nepotism.

A comparison of the two groups of respondents in this regard shows that the Deobandi students were concerned with immediate and short-term problems and the scope of their vision was quite narrow compared to the college students, who were thinking at a far broader level. However, in terms of solutions to the identified problems, both groups were equally clueless.

The Deobandi respondents who overwhelmingly advocated an Islamic system were not clear about how to implement that system in Pakistan. Some of them thought that the *ulama* should become advisors to the government (not unlike the inner caliphs of Shah Waliullah's movement) and thus pave the way for implementing *Shariah*. One of them gave the example of Muhammad bin Abdul Wahhab of Nejd, who had become advisor to a local Arab ruler and guided him to establish a *Shariah*-based government in Arabia. Another student observed that establishing an Islamic government in Pakistan is 'not possible in the presence of the current [mainstream] politicians. We *ulama* should either convince them [politicians] or an Islamic government can be established through the graduates of madaris like Maulana Fazlur Rehman [head of the Deobandi party, JUI].' Similarly, another student said, 'In my view, the government system of the Taliban [in Afghanistan] is very good. However, that system should be introduced here through political means, not by force.'

Some Deobandi respondents approved of the Taliban approach to grabbing power by force before implementing *Shariah*. One of them observed that 'it is imperative to come into power to implement the Islamic system. The approach of Mullah Omar to come into power in Afghanistan was correct. It is permissible to take control [of the government for imposing *Shariah*].' Similarly, one of the Deobandi students praised the Taliban for controlling crime in Afghanistan. He remarked, 'Taliban's system is very good. They established *hadd* [the Islamic system of punishments]. When *hadd* is established, nobody commits a crime. [...] [The Taliban approach] of coming into power through force is permissible.' Another Deobandi student suggested the imposition of a Taliban-style government through the madaris. He observed, 'Pakistan was established in the name of Islam. But the Islamic system has not been implemented here. Since the Taliban implemented the Islamic system [in Afghanistan], it is our desire that their system should be introduced here as well. However, if the Taliban cannot come here themselves, then our madaris should come forward to implement Islam here.'

6.5.3 The educational system

All the Deobandi students showed a peculiar sense of pride and superiority because of their religious qualifications, which distinguished them from the worldly education system of mainstream society. One madrassah student claimed, 'The education we have received is exactly the same provided by the Prophet to his companions. Our education is actually the *Shariah* of the Prophet. Accordingly, we are leading exactly the same life that was lived by the Prophet and his companions. Therefore, in the final analysis, we shall definitely be successful.' This pride is not unlike that of countercultural nonconformists, who believe themselves to have a moral edge on mainstream society (Yinger 1982, 30).

As regards the objectives of the madaris, there was a consensus among the Deobandi students that their institutions were working for the spreading of Islam and dissemination of the message of God to the people. They also believed that their institutions were playing a role in changing and reforming society through the teachings of Islam. One remarkable finding in this regard was that despite all their pride in their religious credentials, the Deobandi students still believed that they would need a degree from mainstream education to find the best jobs. Hence, most of them were simultaneously studying 'worldly' subjects in order to take university examinations as private candidates for a bachelor's degree. A couple of them had already passed their examination. The majority of the Deobandi respondents believed that both the madaris and the mainstream institutions should continue, but the madrassah system should dominate the worldly educational system.

The college students also believed that the objective of madaris was to disseminate Islamic education. However, they did not say that madaris were playing any role in spreading Islam or reforming society. On the contrary, some of them believed that madaris were involved in spreading sectarianism and terrorism in the country. One college student opined, 'Some madaris are involved in Talibanization and are spreading extremism in society. Madaris have also played a major role in sectarianism in Pakistan.'

Similarly, another student pointed out that 'there are some bad people in madaris who tell their students that if they kill other people, they will go to heaven.' However, on the whole, the majority of the college students did not show a very negative attitude about the madrassah education system and believed that these institutions should be allowed to continue alongside mainstream education.

Another notable comparison was established when the respondents from both sides were asked to differentiate a typical madrassah student from a student of a mainstream educational institution. Here, the Deobandi students again brandished their pride and superiority over the mainstream students. One of the Deobandi students declared that madrassah students were the heirs of the Prophet. They believed that madrassah students held knowledge of Islam and had far more religious affinity in their lives than the students of worldly education. While disregarding the courses of Islamic studies taught in mainstream education, one of the madrassah respondents declared that 'if Islamic studies are enough, there was no need for God to send 170,000 [*sic* – historically, it is said to be 124,000] prophets'. Further, they distinguished themselves by observing that they had to play a role in spreading Islam in society whereas the college students could not do it because they lacked Islamic education and were mostly dominated by worldly concerns.

The Deobandi students also considered the overall environment of their madaris to be more Islamic and pious, and felt that the students actually practised religion there, while the mainstream educational institutions conversely have an atmosphere which is devoid of Islamic values and practices. One of the Deobandi students strongly condemned mainstream educational institutions while defending the madaris: 'People say that madaris are producing terrorists. They should tell us what [products] colleges have provided to society. Madaris have at least produced *ulama* and *huffaz*. What has an engineering university produced when the smallest of engineering work has to be completed with foreign support and we have to import every product from the United States and China?'

On the other hand, the college students described the dissimilarity between madrassah and mainstream students from a very different perspective and observed that madrassah students were completely distinct from mainstream society in terms of their appearance, training and thinking. One of them stated that in madaris, 'the administration is run by the *maulvis*, [clerics] who are not properly educated as they themselves are graduates of madaris. They are not aware of what is happening in the world. They have their own distinct world.' Another student believed that 'some *maulvis* were using the madaris and the Quran for financial gains. These people are actually behind the sectarianism [in Pakistan]. In this process, they have pushed us far away from the religion.' Another student referred to this viewpoint on the separation of madaris from the spirit of Islam: 'Madaris have existed for a long time. Earlier madaris were very close to Islam. But these days, their situation has worsened a lot. Nowadays, they have links with terrorism and are involved in using weapons – a situation that has vitiated society.'

While agreeing that madrassah students had more knowledge about Islam, most of the college students observed that the former were far removed from the issues and realities of mainstream society. Although the majority of the college students gave credit to the madrassah students for having a better understanding of religious issues, some of them pointed towards their ignorance of science and other modern subjects. The majority of them agreed that because of this lack of knowledge about modern education, madrassah students were not capable of solving the problems faced by society. One respondent stated, 'The madrassah people do not fit in with the modern world. They are not fit for this age.' Another student observed that madrassah graduates 'were weak in logical thinking as compared to college and university graduates.'

Some of the college students criticized madrassah students for their rigid and extremist views. One of them observed that owing to their intolerance, rigidity and unkind attitude towards common people, madrassah students were worse than the ordinary Muslims of society. (He made this statement in light of his personal experience and observation of his elder brother, who was a madrassah graduate.) Another student criticized the environment of the madaris with respect to the treatment of young students. He himself had once studied at a Deobandi madrassah to learn the Quran by heart. He stated that he had witnessed young students being sexually abused by some teachers and senior students.

At the same time, a couple of college students appreciated madrassah students on the grounds that they were more focused on the hereafter than mainstream students, who pursued a worldly and material approach.

6.5.4 Women's role in society

It was remarkable that respondents both from the madrassah and the college almost agreed on the definition of *purdah* for women. They believed that whole body along with the face of a woman should be covered for observing *purdah* outside her home. The only exception in this regard was that the Deobandi students also included the hands and feet of women in their definition of *purdah*, while some of the college students did not agree with this.

Despite this common ground on the definition of *purdah*, there were fundamental differences between the madrassah and college students about the role of women in society. While the former believed that the only place for a woman was her home, the latter thought that women should be allowed equal opportunities alongside men to play a role in society. All the college students were of the view that women should be educated and should be allowed to work outside their homes. Contrarily, all the Deobandi respondents believed that women should not work outside their homes. However, they conceded that girls may be provided education, especially religious education. But they should observe *purdah* before leaving their homes for the purpose of education. There was only one Deobandi respondent who was flexible on the idea of women working outside their homes: 'A woman can work outside her home while fully observing *purdah* and only when she has to interact with women, not men.'

The overall viewpoint of the Deobandi respondents in this regard can be summed up by the following words of one of the madrassah respondents: 'It is not appropriate for women to work outside their homes. The Prophet said that men should work while the women should stay at home. [...] [However], female education is permissible only if they go to those madaris where both students and teachers are female.'

To sum up, the above-mentioned findings from the journals and interviews not only highlight the conflict between the values and attitudes of the Deobandis and Pakistan's mainstream Muslim society but also verify the observations in previous chapters regarding the countercultural disposition of the DMM. This discord between the DMM and mainstream Pakistani society is aptly represented by the following statement, which was written on the wall of the Deobandi madrassah: 'Islam cannot be implemented in the country until the difference between *maulvi* [madrassah graduate] and mister [mainstream graduate] is removed. Our *ulama* want to implement Islam in the country, whereas all other sections of society and the media are trying to ensure it does not happen.'

EPILOGUE

In most cases, a counterculture lacks the power to destroy its parent society.

Kenneth Westhues, *Society's Shadow: Studies in the Sociology of Countercultures* (1972, 34)

Different scholars have interpreted the DMM from different perspectives. For some, it is an educational movement because it is based in madaris. Others consider it to be a religio-political movement as it hopes to establish an Islamic state in the subcontinent. Still others think that it is purely a religious movement involved in teaching religion and producing *ulama* to revive and spread Islam. The Deobandis themselves generally believe that their movement was launched to protect Islam and its teachings, which were under threat after the rise of British rule in India.

This book has endeavoured to interpret the DMM from a countercultural perspective by highlighting the presence of countercultural trends and tendencies in its 150-year-long history. The origin of the DMM is generally traced back to the eighteenth-century movement of Shah Waliullah, a broad-based Islamic revivalist movement with three components: intellectual, political and social. At the intellectual level, Waliullah's movement was originally a proponent of *ijtihad* and *tatbiq* (intellectual synthesis) of different viewpoints in Islam. The political component of the movement focused on the idea of establishing a model Muslim state in the subcontinent for the implementation of Islam. The social component of Waliullah's movement (which carried a relatively low priority and was largely considered part of the political component) was mainly concerned with purification of the norms and values of Indian Muslims in light of the practices of early Islam in Arabia. Another minor aspect of the social component was criticism of Shia Islam, although this was mostly underemphasized as Waliullah tried to find a common ground between Sunni and Shia Muslims.

When Waliullah's movement was passed on to the next generation of his family, its intellectual component suffered a setback owing to the absence of any scholar who could match the intellect and vision of the founder. Waliullah's son Abdul Aziz could not maintain the broad base of the movement. Gradually, the doors of *ijtihad* and *tatbiq* were closed down as the movement opted for the strict *taqlid* of Hanafi *madhab*. Further, the political component also took a backseat during that time in view of the decline of Muslim rule in India. Interestingly, this lack of intellectual and political rigour was compensated by an increased emphasis on the social component of the movement and by producing more literature to condemn the prevalent practices of Indian Muslims. At the same time, anti-Shia sentiment and literature gained more prominence and acclaim.

By the time control was handed over to the third generation of the Waliullah family, the scope of the movement had further narrowed down. Under the leadership of Waliullah's grandson Muhammad Ismail and his *shaikh* Syed Ahmed, the movement's top priority became its social component with a strong emphasis on condemnation of the popular customs and sociocultural practices of Indian Muslims. Aggressive opposition to Shia Islam also came to the foreground during that period. In fact, it was under the leadership of Ismail and Ahmed that the countenance of Waliullah's Islamic revivalist movement took on a countercultural complexion.

When the founders of the DMM, Muhammad Qasim and Rasheed Ahmed, tried to preserve and revive Waliullah's movement through the establishment of the Darul Ulum Deoband in 1866, the scope of the movement had been confined mostly to its social component, which was originally given the least priority by Waliullah himself. On the contrary, condemnation of the values and practices of mainstream Muslim society had become the major focus of the movement when it was resurrected at Deoband. Another important focus of the movement was its opposition to Shia Islam. The political component of the new movement was placed on the back burner in the face of British rule in India. In other words, the DMM actually resurrected Ismail and Ahmed's movement rather than the original movement of Waliullah. As such, countercultural currents were present in the DMM from the time of its inception.

The DMM has gone through different phases to represent different types of counterculture: ascetic, mystic, activist and extremist. In Pakistan, the DMM originally behaved as an ascetic and mystic counterculture before gradually coming into an activist mode. Since the 1980s, the DMM's unprecedented access to funds and facilities in the wake of the war in Afghanistan has broadened the scope of the movement in terms of reviving Waliullah's political aim to establish an Islamic state. However, when the model Islamic state was finally established by the Deobandi Taliban in Afghanistan, it proved to be neither a model nor Islamic nor even a state in the true sense of these words.

The failure of the Deobandi government in Afghanistan has generally been explained away with respect to different political, religious, ethnic and tribal factors. However, if the historical context of Waliullah's movement is taken into consideration, the Deobandi rule in Afghanistan can be comprehended from a countercultural perspective. It has to be noted that Waliullah's movement dropped its intellectual tradition more than two centuries ago. Gradually, it also lost its original political vision more than a century ago. Since then, it has been growing primarily as a countercultural movement, predominantly identified by its perennial conflict with mainstream Muslim society. By the time the DMM strengthened in Pakistan and Afghanistan, it had become a mere shadow of Waliullah's movement and was first and foremost a counterculture.

After cultivating itself as a counterculture for so many years, when the DMM was given an opportunity to revive its political component through the Taliban government in Afghanistan and a couple of provincial governments in Pakistan, it was naturally very hard for it to shed its countercultural inclinations. The outcome was a picayune and parochial version of political Islam that was more concerned with the prevalent customs, traditions and practices of the majority of Muslims than with building state institutions and improving the socioeconomic standing of its people. Under this narrow version of political Islam, politics and Islam were merely used to support the countercultural vision of the movement, which took precedence over everything else.

It is quite remarkable that as the original scope of Waliullah's movement narrowed down, the countercultural compass of the movement became broader. In Pakistan, the circle of the DMM's countercultural concerns has grown bigger and bigger, especially after its involvement in the Afghan war since the 1980s. Now, the DMM not only condemns the values and practices of mainstream Muslim society but also denounces and challenges the mainstream political and educational systems of the state. Similarly, the mainstream ideas of sports, leisure and entertainment have also been castigated. The state is now being embarrassed by a small group of Deobandi clerics who, every year, challenge the state committee's verdict on the sighting of the new moon to establish the end of fasting and the beginning of Eid. As a result, many Deobandis of the Khyber Pukhtunkhwah province and tribal areas now celebrate Eid on a different date to all other Muslims in Pakistan. Furthermore, the militant wings of the DMM like Lashkar-e-Jhangwi (LeJ) and Sipah-e-Sahaba Pakistan (SSP) have begun to challenge the writ of the state. Apart from attacking Shia Muslims and Sunni visitors to *sufi* shrines, Deobandi militant organizations like Tehreek-e-Taliban Pakistan (TTP) have also bushwhacked the law enforcement agencies, including the armed forces, who are trying to contain the illegal activities of these militants.

The DMM's Impact on Pakistani Society

According to Milton Yinger (1982, 287), 'The impact of countercultures is not automatic, rather it is filtered through human intelligence – or can be.' Similarly, the indirect effects of countercultures are probably more important than the direct and intended effects (Yinger 1982, 307). In this regard, the DMM in Pakistan has largely not been successful in changing the popular customs and sociocultural and religious practices of mainstream Muslim society.

It can be argued that the DMM has managed to influence Muslims in urban areas of Pakistan because several popular customs and practices that it condemns (e.g. the many ceremonies associated with marriage) are no longer followed in big cities. However, the causes for this change vary. In fact, socioeconomic developments and the busy, modern lifestyle of big cities have contributed more to that change than the influence of the DMM. For instance, modern-day matrimonial ceremonies are less exhaustive because urban people have less time to attend all such events. Another reason is the expenses involved.

On the other hand, new customs like celebrating Mother's Day, Father's Day and even Valentine's Day have simultaneously become popular in big cities. The DMM has castigated these new customs with equal or even more vehemence. Similarly, many previously popular sports like pigeon keeping and chess playing have become obsolete in urban areas while giving way to new forms of sports and recreation like cricket and video games. It is interesting that the DMM has condemned not only the old but also the new customs and practices, showing that it is not opposed to any particular activities or practices of mainstream Muslim society as such. In actuality, it is the countercultural character of the DMM that puts it into conflict with the majority of Pakistani Muslims on one pretext or the other.

However, one has to acknowledge at the same time that the DMM has managed to somewhat influence the urban population, especially with respect to the spiritual beliefs and *sufi* practices of folk Islam. Actually, educated urban people who have been trained in physical and social sciences are more prone to the impact of Deobandi criticism of *sufi* Islam. For them, the spiritual and arcane practices of folk Islam appear incompatible with their training in logical and rational thinking. Their bustling and hectic lifestyles leave them with little time to contemplate and understand the spiritual aspect of Islam. However, this Deobandi influence on the urban middle class has led less to conversion than confusion – a situation Yinger (1982, 84) calls a 'crisis of meaning' in mainstream society caused by the impact of a counterculture.

The Deobandi counterculture has managed to have some impact on the members of mainstream society because of two factors. First, it has survived for long time owing to its various streams in Pakistan, which represent different types of counterculture. For example, Deobandi madaris represent an *ascetic* approach that is focused on preserving and practicing the norms and values of the DMM inside a safe and secure environment. On the other hand, the Tablighi Jamaat (Proselytizing group) has continued to influence ordinary Muslims by adopting a prima facie *mystic* approach that concerns itself with the spiritual formation of individuals (Metcalf 1993). The Deobandi mosques and Deobandi political parties like Jamiat-ul-Ulama-e-Islam (JUI) adopt an *activist* approach to put their message across, while the militant groups of the Deobandis try to suppress their opponents through an *extremist* approach.

The second factor that has allowed the DMM to impact mainstream society is its ability to increase its outreach and influence through the explicit and implicit support of Pakistan's all-powerful military establishment, which is also referred as a 'deep state' in the mould of the Turkish *derin devlet*. First, the military government of General Zia-ul-Haq strengthened the DMM to utilize it in the Afghan *jihad* against the Soviets. Then, the military establishment tacitly supported the Deobandis to launch the Taliban in Afghanistan. The Deobandi militants were also used by the 'deep state' to wage *jihad* against India in Kashmir. Later on, the military government of General Pervez Musharraf adopted a soft approach towards the Deobandi militants on the one hand and the Deobandi JUI on the other. The former were allowed to prosper before they were used as leverage to gain political and financial support from the United States. The latter was allowed to lead state governments in two of the four provinces of Pakistan after the 2002 elections.

These two endeavours by the military governments of Generals Zia and Musharraf, who provided a role for the Deobandi counterculture in the mainstream system, had two different types of impact. Yinger (1982, 290) has pointed out that when a counterculture is brought into a system, it may turn out to be either a Trojan Horse a 'mahogany door'. The example of a mahogany door is taken from the story of a man who went to a market and bought a mahogany door because it was too elegant and too inexpensive to resist. He immediately made it the door to his study. The result was, of course, that the rest of the room looked shabby, so he had to redecorate the whole room – which made the rest of the house look shabby. Now the whole house needed to be reconstructed to match that inexpensive and elegant-looking door.

General Zia's venture to bring the DMM into the system proved to be a mahogany door that paved the way for the 'reconstruction' of the whole system in line with the vision of the Deobandis, who were given a vital role in government and politics. General Zia called this 'reconstruction' Islamization because it also provided some legitimacy to his extra-constitutional military government. That so-called Islamization by General Zia's regime under the influence of the Deobandis marked the beginning of the decline of the sociocultural structure of Pakistan. This sociocultural decline was characterized by rising sectarianism, intolerance and extremism. After General Zia's death in 1988, neither the civilian Pakistani ruler nor the powerful military establishment tried to rid Pakistan of the 'mahogany door' and the calls for 'reconstruction' continued.

When General Musharraf gave the Deobandi JUI a major role in Pakistan's politics and simultaneously adopted a soft approach towards the Deobandi militants after the fall of the Afghan Taliban, Pakistan faced the Trojan Horse of counterculture. Since then, the rise of militancy and Talibanization has actually shattered the social fabric of the country. The force and fear of the extremist militant organizations like TTP, LeJ and SSP belonging to the Deobandi sect have prima facie held hostage all the major stakeholders of society as well as the state, who find it hard to openly condemn the pro-Taliban militants. These stakeholders include all the big political parties as well as government, media and civil society organizations. Even the omnipotent military establishment is reluctant to launch a decisive operation against the TTP leadership and other militant organizations based in the difficult terrain of Pakistan's tribal areas that serve as their hideout.

Another reason for the military's reluctance to launch a full fledged operation is that it still believes that these pro-Taliban groups could be used to enhance Pakistan's role in Afghanistan after the withdrawal of NATO forces in 2014. However, this vision is likely to be proved as hollow and disastrous as were its earlier strategies devised to follow its preferred 'non-concept' of 'strategic depth'. Until the military establishment of Pakistan embraces them again, the Deobandi militants continue to sustain themselves through their connections with al-Qaeda on the one hand and with financial support through illegal activities like smuggling, kidnapping and extortion on the other.

Interestingly, the counterculture of the DMM also had the unintended, rather opposite impact of strengthening and reinforcing many of the practices of spiritual Islam in mainstream society. For example, the Barelwis, who represent the majority of Muslims in Pakistan, have become more organized to defend the practices of folk Islam, like celebrating Milad-un-Nabi (the birthday of the Prophet). Milad festivities are now being celebrated with more religious fervour and enthusiasm, especially in the big cities, where large processions are carried out to mark the event. Similarly, several Barelwi groups are now organizing annual meetings to show their strength as well as to preach and reinforce the traditional values and practices of folk Islam. The Barelwis have also effectively used the fast-expanding electronic media to revive the values of folk Islam. The ostensible objective of this demonstration of camaraderie by the majority Barelwi sect is to give menacing signals to the DMM.

As a result of this collision between mainstream society and Deobandi counterculture, 'fanatics of both persuasions' – in the words of Victor Turner (1974, 268) – have come to the fore. In response to the militant Deobandi groups, the Barelwis have also established their own extremist organizations to defend their values and practices.

DMM's Future in Pakistan

As mentioned above, the DMM in Pakistan is a compound of different types of counterculture, i.e. ascetic, mystic, activist and extremist. According to Yinger (1982, 93), the compound of different varieties of counterculture is highly unstable and the lifespan of a pure singular counterculture, like an unalloyed ascetic or an unadulterated activist one, is likely to be longer. On the other hand, Westhues (1972, 20) has observed that isolation from mainstream society mainly contributes to the longevity of a counterculture.

As far as religious countercultural groups are concerned, Yinger (1982, 247) has stated that some of these groups may increase their lifespan when they 'denominationalize' by reducing their isolation and opposition to larger society. Other groups may evolve in the opposite direction and become more isolated and more countercultural. For a time, at least, a group may seem to be moving in both directions, with some branch adapting in some measure to the world around it, while another pushes strongly against the dominant norms. Yinger has also indicated that the most deviant and extreme religious groups are likely to fade away if they are not ready to become part of the very establishment they sought to criticize and change.

In view of the above observations, one can reflect that the militant or the extremist component of the DMM is not likely to last very long, especially if the state and the military establishment do not provide it some tacit support with a view to increasing Pakistan's leverage in post-2014 Afghanistan. Similarly, the activist aspect of the Deobandi counterculture is also likely to be reversed if the state decides to cut it to its actual size, because being a minority sect, Deobandi Islam does not have popular support in mainstream society. Further, the rise of a popular political party which can address the major sociopolitical and economic issues of the people will render Deobandi politics irrelevant. It is remarkable that the people of Pakistan have consistently ignored religious groups in general elections. The only exception was the elections of 2002, when the absence of mainstream leaders like Benazir Bhutto and Nawaz Sharif as well as the tacit support of the 'deep state' allowed the JUI-led Muttahida Majlis-e-Amal to form governments in two provinces.

Without the support of the mighty military establishment of Pakistan, the DMM's counterculture shall presumably be reduced to its pre-1970s status, whereby its ascetic character might prevail upon the whole movement and it will become mainly concerned with the protection and preservation of its madaris. As for the mystic component of the DMM in the form of Tablighi Jamaat (TJ), that is not a pure or true Deobandi counterculture in the sense that participants of *tabligh* missions belong to different religious denominations and do not necessarily agree with the teachings of Deobandi Islam. Moreover, TJ has acquired a global outreach, which has further diluted its identity as a Deobandi counterculture. Currently, TJ is active in at least 165 countries with an estimated membership range of twelve to eighty million (World Almanac of Islamism 2013). However, TJ still holds some connection with the DMM inside Pakistan, where most of the *tabligh* missions are headed by the Deobandis. Similarly, most of the mosques where these groups stay during proselytizing activities belong to the Deobandi sect. Therefore, it is not unlikely that the TJ in Pakistan shall continue to provide the DMM with potential converts to the Deobandi counterculture.

As for the ascetic aspect of Deobandi counterculture, it is represented by the madaris, which are the major source of cohesiveness in the movement. Here again, the key to tackling this counterculture lies with the state. If the government decides to introduce to the mainstream educational institutions (colleges and universities) the kind of religious education and Islamic degrees and titles offered by the madaris, a new crop of modern and broad-minded religious leaders would gradually push the madrassah graduates into the background. Apparently, there is not much need to introduce large-scale changes in the curriculum of the *Dars-e-Nizami* because it is not the syllabus but the mindset that matters most in madaris. After all, the madaris of the Barelwi and Ahle Hadith sects are also teaching more or less the same *Dars-e-Nizami* that is followed by the Deobandi madaris. In the same way, the religious scholars produced in colleges and universities will have a far more tolerant and unprejudiced mindset owing to their interaction with students and teachers of worldly education. The government can then give these modern Islamic scholars the role of prayer leaders and *ulama* in order to break the monopoly of madaris on the religion.

So far, different governments in Pakistan have tried to convince the madrassah management to introduce mainstream subjects and courses in madaris alongside the *Dars-e-Nizami*. This approach has not worked for about the last five decades. Most of the efforts in this regard have been jeopardized by the DMM and will continue to fail because of the DMM's paranoia over state intervention. Yinger (1982, 278) has termed such paranoia the 'strategic dilemma' of countercultural movements in education. They cannot go for drastic change because it would lead to loss of support; neither can they moderate their goals because the movement might be co-opted by mainstream society. Therefore, even if the Deobandis accept the proposal of adding the mainstream educational syllabus to their madaris (most of them have agreed to it in principle), they would have to keep it as the lowest priority while maintaining the superiority of their curriculum and their counterculture. In short, the key to the longevity of the Deobandi counterculture is their madaris, which are isolated from mainstream society not unlike 'a social island existing in society's sea' (Westhues 1972, 20).

As regards fears about the rise of an Afghan-style Deobandi Taliban in Pakistan, the prospects of such a possibility are negligible. Such fears are largely an exaggeration to say the least. The overall social, cultural and religious make-up of Pakistan is entirely different to Afghanistan. The only similarity is the tribal areas of Pakistan (which make up a tiny part of the country), where the Taliban have already made inroads. However, that situation is likely to reverse if the military establishment decides to carry out a sustained operation against the militants in the tribal areas. So far, the military has launched a short-term and selective operation there with the hope of using the local Taliban as a cat's paw in Afghanistan after the withdrawal of NATO forces at the end of 2014.

Otherwise, the military establishment, which actually helped the Deobandis to grow strong in the first place, will never allow the creation to threaten the creator. Militant Deobandi forces like TTP, despite their links with al-Qaeda, are *de minimis* in relation to the state power and military strength of Pakistan. As Westhues (1972, 18) has said, a counterculture lacks the power to destroy its parent state.

To conclude, the rise of the Deobandi counterculture in Pakistan was mainly spawned by the support of the all-powerful military establishment of Pakistan. Without that support, the DMM is not likely to survive in its present form, in which it has parallel streams that represent different varieties of counterculture. According to an editorial in *Dawn*, 'Though there are signs the state may be moving away from its earlier policy of supporting certain militants elsewhere in the country, memories of support for "useful" militants still linger' (19 February 2013). Despite distancing itself from these militant organizations, the 'deep state' still tacitly supports Deobandi-dominated religious organizations like the Defence of Pakistan Council and the All-Pakistan Ulama Council.

In short, the role of the military establishment is most vital vis-à-vis the DMM's future in Pakistan. If the 'deep state' explicitly and comprehensively backs away from the DMM, the movement will soon be restricted to its madaris, which will gradually become isolated from and irrelevant to mainstream society. Similarly, its militant wings will soon fade away once the security forces make up their minds to crush the militants. As for the Deobandi political groups, they will presumably become marginalized and end up allying with bigger political parties to stay relevant. However, if the military establishment of Pakistan maintains an equivocal stance with regard to militants and political groups belonging to Deobandi Islam, the present situation may continue for some time – until some popular and powerful civilian ruler reins in the military establishment and cuts off every type of support to the DMM, thus paving the way for the gradual withering of the Deobandi counterculture.

Appendix I

THE DEOBANDI STANCE VIS-À-VIS MUSLIM GROUPS OTHER THAN THE BARELWIS

It is interesting to note that the DMM has not only condemned the Barelwi sect, which both represents the largest proportion of Pakistani Muslims (more than 60 per cent) and defends the beliefs and practices of millions of followers of folk Islam who claim not to belong to any particular sect. True to its countercultural nature, the DMM has also denounced other Muslim sects of Pakistan like Ahle Hadith and the Shias, who respectively represent about 5 per cent and 15 per cent of Pakistanis. Similarly, the Deobandis have castigated Jamaat-e-Islami, which is not a sect as such but a group of followers of Maulana Maududi.

A. The DMM on Ahle Hadith

Ahle Hadith is a *ghair muqallid* sect not much different from the Salafis of Saudi Arabia. In fact, the terms Ahle Hadith and Salafi are mostly used interchangeably. Ahle Hadith are also called Wahhabis because of their inspiration from the teachings of Muhammad bin Abdul Wahhab (1703–92) of Nejd, the founder of the Salafi movement in Arabia.

The DMM has adopted a fairly soft approach in condemning the Ahle Hadith sect. This may be due to the fact that the forefathers of the DMM like Muhammad Ismail, Syed Ahmed and Rasheed Ahmed were influenced by the teachings of Muhammad bin Abdul Wahhab. In fact, the Deobandi approach regarding the use of terms like *bidah*, *shirk* and *kufr* is not much different from that of the Salafis. However, the DMM has kept its distinct identity intact by not only distancing itself from the Ahle Hadith but also by condemning them at the same time.

The major focus of the DMM's criticism against Ahle Hadith is their *ghair muqallid* approach in *fiqh*. A *ghair muqallid* is the one who does not exclusively follow any of the four *madhabs* of *fiqh*. The Ahle Hadith *ulama* have classified the concept of *taqlid* (following a particular Imam) as *bidah* on the grounds that this practice started many centuries after the Prophet. The Deobandis on the other hand have disagreed with this and have argued that if the stance of Ahle Hadith is accepted, then it would mean that the whole Muslim *ummah*, except for the Ahle Hadith sect (which did not exist for about thirteen centuries after the Prophet), has been on the wrong path. The DMM has criticized this approach as being similar to that adopted by Shias against the companions of the Prophet (Ludhianvi n.d., 29).

The Deobandis have also argued that the Ahle Hadith are not truly *ghair muqallid* in the sense that they do follow one *muhaddith* (expert of the Hadith) or another. However, this is a weak argument because the Deobandis here have used the term *taqlid* in its literal meaning (i.e. following). The religious term *taqlid* is actually applied to the exclusive and strict following of one of the four schools of thought in *fiqh* – i.e. Hanafi, Shafi'i, Maliki and Hanbli. Ahle Hadith do not restrict themselves to any one of these *madhabs* and primarily follow the *sahih* (authentic) Ahadith compiled by different *muhadditheen*.

The Deobandis have also denounced Ahle Hadith on the grounds that they show contempt and disrespect towards the person and teachings of Imam Abu Hanifa, whose *fiqh* the Deobandis follow (Ludhianvi n.d., 31). Another criticism is that their approach towards *ijtihad* is too lenient because it tolerates unqualified Muslims who use their limited knowledge to interpret Islam. Ludhianvi (n.d., 27) has declared Ahle Hadith a dangerous sect in the sense that the fundamental reason behind the rise of atheistic (*mulhid*) and misguided (*gumrah*) sects in Islam has always been the lack of *taqlid*.

Another point of the DMM's ideological difference with Ahle Hadith is that the latter, in its enthusiasm for *ijtihad*, sometimes even ignores *ijma-e-ummat* (consensus of Muslim scholars) – a fundamental source of *fiqh*. Ludhianvi (n.d., 31) has quoted two examples in this regard. One is about Ahle Hadith's declaration as *bidah* the practice of offering twenty *raka* (units) in *tarawih* (Ramadan prayers) – a practice initiated by Caliph Umar and concurred by the *salaf-as-saliheen*. Second, Ahle Hadith *ulama* have disagreed with the consensus of *salaf-as-saliheen* as well as the imams of four *madhabs* regarding divorce. The Ahle Hadith believe that if a husband tells his wife three times in a single meeting that he is divorcing her, then it is considered one divorce and the marriage stays intact until three divorces occur. On the other hand, the *ijma* (consensus) in this regard is that three divorces have occurred in that scenario and the marriage is over (Ludhianvi n.d., 32).

Ludhianvi has concluded that the approach of the Ahle Hadith in these two examples, where they ignore the teachings of *sahaba*, is very similar to that of Shias. This is a very strong criticism in view of the fact that most Deobandis consider Shias to be *kafir*. However, Ludhianvi has not employed the Hadith regarding *tashabbuh bil kuffar* (resemblance with non-believers) to condemn Ahle Hadith. On the other hand, he has repeatedly referred to that Hadith to castigate the popular practices of Sunni Barelwis, which he has linked to Shias.

B. The DMM on Shia Muslims

Renowned Deobandi scholar Abdul Haq declared the Shias *zandiqa* (heretics) for believing their *imams* to be innocent (Haq 2009, vol. 1, 387). He also explained that there are many subsects of Shias and if a subsect refuses to accept the ascendancy of Abu Bakr as the first caliph, or holds a faith that the third caliph Ali has heavenly status like the prophets, or believes that the Quran was altered after the Prophet's death, each of these Shia groups is undoubtedly *kafir*. He asserted that 'it is illegitimate for Muslims to interact and develop relationships with such Shias or even attend their death prayers' (Haq 2009, vol. 1, 386).

In another *fatwa*, Haq (2009, vol. 5, 338) even pronounced it impermissible for Muslims to greet Shias and consume the meat of an animal that has been slaughtered by a Shia.

The DMM's castigation of Shia Islam is mainly based on the following three issues.

i. Concept of imamate

According to Ludhianvi (n.d., 15–18), Shias believe that God sent imams after the Prophet. These imams are considered pure and innocent like the prophets. They hold the power to implement *Shariah*. They can even suspend or cancel any order given in the Quran. There are twelve imams in Shia Islam; hence they are called *Athna Ashri* (Twelver) or *Imamia* Shia. Although there are many small sects in Shia Islam (e.g. Ismaili, Zaidi, etc.), Athna Ashri are the largest group and are considered the mainstream Shias.

The Deobandis believe that this concept of imamate was introduced by the Jews under the leadership of Abdullah ibn Saba, a hypocrite Muslim who presented himself as the supporter of Ali and propagated the right of the latter to become the caliph in place of Usman. The Deobandis see this Shia concept of imamate as a rebellion and conspiracy against Islam as well as against the finality of the Prophethood of Muhammad (PBUH). They believe this concept to be the source of inspiration for all the false prophets, such as Mirza Ghulam Ahmed, founder of the Qadiyani religion.

ii. Hatred and enmity vis-à-vis sahaba

According to the Deobandis, Shias believe that all the companions (*sahaba*) of the Prophet who took *bay'ah* of Abu Bakr after the Prophet's death became *murtad* (apostate), because the caliphate was the right of Ali, who is the first of the twelve imams of Shia (Ludhianvi n.d., 18). The DMM has castigated this Shia belief on the grounds that it will lead to the negation of Islam because if *sahaba* are condemned as *murtad* then the fundamental sources of *fiqh* like the Hadith, *ijma*, *qiyas* (deductive analogy) and *ijtihad* would too be compromised.

iii. Changes in the Quran

According to Deobandi literature, Shias believe that the Quran followed by Muslims is not the actual Quran that was revealed to the Prophet. The present Quran does not include the verses which support the imamate of Ali because Caliph Usman removed them during the compilation of the Quran. Shias are also said to believe that the complete version of the original Quran is in the possession of their 12th imam, who is alive but has been *ghaib* (absent) for about 1200 years. He will appear before the world near the *Qiyamah* (Ludhianvi n.d., 20–21).

Shias, on the other hand, have come up with their own arguments to defend their position against the above-mentioned Deobandi criticism. Many Shia scholars have clearly declared that the current Quran is the final and true Quran. Similarly, they have refused to accept Deobandi allegations regarding the concept of imamate and declaring *sahaba* as *murtad*. However, the Deobandis have not accepted the viewpoint of Shia scholars, who they believe to be lying in line with the Shia practice of *taqiyya* (religious dissimulation). According to Hassan Ja'afri, a renowned Shia scholar, *taqiyya* is a legal dispensation, which allows a person to hide his religious beliefs in order to protect his life, respect and wealth (Akbar 2010, 297).

Based on condemnation of Shia beliefs on the aforementioned three issues, the Deobandi *ulama* and their predecessors have always denounced Shia Islam. Shah Waliullah and Shah Abdul Aziz strongly condemned Shia beliefs, especially their concept of imamate. Muhammad Ismail and Syed Ahmed then stopped by force Shia practices like *taziyah* of Muharram. Later, Muhammad Qasim and Rasheed Ahmed, the founders of the DMM, also castigated these Shia beliefs. However, none of these *ulama* tried to categorically declare Shias non-Muslims. But as the ambit of the DMM gradually became more parochial, the views of the Deobandis became more rigid and brazen.

This situation became worse after the rise of Shia Islam in the wake of the Iranian revolution and the simultaneous exposure of the Deobandis to the Afghan *jihad* against the Soviets. Then the DMM's approach regarding Shias became more aggressive and extremist. It was actually against this backdrop that Manzoor Naumani, a renowned Deobandi scholar, issued a *fatwa* in December 1987 declaring Shias *kuffar* (non-believers). This *fatwa* was endorsed by hundreds of prominent Deobandi *ulama* in both India and Pakistan. Maulana Wali Hassan, Deobandi grand mufti of Pakistan, issued a separate *fatwa* in this regard whereby he wrote, '*Athna Ashri* Shias are *kafir*. Their marriage with Muslims is *haram*. Muslims should not participate in the funeral prayers of Shias. An animal slaughtered by a Shia is not *halal* for Muslims. It is not permissible to bury Shias in the graveyards of Muslims. In short, Shias must be treated as non-Muslims' (Hassan 1988).

Since the 1980s, several extremist Deobandi organizations have been established whose major objective is to have Shias declared non-Muslims just like the Qadiyanis. Since then, the Deobandis have been actively involved in sectarian clashes with Shias. Both sects support their own armed groups and militant organizations. Thousands of Muslims have died in these sectarian clashes, which continue to date. Most of the sectarian militant groups have been banned by the government without much improvement in the situation. Such groups either continue to operate underground or reorganize themselves under new names. The killing strategies of Shia and Deobandi organizations are different. Shias generally target a particular Deobandi scholar or leader who enjoys wide influence over the people. The Deobandis on the other hand kill not only Shia scholars but also ordinary Shias.

In places like Balochistan, the banned Deobandi organizations Lashkar-e-Jhangwi and Sipah-e-Sahaba Pakistan have indiscriminately killed people travelling on Iran-bound buses on the understanding that the buses were carrying Shia pilgrims. Similarly, hundreds of Hazara Shias have been killed by Lashkar-e-Jhangwi in Quetta. In Karachi, where banned groups are not allowed to operate, extremist Deobandis have reorganized themselves under the name of Ahle Sunnat wal Jamaat – a term which was generally used for the Barelwis until very recently.

C. The DMM on Jamaat-e-Islami

The DMM opposed Maulana Maududi and his party Jamaat-e-Islami (JI) well before the partition of India. The Deobandis believed that Maududi was not a good Muslim; that his writings were sub-scholarly; that he was disrespectful to the prophets and *sahaba*, especially Caliph Usman; and that he created a lot of *bidah* and hence mutilated the spirit of Islam (Pirzada 2000, 101). These views were shared by prominent Deobandi *ulama* like Hussain Madni, Kifayatullah, Qari Tayyab, Mufti Shafi and Zafar Usmani. Mufti Mahmood of JUI once ruled Maududi as outside the pale of Islam and 'an American agent' (Pirzada 2000, 102).

Later on, Deobandi scholars in Pakistan like Abdul Haq also condemned Maududi for showing disrespect and indiscretion towards prophets, *sahaba* and imams as well as for his hauteur about his own views and *ijtihad* (Haq 2009, vol. 1, 404–8). In the light of the *fatawa* by past DMM leaders like Hussain Ahmed Madni and Ahmed Ali Lahori, Abdul Haq considered Maududi and his Jamaat-e-Islami to be misguided (*gumrah*). He further declared Maududi to be undesirable and damaging for Muslims, who should stay away from his ideas.

Ludhianvi (n.d., 122–83) in a long commentary has condemned the philosophy and teachings of Maududi on the following grounds.

i. Ghair muqallid approach

Maududi strictly opposed the concept of *taqlid* and even described it as wrongful and sinful for an educated person. However, his non-*taqlid* is different from Ahle Hadith, whose major emphasis is on the Quran and Hadith. Maududi, however, has differentiated between the Hadith (discussion of the words, deeds or tacit approvals of the Prophet) and the Sunnah (practices of the Prophet). He has put more emphasis on Sunnah than Hadith. Ludhianvi has vehemently opposed this approach and has placed Maududi in the same league as that of Ghulam Ahmed Pervaiz and Mirza Qadiyani, whose followers have been declared non-Muslims.

ii. Disrespect towards prophets and sahaba

The Deobandis have condemned the writings of Maududi on the grounds that he used language to describe prophets and *sahaba* that is generally reserved for ordinary people and worldly rulers. The Deobandis have declared this lack of reverence on the part of Maududi to be similar to that of Shias. It is interesting to note that Muhammad Ismail, one of the forefathers of the DMM, also used similar language for prophets and saints to highlight the concept of *tawhid*. But the Deobandis defended him against the scathing criticism of the Barelwi *ulama*.

iii. Anti-tasawwuf approach

Maudūdi strongly opposed the concept of *tasawwuf* and spirituality in Islam. He condemned the practice of *tasawwuf* by likening it to opium addiction and criticized all

Muslim scholars including Deobandi forefathers like Shah Waliullah and Muhammad Ismail, who were alleged to have failed in keeping their movements uncontaminated from the 'disease of *sufism*' (Maududi n.d., 146).

Against this criticism, the Deobandis have not only defended their forefathers but also the institution of *tasawwuf* itself. It is interesting that in opposing the views of Maududi, the Deobandis have gone to the extent of accepting the concept of *tasawwuf* (Ludhianvi n.d., 163), which they had earlier opposed in condemnation of the folk Islam represented by the Barelwis and other Muslims of the subcontinent. The DMM's approach in its criticism of Maududi's views about *tasawwuf* is actually not much different from the one the Barelwis adopted against the DMM's views on the practices of folk Islam.

iv. Political Islam

Maududi, like the Egyptian Ikhwan ul Muslimeen, believed that Islam was fundamentally a political movement and establishing Islamic rule was akin to worship (*ibadah*). He went to the extent of stating that obligatory prayers, *zakat* (Islamic tax) and *hajj* (pilgrimage) in fact prepare a Muslim for the actual *ibadah* of establishing Islamic rule (Ludhianvi n.d., 160).

The Deobandis, on the other hand, have divided Islam into different compartments like faith, worship, conduct, socialization and politics. They have condemned Maududi's sole focus on political Islam as a dangerous mistake and an intellectual deviation that has undermined other vital pillars of Islam.

Apart from the above issues, the DMM has also criticized Maududi on the grounds that he did not learn Islam from any established scholar or institution and hence could not develop a proper understanding of the religion. Further, he was too influenced by the modern world to present Islam in its original configuration. Therefore, he introduced changes and reforms to Islam in order to satisfy modern minds. In this regard, he was not much different from those Muslim scholars who try to find compatibility between the Islamic system of governance and modern democracy (Ludhianvi n.d., 181–3).

Appendix II

COUNTERCULTURAL EXPOSITION OF THE DEOBANDI TALIBAN

There is no doubt that the Taliban movement in Afghanistan is a Deobandi movement. It was launched through Pakistan's Deobandi party, Jamiat-ul-Ulama-e-Islam (JUI) in 1994 with the support of Pakistan's military establishment and Saudi Arabia (Rashid 2008, 72). Most of the leadership and fighting forces of the Taliban had studied in Pakistan's Deobandi madaris (Rashid 2008, 1, 32, 89, 92). Many Deobandi madaris of Pakistan regularly dispatched their students to Afghanistan to fight alongside the Taliban (Rashid 2008, 53, 59, 78, 91). Several *ulama* of Deobandi madaris in the NWFP and Karachi developed close links with the leadership of the Taliban, and these *ulama* provided guidance to the Taliban regarding imposition of *Shariah*. In other words, the *Shariah* imposed by the Taliban in Afghanistan actually represented the Deobandi version of Islam. As such, a closer look at the Taliban version of Deobandi *Shariah* shall bring forth the true countercultural character of the DMM.

The following discussion about the measures taken by the Taliban to impose *Shariah* in Afghanistan clearly reveals the countercultural complexion of the Deobandi movement. This discussion heavily borrows from Ahmed Rashid's critically acclaimed book, *Taliban: Islam, Oil and the New Great Game in Central Asia.*

After coming into power, the Taliban immediately implemented the Deobandi interpretation of *Shariah.* They closed down girls' schools and restricted women's movement outside their homes, smashed TV sets, forbade a whole array of sports and recreational activities and ordered all males to grow long beards (Rashid 2008, 29). At the same time, they established a religious police force called Amr bil Maroof wa Nahi anil Munkar (Promotion of good/virtue and prevention of evil/vice) to announce and implement various measures as part of its Islamization campaign. This religious police force was modelled on a similar government organization in Saudi Arabia (Rashid 2008, 105–6). It is not a coincidence that the Deobandi provincial government in the NWFP also unsuccessfully tried to replicate this model through the Hasba Bill in 2003.

One of the first Taliban decrees in Afghanistan was to ban every conceivable kind of entertainment and cultural activity including music, TV, Internet, videos, painting, playing cards, kite flying, pigeon keeping and most sports and games including football (later allowed with some conditions) and chess (Rashid 2008, 2, 219). They also issued a *fatwa* stipulating that men should grow beards the exact length of one's fist – an absurd decision considering growth of facial hair differs from person to person and some ethnic groups like the Hazaras have naturally very thin facial hair. Apart from that, there is difference of opinion among various Muslim sects about the length of beards. On one extreme is the Ahle Hadith sect, which forbids clipping the beard at all. On the other extreme are those who follow theologians like Egyptian Sheikh Mahmoud Shaltout, who issued a *fatwa* stating that everything relating to clothing and physical appearance, including beards and shaving, is a habit unrelated to *Shariah* and it should be adopted according to one's living environment (Al-Arabia 2013).

The Taliban banned all sports for Afghan women, who were particularly discriminated against by decrees issued from time to time in the name of preventing obscenity and vulgarity. They closed down all girls' schools and colleges and banned women from work (Rashid 2008, 2, 50). The religious police went on a rampage forcing all women off the streets. They ordered householders to blacken their windows so women would not be visible from the outside (Rashid 2008, 70). Women were also banned from wearing make-up and high heels or making a noise with their shoes while walking. The Taliban police not only flogged men for not having long beards but also beat women for not properly wearing the *burqa* – a long tent-like dress covering the whole body from head to toe (Rashid 2008, 105–6). Most of these measures were neither in line with the spirit of Islam nor the teachings of the Prophet, whose 'supreme and unmistakable' achievement has been the emancipation of women (Maikash 2006, 145).

The Taliban did not recognize the very idea of culture. They banned Nawroz, the traditional Afghan new year celebrations, as un-Islamic. An ancient spring festival, Nawroz marks the first day of the Persian solar calendar, when people visit the graves of their relatives. The religious police forcibly stopped people from doing so (Rashid 2008, 116). This was perhaps in line with the Deobandi stance against the practice of visiting graves, which they link to *shirk* and *bidah*. The Taliban also issued a list of permissible Muslim names for newborn babies (Rashid 2008, 70). This was also inferred from the teachings of the forefathers of the DMM, who had forbidden many popular Muslim names for being indicative of *shirk*, as mentioned in Chapter 2.

The Taliban also banned singing and dancing at weddings, which for centuries had been major occasions from which hundreds of musicians and dancers made a living. According to the education minister Mullah Abdul Hanifi, the Taliban 'opposed music because it creates a strain in the mind and hampers the study of Islam' (Rashid 2008, 115). They also opposed the popular practices of *sufism*, which has long been a part of the history and tradition of Afghanistan and has been a moderating factor for Islam in multi-ethnic Afghan society (Rashid 2008, 84). After they occupied Herat, the Taliban barred people from visiting the shrines of *sufi* saints, of which Herat had an abundance (Rashid 2008, 113).

Like true Deobandis, the Taliban treated all Shia Muslims as *munafiqeen* or hypocrites who were beyond the pale of Islam. In 1997, after the fall of Mazar-e-Sharif, a Shia-dominated city, the Taliban mullahs proclaimed from the mosques that the city's Shias had three choices: convert to Sunni Islam, leave for Shia Iran or die. For a time, they also banned Ashura – a Shia religious event to mourn the martyrdom of the Prophet's grandson in the month of Muharram. Later, a small Taliban unit accompanied by Pakistani militants of Sipah-e-Sahaba Pakistan (SSP) killed 11 Iranian diplomats in Mazar-e-Sharif (Rashid 2008, 69, 74, 117).

The Taliban offered sanctuary to the Deobandi militants of SSP, the most virulent anti-Shia group in Pakistan, after the government launched a crackdown against them in 1998. Hundreds of SSP militants were then trained at the Khost training camp, which was run by the Taliban and Usama bin Laden. The Taliban also gave refuge to Iranian group Ahle Sunnah wal Jamaat (ASWJ), which recruited Iranian Sunni militants from the Khorasan and Sistan provinces (Rashid 2008, 92, 203). Interestingly, the SSP adopted the name ASWJ to survive after it was declared a banned outfit in Pakistan.

After coming into power, the Taliban also strongly condemned the instruments of mainstream politics. Mullah Wakil, the aid and confidant of Taliban leader Mullah Omar declared that *Shariah* does not allow politics or political parties. He also stated that the Taliban rejected general elections because they were incompatible with *Shariah*. The attorney general of the Taliban government declared that they did not need a constitution because *Shariah* was their constitution (Rashid 2008, 43, 102, 107). The TTP in Pakistan also followed their Afghan mentors when they threatened to sabotage the elections in Pakistan in 2013.

Apart from taking the above-mentioned measures, the Taliban were so carried away by the countercultural mindset of the DMM that they even banned innocuous social customs and cultural practices which had nothing to do with their concept of 'vice and virtue' as such. For example, when they allowed limited sports for men, they directed onlookers to refrain from the impulsive practice of clapping and instead chant 'Allah-o-Akbar' (God is great). They banned Labour Day on 1 May by declaring it a communist holiday, which is historically incorrect. They also opposed Western dress. One of Taliban-supported Deobandi groups, Harkat-ul-Ansar, banned jeans and jackets in Kashmir. The Taliban were so obsessed with contradiction and condemnation of common practices and popular custom that they even restricted any show of festivity at Eid, the principal Islamic celebration. Similarly, they refused to follow the prevalent work habits and office schedules. When in power, the Taliban ministers and officials attended their offices for only four hours from 8 a.m. to 12 p.m. (Rashid 2008, 101, 107, 116, 137).

The Deobandi Taliban were not trained in the history and traditions of Islam. Neither were they sensitive to the culture and history of their own country. They were poorly tutored in Islamic and Afghan history, knowledge of *Shariah* and the Quran and even recent political and theoretical developments in the Muslim world. While Islamic radicalism in the twentieth century has a long history of scholarly writing and debate, the Taliban have no such historical perspective or tradition. Their exposure in this regard is minimal and their sense of their own history is even less. This has created an obscurantism which allows no room for debate even with fellow Muslims. They are vehemently opposed to modernism and have no desire to understand or adopt modern ideas of progress or economic development, and so they failed to issue an agenda on how they intended to set up a representative government or foster economic development. They have simply refused to define the state they want to constitute and rule over, largely because they have no idea what they want (Rashid 2008, 93, 101, 212).

According to Rashid (2008, 87–8), the Taliban interpretation of Islam, *jihad* and social transformation was an anomaly in Afghanistan because the movement's rise echoed none of the leading Islamist trends that had emerged through the anti-Soviet war.

The Taliban were neither radical Islamists inspired by the Ikhwan, nor mystical *sufis*, nor traditionalists. They fitted nowhere in the Islamic spectrum of ideas and movements that had emerged in Afghanistan between 1979 and 1994. The Taliban represented nobody but themselves and they recognized no Islam except their own. But they did have an ideological base – an extreme form of Deobandism being preached by Pakistani Deobandis in Afghan refugee camps inside Pakistan.

In short, the Taliban interpretation of Islam was narrow, negative and destructive. They considered the practices and beliefs of their society to be wrong. Rashid (2008, 211–12) has argued that the Taliban interpretation divested Islam of all its legacies except theology. Islamic philosophy, science, arts, aesthetics and mysticism were ignored. Thus the rich diversity of Islam, its polyvocal tradition and the essential message of the Quran – to build a civil society that is just and equitable and in which rulers are responsible for their citizens – was forgotten. On the contrary, the Taliban as rulers of Afghanistan implemented an extreme and narrow interpretation of *Shariah* that placed them in direct conflict with the majority of citizens. In the words of Rashid (2008, 107), 'The Taliban were right, their interpretation of Islam was right and everything else was wrong and an expression of human weakness and a lack of piety.' All this aptly applies to the DMM as a whole.

Appendix III

INTERVIEW GUIDE

1. Greetings and introduction.
2. Brief information about the research and its objectives.
3. Verbal consent of the interviewee.
4. Personal information about the interviewee (name, age, place of residence).
5. How do you look at the cultural values and customs in Pakistan especially with respect to marriage, death, birthday events, dress, etc.? Are these values in conflict with Islam?
6. Do you watch television and use the Internet? If not, why?
7. What do you think about the political system in Pakistan and what, in your opinion, is the best system of governance and how can it be introduced in Pakistan?
8. What do you think about the education system in Pakistan and how do you compare the madaris with the mainstream education system?
9. What are your views about *sufism*/spiritualism in Islam? How do you look at the practice of visiting shrines of saints?
10. What are your views about the suicide attacks and bombings in Pakistan?
11. What do you think about the current status and role of women in Pakistani society?
12. What are your views on Pakistan's foreign policy especially with reference to India, Afghanistan, Europe, the United States and the Muslim world?
13. What are the three biggest challenges faced by Pakistan and what solutions do you recommend?
14. What are the major differences between *madrassah* and college students?

GLOSSARY OF ISLAMIC TERMS

adhan: call for the daily prayers. The person who calls the *adhan* is called a *mu'adhin*, who calls the *adhan* five times a day before Muslims are to perform their daily *salah* (prayer). The *adhan* is composed of specific words and phrases to be recited loudly in the Arabic language so that the neighbours can recognize the time schedule for the prayers.

alim (plural *ulama*): a man of knowledge; a scholar, especially in the sciences of Islam.

ahl al-hall wal-aqd: literally 'the people of loosing and binding', i.e. the *ulama* (scholars), leaders and army commanders who make binding decisions for the community.

Amr bil Maroof wa Nahi anil Munkar: the Afghan Taliban's religious police force; literally 'promotion of good/virtue and prevention of evil/vice', a duty for all Muslims prescribed in the Quran.

ameerul momineen: commander of the believers. This title is given to Islamic leaders.

Arafa: a plain 15 miles to the east of Makkah. One of the essential rites of *hajj* is to stand on Arafa on the ninth of Dhul-Hijjah, the twelfth month of the Islamic lunar calendar.

Ashura: the tenth day of Muharram, first month of the Muslim lunar calendar. It is a highly desirable day to fast.

Athna Asharis: 'Twelvers' or mainstream Shias who believe in 12 imams.

ayah (plural *ayaat*): a verse of the Quran. It literally means 'sign' and also refers to the signs one sees in the Creation.

barzakh: literally 'partition' or 'barrier'; usually it means life in the grave, which is a partition between life on earth and life in the hereafter.

bay'ah: literally means the striking together of the hands of two contacting parties to ratify a contract. It is an act of swearing allegiance to a spiritual or political leader.

bayyinah (plural *bayyinat*): a piece of evidence which is clear and demonstrates the truth; testimony. Such clear demonstrative evidence reinforces belief.

bidah: 'innovation' in Muslim ritual practice or beliefs, changing the original practice of the Prophet, something introduced into Islam after the formative period.

darul harb: abode of war, a territory under the hegemony of unbelievers which is hostile to the Muslims living in its divine.

darul Islam: abode of Islam, the Muslim nation.

dhikr: remembrance of God; commonly refers to invocation of Allah by repetition of His names or particular formulae.

deen: religion in general; the life transaction (literally the debt between two parties); the way of life and the system of conduct based on recognizing God as one's sovereign and committing oneself to obey Him.

dua: making supplication to Allah.

Eid: The word Eid is an Arabic word meaning festivity, celebration, recurring happiness and feast. In Islam, there are two major Eids – namely, the feast of Ramadan (Eid-ul-Fitr) and the Feast of Sacrifice (Eid-ul-Adha). The first Eid is celebrated by Muslims after fasting the month of Ramadan as a matter of thanks and gratitude to Almighty Allah. It takes place on the first day of Shawwal, the tenth month of the lunar calendar. The second Eid is the Feast of Sacrifice and it is to be celebrated in memory of Prophet Abraham (PBUH) trying to sacrifice his son Ismail (Ishmael). This Eid lasts for four days between the 10th and 13th day of Dhul-Hijjah.

fardh: an obligatory act of worship or practice as defined by Islamic law (i.e. *Shariah*). Doing *fardh* is considered a good deed, while not doing it is a bad deed or a sin.

fatwa (plural *fatawa*): an authoritative, advisory statement on a point of law.

fiqh: the science of Islamic jurisprudence and application of *Shariah*. The meaning of the word *fiqh* is understanding, comprehension, knowledge and jurisprudence in Islam. A jurist is called a *faqih*, who is an expert in matters of Islamic legal matters. The most famous scholars of *fiqh* in the history of Islam are the founders of the four schools of thought in Islam: Imam Malik, Imam Ash-Shafi'i, Imam Abu Hanifa and Imam Ahmad.

fisq: deviant behaviour; leaving the correct way or abandoning the truth; disobeying Allah; immoral behaviour.

fitnah: The word *fitnah* comes from an Arabic verb which means 'to seduce, tempt or lure'. There are many shades of meaning, mostly referring to a feeling of disorder or unrest. Variations of the word *fitnah* are found throughout the Quran to describe the trials and temptations that may face believers. The term has also been used to describe divisions which occurred in the early years of the Muslim community. In modern usage, it is used to describe forces that cause controversy, fragmentation, scandal, chaos or discord within the Muslim community, disturbing social peace and order.

ghaib: the unseen, un-manifest, that which is hidden from the eyes whether or not it is perceived by the heart; or it can be something which is beyond any sort of perception, such as the future.

Gog and Magog: two evil empires or nations mentioned in the Quran and Hadith in connection with the Final Hour.

Hadith: Reports on the sayings and traditions of Prophet Muhammad (PBUH).

hajj: pilgrimage to Makkah. A Muslim is to perform *hajj* at least once in his/her life, if means and health allow. There are rules and regulations and specific dress to be followed. It is to take place during the last month of the lunar calendar called Dhul Hijjah.

Hajr-e-Aswad: the black stone set in one corner of the Ka'bah in Makkah, which the pilgrims are supposed to kiss during *tawaf* (circumambulation) of Ka'bah.

halal: something that is lawful and permitted in Islam.

halaqah: a circle of people gathered for the purpose of study of Islam.

haram: something which is unlawful or prohibited in Islam. Doing *haram* counts as a bad deed and not doing it counts as a good deed.

Hijaz: the region along the western seaboard of Arabia in which Makkah, Madinah, Jeddah and Taif are situated.

ijma: consensus, particularly of the people of knowledge among the Muslims on matters of *fiqh*.

ijtihad: the exercise of independent judgement in Islamic law. Attempting to uncover Allah's rulings on issues in light of sources of *Shariah*, i.e. the Quran, the Sunnah, *ijma*, *qiyas*.

imam: a leader, especially in prayer. An imam is a religious leader. Any person who leads a congregational prayer is called an imam. A religious leader who also leads his community in political affairs may be called an imam, an ameer, or a caliph.

iman: faith and trust in Allah.

Islam: submission to the will of Allah, the way of life embodied by all the prophets, given its final form in the guidance brought by Prophet Muhammad (PBUH). Islam is an Arabic word, the root of which is *silm* and *salam*. It means among other things: peace, greeting, salutation, obedience, loyalty, allegiance and submission to the will of the Creator of the Universe.

Ismailis: the 'Sevener' Shia followers of Ismail, son of Imam Ja'far Sadiq. They assert that Ismail completed the cycle of seven imams, after which the era of hidden imams began and the latter send out emissaries. They believe that if the imam is not manifest (*qa'im*), then his emissary or proof (*hujjah*) must be manifest.

jahiliyyah: literally meaning ignorant, it refers to the pre-Islamic era that existed in Arabia. It is a combination of views, ideas and practices that totally defy and reject the guidance sent down by God through His prophets.

jihad: an Arabic word, the root of which is *jahada*, which means to strive for a better way of life. It is a struggle, particularly fighting in the way of Allah to establish Islam.

jinn: invisible, non-human creatures created by God from smokeless fire. They are spiritual beings that inhabit the heavens and the earth.

jizya: a protection tax payable by non-Muslims as a tribute to a Muslim ruler, traditionally 4 dinars or 40 dirhams per year.

Ka'bah: the first house of worship built for mankind. It was originally built by Adam and later on reconstructed by Abraham and Ismail. It is a cubed shaped structure based in the city of Makkah to which all Muslims turn to in their five daily prayers.

kafir: (plural *kuffar*) a person who rejects Allah and his messenger Muhammad (PBUH). The opposite is a believer or *momin*.

khanqah: also called *zaviyah*, a place where seekers of Allah live and meet.

kufr: disbelief; to cover up the truth; to reject Allah and refuse to believe that Muhammad is his messenger.

Madhab: a school of law founded on the opinion of a *faqih*. The four main schools are now Hanafi, Maliki, Shafi'i and Hanbli. There are also other *madhabs* which have ceased to exist: the Awza'i, Zahiri, Jariri (from Ibn Jarar at-Tabari) and the *madhab* of Sufyan ath-Thauri. The Shias also designate their *fiqh* as the Imami or Ja'fari *madhab* after Imam Ja'far Sadiq.

madrassah (plural *madaris*): a traditional place of study and learning.

Madinah: the first city-state that came under the banner of Islam. It is where the Prophet Muhammad's (PBUH) mosque and grave are situated.

mahram: A *mahram* refers to the group of people whom it is unlawful for a woman to marry due to marital or blood relationships. These people include: i) her seven permanent *mahrams* due to blood relationships: her father, her son (who has passed puberty), her brother, her uncle from her father's side, her brother's son, her sister's son and her uncle from her mother's side; ii) her *radha'i mahrams*, due to sharing the same nursing milk when she was an infant; their status is similar to the permanent seven *mahrams*; iii) her (in-law) *mahrams* because of marriage: her husband's father (father-in-law), her husband's son (stepson), her mother's husband (stepfather) and her daughter's husband.

makruh: abominable, reprehensible but not unlawful in *Shariah*. Not doing *makruh* counts as a good deed but doing it does not count as a bad deed.

Milad or ***Maulud*** or ***Maulid***: a time, place or celebration of birth, especially that of the Prophet Muhammad (PBUH), who was born on the 12th of Rabi ul Awwal (third month of the Muslim calendar) in 571 CE.

minbar: steps on which the imam stands to deliver his *khutba* or sermon.

mubah: permissible, permitted, something for which there is neither reward nor punishment. It is also called *ja'iz*.

mujaddid: renewer, restorer of the *deen*. It is said that one comes every hundred years or so.

muqallid: one who practices *taqlid*, not performing *ijtihad*, but instead following the legal opinion already arrived at by a *mujtahid*.

mufti: someone qualified to give legal opinion or *fatwa*.

Muharram: the first month of the Muslim lunar year.

munafiq (plural *munafiqeen*): a hypocrite; someone who outwardly professes Islam on the tongue but inwardly rejects Allah and His Messenger.

murtad: an apostate from Islam; a recanter.

mustahab: what is recommended but not obligatory in acts of worship in *Shariah*.

mushrik: a polytheist; someone who commits *shirk* by ascribing partners to Allah.

Muslim: someone who follows the way of Islam, not abandoning what is obligatory while keeping within the bounds set by Allah and following the Sunnah as much as possible.

Muzdalifah: a place between Arafa and Mina where the pilgrims returning from Arafa spend a night in the open.

nafl or ***nafila***: supererogatory or voluntary act of worship.

pir: Persian for *murshid*, a spiritual guide.

purdah: (Persian: curtain) the religious and social practice of female seclusion prevalent among some Muslim communities in Pakistan, Afghanistan and India. It takes two forms: physical segregation of the sexes and the requirement that women cover their bodies so as to cover their skin and conceal their form.

qabr (plural *quboor*): grave.

qadhi: a judge qualified to judge all matters in accordance with *Shariah* and to dispense and enforce legal punishments.

qawwali: *sufi* singing in Urdu and Persian.

qibla: the direction Muslims face during *salah* (prayer) that is towards the Ka'bah in Makkah.

Qiyamah: Day of Judgment; the arising of people at the Resurrection.

qiyas: logical deduction by analogy; reaching a legal decision on the basis of evidence (a precedent). *Qiyas* is one of the four main fundamental principles utilized for reaching a judgement. Other three are the Quran, the Sunnah and *ijma.*

Ramadan: the month of prescribed fasting for Muslims. It is in the ninth month of the Muslim calendar.

riba: usury, which is *haram* in all its forms since it involves obtaining something for nothing through exploitation.

sadaqah: non-obligatory alms; charitable giving in the cause of Allah. Fasting at Ramadan is one of the five pillars of Islam (the other four are *shahadah* – i.e. declaring that there is no God except Allah and Muhammad is His Prophet – praying five times a day, paying *zakat* and performing *hajj*).

sahaba (singular *sahabi*): literally companions, the Muslims who saw the Prophet at least once.

sahih: healthy and sound with no defects, a term used to describe an authentic Hadith.

salah: prayer, particularly the five daily obligatory prayers i.e. Fajr (dawn), Zuhr (noon), Asr (afternoon), Maghrib (sunset), and Isha (late night). There are non-obligatory prayers as well. *Salah* is an Arabic word to mean a spiritual relationship and communication between the creature and his Creator.

sama: a listening session; listening to *sufi* music and poetry about Allah so that the heart may open.

satr (*awrah*): the private parts of the body which it is indecent to expose in public. For men, this is from the navel to the knee. For women, it is all of her body except the hands, feet and face.

shaikh: in *sufism*, the spiritual teacher who guides one from knowledge of one's self to the knowledge of one's Lord.

Shariah: literally 'the road'; the legal modality of a people based on the revelation of their Prophet. The final *Shariah* is that of Islam.

Shia: literally a party or faction, specifically the party who claim that Ali should have succeeded the Prophet as the first caliph and that the leadership of the Muslims belonged to his descendants.

shirk: the unforgivable wrong action of worshipping something or someone other than Allah or associating something or someone as a partner with Him.

siratul mustaqeem: literally the straight path, the path that the Prophet demonstrated to the mankind by way of the Quran; the path that leads to the Paradise.

suffah: a raised platform that was used by the Prophet as a welcoming point for newcomers or destitute people. It was the veranda of his mosque.

sufi: a Muslim mystic.

Sunnah: literally the customary practice of a person or group of people. It has come to refer to the practice of Prophet Muhammad (PBUH) and to the first generation of Muslims.

surah: a chapter of the Quran. There are 114 chapters in the Quran, each of which is called a *surah*.

Sunni: the main body of Muslims who recognize and accept the first four caliphs of Islam.

tabi'un: 'followers'; the second generation of early Muslims who did not meet Prophet Muhammad (PBUH) and learned the *deen* of Islam from his companions (*sahaba*).

tabi'ut tabi'een: 'followers of the followers'; the generation after the *tabi'un* who did not meet any of the *sahaba*.

tafsir: commentary and explanations of the meanings of the Quran.

tajvid: the art of reciting the Quran in accordance with the rules of *nutq* (pronunciation and intonation and giving each consonant its full value).

taqiyya: concealment of one's views to escape persecution. It was obligatory for the secret agents of some of the more extreme Ismaili Shia groups.

taqlid: imitation; following the opinion of a *mujtahid*, without considering the evidence (*daleel*).

tarawih: prayers at night in the month of Ramadan.

tasawwuf: Arabic term for *sufism*, the science of the journey towards the Lord.

tatbiq: Shah Waliullah's doctrine whereby the principles of Islam were reconstructed and reapplied in accordance with the Quran and the Hadith with the objective of creating synthesis between different viewpoints.

tawhid: the doctrine of Allah's oneness. It is the basis of Islam.

tawaf: circumambulation of the Ka'bah, repeated seven times, usually done during *umrah* or *hajj*.

tawassul: to seek the assistance of a person of virtue in praying to Allah.

taziyah: Shia performance of mourning to mark the death of Imam Hussain, grandson of the Prophet.

ulama (singular *alim*): the learned, knowledgeable people in Islam.

ummah: the body of Muslims as one distinct community.

wahdatul wajud: unity of being. There is only One Self, which is manifested in multiplicity. Allah is one in His *zaat* (being), *sifaat* (attributes) and *af'aal* (functions). There is only One Entity in existence and multiplicity appears through relations between non-essential entities. In other words, there is no true existence except for Allah.

wahdatush shahud: unity of consciousness, unity of direct witnessing. This concept holds that Allah and His creation are entirely separate and there is a true existence of creature and universe which are separate from Allah.

walima: a feast accompanying a wedding to be arranged by the groom's family.

wasilah: the means of intercession (*tawassul*) through which a Muslim supplicates to Allah and seeks nearness to Him. Wasilah can be good deeds, holy places or pious persons (living as well as dead).

waqf (plural *auqaf*): pious trust; an unalienable endowment for a charitable purpose that cannot be given away or sold to anyone.

wudhu: ritual washing to be pure for prayer (*salah*).

zakat or ***zakah***: compulsory wealth tax paid on certain forms of wealth: gold and silver, staple crops, livestock and trading goods. It is to be used for the welfare of society in the eight categories mentioned in the Quran: the poor, the needy, the sympathizers, the captives, the debtors, the cause of Allah, the wayfarers, and for those who are to collect it.

REFERENCES

9/11 Commission. 2004. *The 9/11 Commission Report: Final Report of the National Commission on Terrorist Attacks Upon the United States (9/11 Report)*. Washington, DC: GPO.

Abbasi, I. H. 2004. *Deeni Madaris: Mazi, Haal, Mustaqbil* [Religious schools: Past, present, future]. Karachi: Maktaba-e-Umaf Farooq.

Abbasi, M. R. 2001. 'Dini Sahafat mein *As-Sayyanah* ka Kirdar' [Role of *As-Sayyanah* is religious journalism]. *As-Sayyanah* 10(3): 42–55.

Abbott, F. 1962. 'The Decline of the Mughal Empire and Shahwaliullah'. *Muslim World* 52(2): 115–23. Online: http://onlinelibrary.wiley.com/doi/10.1111/j.1478-1913.1962.tb02602.x/abstract (accessed 24 August 2011).

Adorno, T. 1974. 'Theses against Occultism'. *Telos*, Spring: 7–12.

Agha, S. B. 2009. 'Yom-e-Siyah aur Murawwajah Tariqa-e-Soag: Islami Nuqta-e-Nazar se' [Black day and the customary practice of mourning from an Islamic viewpoint]. *Bayyinat* 72(12): 41–3.

Ahadees.com. Quran (English translation). http://ahadees.com/english-translation.html (accessed February 2013).

Ahmad, M. 1991. 'The Politics of War: Islamic Fundamentalisms in Pakistan'. In *Islamic Fundamentalisms and the Gulf Crisis*, ed. J. Piscatori, ch. 8. Chicago: American Academy of Arts and Sciences.

______. 2004. 'Madrassa Education in Pakistan and Bangladesh'. In *Religious Radicalism and Security in South Asia*, ed. S. P. Lamiaye, R. G. Wirsing and M. Malik, 101–15. Honolulu: Asia-Pacific Center for Security Studies. Online: http://www.globalwebpost.com/farooqm/study_res/bangladesh/mumtaz_madrassah.pdf (accessed 28 May 2013).

Ahmed, A. S. 2002. 'Ibne Khuldun's Understanding of Civilizations and the Dilemmas of Islam and the West Today'. *Middle East Journal* 56(1): 20–45. Online: JSTOR database (accessed 5 June 2011).

Ahmed, R. 2008. 'Digital Tasveer aur Tableegh-e-Deen' [Digital picture and proselytization of religion]. *Bayyinat* 71(6): 37–43.

Ajiz, M. H. 2010. 'Afghanistan: Amrika ke Liye Aik Naya Viet Nam' [Afghanistan: A new Vietnam for the United States). *Al-Qasim* 14(2): 19–22.

Akbar, S. 2010. *Pakistan Ke Dini Masalik* [Religious sects of Pakistan]. Islamabad: Al-Baseerah.

Akhtar, N. H. 2009. 'Lord Macaulay ka Nizam-e-Taleem aur uss ke Asraat-o-Nataij' [Lord Macaulay's system of education and its effects and consequences]. *Bayyinat* 72(11): 42–7.

Alam, A. 2003. 'Understanding Madrasas'. *Economic and Political Weekly* 38(22): 2123–6.

Alan, C. 2005. 'The Hidden Roots of Wahhabism in British India'. *World Policy Journal* 22(2): 87–93.

Al-Arabia News. 2013. 'To Beard or Not to Beard Is Not the Question'. 8 January. Online: http://english.alarabiya.net/articles/2013/01/08/259372.html (accessed 8 January 2013).

Ali, A. M. A. 2005. 'Roodad: Pehla Makki Shaikh-ul-Islam Seminar' [Narrative of the first seminar on Makki Shaikh-ul-Islam]. *As-Sayyanah* 14(5): 26–33.

Ali, G., and I. Khattak. 2003. 'MMA to Set Up Taliban-Style Ministry'. *Daily Times*, 30 January. Online: http://www.dailytimes.com.pk/default.asp?page=story_30-1-2003_pg7_11 (accessed 12 December 2013).

Ali, J. 2003. 'Islamic Revivalism: The Case of the Tablighi Jamaat'. *Journal of Muslim Minority Affairs* 23(1): 173–81. Online: EBSCO Publishing database (accessed 4 June 2011).

Ali, S. H. 2008. 'Pakistani Madrassahs and Rural Underdevelopment: An Empirical Study of Ahmedpur East'. In *Madrasas in South Asia: Teaching Terror?*, ed. J. Malik, ch. 5. London and New York: Routledge.

______. 2009. *Islam and Education: Conflict and Conformity in Pakistan's Madrassahs*, Karachi: Oxford University Press.

Al-Khateeb, W. M. A. n.d. *Mishkat-ul-Masabeeh*. Urdu translation by Abidur Rehman Kandhalwi. Karachi: Dar-ul-Isha'at.

Allahabadi, Q. Z. 2005. 'Salook-o-Tasawwuf Aur Bait-o-Tariqat'. *Al-Qasim* 9(2): 13–20.

Al-Mustafa, M. R. 2010. *Milad-e-Mustafa* [Milad of the Prophet]. Lahore: Zavia.

Ambethwi, K. A. 1995. 'Islami Madaris'. *Bayyinat* 57(7): 12–18.

Andrabi, T., A. Khawaja, J. Das and T. Zajonc. 2005. 'Religious School Enrolment in Pakistan: A Look at the Data'. Harvard working paper. Online: http://www.hks.harvard.edu/fs/akhwaja/papers/madrassa_CER_dec05.pdf (accessed 5 June, 2011).

Amin, N. M. 2010. *Kia Salat-o-Salam aur Mahfil-e-Milad Bidat Hai?* [Is offering peace and blessings for the Prophet and holding Milad meetings *bidah*?] Karachi: Tahaffuz-e-Nazriyat-Deoband Academy.

Ansari, M. A. 2006. 'Dini Madaris: Islami Tehzeeb aur Riwayat ke Ameen' [Religious madaris: Custodians of the Islamic civilization and traditions]. *Bayyinat* 69(6): 34–43.

Anzar, U. 2003. 'Islamic Education: A Brief History of Madrassas with Comments on Curricula and Pedagogical Practices'. Online: http://schools.nashua.edu/myclass/fenlonm/block1/Lists/DueDates/Attachments/10/madrassah-history.pdf (accessed 30 April 2011).

Arif, M. S., A. Ali and A. M. Dinpuri. 2010. 'Fatwa: Chehra ke Purdah par Chand Ashkalat ka Jawab' [Answer to some intricacies about the *purdah* of face]. *Bayyinat* 73(8): 53–64.

Arjomand, S. A. 1999. 'The Law, Agency and Policy in Medieval Islamic Society: Development of the Institutions of Learning from the Tenth to the Fifteenth Century'. *Comparative Studies in History and Society* 41(2): 263–93. Online: JSTOR OneSearch, UWA Research Repository (accessed 19 January 2014).

Arshad, M. 2005. 'Tradition of Madrasa Education'. In *Madrasas in India: Trying to Be Relevant*, ed. A. Wasey, ch. 2. New Delhi: Global Media.

Aslam, M. U. 2008. 'Tasveer Sazi: Butt-Parasti ka Pehla Zeenah' [Picture making: The first step towards idol worship]. *Bayyinat* 71(11): 41–4.

Athar, T. M. 1999. 'Dini Madaris: Taliban ki Chhaoniyaan' [Religious madaris: Garrisons of the Taliban]. *Al-Qasim* 3(7): 7–9.

______. 2000. 'Jamhoori Nizam ka Nifaz: Dohray Nizam ki Duhai' [Implementation of a democratic system: An outcry for a duplicitous system]. *Al-Qasim* 4(1): 7–10.

Attari, M. Z. 2009. *Haq Par Kaun?* [Who is right?] Rawalpindi: Islamic Book Corporation.

Aziz, A. S. n.d. *Tohfa-e-Athna Ashari* [Gift of Twelver Shias]. Karachi: Darul Ishaat.

Barelwi, A. R. K. n.d. *Kanz-ul-Iman*. Urdu translation and exegesis of Quran. Lahore: Zia-ul-Quran.

Barkat, J. 2001. 'Islam Mein Aurat ka Rutbah' [Status of women in Islam]. *As-Sayyanah* 10(5): 25–8.

Bashir, A. H. K. 2006. *Barr-e-Saghir Mein Islam ki Aamad-o-Isha'at aur Islami Aqaid-o-Nazariyat* [Arrival and spread of Islam in the subcontinent and Islamic beliefs and ideologies]. Gujrat: Haqq Chaar Yaar Academy.

Bayat, A. 2005. 'Islamism and Social Movement Theory'. *Third World Quarterly* 26(6): 891–908. Online: JSTOR OneSearch, UWA Research Repository (accessed 11 April 2014).

Beckford, J. A. 1983. 'The Restoration of "Power" to the Sociology of Religion'. *Sociological Analysis* 44(1): 11–31. Online: JSTOR OneSearch, UWA Research Repository (accessed 11 April 2014).

Bergen, P., and S. Pandey. 2006. 'The Madrassa Scapegoat'. *Washington Quarterly* 29(2): 117–25. Online: http://www.twq.com/06spring/docs/06spring_bergen.pdf (accessed 4 May 2011).

Berkey, L. P. 2007. 'Madrasas Medieval and Modern: Politics, Education and the Problem of Muslim Identity'. In *Schooling Islam: The Culture and Politics of Modern Muslim Education*, ed. R. W. Hefner and M. Q. Zaman, ch. 2. Princeton, NJ: Princeton University Press.

Bewley, A. 1998. *A Glossary of Islamic Terms*, London: Ta-Ha.

Bhatti, A. U. 2010. 'Hakim-ul-Ummat Maulana Ashraf Ali Thanvi Sahib ka Islah-Tasawwuf mein Kirdar' [Role of the 'thinker of the nation' Maulana Ashraf Ali Thanvi in reforming tasawwuf]. *As-Sayyanah* 20(5): 35–41.

Binder, L. 1961. *Religion and Politics in Pakistan*. Berkeley: University of California Press.

Binouri, M. Y. 1997. 'Takhleeq-e-Kainat ka Maqsad' [The goal of the creation of the universe]. *Bayyinat* 59(10): 3–5.

______. 2010. 'Ulama-o-Talaba Ke Khilaf Sazish' [Conspiracy against the religious scholars and students]. *As-Sayyanah* 2(5): 16–19.

______. 2012. 'Rahnuma-e-Qom ke Hathon Islami Tehzeeb-o-Aqdar ki Pamali' [Ruination of the Islamic civilization and values by the national leaders]. *Bayyinat* 75(4): 3–12.

Buchdahl, D. 1977. 'The Past, the Counterculture and the Eternal-Now'. *Ethos* 5(4): 466–83.

Bukhari, M. I. 2004. *Sahih Bukhari*, vols 1–8. Urdu translation by Dawood Raz. Delhi: Markazi Jamiat-e-Ahle-Hadith Hind.

Bukhari, S. T. 1999. 'Murawwajah Taqweem: Aik Gunah-e-Be-Lazza' [Customary calendar: An insipid sin]. *Al-Qasim* 3(4): 23–5.

______. 2002. 'Neck-Tie Pehan'na Islam mein Haram Hai' [Wearing a necktie is forbidden in Islam]. *Al-Qasim* 6(7): 21–2.

Butt, Z. D. 2006. *Shah Waliullah ka Qafla* [Caravan of Shah Waliullah]. Lahore: Idara-e-Adab-e-Itfaal.

Candland, C. 2008. 'Pakistan's Recent Experience in Reforming Islamic Education'. In *Madrasas in South Asia: Teaching Terror?*, ed. J. Malik, ch. 6. London: Routledge.

Chishti, A. K. 2010. 'Criminal Silence and the Business of Fatwas'. *Daily Times*, 27 October. Online: http://www.dailytimes.com.pk/default.asp?page=2010%5C10%5C27%5Cstory_27-10-2010_pg7_27 (accessed 10 December 2013).

Christiansen, J. 2009. 'Four Stages of Social Movements'. *EBSCO Research Starters*. Online: http://www.ebscohost.com/uploads/imported/thisTopic-dbTopic-1248.pdf (accessed 4 November 2013).

Clecak, P. 1973. *Radical Paradoxes: Dilemmas of the American Left 1945–1970*. New York: Harper & Row.

Cohen, J. L. 1985. 'Strategy or Identity: New Theoretical Paradigms and Contemporary Social Movements'. *Social Research* 52 (4): 663–716. Online: JSTOR OneSearch, UWA Research Repository (accessed 11 April 2014).

Cohen, S. P. 2000. 'Pakistan's Fear of Failure'. *Wall Street Journal* (Asia), 23 October.

Coulson, A. 'Education and Indoctrination in the Muslim World'. *Policy Analysis* 511 (2004): 1–36.

Daily Times. 2003. 'Talibanization of NWFP'. Editorial, 25 May. Online: http://www.dailytimes.com.pk/default.asp?page=story_25-5-2003_pg3_1 (accessed 12 December 2013).

______. 2008. 'Suicide Bombing Un-Islamic: Only State Can Declare Jihad' (*fatwa*). *Daily Times*, 15 October. Online: http://www.dailytimes.com.pk/default.asp?page=2008%5C10%5C15%5Cstory_15-10-2008_pg1_2 (accessed 11 December 2013).

Daily Express. 2007. 'Supreme Court ne Hasba Bill ki do shiqein aain se mudsadam qarar de dein' [Supreme court declares two sections of Hasba Bill unconstitutional]. 21 February. Online: http://express.com.pk/epaper/PoPupwindow.aspx?newsID=1100131033&Issue=NP_LHE&Date=20070221(accessed 14 December 2013).

Daily Times. 2003. 'Vigilante Operation against Cable Operators'. 11 January. Online: http://www.dailytimes.com.pk/default.asp?page=story_11-1-2003_pg7_24 (accessed 12 December 2013).

______. 2005. 'SC Declares Key Hasba Sections Unconstitutional'. 5 August. Online: http://dailytimes.com.pk/default.asp?page=story_5-8-2005_pg1_1 (accessed 14 December 2013).

Dawn. 2013. 'Timeline: Hazara Killings in Balochistan'. 11 January. Online: http://dawn.com/2013/01/11/timeline-hazara-killings-in-balochistan/ (accessed 13 January 2013).

______. 2014. 'Maulana Samiul Haq Distances Himself from Taliban Talks'. 22 January. Online: http://www.dawn.com/news/1081973/maulana-samiul-haq-distances-himself-from-taliban-talks (accessed 1 April 2014).

Darkhawasti, S. D. 2012. 'Tasveer ki Hurmat Quran-o-Sunnat ki Roshni Mein' [Impermissibility of pictures in the light of the Quran and Sunnah]. *Bayyinat* 75(9): 59–61.

Dalrymple, W. 2005. 'Inside the Madrasas'. *New York Review of Books* 52(19). Online: http://www.nybooks.com/articles/archives/2005/dec/01/inside-the-madrasas/#fnr10 (accessed 19 January 2014).

Debats, D. L., and B. F. Bartelds. 1996. 'The Structure of Human Values: A Principal Components Analysis of the Rokeach Value Survey (RVS)'. Dissertation, University of Groningen. Online: http://www.dissertations.ub.rug.nl/FILES/faculties/gmw/1996/d.l.h.m.../c5.pdf (accessed 7 November 2013).

De la Porta, D., and M. Diani. 2006. *Social Movements: An Introduction*, 2nd ed. Malden, MA: Blackwell.

Durrani, M. R., ed. 2001. *Darul Ulum Deoband: Ahyaiy Islam ki Alamgeer Tehrik* (Deoband Madrassah: Global Movement for the Revival of Islam). Lahore: Jamiat.

Eickelman, D. E., and J. Piscatori. 1996. *Muslim Politics*. Princeton, NJ: Princeton University Press.

Fair, C. 2009. *The Madrassah Challenge: Militancy and Religious Education in Pakistan*. Lahore: Vanguard.

Faizi, S. F. H. 1970. *Pakistan: A Cultural Unity*. Lahore: Sh. Muhammad Ashraf.

Farooq, M. 1998. 'Jihad Ghalba-e-Islam ki Rooh aur Waqt ki Zaroorat Hai' [Jihad is the spirit of Islam and the need of the hour]. *Al-Qasim* 2(3): 44–5.

Faruqi, Z. H. 1963. *The Deoband School and the Demand for Pakistan*. London: Asia Publishing House.

Fatwa, 2001. 'Afghanistan par Amreeki Hamla Riyasti Dehshat Gardi Hai' [The US attack on Afghanistan is state terrorism]. *As-Sayyanah* 10(11): 61–2.

Feldman, H. 1967. *Revolution in Pakistan: A Study of the Martial Law Administration*. London: Oxford University Press.

Gangohi, R. A. n.d. *Fatawa-e-Rasheedia*, vols 1–3. Karachi: Dar-ul-Ishaat.

______. n.d. *Imdad-us-Sulook*. Lahore, Karachi: Idara-e-Islamyat.

Gecas, V. 2008. 'The Ebb and Flow of Sociological Interest in Values'. *Sociological Forum* 23(2): 344–50.

Gilani, S. M. A. [1966] 2006. *Barr-e-Sagheer Pak-o-Hind mein Musalmano ka Nizam-e-Taleem-o-Tarbiyat* [System of education and training of Muslims in the subcontinent]. Lahore: Almeezan.

______. n.d. *Sawaneh-e-Qasmi* [Biography of Muhammad Qasim], vols 1–2. Deoband: Darul Ulum Deoband.

Goldberg, J. 2000. 'Inside Jihad U: The Education of the Holy Warrior'. *New York Times* (Magazine), 25 June 2000. Online: http://www.nytimes.com/2000/06/25/magazine/inside-jihad-u-the-education-of-a-holy-warrior.html?pagewanted=all&src=pm (accessed 11 March 2013).

Gul, I. 2009. *The Most Dangerous Place: Pakistan's Lawless Frontier*. New York: Penguin.

Gumthalvi, A. K. 2008. 'Mah-e-Sha'ban ke Muta'liq Ahkam aur Fazail' [Etiquettes and Commandments for the Month of Sha'ban]. *As-Sayyanah* 18(5): 22–9.

Haenfler, R. 2004. 'Collective Identity in the Straight Edge Movement: How Diffuse Movements Foster Commitment, Encourage Individualized Participation, and Promote Cultural Change'. *Sociological Quarterly* 45(4): 785–805.

Haidri, A. S. 2009. 'Muharram ke Mahinay mein Qayam-e-Amn ki aik Mufeed Tajweez' [A useful proposal to establish peace in the month of Muharram]. *Al-Qasim* 13(1): 46–9.

Halim, A. 1998. 'Bid'at-Muharram ka Tareekhi Pas-Manzar' [Historical background of the innovations of the month of Muharram]. *Bayyinat* 61(1): 51–7.

Hallaq, W. B. 2005. *The Origins and Evolution of Islamic Law*. London: Cambridge University Press.

Hanbal, A. B. n.d. *Musnad Imam Ahmad bin Hambal*, vols 1–14. Urdu translation by Muhammad Zafar Iqbal. Lahore: Maktabah Rehmania.

Hannigan, J. A. 1991. 'Social Movement Theory and the Sociology of Religion: Toward a New Synthesis'. *Sociological Analysis* 52(4): 311–31. Online: JSTOR OneSearch, UWA Research Repository (accessed 11 April 2014).

Haq, A. 1972. *The Faith Movement of Mawlana Muhammad Ilyas*. London: George Allen and Unwin.

______. 1998. 'Tehreek-e-Taliban Waziristan'. *Al-Qasim* 2(3): 6–8.

______. 2004. 'Ashraaf-e-Ummat Kaun Hain?' [Who are the elite of the nation?]. *Al-Qasim* 7(10): 38–47.

______. 2009. *Fatawa-e-Haqqania*, vols 1–4. Akora Khattak: Maktaba Syed Ahmed Shaeed.

Haq, I. 1996. 'Istafta ba-silsilah Islami Programme ki Video Filmsazi' [Fatwa regarding video filmmaking of Islamic programmes]. *Bayyinat* 58(11): 57–63.

Haqqani, A. Q. 1998b. 'Imarat-e-Islami Afghanistan Dini Madaris ka Naqd Samrah hai' [Islamic emirate of Afghanistan is the immediate result of madaris]. *Al-Qasim* 2(6): 11–12.

______. 1998a. 'Iran, Taliban se Larzah bar-Andam kiyun?' [Why is Iran afraid of the Taliban?]. *Al-Qasim* 2(7): 32–4.

______. 1998b. 'Karachi ko Taliban ke Hawalay kia Jaiy' [Karachi may be handed over to Taliban]. *Al-Qasim* 2(3): 2–4.

______ 1999a. 'Murawwajah Khel: Insaniyat ki Akhlaqi Maut ka Samaan' [Customary sports: Source of moral death of humanity]. *Al-Qasim* 3(2): 2–4.

______. 1999b. 'Islami Nizam-e-Hayat ki Tashkeel' [Construction of the Islamic system of life]. *Al-Qasim* 2(8–9): 53–6.

______. 2002. 'Kharjah Policy ke Ahdaf: Quran-o-Sunnat ki Roshni Mein' [Objectives of foreign policy in the light of the Quran and Sunnah]. *Al-Qasim* 6(5): 3–4.

______. 2005. 'Islamic Modernism Kia Hai?' [What is Islamic modernism?]. *Al-Qasim* 9(3): 8–11.

______. 2008a. 'Intakhabat: Qom kiya Faisla Karay?' [Elections: What should the nation decide?] *Al-Qasim* 11(9): 3–5.

______. 2008b. 'Intakhabat 2008: Faraib Khurdah Shaheen' [Elections 2008: The deluded eagles]. *Al-Qasim* 11(11): 3–6.

______. 2008c. 'Nizam Nahi, Imam Badlo' [Change the leader, not the system]. *Al-Qasim* 12(3): 3–6.

______. 2009a. 'Hakoomat nahi, Nizam-e-Hakoomat ki Tabdeeli Zaruri Hai' [Not the government, but the system of the government needs to be changed]. *Al-Qasim* 13(2): 3–6.

______. 2009b. 'Zardari, Gilani, Kayani, Iftikhar aur Sharif Baradran Nahi, Aik Umar bin Abdul Aziz ki Zarurat Hai' [Not Zardari, Gilani, Kayani, Iftikhar and Sharif brothers but one Umar bin Abdul Aziz is needed]. *Al-Qasim* 13(4): 3–8.

______. 2010. 'Dini Madaris ka Tahaffuz' [Protection of madaris]. *Al-Qasim* 14(7–8): 3–8.

Hardy, P. 1971. *Partners in Freedom and True Muslims: The Political Thought of Some Muslim Scholars in British India 1912–1947*. Sweden: Studentlitteratur, Scandinavian Institute of Asian Studies.

Hasan, Z. 1950. *Arwah-e-Salasa*. Maktaba Saharanpur.

Hasba Bill. 2005. Online: http://www.dawn.com/news/148019/text-of-hasba-bill/1 (accessed 14 December 2013).

Hassan, W. 1988. 'Hazrat Maulana Wali Hassan Saheb Ka Fatwa' [Fatwa by Mufti Wali Hassan against Shias]. *Al-Bayyinat* 51(3): 77–80.

Herald. 2012. 'Readers Ask: Interview with Police Chief of Balochistan Province'. 44(5) (May): 55.

Hitlin, S., and J. A. Piliavin. 2004. 'Values: Reviving a Dormant Concept'. *Annual Review of Sociology* 30: 359–93.

Hopper, R. D. 1950. 'The Revolutionary Process: A Frame of Reference for the Study of Revolutionary Movements'. *Social Forces* 28(3): 270–80.

Hunter, W. W. [1871] 1974. *The Indian Musalmans: Are They Bound in Conscience to Rebel Against the Queen?* Lahore: Premier Book House.

Hussain, K. 2013. 'Fazlullah's Ascent'. *Dawn*, 19 November. Online: http://www.dawn.com/news/1057083 (accessed 10 December 2013).

Hussain, Z. 2007. *Frontline Pakistan: The Struggle with Militant Islam*. New York: Columbia University Press.

______. 2014. 'A State of Fear'. *Dawn*, 29 January. Online: http://www.dawn.com/news/1083386/a-state-of-fear (accessed 29 January 2014).

Husaini, Q. Z. 1993. 'Tasveer Kashi and Tasveer Kushi' [Picture making or picture breaking]. *Bayyinat* 56(5): 47–9.

Ibrahim, M. 2011. *Nafi-e-Sama-e-Mauta* [Negation of the listening by the dead]. Bajaur: Madrassah Zia-ul-Quran Mukhbatiah.

Ikram, S. M. 1970. *Modern Muslim India and the Birth of Pakistan, 1858–1951*. Lahore: Sh. Muhammad Ashraf Publishers.

______. 2011. *Rood-e-Kausar*. Lahore: Idaa Saqafat-e-Islamia.

Ikram, S. M., and P. Spear, eds. 1955. *The Cultural Heritage of Pakistan*. London: Oxford University Press.

Iqbal, M. 2007. 'Nizam-e-Khilafat ki Zaroorat aur Fawaid' [The need and benefits of the caliphate system]. *Al-Qasim* 11(5): 59–60.

______. n.d. *Armaghan-e-Hijaz*. Allama Iqbal Cyber Library, online: http://iqbalcyberlibrary.net (accessed 6 November 2014).

Islam101. 'Glossary of Islamic Terms'. Online: http://www.islam101.com/selections/GLOSSARY0.html (accessed 10 June 2014).

Islamic Centre of New Castle, Australia. 2014. 'Glossary of Islamic Terms and Concepts'. Online: http://islamiccentre.org.au/education/glossary-of-islamic-terms-and-concepts/ (accessed 9 June 2014).

Ismail, S. M. n.d. *Taqwia tul Iman* [Strengthening of faith]. Lahore: Al-Maktabatus-Salafiya.

Ismail, M. 1993. 'Ilm-e-Deen aur Taleem-e-Niswan' [Religious knowledge and female education]. *Bayyinat* 56(2): 31–6.

Jaaisi, S. A. A. 2007. *Shah Waliullah aur Tasawwuf* [Shah Waliullah and *sufism*]. Karachi: Jamiat-e-Isha'at Ahle Sunnat.

Jabbar, A. 1999. 'Tehreek-e-Taliban aur Jihad-e-Kashmir' [Taliban movement and *jihad* in Kashmir]. *Al-Qasim* 3(3): 13–14.

Jamal, A. 2004. 'Politics of Fatwas'. *Pakistan Link*, 11 November. Online: http://pakistanlink.org/Commentary/2004/Nov11/05.htm (accessed 10 December 2013).

Jamal, N. 2012. 'Jhang: The War Diaries'. *Herald* 44(5) (May): 52–4.

Jamia Ashrafia. http://www.jamiaashrafia.org (accessed 29 December 2013).

Jamia-tul-ulum-ul-Islamiah. http://www.banuri.edu.pk (accessed 29 December 2013).

Jafferlot, C., ed. 2002. *A History of Pakistan and Its Origins*. London: Anthem.

Jawwad, R. 2013. 'Apas ki Baat with Najam Sethi'. YouTube video. Online: http://www.youtube.com/watch?v=aGzh_IrmlFU (accessed 3 November 2013).

Jonsson, B. 1981. 'Notes on Counter Culture and Societal Change'. In *Spontaneity and Planning in Social Development*, ed. U. Himmelstrand, ch. 9. London: Sage.

Kafeel, M. 2000. 'Rasmon ki Zanjeer se Azadi' [Freedom from the clutches of custom]. *As-Sayyanah* 9(17): 52–4.

Kamran, M. 2007. 'Hasba Bill Partially Unconstitutional: SC'. *Daily Times*, 21 February. Online: http://www.dailytimes.com.pk/default.asp?page=2007%5C02%5C21%5Cstory_21-2-2007_pg1_3 (accessed 12 December 2013).

Karim, Q. A. 1993. 'Pakistan ka Adm-Istehkam: Quran-o-Sunnat ki Roshni Mein' [Pakistan's instability in the light of the Quran and Sunnah]. *Bayyinat* 56(3): 17–31.

Karim, S. B. A. 1998. 'Taziyah ki Tareekhi aur Shari'i Hasiyyat' [Historical and religious position of *taziyah*]. *Bayyinat* 61(1): 33–42.

Kashmiri, S. A. 2004. 'Madaris: Ulum-e-Nubawwat ke Sarchashmay' [Madaris: Fountainheads of the knowledge of Prophethood]. *Al-Qasim* 8(6): 31–5.

Khattak, D. 2013. 'Who Is Mullah Fazlullah?'. *Foreign Policy*, 8 November. Online: http://southasia.foreignpolicy.com/posts/2013/11/08/who_is_mullah_fazlullah#sthash.NwyYLnSX.MKNmFW7m.dpbs (accessed 10 December 2013).

Khalid, H. 1995. 'Dini Madaris Kay Khilaf Propaganda Ke Asbab' [Reasons behind the propaganda against the madaris]. *Bayyinat* 58(7): 51–5.

Khalid, S. M. 2002. *Dini Madaris mein Taleem: Kaffiat, Masa'il Imkanaat* [Education in madaris: Situation, problems, possibilities]. Islamabad: Institute of Policy Studies.

Khan, M. A. 1967. *Friends Not Masters: A Political Autobiography*. New York: Oxford University Press.
Khan, N. 1999. 'Naujawanon ki Tabahi ka Zimmadar kon?' [Who is responsible for the destruction of the youth?]. *Al-Qasim* 2(12): 38–41.
Khan, S. A. K. 1903. *Asbab-e-Baghawat-e-Hind* [Causes of Indian revolt]. Agrah: Matba Mufeed-e-Aam.
Khan, S. U. 2008. 'Fitnon ki Baarish' [Rain of tribulations]. *Al-Qasim* 12(5–6): 17–25.
Klineberg, O., M. Zavalloni, C. Louis-Guerin and J. Ben-Brika. 1979. *Students, Values, and Politics: A Crosscultural Comparison*. New York: Free Press.
Knapp, M. G. 2003. 'The Concept and Practice of Jihad in Islam'. *Parameters* 33(1): 82–94. Online: ProQuest Research Library New Platform (accessed 13 November 2013).
Ludhianvi, M. Y. 1994. 'Sadr-e-Pakistan ki Khidmat mein Chand Guzarishat' [A few requests to the president of Pakistan]. *Bayyinat* 56(9): 3–19.
______. 1997. 'Ghair-Shari'i Hakoomat ki Bartarfi aur Maujooda Hukmranon se Khadshat' [Dismissal of the non-religious government and misgivings about the present rulers]. *Bayyinat* 59(9): 3–7.
______. 1998. Dini Madaris kay Khilaf Hakoomat kay Azaaim [Designs of the government against the madaris]. *Bayyinat* 60(11): 3–9.
______. 2009. 'Jadeed Taleem aur uss ke Nataij' [Modern education and its consequences]. *Bayyinat* 72(17): 14–23.
______. n.d. *Ikhtalaf-e-Ummat Aur Sirat-e-Mustaqeem* [Disagreement in ummah and the straight path]. Lahore: Maktaba-e-Madinah.
Madni, S. H. A. 1954. *Naqsh-e-Hayat* [Imprint of life]. Karachi: Darul Isha'at.
______. n.d. *Safar Nama Aseer-e-Malta* [Travelogue of a prisoner of Malta]. Lahore: Tayyab.
Madrassah Darul Ulum Deoband. http://www.darululoom-deoband.com (accessed 14 May 2011).
Maikash, M. A. K. 2006. *Tareekh-e-Islam* [History of Islam]. Lahore: Maktaba-e-Aala Hazrat.
Maley, W. 1998. *Fundamentalism Reborn? Afghanistan and the Taliban*. London: Hurst.
Malik, I. H. 1997. *State and Civil Society in Pakistan: Politics of Authority, Ideology and Ethnicity*. London: MacMillan.
Malik, J. 1996. *Colonialization of Islam: Dissolution of Traditional Institutions in Pakistan*. Lahore: Vanguard.
______, ed. 2008. *Madrasas in South Asia: Teaching Terror?* London and New York: Routledge.
Mamay, S. 1991. 'Theories of Social Movement and Their Current Development in Soviet Society', ed. Jerry Eades and Caroline Schwaller. Transitional Agendas: Working papers from the Summer School for Soviet Sociologists. Online: http://lucy.ukc.ac.uk/csacpub/csacmonog.html (accessed 4 November 2013).
Mansoor, A. L. S. 2011. 'Dini Madaris mein Dunyawi Taleem ka Riwaj Parr Janay k Awaqib-o-Nataij' [Effects and consequences of the prevalence of worldly education in madaris]. *Bayyinat* 75(11): 25–36.
Meeruthi, M. A. I. 1908. *Tazkira-tur-Rasheed* [Mention of Rasheed Ahmed]. Lahore: Idara-e-Islamyat.
Metcalf, B. 1978. 'The Madrasa at Deoband: A Model for Religious Education in Modern India'. *Modern Asian Studies* 12(1): 111–34.
______. 1982. *Islamic Revival in British India: Deoband 1860–1900*. Princeton, NJ: Princeton University Press.
______. 1993. 'Living Hadith in the Tablighi Jama'at'. *Journal of Asian Studies* 52(3): 584–608. Online: JSTOR database (accessed 3 June 2011).
______. 2002. *A Concise History of India*. Cambridge: Cambridge University Press.
______. 2007. 'Madrasas and Minorities in Secular India'. In *Schooling Islam: The Culture and Politics of Modern Muslim Education*, ed. R. W. Hefner and M. Q. Zaman, ch. 4. Princeton, NJ: Princeton University Press.
Mian, S. M. 1957. *Ulmaa-e-Hind ka Shandaar Mazi* [Glorious past of religious scholars of India], vols 1–6. Karachi: Maktaba-e-Rasheedia.
______. 1988. *Tehreek-e-Shaikh-ul-Hind* [Movement of the elder of India]. Karachi: Maktaba-e-Rasheedia.

Miller, F. D. 1999. 'The End of SDS and the Emergence of Weatherman: Demise through Success'. In *Waves of Protest: Social Movements since the Sixties*, ed. J. Freeman and V. Johnson, 303–24. Lanham, MD: Rowman & Littlefield.

Mir, A. 2004. *The True Face of Jehadis*. Lahore: Mashal Books.

Mishkaat Sharif [Book of Hadith]. n.d. Translation by Abidur Rehman Kandhalwi. Karachi: Dar-ul-Isha'at.

Mohsin, C. 2008. 'Mullah Military Alliance'. *Pakistan Christian Post*. Online: http://www.pakistanchristianpost.com/viewarticles.php?editorialid=166 (accessed 2 November 2013).

Muawiyah, A. M. 2003. 'Milad, Seerat aur Musalman' [Milad, the Prophet's life and the Muslims]. *As-Sayyanah* 12(5): 30–32.

______. 2008. 'Siyasat-e-La-Deen' [Irreligious politics]. *Bayyinat* 71(11): 42–5.

Muawiyah, M. T. 2000. 'Jin ska Shaitan' [Satan of sex]. *Al-Qasim* 3(12): 29–30.

Muhammad, F. 2009. 'Asr-e-Hazir ke Challenge aur Ulama-e-Karaam ki Zimme-dariyan' [Challenges of the present age and the responsibilities of the religious scholars]. *Bayyinat* 72(5): 41–9.

______. 1998. 'Dini Madaris aur Nadaan Hukmran' [Religious madaris and senseless rulers]. *Bayyinat* 61(2): 51–4.

Mukhtar, H. U. 1995. 'She'r ka Hukm' [Commandments about Poetry]. *Bayyinat* 57(7): 11–15.

Murphy, E. 2013. *The Making of Terrorism in Pakistan: Historical and Social Roots of Extremism*. London: Routledge.

Musgrove, F. 1974. *Ecstasy and Holiness: Counterculture and the Open Society*. London: Methuen.

Muslim, I. 2004. *Sahi Muslim*, vols 1–6. Urdu translation by Waheed-uz-Zaman. Lahore: Naumani Kutab Khana.

Nadwi, S. A. H. n.d. *Karwan-e-Iman-o-Azeemat* [Caravan of faith and steadfastness]. Karachi: Majlis-e-Nashriyat-e-Islam.

Naeem, F. S. 2009. 'Sufisim and Revivalism in South Asia: Mawlana Ashraf 'Ali Thanvi of Deoband and Mawlana Ahmad Raza Khan of Bareilly and Their Paradigms of Islamic Revivalism'. *The Muslim World* 99(3): 435–51. Online: Wiley Online Library database (accessed 29 March 2011).

Naeemi, A. Y. K. n.d. *Jaa'al Haq* [Coming of the truth]. E-book: Ala Hazrat Network.

Nagarkar, V. V. 1975. *Genesis of Pakistan*. Bombay: Allied Publishers.

Naumani, M. M. 1988. 'Muqaddimah'. *Bayyinat* 51(3): 17–62.

Nasim, Q. M. 2009. 'Shab-e-Qadr'. *Al-Qasim* 13(9–10): 60–63.

Niazi, M. I. H. K. 2012. *Mazaraat Aur Bidat* [Shrines and *bidah*]. Karachi: Welcome Book Port.

Nishapuri, A. 2012. 'Why Did Takfiri Deobandis of Sipah Sahaba Sill Senior Deobandi Scholar Mufti Nizamuddin Shamzai?'. *Let Us Build Pakistan*, 12 December. Online: http://lubpak.com/archives/233399 (accessed 11 December 2013).

Nizami, M. A. n.d. *Khoon Kay Aansoo* [Tears of blood]. Lahore: Progressive Books.

Nojumi, N. 2002. *The Rise of the Taliban in Afghanistan: Mass Mobilization, Civil War and the Future of the Region*. New York: Palgrave.

Ojha, P. N. 1975. *North Indian Social Life During Mughal Period*. Delhi: Oriental.

Okon, E. E. 2013. 'Jihad: Warfare and Territorial Expansion in Islam'. *Asian Social Science* 9(5). Online: Academic Search Primer database (accessed 13 November 2013).

Olesen, A. 1995. *Islam and Politics in Afghanistan*. Richmond: Curzon Press.

Parsons, T. 1951. *The Social System*. London: Routledge and Kegan Paul.

Pemberton, K. 2009. 'An Islamic Discursive Tradition on Reform as Seen in the Writing of Deoband's Mufti Muhammad Taqi Usmani'. *The Muslim World* 99(3): 452–77. Online: Wiley Online Library database (accessed 29 March 2011).

Pew Research Centre. 2002. *What the World Thinks in 2002*. Online: http://www.pewglobal.org/files/2002/12/2002-Report-Final-Updated.pdf (accessed 12 December 2013).

______. 2012. *Pakistani Public Opinion Ever More Critical of US*. Online: http://www.pewglobal.org/files/2012/06/Pew-Global-Attitudes-Project-Pakistan-Report-FINAL-Wednesday-June-27-2012.pdf (accessed 12 December 2013).

Pirzada, S. A. S. 2000. *The Politics of the Jamiat Ulema-e-Islam Pakistan (1971–77)*. Karachi: Oxford University Press.

Pirzada, Y. 2013. 'Barrhak Lagana Mana Hai!' [Bragging is prohibited]. *Jang*, 20 November. Online: http://jang.com.pk/jang/nov2013-daily/20-11-2013/col3.htm (accessed 11 December 2013).

Qadir, A. 2012. 'Ta'ziyat ka Sahi Tariqah' [Correct method of condolence]. *As-Sayyanah* 22(8): 34–8.

Qadir, A., A. M. Dinpuri and M. I. Haq. 1998. 'Bachiyoun ke Dini Madaris ka Qiyam aur unn Bachiyoun ki Taleem ka Hukm' (*fatwa*). [Establishing girls' madaris and commandment about girls' education]. *Bayyinat* 60(12): 49–58.

Qadri, M. T. 2005. *Al-Bidah I'nd-al-Aimma wal Muhaddiseen* [*Bidah* in the eyes of imams and Hadith experts]. Lahore: Minhaj-ul-Quran.

______. 2007. *Lafz Bidat ka Itlaq: Ahadees-o-Aasar ki Roshni Mein* [Application of the word *bidah* in the light of Ahadith and causatum of companions in the eyes of imams and hadith experts]. Lahore: Minhaj-ul-Quran.

______. 2010. *Kia Milad-un-Nabi Manana Bidat Hai?* [Is celebrating the Prophet's birth anniversary a *bidah*?] Lahore: Minhaj-ul-Quran.

Qasmi, B. S. 2002. Nizam-e-Islami se Jamhooriat ka Takrao (Clash of Democracy with the Islamic System). *Al-Qasim* 6(5): 14–17.

Qasmi, M. Z. 2007. 'Internet ki Hilakat Khaiziyan aur unn se Bachnay ki Tadabeer' [Devastating effects of the Internet and the techniques to avoid it). *Al-Qasim* 11(3): 31–5.

Qawi, A. 2011. 'Islam mein Nangay Sar Rehna Tehzeeb ke Khilaf Hai' [It is uncivil in Islam to keep the head uncovered]. *Al-Qasim* 15(12): 27–32.

Quddus, A. 1991. 'Masail-o-Fazail-eMuharram-ul-Haram' [Issues and sanctifications of the holy month of Muharram]. *As-Sayyanah* 1(4): 23–7.

Qureshi, M. A. 2008. 'Islam Mein Purday ki Ahmiyat' [Importance of *purdah* in Islam]. *Bayyinat* 71(4): 45–8.

Rahim, F. 2011. 'Hadiya aur Tohfay ke Zariye Apas mein Mohabbat-o-Ulfat Paida kijiay' [Create love and affection among yourselves through gifts and offering]. *As-Sayyanah* 21(4): 18–21.

Rahman, K. 2009. 'Madrasas in Pakistan: Role and Emerging Trends'. In *Islam and Politics: Renewal and Resistance in the Muslim World*, ed. A. Pandya and E. Laipson, ch. 5. Washington, DC: Henry L. Stimson Centre.

Rahman, K., and S. R. Bukhari. 2006. 'Pakistan: Religious Education and Institutions'. *The Muslim World* 96(2): 323–39. Online: Wiley Online Library database (accessed 31 March 2011).

Raja, M. 2013. 'Pakistani Victims: War on Terror Toll Put at 49,000'. *Daily Times*, 27 March. Online: http://tribune.com.pk/story/527016/pakistani-victims-war-on-terror-toll-put-at-49000 (accessed 10 December 2013).

Rana, M. A. 2009. 'Mapping the Madrassa Mindset: Political Attitudes of Pakistani Seminaries' n.p. Re: Paper on Madrassah Mindset, e-mail to the author (amir@san-pips.com), 27 September (11 October 2010).

Rana, A. 2003. 'JUI-S Wants to Expel Shia TI'. *Daily Times*, 16 October. Online: http://www.dailytimes.com.pk/default.asp?page=story_16-10-2003_pg7_3 (accessed 13 December 2013).

Rashdi, Z. 2009. 'Madrassah Qaim Hai aur Qiyamat tak Qaim Rahay Ga' [Madrassah holds its ground and would stay till the day of resurrection]. *Al-Qasim* 13(9–10): 11–13.

Rashid, A. 1998. 'Pakistan and Taliban'. In *Fundamentalism Reborn? Afghanistan and the Taliban*, ed. W. Maley, ch. 4. London: Hurst and Company.

______. 2002. *Jihad: The Rise of Militant Islam in Central Asia*. Lahore: Vanguard.

______. 2010. *Taliban: Militant Islam, Oil and Fundamentalism in Central Asia*. London: Yale University Press.

Rauf, A. 2011. 'Ashra-e-Zil-Hajjah: Takbeer-e-Tashreeq aur Qurbani ke Masail' [Ten days of the month of Zil-Hajj: Reciting exaltation and glorification of Allah and the issues regarding sacrifice]. *As-Sayyanah* 21(9): 44–53.

Raz, M. D. 2004. *Sahih Bukhari*, vols 1–8. Urdu translation. Delhi: Markazi Jamiat-e-Ahle-Hadith Hind.

Rehman, A. 2001. 'Purdah ke Mauzoo' Par Jamai' aur Dilchasp Mazmoon' [An in-depth and interesting essay on the topic of purdah]. *As-Sayyanah* 10(10): 49–52.

Rehman, G. 1999. 'Islami Inqalab ke liye Jihad Na-guzeer ho Gaya Hai' [Jihad becomes obligatory for Islamic revolution]. *Al-Qasim* 3(5): 36–7.

Rehman, H. 2003. 'Taliban-e-Ilm-e-Nabuwwat: Maqam, Zimme Dariyan aur Faraiz' [Students of the knowledge of the Prophethood: Staus, responsibilities and obligations]. *Al-Qasim* 7(4): 23–33.

Rehman, H. F. 1997. *Haji Imdadullah Mahajir Makki aur un ke Khalafa* [Imdadullah and his disciples]. Karachi: Majlis-e-Nashriyaat-e-Islam.

Rehman, S. 2003. 'Madaris Ka Nizam: Afadiyat aur Barkaat' [Madaris system: Benefits and blessings]. *As-Sayyanah* 12(11): 34–8.

Rehman, T. 2004. *Denizens of Alien Worlds: A Study of Education Inequality and Polarization in Pakistan.* Karachi: Oxford University Press.

______. 2008. 'Madrasas: The Potential for Violence in Pakistan?'. In *Madrasas in South Asia: Teaching Terror?*, ed. J. Malik, ch. 4. London and New York: Routledge.

Reich, C. A. 1970. *The Greening of America.* New York: Random House.

Riaz, A,. 2008. *Faithful Education: Madrassahs in South Asia.* London: Rutgers University Press.

Rizwi, S. M. [1976] 2005. *Tareekh-e-Daru-Ulum Deoband* [History of Darul Ulum Deoband], vols 1–2. Karachi: Idara-e-Islamyat.

Robertson, R. 1989. 'Globalization, Politics and Religion'. In *The Changing Face of Religion*, J. Beckford and T. Luckmann, 10–23. London: Sage.

Robinson, F. 1974. *Separatism among Indian Muslims: The Politics of the United Provinces' Muslims, 1860–1923.* London: Cambridge University Press.

Rose, J. D. 1982. *Outbreaks: The Sociology of Collective Behavior.* New York: Free Press.

Roszak, T. 1968. *The Making of a Counter Culture: Reflections on the Technocratic Society and Its Youthful Opposition.* London: Faber and Faber.

Saeed, A. 2002. 'Gana Aik Sangeen Gunah Hai' [Music is an extreme sin]. *As-Sayyanah* 11(4): 26–30.

Safi, S. 2013. 'Taliban se Muzakarat aur Tareekh ka Sabaq' [Negotiations with the Taliban and lesson of history]. *Jang*, 10 September. Online: http://jang.com.pk/jang/sep2013-daily/10-09-2013/col2.htm (accessed 11 December 2013).

Sahibzada, S. B. A. 2008. 'Bhook Hartal ya Khud Kashi: Islami Nuqta-e-Nigah Se' [Hunger strike or suicide: An Islamic perspective]. *Bayyinat* 71(11): 33–5.

Sanyal, U. 2008. *Ahl-I Sunnat Madrasa: The Madrasa Manzar-I Islam, Bareilly, and Jamia Ashrafiyya, Mubarakpur.* New York: Routledge.

Shahjahanpuri, A. S., ed. 2004. *Buzurgaan-e-Darul Ulum Deoband* [Elders of Deoband Madrassah]. Lahore: Jamiat.

Shehzad, M. 2012. 'MMA is Back'. *Friday Times* 24(38). Online: http://www.thefridaytimes.com/beta3/tft/article.php?issue=20121102&page=4 (accessed 13 December 2013).

Schwartz, S. H. 2006. 'A Theory of Cultural Value Orientations: Explication and Applications'. *Comparative Sociology* 5(2): 137–82.

Schwartz, S. H., G. Melech, A. Lehrnami, S. Burgess, M. Harris and V. Owens. 2001. 'Extending the Cross-Cultural Validity of the Theory of Basic Human Values with a Different Method of Measurement'. *Journal of Cross-Cultural Psychology* 32(5): 519–42.

Shafi, M. 2007. 'Intakhabat mein Vote, Voter aur Umeedwar ki Shari'i Hasiyyat' [Religious position of the vote, voters and candidates in elections]. *As-Sayyanah* 17(9): 5–10.

Shahid, S. 2012. 'The Great Game Replay'. *Herald* 44(5) (May): 46–51.

Shakir, H. A. 2002. 'Phoonkon se Yeh Chiragh Bujhaya Na Jaiy Ga' [This lamp shall not be put out by blowing air from the mouth]. *Al-Qasim* 6(4): 22–3.

Sikand, Y. 2006. 'The Tablighi Jama'at and Politics: A Critical Appraisal'. *The Muslim World* 96(1): 175–95. Online: Wiley Online Library database (accessed 31 March 2011).

Sindhi, U. 2002. *Shah Wali Allah aur unka Falsafa* [Shah Wali Allah and his philosophy]. Lahore: Sindh Sagar Academy.

______. [1944] 2008. *Shah Wali Allah aur unki Siyasi Tehreek* [Shah Wali Allah and his Political Movement]. Lahore: Sindh Sagar Academy.

Singer, P. W. 2001. 'Pakistan's Madrassahs: Ensuring a System of Education, Not Jihad'. Brookings Institution analysis paper, no. 14, November 2001. Online: http://www.brookings.edu/views/papers/singer/20020103.pdf (accessed 29 April 2011).

Slater, P. E. 1971. *The Pursuit of Loneliness: American Culture at the Breaking Point.* Boston: Beacon Press.

Smith, W. C. 1943. *Modern Islam in India: A Social* Analysis. Lahore: Minerva Book Shop.

Social Policy and Development Centre (SPDC). 2003. *Social Development in Pakistan: The State of Education.* SPDC Annual Review. Online: http://www.spdc.org.pk/Publications/Annual%20 Reviews/AR-5.pdf (accessed 3 January 2014).

Soomro, K. M. 2005. 'Islami Saal-e-Nau ka Aghaz' [The beginning of the Islamic new year]. *Al-Qasim* 11(10): 46–7.

South Asia Terrorism Portal. 2013. 'Fatalities in Terrorist Violence in Pakistan'. Online: http://www.satp.org/satporgtp/countries/pakistan/index.htm (accessed 31 May, 2013).

Spates, J. L. 1983. 'The Sociology of Values'. *Annual Review of Sociology* 9: 27–49.

Spini, D. 2003. 'Measurement Equivalence of 10 Value Types from the Schwartz Value Survey across 21 Countries'. *Journal of Cross-Cultural Psychology* 34(1): 3–23.

Stern J. 2000. 'Pakistan's Jihad Culture'. *Foreign Affairs* 79 (6): 115–26.

Tariq, A. 1998. 'Woman's Satr'. *Islamic Voice* 12-08 (140). Online: http://www.islamicvoice.com/august.98/dialogue.htm (accessed 31 December 2013).

Taylor, D. 1983. 'The Politics of Islam and Islamization in Pakistan'. In *Islam in the Political Process*, ed. J. Piscatori, ch. 10. Cambridge University Press.

Thanvi, A. A. 1980. *Hifz-ul-Iman* [Protection of the faith]. Lahore: Subhani Academy.

______. 1992. 'Tafseel-ut-Tauba' [Details of repentance]. *As-Sayyanah* 6(1): 7–15.

______. 1994. 'Tatheer-e-Ramzan' [Purification of Ramadhan]. *As-Sayyanah* 2(3): 7–18.

______. 2001a. 'Rasm-o-Riwaj ke Khatam Karnay ke Tariqay' [Methods to eliminate customs and traditions]. *As-Sayyanah* 10(12): 15–18.

______. 2001b. 'Milad-un-Nabi'. *As-Sayyanah* 10(6): 20–24.

______. 2002. *Islah-ur-Rusoom* [Reformation of the customs]. Karachi: Dar-ul-Ishaat.

______. 2003. 'Zikr-e-Rasool' [Mention of the Prophet]. *As-Sayyanah* 12(5): 14–21.

______. 2003a. 'Aurtoun Ka Course aur Nizam-e-Taleem' [Syllabus and educational system for women]. *As-Sayyanah* 12(2): 11–17.

______. 2003b. 'Europe aur Amreeka Walon ka Iqrar' [Confession by the Europeans and Americans]. *As-Sayyanah* 12(3): 17–21.

______. 2004. 'Bachay ki Paidaish par Rasmi Tor par Lain Dain' [Customary exchanges on childbirth]. *As-Sayyanah* 13(5): 11–14.

______. 2005. 'Purdah Kay Ahkaam' [Commandments about *purdah*]. *As-Sayyanah* 14(10): 15–19.

______. 2007. 'Purdah Kis Umar se Hona Munasib Hai?' [What should be the starting age for observing *purdah?*] *As-Sayyanah* 17(3): 14–19.

______. 2008a. 'Islah-e-Khawateen' [Reforming women]. *As-Sayyanah* 18(6): 13–15.

______. 2008b. 'Aurtoun ko Mantaq aur Falsafa Parrhana' [Teaching logic and philosophy to women]. *As-Sayyanah* 18(5): 13–16.

______. 2011. 'Milad-un-Nabi'. *As-Sayyanah* 21(2): 12–24.

______. 2012. 'Tatheer-e-Ramzan: Mah-e-Ramzan ke Aadab-o-Ahkam' [Purifiying Ramadhan: Etiquettes and commandments for the month of Ramadhan]. *As-Sayyanah* 22(7): 18–36.

Thanvi, N. H. 2001. 'Pakistan ke Qiyam aur uss ki Tameer par Aik Nazar' [A look at the founding and construction of Pakistan]. *As-Sayyanah* 10(8): 11–25.

Thanvi, T. H. 2013. 'Tehreek-e-Pakistan ke Mukhalif Ulama bhi Mukhlis Thay' [The ulama who opposed the Pakistan Movement were also sincere]. *Jang*, 23 December. Online: http://jang.com.pk/jang/dec2013-daily/23-12-2013/col11.htm (accessed 30 December, 2013).

Tirmazi, A. Q. 2007. 'Mazar-e-Ashraf ki Be-Hurmati' [Desecration of the tomb of Ashraf Thanvi]. *As-Sayyanah* 2(17): 34–9.

______. 2011. 'Masail-Fazail-eMuharram-ul-Haram' [Etiquettes and commandments for the month of Ramadhan]. *As-Sayyanah* 21(10): 27–32.

Troll, C. W. 1994. 'Two Conceptions of Da'wa in India: Jama'at-i-Islami and Tablighi Jama'at'. *Archives du sciences sociales des religions* 39(87): 115–33. Online: JSTOR database (accessed 3 June 2011).

Turner, R. H, and L. M. Killian. 1972. *Collective Behavior*, 2nd ed. Englewood Cliffs, NJ: Prentice-Hall.

Turner, V. W. 1974. *Dramas, Fields and Metaphors*. New York: Cornell University Press.

University of Michigan. 2013. *The Birthplace of the Arab Spring: Values and Perceptions of the Tunisian Public in a Comparative Perspective*. Final Report, December 2013. Online: http://mevs.org/files/tmp/Tunisia_FinalReport.pdf (accessed 15 January 2014).

Usmani, M. T. 2002. 'Libas ke Mutaliq Shar'I Usool' [Religious principles regarding dress]. *As-Sayyanah* 11(6): 37–40.

______. 2005. *Hamara Taleemi Nizam* [Our education system]. Karachi: Maktaba Darul Ulum.

Westhues, K. 1972. *Society's Shadow: Studies in the Sociology of Countercultures*. Toronto: McGraw-Hill Ryerson.

______. 1982. *First Sociology*. New York: McGraw-Hill.

White, J. T. 2008. *Pakistan's Islamist Frontier: Islamic Politics and US Policy in Pakistan's North West Frontier*. Arlington: Centre on Faith and International Relations.

Wifaqul Madaris Al-Alabiyya. http://www.wifaqulmadaris.org (accessed 14 February 2011).

World Almanac of Islamism. 2013. 'Tablighi Jama'at'. Online: http://almanac.afpc.org/tablighi-jamaat (accessed 6 January 2014).

Wuthnow, R. 1982. 'World Order and Religious Movements.' In *New Religious Movements: A Perspective for Understanding Society*, ed. E. Barker, 47–65. Lewiston, NY: Mellen.

______. 2008. 'The Sociological Study of Values'. *Sociological Forum* 23(2): 333–43.

Yaran, C. S. 2007. *Understanding Islam*. Edinburgh: Dunedin Academic Press.

Yinger, M. J. 1982. *Countercultures: The Promise and the Peril of a World Turned Upside Down*. New York: The Free Press.

______. 1960. 'Contraculture and Subculture'. *American Sociological Review* 25(5): 625–35.

Zafar, M. A. 2003. 'Hakim-ul-Ummat Maulana Asharaf Ali Thanvi aur Jamhooriat' [The thinker of the nation, Maulan Asharaf Ali Thanvi and democracy]. *As-Sayyanah* 12(3): 50–52.

Zahid, M. 1994. 'Qiyam-e-Pakistan: Chand Qabil-e-Tawajjauh Pehlu' [Making of Pakistan: Some attention-worthy aspects]. *As-Sayyanah*2(3): 40–53.

______. 1999. 'Wajpayee Ka Daurah-e-Lahore: Amrika se Muhtat Rahiye' [Wajpayee's Lahore visit: Beware of America]. *As-Sayyanah* 8(3): 3–6.

______. 2001. 'Chhaaj Tou Bolay' [Pot calling the kettle black]. *As-Sayyanah* 10(6): 3–6.

______. 2002. 'Dini Madaris Aham Milli Zaroorat Hain' [Madaris are an important need of the nation]. *As-Sayyanah* 11(2): 3–10.

______. 2007. 'Kia Jamhooriat Bil-kulliah Khilaf-e-Shariat Hai?' [Is democracy totally against the Shariah?]. *As-Sayyanah* 17(7): 409.

Zaman, M. Q. 2007. 'Tradition and Authority in Deobandi Madrasas in South Asia'. In *Schooling Islam: The Culture and Politics of Modern Muslim Education*, ed. R. W. Hefner and M. Q. Zaman, ch. 3. Princeton, NJ: Princeton University Press.

INDEX